DICTIONARY OF LEGAL TERMS

A Simplified Guide to the Language of Law

by Steven H. Gifis
Associate Professor of Law
Rutgers University School of Law/Newark

BARRON'S EDUCATIONAL SERIES, INC.
Woodbury, New York • London • Toronto • Sydney

All inquiries should be addressed to:
Barron's Educational Series, Inc.
113 Crossways Park Drive
Woodbury, New York 11797

Library of Congress Catalog Card No. 83-2726
International Standard Book No. 0-8120-2013-8

Library of Congress Cataloging in Publication Data
Gifis, Steven H.
Dictionary of legal terms.

1. Law—United States—Dictionaries. I. Title.
KF156.G5 1983 340'.03'21 83-2726
ISBN 0-8120-2013-8

PRINTED IN THE UNITED STATES OF AMERICA

45 550 9876543

CONTENTS

Translating "legalese" is big business. Too often we're forced to depend on lawyers to define even the most common legal terms. That's why I've had a special edition of the *Dictionary of Legal Terms* published for HALT members. This book presents clear and concise explanations of the legal terms that you encounter daily.

HALT is committed to making the legal system more accessible. And, plain English is the key to that access. Through the use of HALT's *Citizens Legal Manuals* , the *Dictionary of Legal Terms* and other self-help material, you can regain control over your legal affairs.

More than anything, I'd like to tell you that you won't need this book for very long. But legal reform is an evolutionary process that requires the dedication and time of concerned people like you and all HALT members.

Although half the states have passed plain English laws, much more work is needed to broaden these reforms and pass them nationwide. With your support HALT is actively working toward that goal.

Glenn Nishimura
Executive Director
HALT / Americans for Legal Reform

PREFACE

Professions tend to insulate themselves from lay understanding by the development of specialized jargon. The legal profession has achieved this insulation so successfully that the uninitiated is overwhelmed by the incomprehensibility of his or her lawyer's prose. Despite the increasing pervasiveness of law into every facet of modern life, the special language of the law remains a barrier to nonlawyers. In recent years "plain language" statutes have been passed by several states, requiring that consumer contracts, such as residential leases, be written in plain, everyday language. Yet, even with these reforms, the language of the lawyer often remains a mystery to the client.

The lawyer's language is replete with words having particular meanings. Thus, a lawyer "moves" to "evict a holdover tenant" when his or her client wants to kick the tenant out. The lawyer seeks to "partition a co-tenancy" gone sour and to "compel an accounting" to the "aggrieved party." A client's home is destroyed by earthquake and the insurance company refuses to pay. An attorney asks if the "risk" of earthquake is included in the insured's policy and, if not, whether "representations" were made to the homeowner that would support an action to "reform" the policy or that might create an "estoppel" against the company's denial of "liability." A merchant finds an umbrella in a coat rack; the attorney asks whether it has been "abandoned" or "mislaid" and explains to the merchant the "duty" that the law imposes upon a "finder" of "lost property."

In 1975 I authored a paperback law dictionary primarily for law students who were trying to comprehend what I and their other law professors were saying. That book has been used by tens of thousands of law students. It is hoped they have found it of assistance in understanding the baffling new world of law. Paralegals, legal secretaries and other professionals who regularly interact with lawyers have also purchased the law dictionary. It occurred to me, however that the greatest need for communication existed between the lawyer and the client.

And, even for the general citizens, it seemed to me that comprehending the ordinary newspaper article had to be growing more and more difficult as the news of the day became more and more entangled with legal jargon. The available law dictionaries were either too sophisticated for the average lay person or too simplistic and incomplete to be helpful. The purpose of this book is to provide a ready, accessible and useful source of understanding of the language of law and law-related processes and concepts.

The text of the book has been drawn in large part from the earlier publication *Law Dictionary*. The definitions have been re-drafted in lay terms and the citations to authority have been deleted. Users of this book who need a more detailed explanation of a term may find resort to the *Law Dictionary* appropriate. And, in addition to the greater readability of the text, many new terms were added that law students might not encounter in their studies and that might not be thought of as technically "legal terms" but that have special meaning and arise in legal contexts. Hundreds of definitions have been added from the fields of securities, finance and taxation, which will assist the average person in understanding the business section of a newspaper. Abbreviations such as "N.O.V." have been defined so that the user will not have to fumble through many other sources until he or she discovers that the phrase refers to non obstante verdicto.

Although the book is titled a *Dictionary of Legal Terms* and may be used as one would use any other dictionary, it is contemplated that the user may want to skim through the book from time to time, stopping to read definitions touching upon jargon that he or she has noticed but not comprehended. In this fashion the book will be a primer for the lay person and hopefully will bridge the communication gap between the reader and the law.

STEVEN H. GIFIS

Hopewell, New Jersey

ACKNOWLEDGMENTS

A number of persons contributed to this project. The financial and securities terms were drafted by Michael B. Perkins, C.F.A.; the taxation terms, by David Mills, Esq. The task of editing the *Law Dictionary* into a layman's version was handled very ably by Keith Roberts, Esq., and significant editorial assistance was rendered by Alan Dexter Bowman, Esq., and Joseph C. Mahon, Esq. The examples were drafted by Andrew Levine, Rutgers School of Law-Newark, Class of 1984. The overall editing of the entire manuscript was performed with great skill and precision by my wife, Susan Pollard Gifis, Esq. Finally, the entire manuscript was typed and retyped with great care and cheerfulness by my secretary, Angela DiPierro. Without the contributions of all of these persons, this book would not have been produced.

PRONUNCIATION GUIDE

The decision as to which Latin words, maxims and expressions should be included in this dictionary, in view of the thousands that the user might encounter, was necessarily a somewhat arbitrary one; but an earnest effort has been made to translate and, where appropriate, to illuminate those terms and phrases considered likely to be crucial to a full understanding of important legal concepts. Hopefully, there are no significant omissions and we have erred only on the side of overinclusiveness.

Each of the Latin and French words and phrases—at least those that continue to be recognized as such and have not become, functionally, a part of the English language—includes a phonetic spelling designed to assist the user in the pronunciation of terms that are probably unfamiliar to her or him. The purpose in providing this pronunciation guide, however, has not been to indicate the "correct" mode of pronouncing the terms; rather, the goal has been to afford the user a guide to an acceptable pronunciation of them. In the case of Latin words, therefore, neither the classic nor the ecclesiastical pronunciation has been strictly followed; instead, the phonetic spellings provided herein reflect the often considerable extent to which pronunciation has been "Anglicized" and/or "Americanized," partly through widespread legal usage.

Of course, such a system is anything but uniform, and adoption of it is clearly hazardous from the standpoint of general acceptance as well as that of scholarship. Many, if not most, of these terms have alternative pronunciations in common usage throughout the English-speaking legal world, and there has been some deference to classical or ecclesiastical pronunciation and, hopefully, to consistency. Thus, the choices made here, while in most cases meant to reflect the most commonly accepted pronunciation, inevitably have been the product of the author's personal preferences.

The phonetic symbols employed herein were drawn from what the author perceives as a commonly recognized and understood "system." The following guide should be of some assistance in interpreting them.

Vowels

ă as in *ă*t
ä as in *ä*rmy
ȧ as in *a*rrive
ā as in *ā*pe
aủ as in *ou*t

ĕ as in *ĕ*gg
ē as in *ē*vil
ė as in *ea*rn

ĭ as in *ĭ*ll
ī as in *ī*ce

ŏ as in *ŏ*x
ô as in *o*rgy
ō as in *ō*pen

ŭ as in *ŭ*p
û as in *û*rge
ū as in r*û*de

Consonants

g as in *g*as

j as in *j*ump or as the *g* in rouge or bourgeois

KEY TO EFFECTIVE USE OF THIS DICTIONARY

Alphabetization: The reader should note carefully that all entries have been alphabetized letter by letter rather than word by word. Thus *ab initio,* for example, is located between *abeyance* and *abortion,* rather than at the beginning of the listings. In the same manner, *actionable* appears before, not after *action ex delicto*.

Brackets: Material in brackets [thus] represents an alternate expression for the preceding phrase. For example, "Federal Bureau of Investigation [F.B.I.]" indicates that F.B.I. is another way of expressing the entry for Federal Bureau of Investigation. When the reader is referred to a different main entry for the definition of a particular word, brackets are also used to indicate that the word to be defined appears as a subentry of the main word to which the reader is referred. Thus, **"COMPENSATORY DAMAGES** See **damages** [ACTUAL DAMAGES]" indicates that the definition of compensatory damages appears under the sub entry **ACTUAL DAMAGES,** which in turn is found under the heading **DAMAGES.**

Cross References: **Boldface type** has been used within the text of the definitions and at the end of them, to call attention to terms that are defined in the dictionary as separate entries and that should be understood and, if necessary, referred to specifically, in order to assure the fullest possible comprehension of the word whose definition has been sought in the first instance.

Terms emphasized in this manner include many that appear in the dictionary only in a different form or as a different part of speech. For example, although the term "alienate" may appear in boldface in the text of a definition, it will not be found as a separate entry, since it is expected that the reader can readily draw the meaning of that term from the definition given for the word "alienation"; likewise, the reader coming across the word "estop" printed in boldface should not despair upon discovering that it is not in fact an entry here, but should instead refer to the term "estoppel."

Also, the reader must not assume that the appearance of a word in regular type precludes the possibility of its having been included as a separate entry, for by no means has every such word been printed in boldface in every definition. Terms emphasized in this manner include primarily those an understanding of which was thought to be essential or very helpful in the reader's quest for adequate comprehension. Many terms that represent very basic and frequently used concepts, such as "property," "possession" and "crime," are often printed in regular type. Furthermore, boldface is used to emphasize a word only the first time that that word appears in a particular definition.

Examples: Examples have been included to clarify many terms. Where these appear, they are clearly marked *"EXAMPLE:"*.

Gender: Where masculine nouns and pronouns have been used, they are intended to refer to both men and women and should be so read.

Subentries: Words printed in boldface **SMALL CAPITALS** include:

(1) those whose significance as legal concepts was not deemed sufficiently substantial to warrant their inclusion in the dictionary as separate entries, though some explanation or illumination was throught desirable, and

(2) those which, though important, are most logically and coherently defined in the context of related or broader terms.

Words emphasized in this manner either have been separately and individually defined in the manner of "subcategories" or have been defined or illustrated, implicitly or explicitly, within the text of the definition of that main entry.

DICTIONARY OF LEGAL TERMS

A

ABANDONMENT the intentional giving up of rights or property with no future intention to regain title or possession.

EXAMPLE: Paul finishes reading his newspaper while waiting for a doctor to see him. Upon leaving the doctor's office, Paul intentionally decides not to take the paper with him. Paul *abandons* the newspaper. Had he merely forgotten the paper and returned to the office to retrieve it, he would not be considered to have abandoned the property.

ABATABLE NUISANCE see **nuisance.**

ABATEMENT generally, a lessening or reduction: also, either a termination or a temporary suspension of a lawsuit. An ABATEMENT OF A LEGACY means that the **legacy** to a **beneficiary** is either reduced or completely eliminated because of debts that must first be paid out of the decedent's estate. An ABATEMENT OF TAXES is a tax rebate or decrease.

ABDUCTION the criminal or wrongful act of forcibly taking away another person through **fraud,** persuasion or violence. (Compare **kidnapping.**)

ABET see **aid and abet.**

ABEYANCE an undetermined or incomplete state of affairs; in property law, the condition of a **freehold** or estate in **fee** when there is no existing person in whom the estate **vests.**

ABILITY TO STAND TRIAL see **competent.**

AB INITIO *(ăb ĭn-ĭ'-shē-ō)* Lat.: from the beginning. Commonly used in referring to the time when an action or instrument or interest in property becomes legally valid.

ABORTION the premature termination of a pregnancy; may be either spontaneous (miscarriage) or induced. A woman enjoys a constitutional right to have an abortion during the first trimester of her pregnancy. During the second trimester, however, the state may regulate the abortion procedure, and during the third trimester the state may even proscribe abortion except where medically necessary to preserve the health of the mother.

ABRIDGE to shorten, condense; to diminish.

ABROGATE to annul, repeal, put an end to; to make a law void by legislative repeal.

ABSCOND to travel secretly out of the **jurisdiction** of the courts, or to hide in order to avoid a legal **process** such as a lawsuit or arrest.

ABSQUE HOC *(äb'-skwā hŏc)* Lat.: without this. If it had not been for this; a phrase used to introduce a denial in a pleading.

ABSTENTION [DOCTRINE] the policy that a federal district court may decline to exercise its **jurisdiction** and may allow a state court to decide a federal constitutional question or questions of state law. Abstention is based on **comity** and is intended to restrict federal court interference in state proceedings. See **federalism.**

EXAMPLE: A prisoner in a state prison brings a lawsuit in federal district court claiming that under federal law he is entitled to have access to a law library. The state in which the prisoner is jailed may require by law that each state prison maintain an adequate law library. The federal court applies the *abstention doctrine* in refusing to hear the case, instructing the prisoner to raise the issue in a state court.

ABSTRACT OF RECORD a condensed history of a case, taken from the trial court records and prepared for use by the **appellate court.**

ABSTRACT OF TITLE a short history of **title** to land, noting all **conveyances,** transfers, **grants, wills** and judicial proceedings, and all **encumbrances** and **liens,** together with evidence of satisfaction and any other facts affecting title.

EXAMPLE: John wants to sell a parcel of land to Bill. In order to protect himself from claims by any other persons concerning that parcel, Bill insists that John provide an *abstract of title* before Bill purchases the land. Only with that abstract can Bill be satisfied that John is the rightful owner of the property. Bill can also purchase a policy of title insurance to protect himself from any problems that develop arising from ownership in the land. The insurance will be based on the abstract of title.

ABUSE OF DISCRETION on appeal, the characterization by a reviewing court of a lower court or administrative agency decision or ruling as arbitrary and unreasonable, leading the reviewing court to overturn the decision. See **discretion.**

ABUSE OF PROCESS improper use of a legal **process;** for example, serving a **summons** to frighten the recipient or to prompt a response from him, where no **suit** has been filed, or filing a lawsuit for an improper purpose.

EXAMPLE: Nick desperately needs information from Sam to aid Nick in preparing for a lucrative business deal. Sam refuses to provide that information because of its confidential nature. Nick files a lawsuit against Sam so he can acquire the information by claiming that he needs it in connection with the lawsuit. Nick has thus participated in an *abuse of process* because he used service of summons, which is a legal process, to institute a lawsuit, for the sole purpose of acquiring information not otherwise lawfully available to him.

ABUT to adjoin, touch boundaries, border on.

ACCELERATION 1. the hastening of the time for **enjoyment** of a **remainder** interest due to the premature termination of a **preceding estate;** 2. the process by which, under the terms of a **mortgage** or similar obligation, an entire debt is to be regarded as due upon the borrower's failure to pay a single installment or to fulfill some other duty. See **acceleration clause.**

ACCELERATION CLAUSE a provision in a **contract** or document that, upon the happening of a certain event, a person's expected interest in the property will become **vested** sooner than expected. Often found in **installment contracts,** this clause, if invoked, causes the entire debt to become due upon a party's failure to make payment on time.

EXAMPLE: David signs a loan agreement with the bank, promising to repay the bank in monthly payments over a three-year period. The agreement includes an *acceleration clause* which provides that if Dave fails to pay the required amount for any month or months, the bank can demand that Dave repay the remaining amount of the loan in one payment.

Although acceleration clauses are frequently found in loan or mortgage agreements, they are not generally resorted to until other methods of repayment are attempted.

ACCEPTANCE the voluntary act of receiving something or of agreeing to certain terms. 1. In contract law, acceptance is consent to the terms of an **offer,** creating a binding **contract.**

EXAMPLE: A homeowner contracts with an aluminum siding company to cover the house with new siding. The homeowner is not happy with two of the clauses in the contract, but the company is unwilling to change the clauses. When the homeowner signs the contract with the clauses unchanged, his signature acts as an *acceptance* of those clauses as they are printed. The fact that he has questioned those clauses has no effect on their validity as part of the contract.

2. In real property law, acceptance is essential to completion of a gift **inter vivos.** 3. "Acceptance" by a bank of a check or other **negotiable instrument** is a formal procedure whereby the bank on which the check is drawn promises to honor the **draft** by paying the payee named on the check.

ACCESSORY a person who aids or contributes to a crime as a subordinate. An accessory performs acts that aid others in committing a crime or in avoiding apprehension. In some jurisdictions an accessory is called an **aider and abettor.** See also **accomplice; conspirator.** Compare **principal.**

ACCESSORY AFTER THE FACT a person who harbors or assists a criminal knowing that he or she has committed a **felony** or is sought in connection with a crime.

ACCESSORY BEFORE THE FACT a person who incites, counsels or orders another to commit a crime, but who is not present when it is committed.

ACCOMMODATION INDORSEMENT see **indorsement.**

ACCOMMODATION MAKER [OR PARTY] one who, as a favor to another, signs a **note** as acceptor, **maker** or **indorser,** without receiving compensation or other benefit, and who thus guarantees the debt of the other person.

ACCOMPLICE one who voluntarily joins another in committing a crime. An accomplice has the same degree of liability as the **defendant.** See also **accessory; aid and abet; conspirator.** Compare **principal.**

ACCORD AND SATISFACTION the payment of money or other valuable consideration (usually less than the amount owed) in exchange for **extinguishment** of a debt. There must be an express or implied agreement that accepting the smaller sum discharges the obligation to pay the larger sum.

ACCOUNTING METHOD the method used by a business (**corporation, partnership** or **sole proprietorship**) in keeping its books and records for purposes of computing income and **deductions** and determining taxable **income.**

ACCRUAL METHOD an accounting method under which income is subject to tax when the right to receive such income becomes fixed, and deductions are allowed when the obligation to pay becomes fixed, regardless of when the income is actually received or when the obligation is actually paid. The accrual method must be utilized by any business taxpayer that has inventory.

CASH METHOD an accounting method under which income is subject to tax when received and deductions are allowed when paid.

ACCOUNTS PAYABLE the list of moneys currently owed by the debtor to the creditor. This list is kept in the ordinary course of the debtor's business. See **accounts receivable.**

ACCOUNTS RECEIVABLE a list of moneys owed on current accounts to a **creditor,** which is kept in the normal course of the creditor's business and represents unsettled claims and transactions. See **accounts payable.**

ACCRETION 1. the act of adding something to property, as when a co-**heir** or co-**legatee** dies or rejects his or her inheritance or legacy, thereby increasing the shares of the other heirs or legatees.

EXAMPLE: A father's will leaves equal amounts of a bank account to his son and daughter. If the son takes his share, the added tax burden on him will virtually eliminate all of his gains. He therefore decides to reject the legacy. The daughter benefits by the *accretion* in the amount of the bank account the father left her if the son's share goes to her.

2. the gradual, imperceptible addition of soil to the shore by the natural action of waters. Compare **avulsion.** 3. in situations involving a **trust,** any addition to principal or income that results from an extraordinary occurrence, that is, an event that, while foreseeable, rarely occurs.

ACCRUE 1. to accumulate, become due, as **interest** added to **principal.** ACCRUED INTEREST is the interest that has become due, whether or not it has been paid. 2. in a **cause of action,** to come into existence as an enforceable claim. For example, the pedestrian's cause of action against the driver accrues when the driver hits and injures the pedestrian.

ACCUSATION a **charge** of wrongdoing against a person or corporation, in the form of an **indictment, presentment, information,** etc.

ACCUSE to institute legal proceedings charging someone with a crime.

ACCUSED the person charged with a crime; the **defendant.**

ACQUIT 1. to set free from an **accusation** of guilt by a verdict of not guilty; 2. in older **contract** terminology, to release from a debt or other obligation.

ACQUITTAL a legal finding that an individual charged with a crime is not guilty and is therefore set free.

ACTIO *(äk'-tē-ō)* Lat.: action. Used to refer to legal **proceedings,** law**suit, process, action,** permission for a suit.

ACTION a court proceeding wherein one party **prosecutes** another party for a wrong done, or for protection of a right or prevention of a wrong.

ACTIONABLE forming the legal basis for a **civil action,** such as wrongful conduct.

ACTION EX DELICTO a **cause of action** based on a **tort.**

ACTIO NON *(äk'-tē-ō nŏn)* Lat.: no action. In **pleading,** a Latin term referring to a nonperformance, **nonfeasance;** also, a **nonsuit.**

ACT OF GOD a violent and catastrophic event caused by forces of nature, which could not have been prevented or avoided by foresight or prudence. Proof that an injury was caused by an act of God demonstrates that **negligence** was not the cause; and an act of God that makes performance of a contractual **duty** impossible may excuse performance of that duty. See **impossibility.**

ACTUAL VALUE see **market value.**

ACTUARY one who calculates insurance and property costs, especially, the cost of life insurance risks and insurance premiums.

ACTUS REUS *(äkt'-ŭs rā'-ŭs)* Lat.: the criminal act. More properly, the physical act that had been declared a crime. In murder, the actus reus is **homicide;** in burglary, it is breaking into another's home at night; in check **forgery,** it is presenting the forged check for payment.

AD DAMNUM *(äd däm'-nŭm)* Lat.: to the damage. The amount of **damages** demanded in a civil suit.

ADDITUR *(ăd'-dĭ-tûr)* Lat.: it is increased. An increase by the court in the amount of **damages** awarded by the jury, which is done with the defendant's consent in return for the plaintiff's agreeing not to seek a new trial.

ADEMPTION the extinction or withdrawal of a **devise** or **bequest** by some act of the decedent clearly indicating an intent to revoke it, e.g., by giving away during his life the property to be devised or bequeathed.

ADHESION CONTRACT a contract so heavily restrictive of one party, while so nonrestrictive of another, that doubts arise as to whether it is a voluntary agreement. The term signifies a grave inequality of bargaining power that may lead the contract to be declared invalid. The concept often arises in standard-form printed contracts submitted by one party to the other on a take-it-or-leave-it basis. See also **overreaching; unconscionable.**

AD HOC *(ăd hŏk)* Lat.: for this, for this particular purpose. An ad hoc committee is one commissioned for a special purpose; an ad hoc attorney is one designated for a particular client in a special situation.

ADJECTIVE LAW the rules of legal practice and **procedure** that make **substantive law** effective. Adjective law determines the methods of enforcing the legal rights created and defined by substantive law. For instance, **service of process** is a matter of adjective law.

ADJOURN to postpone; to delay briefly a court proceeding through **recess.** An adjournment for a longer duration is termed a **continuance.** A session postponed indefinitely is termed an ADJOURNMENT SINE DIE. See **sine die.**

The term has a special meaning in the rules of legislatures which adjourn between legislative sessions, but recess for periods, of whatever duration, within a single session.

ADJUDICATION the determination of a controversy and pronouncement of **judgment.**

ADJUSTER one who determines the amount of an insurance claim and then makes an agreement with the insured as to a settlement.

AD LITEM *(ăd lī'-tĕm)* Lat.: for the suit. For the purposes of the lawsuit being prosecuted. See **guardian** [**GUARDIAN AD LITEM**].

ADMINISTRATIVE AGENCY see **regulatory agency.**

ADMINISTRATIVE HEARING see **hearing.**

ADMINISTRATIVE LAW JUDGE the presiding officer at an administrative **hearing,** whose power is essentially one of recommendation. In the federal system, he can administer **oaths,** issue **subpoenas,** rule on **evidence,** take **depositions** and make or recommend decisions, which can be appealed first to the federal agency for which he hears cases and then to a court of law.

ADMINISTRATIVE PROCEDURE ACT [APA] an act designed to create uniformity and provide guidelines regarding the rule-making and adjudicative proceedings of administrative agencies, intra-agency and judicial review, public access to agency rules and decisions, and personal information collected by an agency.

ADMINISTRATOR someone appointed to handle the affairs of a person who has died without leaving a **will.** If the decedent left a will, an **executor** performs the same function.

ADMIRALTY AND MARITIME JURISDICTION jurisdiction over all actions related to events occurring at sea, including transactions relating to commerce and navigation, to damages and injuries upon the sea, and to all maritime contracts, and **torts.** In most cases, admiralty and maritime jurisdiction in the U.S. is given to the federal courts.

ADMIRALTY COURTS **tribunals** that hear cases involving **maritime law,** the law governing disputes arising on or in relation to seagoing ships.

ADMISSIBLE EVIDENCE evidence that may be introduced in court to aid the **TRIER OF FACT**—i.e., the judge or jury—in deciding the **merits** of a case. Each jurisdiction has established rules of evidence to determine what evidence is admissible. A judge may exclude otherwise admissible evidence when he determines that its **PROBATIVE VALUE** is outweighed by such factors as undue consumption of time, prejudice, confusion of issues or a danger that the jury will be misled. A lurid, gory photograph, for example, depicting the scene of the crime, the weapon used or the injury to the victim may have very high probative value as to several issues in a criminal trial, but since it may cause undue prejudice in the minds of the jurors, it will be excluded if there is any other way to prove the necessary facts.

ADMISSION the voluntary acknowledgment that certain facts are true; a statement by the **accused** or by an **adverse party** that tends to support the charge or claim against him but is not necessarily sufficient to establish guilt or liability.

In civil procedure, an admission is a pretrial **discovery** device by which one party asks another for a positive affirmation or denial of a **material** fact or **allegation** at issue.

ADOPT to agree to, appropriate, borrow, derive from, make use of; the formal process terminating legal rights between a child and his or her natural parents and creating new rights between the child and the adopting parents. See **adoption.**

ADOPTION the legal process by which the parent/child relationship is created between persons not so related by blood. The adopted child becomes the heir and is entitled to all other privileges belonging to a natural child of his adoptive parent.

AD TESTIFICANDUM *(ăd tĕs-tĭ-fĭ-căn'-dūm)* Lat.: for testifying. A person sought ad testificandum is sought to appear as a witness. See **subpoena [AD TESTIFICANDUM].**

ADULTERY voluntary sexual intercourse between a married person (or, under common law, a married woman) and someone other than his or her spouse. Adultery is grounds for divorce, in which case the person who committed the act with the estranged spouse is called a **CORRESPONDENT;** it is also a criminal offense.

AD VALOREM *(ăd và-lô'-rĕm)* Lat.: according to value. Commonly used to designate an assessment of taxes against property at a certan rate upon its value.

AD VALOREM TAX see **tax [VALUE ADDED TAX].**

ADVANCEMENT a *gift* given by a parent to his or her child that is intended to represent all or part of the child's share of the estate in the event the parent dies **intestate.**

EXAMPLE: The mother's will provides that her son receive $20,000 upon her death. During her life, the son requires money to start up his new business. The mother gives him $10,000 without requiring repayment but informs the son that the money reduces the amount to which he will be entitled upon her death. The $10,000 constitutes an *advancement*.

ADVERSARY opponent or **litigant** in a legal controversy or **litigation.** See **adverse party.**

ADVERSARY PROCEEDING a hearing involving a **controversy** between two opposing parties, the outcome of which is expected to be favorable to only one of the parties.

ADVERSE INTEREST an interest contrary to and inconsistent with that of some other person.

ADVERSE PARTY the opposing party in a lawsuit. See **adversary.**

ADVERSE POSSESSION a method of acquiring legal **title** to land through actual, continuous, open occupancy of the property, for a prescribed period of time, under claim of right, and in opposition to the rights of the true owner. See **hostile possession; notorious possession.**

EXAMPLE: Jim owned an empty piece of land next to his house. Paul, a neighbor, built an extension on his home which overlapped a considerable amount of Jim's land. For over fifteen years, Jim never said anything to Paul about building on his property, but after a dispute arose, Jim told Paul to remove any part of the extension that was on Jim's land. A court would find that Paul's continuous use of the property, which Jim always knew about, meant that Paul had legal title to the land by *adverse possession*.

ADVISORY OPINION a formal opinion by a judge, court or law officer upon a question of law submitted by a legislative body or government official but not presented in an actual court case or **adversary proceeding.** Such an opinion has no binding force as law.

ADVOCACY the active taking up of a legal cause; the art of persuasion. A legal advocate is a lawyer.

AFFIANT a person who makes and signs a written statement under oath **[affidavit].**

AFFIDAVIT a written statement made under **oath** before an officer of the court, a **notary public** or other person legally authorized to certify the statement.

EXAMPLE: As part of the defendant's sentence, the judge intends to include a large dollar amount for restitution to the victim. Rather than conduct a trial to determine the defendant's ability to pay the fine, the judge permits the defendant to file an *affidavit* outlining his financial situation. The affidavit also includes the defendant's name, address, age and other technicalities required by law, and an acknowledgment of the truthfulness of the statements made. A legally authorized person is required to administer an oath to the signor (called the **affiant**) and witness his signature.

AFFIRM to approve or confirm; refers to an **appellate court** decision that a lower court judgment is correct and should stand.

AFFIRMATIVE ACTION a positive step taken to correct conditions resulting from past discrimination or from violations of a law.

AFFIRMATIVE ACTION PROGRAMS hiring practices and other employment programs adopted to eliminate discrimination in the employment of minority persons. Such programs are required by federal law.

AFFIRMATIVE DEFENSE see **defense.**

AFFIX 1. to attach to. In real estate, to attach something permanently to the land (e.g., a tree or an addition to a building). 2. to inscribe (e.g., a signature is affixed to a document).

A FORTIORI *(ä fôr-shē-ô'-rē)* Lat.: with stronger reason. An inference that because a certain conclusion or fact is true, then the same reasoning makes it even more certain that a second conclusion is true.

EXAMPLE: Dan is accused of aiding in a bank robbery in which all of the participants were over six feet tall. One suspect has already been cleared by police because he is only five feet six inches. Since Dan is only five feet two inches, *a fortiori* he could not have participated in the robbery and will also be cleared.

AFTER-ACQUIRED PROPERTY 1. in commercial law, property acquired by a debtor after he has entered into an agreement in which other property is put up as **security** for a loan. Commonly used in security agreements, such a clause subjects any additional property to the creditor's mortgage or other interest and makes it clear that improvements, repairs and additions made after the agreement are included as part of the security. 2. in **bankruptcy** law, property acquired by the bankrupt after he has filed to be declared a bankrupt. This property is generally free of all claims of the bankrupt's creditors.

AFTER-ACQUIRED TITLE a property law doctrine that says that if a person without good **title** to land sells it and then subsequently gets good title to it, the title will automatically go to the one who had bought the land.

AGAINST THE [MANIFEST] [WEIGHT OF THE] EVIDENCE a determination by the trial judge that the jury's **verdict** is against the clear weight of the evidence presented, is based upon false evidence, or will result in a **miscarriage of justice,** or that the jury has acted mistakenly or improperly, in which case it is his or her duty, upon motion, to set aside the verdict and grant a new trial. See **n.o.v.** Compare **directed verdict.**

AGE DISCRIMINATION the denial of privileges as well as other unfair treatment of employees on the basis of age, which is prohibited by federal law under the Age Discrimination Unemployment Act of 1967. This act was amended in 1978 to protect employees up to 70 years of age.

AGENCY a relationship in which one person **(agent)** acts on behalf of another **(principal)** with the authority of the latter. Compare **partnership.**

AGENT one who is authorized by another person to act in that person's behalf. The acts of an agent are binding on his **principal.**

EXAMPLE: Kim, an artist, instructs Dan to sell her paintings to various art galleries and to private parties. Dan is considered Kim's *agent,* regardless of whom he sells to, since he will have **apparent authority** to act on her behalf.

AGGRAVATED ASSAULT see **assault.**

AGGRIEVED PARTY one who has been injured or has suffered a loss. A person is aggrieved by a **judgment, order** or **decree** whenever it operates prejudicially and directly upon his or her property, monetary or personal rights.

AGREEMENT mutual assent between two or more legally **competent** persons, ordinarily leading to a **contract.** In common usage, it is a broader term than contract, **bargain** or **promise,** since it includes executed **sales, gifts** and other transfers of **property,** as well as promises without legal obligation. While agreement is often used as a synonym for contract, some authorities narrow it to mean only mutual assent.

AID AND ABET to knowingly encourage or assist another in the commission or attempted commission of a crime. See also **accessory; accomplice; conspirator.** Compare **principal.**

ALEATORY uncertain; risky. An ALEATORY CONTRACT is an agreement in which performance by one party depends upon an uncertain or contingent event—for example, a fire insurance contract is aleatory because it is uncertain when or if benefits will be paid.

ALIAS "otherwise known as"; an indication that a person is known by more than one name. "AKA" and "a/k/a" mean "also known as" and are used in **indictments** to introduce the listing of an alias.

ALIBI an excuse that proves the physical impossibility that a suspected person could have committed the crime.

ALIEN one who is not a citizen of the country in which he lives. A RESIDENT ALIEN is a person who has been admitted to permanent resident status but has not been granted citizenship. An ILLEGAL ALIEN is a noncitizen who has not been given permission by immigration authorities to reside in the country in which he is living.

ALIENATION in real property law, the voluntary transfer of **title** and **possession** of **real property** to another person. The law recognizes the power to alienate (or transfer) property as an essential ingredient of **fee simple** ownership of property and generally prohibits unreasonable restraints on alienation.

ALIENATION OF AFFECTIONS a **tort** based upon willful and malicious interference with the marriage relationship by a third party, causing mental anguish, loss of social position, disgrace, embarrassment or actual monetary loss. (Most states no longer recognize this as the basis for a lawsuit.) If the interference is in the nature of adultery, the tort is called CRIMINAL CONVERSATION. However, it may result from lesser acts which deprive the other spouse of affection from his marital partner. See **consortium.**

ALIMONY court-ordered payment for the support of one's estranged spouse in the case of **divorce** or separation. For federal income tax purposes, alimony payments are **deductions** to the paying spouse and **income** to the receiving spouse if they are payable over an indefinite period, or over a definite period lasting more than ten years.

CHILD SUPPORT, the amount of money the court requires one spouse to pay to the other who has **custody** of the children born of the marriage, may be imposed by the court with or without an award of alimony.

ALIQUOT *(ä'-lē-kwō)* Lat.: an even, fractional part of the whole. In a **trust,** it is a particular fraction of the whole property involved, as distinguished from a general interest.

ALIUNDE *(äl-ē-ŭn'-dā)* Lat.: from another source; from elsewhere; from outside. ALIUNDE RULE refers to the doctrine that a **verdict** may not be **impeached** by evidence offered by a juror unless the foundation for introducing the evidence is laid first by competent, **admissible evidence** from another source.

ALLEGATION in a **pleading,** an assertion of fact; a statement of the issue that the contributing party expects to prove. See **averment.**

ALLEN CHARGE an instruction by the court to a jury that is having difficulty reaching a **verdict** in a criminal case, to encourage the jury to make a renewed effort to arrive at a decision. Because it may have a coercive effect upon the jury, some jurisdictions no longer permit the instruction to be given after the jury reports a deadlock.

ALLOCUTION the requirement in **common law** that, following the **verdict** of conviction, the judge ask the **defendant** to show legal cause why sentence should not be pronounced. It continues to be part of the **sentencing** procedure in a majority of states and is a mandatory part of a valid sentencing in the federal system. The modern allocution does not ask the defendant why sentence should not be imposed but rather asks if he or she has anything to say in his or her own behalf in mitigation of punishment. See **mitigating circumstances.**

ALLODIAL owned freely; not subject to the restriction on **alienation** that existed in feudal law.

ALLUVION a deposit of sedimentary material (earth, sand, gravel, etc.) that has accumulated gradually and imperceptibly along the bank of a river or the sea. Alluvion is the result of **accretion** and is considered part of the property to which it has become attached. See also **avulsion.**

ALTERNATIVE PLEADING in **common law,** a pleading that alleged facts so inconsistent that it was difficult to determine upon which set of facts the person pleading intended to rely. Alternative pleading is generally permitted under modern procedure.

EXAMPLE: Paul is accused of murder. At his trial, he *alternatively pleads* the insanity defense and self-defense. The two are alternatives: the insanity plea means that Paul admits the murder but claims that his mental state prevents him from being criminally responsible, while the plea of self-defense means that he was justified in using deadly force in the particular circumstance.

AMEND to alter. One amends a statute by changing (but not abolishing) an established law. One amends a **pleading** by adding to or subtracting from an already existing pleading.

EXAMPLE: Lisa sues a manufacturing company for injuries resulting from a defect in one of their products. After she files her papers with the court, she discovers new facts which indicate that the company was negligent in developing the product. Lisa seeks to *amend* her pleading to include these new facts, and, as is generally the case, she is permitted to amend.

AMERICAN CIVIL LIBERTIES UNION [ACLU] a national organization, founded in 1920, that seeks to enforce and preserve the rights and civil liberties guaranteed by the federal and state constitutions. Its activities include handling cases, opposing allegedly repressive legislation and publishing reports and informational pamphlets.

AMERICAN DEPOSITORY RECEIPT [ADR] a receipt issued by American banks to domestic buyers as a convenient substitute for direct ownership of stock in foreign companies. ADR's are traded on **stock exchanges** and in **over-the-counter markets** like stocks of domestic companies. **Rights, offers,** stock **dividends** and similar adjustments to the underlying shares are paid in cash or ADR dividends by the bank.

AMICUS CURIAE *(ȧ-mē'-kŭs kyū'-rē-ī)* Lat.: friend of the court. A qualified person who is not a party to the **action** but gives information to the court on a question of law. The function of an amicus curiae is to call attention to some information that might escape the court's attention. An **AMICUS CURIAE BRIEF** (or **AMICUS BRIEF**) is one submitted by someone not a party to the lawsuit, to give the court information needed to make a proper decision, or to urge a particular result on behalf of the public interest or of a private interest of third parties who will be indirectly affected by the resolution of the dispute. Thus, a court might permit a group of retarded citizens to participate in a proceeding brought by a prisoner rights group to challenge a statute authorizing the expenditure of funds for the construction of prisons and mental health facilities, since invalidation of the statute would adversely affect the interests of retarded citizens.

AMNESTY a **pardon** extended to a group of persons excusing them for offenses against the government. See also **executive clemency.**

EXAMPLE: In an attempt to end the dissension caused by the Vietnam War, President Carter granted *amnesty* to all draft evaders on certain conditions. Those individuals entitled to amnesty were absolved of liability for selective service violations.

AMORTIZATION the reduction of a **debt** by periodic charges to assets or liabilities, such as payments on mortgages.

EXAMPLE: A landlord paves the parking lot for an apartment building. In charging each tenant rental for a parking space, the landlord *amortizes* the cost of the pavement so that, over a period of time, the tenant actually pays for the work. If the landlord had borrowed the money to fund the improvement, the landlord would amortize the loan by paying it back over a fixed period of time.

In accounting statements, the term usually refers to charges against investments in intangibles such as patents, copyrights, goodwill, organization, expenses, etc. Compare **depreciation.**

ANCILLARY JURISDICTION the jurisdiction under which a federal court is permitted to decide an entire controversy (including matters which it would not have authority to consider were they raised independently) if the controversy contains other issues that the law specifically authorizes federal courts to decide. Thus, when the court has jurisdiction of the principal action, it may also hear any ancillary proceeding, regardless of any other factor that would normally determine jurisdiction. Compare **pendent jurisdiction.**

ANIMO *(ăn'-ĭ-mō)* Lat.: intentionally.

ANIMO TESTANDI *(tĕs-tăn'-dē)* with the intention to make a **will.**

ANIMO REVOCANDI *(rĕ-vō-kăn'-dē)* with the intention to revoke.

ANIMO REVERTENDI *(rĕ-vĕr-tĕn'-dē)* with the intention to return.

ANNUAL REPORT a formal financial statement issued yearly. The annual report of publicly owned corporations must comply with **SEC** reporting requirements, which include **balance sheet, income statement** and cash flow reports audited by an independent certified public accountant.

ANNUITANT one who receives the benefits of an **annuity.**

ANNUITY a fixed sum payable periodically, subject to the limitations imposed by the grantor—generally, either for life or for a number of years.

ANNUL to make void; to dissolve that which once existed, as to annul a marriage. Annulment wipes out or invalidates the entire marriage, whereas **divorce** only ends the marriage from that point on and does not affect the former validity of the marriage.

ANSWER the **defendant's** principal **pleading** in response to the **plantiff's complaint.** It must contain a **denial** of all the **allegations** the defendant wishes to dispute, as well as any affirmative **defenses** by the defendant and any **counterclaim** against the plantiff.

ANTICIPATORY BREACH breaking a contract before the actual time of required performance. It occurs when one person repudiates his contractual obligation before it is due, by indicating that he will not or cannot perform his contractual duties.

EXAMPLE: Steven contracted with a fuel oil company to supply heating oil to it. The contract called for twelve monthly deliveries over a year period. After three months, Steven realized the contract would be too costly for him to continue supplying the oil. He informed the company that he would not deliver the oil at the next delivery date. His action constitutes an *anticipatory breach* of his contract with the fuel oil company.

Where anticipatory repudiation is by conduct rather than by declaration, it may be called VOLUNTARY DISABLEMENT.

ANTILAPSE STATUTES statutes that allow the **heirs** of a devisee or **legatee** who predeceases the **testator** to inherit what the testator had **bequeathed** to the deceased devisee or legatee. Under common law, a bequest lapsed upon the death of the specified recipient, so that, in particular, when a parent died before the testator/grandparent, the grandchildren were disinherited.

ANTITRUST LAWS statutes that promote free competition by outlawing such things as **monopolies,** price discrimination, and collaboration, for the purpose of **restraint of trade,** between two or more business enterprises in the same market. The two major U.S. antitrust laws are the SHERMAN ACT and the CLAYTON ACT.

A POSTERIORI *(ä pŏs-tĕr-ē-ô'-rē)* Lat.: from the most recent point of view. Relates to knowledge gained through actual experience or observation, rather than through logical conclusions. Compare **a priori.**

APPARENT AUTHORITY a reference to the doctrine that a **principal** is responsible for the acts of his **agent** where the principal by his words or conduct suggests to a third person that the agent may act in the principal's behalf, and where the third person believes in the authority of the agent.

EXAMPLE: A business organization that sells athletic equipment used Tim, a local sports star, to advertise and promote their products. His actions made it seem that he was part of the business, and the business did nothing to qualify that image. A manufacturer contracted with Tim to supply the business with various types of equipment under their belief that Tim was a part of that business. Although the business may not want that equipment, they are forced to purchase it. Tim's *apparent authority* as agent of the business organization was due to the organization's acquiescence, and this false impression obliges them to act in accordance with the contract.

APPEAL a request to a higher court to review and reverse the decision of a lower court. On appeal, no new evidence is introduced; the higher court is limited to considering whether the lower court erred on a question of law or gave a decision plainly contrary to the evidence presented during trial. Unless special permission is granted by the higher court to hear an **interlocutory** appeal, an appeal cannot be made until the lower court renders a final **judgment.**

APPEARANCE the required coming into court of a plaintiff or defendant in an **action** either by himself (**PRO SE**) or through his attorney. An appearance involves a voluntary submission to the **jurisdiction** of the court.

EXAMPLE: Sue is arrested for possessing more than 25 grams of marijuana. Once she employs an attorney, the attorney files a notice of *appearance* with the court stating that he or she is Sue's attorney and will represent her in the forthcoming trial.

GENERAL APPEARANCE a party's appearance at a **proceeding** for any reason other than for questioning the court's jurisdiction.

SPECIAL APPEARANCE an appearance for the sole purpose of questioning the **jurisdiction** of the court over the defendant and the authority of the court to compel his appearance for any other purpose.

EXAMPLE: A seller agrees to provide a buyer with certain goods. One clause in the contract states that, if the goods are defective, the buyer can only sue in the seller's home state. The goods turn out to be defective, but the buyer files suit in a court in the buyer's home state. The seller makes a *special appearance* in the court only for the purpose of challenging that court's jurisdiction based on the clause in the contract. By such an appearance, the seller does not acknowledge the court's right to entertain the buyer's suit against him.

COMPULSORY APPEARANCE an appearance compelled by service of **process.**

VOLUNTARY APPEARANCE an appearance by one who has not been required to appear by service or process.

APPEARANCE DE BENE ESSE see **de bene esse.**

APPELLANT the party to a lawsuit who appeals the decision to a higher court. See **plaintiff** [PLAINTIFF IN ERROR]. Compare **appellee.**

APPELLATE COURT [APPEALS COURT] a court having authority to review the law applied by a lower court in the same case. In most instances, the trial court first decides a lawsuit, with review of its decision then available in an appellate court.

APPELLATE JURISDICTION see **jurisdiction.**

APPELLEE the party prevailing in the lower court who argues, on **appeal,** against setting aside the lower court's **judgment.** In some state courts this party is referred to as the **respondent.** See **defendant** [DEFENDANT IN ERROR]. Compare **appellant.**

APPOINTMENT OF RECEIVER the placing, by court order, of contested property in the hands of a **receiver** in order to protect someone's ownership or **trust** interests in said property or funds. For instance, the **creditor** of a **bankrupt** can have the bankrupt's **assets** placed in the **custody** of a receiver to stop the bankrupt from selling the assets for cash or to prevent other creditors from seizing the assets.

APPOINTMENT, POWER OF see **power of appointment.**

APPORTION to divide fairly or proportionately, according to the parties' respective interests.

APPRAISAL RIGHTS a **statutory** remedy available in many states to minority stockholders [SHAREHOLDERS] who object to an extraordinary action taken by the **corporation** (such as a **merger**). This remedy requires the corporation to repurchase the stock of dissenting stockholders at a price equivalent to its value immediately prior to the extraordinary corporate action.

APPRAISE to estimate the value of property. Compare **assess.**

APPRECIATE 1. increase in value; 2. to understand the significance of something; in criminal law, used in some statutes as part of the insanity test, to signify that the defendant understands the wrongfulness of his or her conduct.

APPRECIATION the excess of the fair market value of property over the taxpayer's **basis** in such property.

UNREALIZED APPRECIATION the amount of appreciation in property that has not yet been subject to tax. See **realization.**

APPROPRIATE 1. to set apart for, or assign to, a particular purpose or use; 2. to wrongfully use or take the property of another.

APPROPRIATION the designation of funds for a specific government expenditure.

APPURTENANT attached to something else. In property law, the term refers especially to the attachment of a restriction (e.g., an **easement** or **covenant**) to a piece of land, which benefits or restricts the owner of such land in his use and enjoyment. To illustrate: if A allows B the right-of-way over A's land so that B has access to the highway, this is an easement appurtenant to B's land. See **easement** [EASEMENT APPURTENANT].

A PRIORI *(ä prē-ô'-rē)* Lat.: from the former, from the first. Modern usage has deviated significantly from the Latin. An a priori conclusion or judgment is one that is necessarily true, that is neither proved by nor capable of being disproved by experience, and that is known to be true by a process of reasoning independent of all factual evidence.

The term is commonly used to indicate a judgment that is widely believed to be certain, or that is introduced presumptively, without analysis or investigation. Thus to accuse someone of having assumed a fact or conclusion a priori is often to disparage him or her for having failed to support a judgment through evidence or analysis. Compare **a posteriori.**

ARBITER *(är'-bĭt-ėr)* Lat.: referee. A person (other than a judicial officer) appointed by the court to decide a controversy according to the law. Unlike an **arbitrator,** the arbiter needs the court's confirmation of his decision for it to be final.

ARBITRAGE a financial transaction involving the simultaneous purchase of currency, **securities** or goods in one market and their sale in a different market with a profitable price or yield differential. True arbitrage positions are completely HEDGED—that is, the performance of both sides of the transaction is guaranteed at the time the position is assumed—and are thus without risk of loss.

ARBITRATION submitting a controversy to an impartial person, the **arbitrator,** chosen by the two parties in the dispute to determine an equitable settlement. Where the parties agree to be bound by the determination of the arbitrator, the process is called BINDING ARBITRATION.

In labor law, arbitration has become an important means

of settling disputes, and the majority of labor contracts provide for arbitration of disputes over the meaning of contract clauses.

COMPULSORY ARBITRATION, in which the parties are forced to agree, is generally not provided for in federal law. The states, however, have increasingly provided for compulsory arbitration in areas beyond the control of federal law, such as police and firefighters' contracts.

ARBITRATOR an impartial person chosen by the parties to solve a dispute between them, who is empowered to make a final determination concerning the issue(s) in controversy, who is bound only by his own **discretion,** and from whose decision there is no appeal.

ARGUENDO *(är-gyū-ĕn'-dō)* Lat.: for the sake of argument.

EXAMPLE: Ace Chemical Company is accused of dumping toxic wastes in a canal outside the city. Although the company does not want to admit that it polluted the canal, for public relations reasons it is willing to pay the cleanup costs. In approaching the city to determine the dollar figure for those costs, the company will state, "Assuming, *arguendo,* that we did pollute the canal, how much will the cleanup cost?" By "assuming arguendo," the company avoids admitting guilt and moves on to the more important questions of cleanup.

ARGUMENT a course of reasoning intended to establish a position and to induce belief.

ARM'S LENGTH a relatively equal bargaining position between contracting parties, in which the agreement reached is seen as free of one-sidedness, **duress, unconscionability** or **overreaching** by either party.

ARRAIGN to bring a defendant to court to answer the charge under which an **indictment** has been handed down.

ARRAIGNMENT an initial step in the criminal process in which the defendant is formally charged with an offense, given a copy of the **complaint, indictment, information** or other accusatory instrument, and informed of his constitutional rights, including the **pleas** he may enter. Where the appearance is shortly after the arrest, it may properly be called a **presentment** since often no plea is taken. Compare **preliminary hearing.**

ARREARS that which is unpaid although due to be paid. A person in arrears is behind in payment.

ARREST to deprive a person of liberty by legal authority; in the technical criminal law sense, to seize an alleged or suspected offender to answer for a crime.

ARREST OF JUDGMENT the court's withholding of **judgment** because of some error in the **record.**

ARSON the willful and malicious burning of another's house; sometimes expanded by statute to include acts similar to burning (such as exploding) or the destruction of property other than dwellings.

ARTICLES OF IMPEACHMENT a formal statement of the grounds upon which the removal of a public official is sought, similar to an **indictment** in an ordinary criminal proceeding. In the federal system, articles of **impeachment** are voted by the House of Representatives, with the trial occurring before the Senate.

ARTICLES OF INCORPORATION the document that creates a private corporation, according to the general corporation laws of the state.

ARTIFICE a **fraud** or a cunning device used to accomplish some wrong; usually implies craftiness or deceitfulness.

ARTIFICIAL PERSON see **corporation.**

AS IS a commercial term denoting agreement that buyer shall accept delivery of goods in the condition in which they are found on inspection prior to purchase, even if they are damaged or defective.

ASPORTATION see **caption; trespass** [**TRESPASS DE BONIS ASPORTATIS**].

ASSAULT an attempt or apparent attempt to inflict bodily injury upon another by using unlawful force, accompanied by the apparent ability to injure that person if not prevented. An assault need not result in a touching so as to constitute a **battery.** Thus, no physical injury need be proved to establish an assault. An assault may be either a civil or criminal offense. Some jurisdictions have defined criminal assault to include battery—the actual physical injuring.

AGGRAVATED ASSAULT an assault where serious bodily injury is inflicted on the person assaulted; an assault with a dangerous or **deadly weapon.**

ASSESS 1. to determine the value of something; 2. to fix the value of property on the basis of which property taxes will be calculated. Compare **appraise.**

ASSESSMENT OF DEFICIENCY in general, the amount of tax determined to be due after an appellate review within the **Internal Revenue Service** and a **Tax Court** adjudication (if requested).

JEOPARDY ASSESSMENT an immediate assessment of the deficiency by the Internal Revenue Service without appellate review and Tax Court hearing, which is permitted if, in the opinion of the Internal Revenue Service, the assessment and collection of a deficiency would be jeopardized by delay.

ASSET anything owned that has monetary value; any interest in **real property** or **personal property** that can be used for payment of *debts*.

EXAMPLE: Jane wants to borrow a sizeable amount of money to build a summer house in the mountains. Although banks are generally unwilling to lend money for such projects, they will lend to Jane because she has substantial *assets*, including ownership of several buildings and a large number of stocks. Such assets are generally pledged as **collateral.** With respect to real property, Jane might give the bank a mortgage as a form of collateral.

Assets appear as one of three major **balance sheet** categories and are counterbalanced by **liabilities** and **net assets.** In corporations, net assets are usually referred to as shareholder's equity or **book value.**

CURRENT ASSETS for accounting purposes, property that can be easily converted into cash, such as marketable **securities, accounts receivable** (goods or services sold but not paid for) and inventories (raw materials, work in process and finished goods intended for future sale).

FIXED ASSETS in accounting, property used for production of goods and services, such as plant and machinery, buildings, land, mineral resources.

Other categories of assets include intangibles, such as **goodwill,** patent rights and acquisition costs in excess of fair market value, and tangibles, such as long-term investments in other companies, long-term receivables, insurance owned.

ASSIGN to transfer one's **interest** in property, contract or other rights to another.

ASSIGNED RISK in automobile insurance, a class of persons to whom insurance companies will not issue policies voluntarily, usually because their record of prior accidents has made them a high risk, and who therefore are assigned by state law to insurance companies and must pay higher rates. Many states have FINANCIAL RESPONSIBILITY LAWS that prohibit such persons from driving unless adequate insurance has been obtained.

ASSIGNMENT the transfer to another of one's **interest** in a right or property.

ASSIGNMENT FOR BENEFIT OF CREDITORS a **debtor's** transfer of his property to another party to be held in **trust** and applied to the debts of the assignor (debtor).

ASSIGNMENT OF A LEASE the transfer of the **lessee's** entire interest in the **lease,** by which the assignee of the lease becomes primarily liable for any rent required to be paid under the lease, and the assignor (original lessee) remains secondarily liable for the rent if the assignee does not pay it.

ASSIGNMENT OF ERROR the **appellant's** declaration or complaint against the trial judge that he committed an **error** in the lower court proceedings. Assignments of error establish the issues to be argued on **appeal.**

ASSIGNMENT OF INCOME a taxpayer's direction that income earned by him be paid to another person, so that it will be considered the other person's income for federal tax purposes. An effective assignment of income would be to transfer a share of dividend-paying stock *before* the dividend declaration date—in such a case the dividend would be taxed to the transferee; an ineffective assignment of income would be to transfer the share *after* the dividend declaration date—here the dividend would be taxed to the transferor.

ASSIGNS [ASSIGNEES] all those who take from another by deed upon the transfer of real property, or under a will, or, in the absence of a valid will, those who inherit the property of the **intestate** by operation of law. See **descent.**

ASSOCIATE JUSTICE a member of the United States Supreme Court, other than the **Chief Justice;** the title held by a judge, other than the presiding judge, on the highest court of some states.

ASSOCIATION a group of persons joined together for a certain object.

ASSUMPSIT *(ȧ-sŭmp'-sĭt)* Lat.: he promised; he undertook. In contract law, the term signifies an express or implied promise or undertaking, made either orally or in writing not under **seal.** The term refers especially to one of the old **forms of action** in **common law** comprising an action in **equity** and applicable to almost every case in which money had been received that in equity and good conscience ought to have been refunded.

ASSUMPTION OF MORTGAGE see **mortgage.**

ASSUMPTION OF RISK 1. in torts, an affirmative **defense** used by the defendant in a **negligence** suit, claiming that plaintiff had knowledge of an obviously dangerous condition or situation and yet voluntarily exposed himself to the hazard, thereby relieving the defendant of legal responsibility for any resulting injury; 2. in contract law, the agreement by an employee to assume the risks of ordinary hazards arising out of his occupation.

Contributory negligence arises when plaintiff fails to exercise due care, while assumption of risk arises regardless of the care used and is based fundamentally on consent.

ASSURED see **insured.**

ASYLUM a shelter for the unfortunate or afflicted—the insane, the crippled, the poor. A **POLITICAL ASYLUM** is a state that accepts a citizen of another state to shelter him from prosecution by that other state.

AT LAW that which pertains to or is governed by the rules of law, as distinguished from the rules of equity; according to the rules of the **common law.** In England, and later in the United States, courts of law developed strict rules establishing the kinds of **causes of action** that could be maintained and the kinds of remedies that were available. Courts of equity established different rules and remedies, partly to mitigate the rigors of the law courts. "At law" and "in equity" thus refer to two different bodies of **jurisprudence.**

The term also may be used to mean by **operation of law.**

ATROCIOUS outrageously wicked and vile. An atrocious act demonstrates depraved and insensitive brutality and exhibits a senselessly immoderate use of extreme violence for a criminal purpose.

ATTACHMENT a legal **proceeding** by which a defendant's property is taken into custody and held for payment of a **judgment** in the event plaintiff's demand is later established and judgment is rendered in his favor.

ATTAINDER in common law, the elimination of all civil rights and liberties, and the forfeiture of property, caused by one's conviction for a **felony** or **capital offense.** See **bill of attainder.**

ATTAINDER, BILL OF see **bill of attainder.**

ATTEMPT an **overt act,** beyond mere preparation, moving directly toward the actual commission of a criminal offense. The attempt to accomplish a criminal act is often made a crime itself, separate and distinct from the crime that is attempted. See **inchoate.** Compare **conspiracy.**

ATTEST to affirm as true; to sign one's name as a witness to the execution of a document; to bear witness to.

EXAMPLE: Where a person writes a will, that person must understand the nature of what he or she is doing when the will is signed and what the various provisions of the will mean. The laws of most states require that at least two persons *attest* to, or formally confirm, the writer's ability to meet these requirements. These persons are witnesses to the will.

ATTORNEY-CLIENT PRIVILEGE see **privileged communication.**

ATTORNEY, POWER OF see **power of attorney.**

ATTORNEY GENERAL the chief law enforcement officer of the federal government or of a state government.

ATTORNEY'S FEE the attorney's charge for his services in representing a client; also, the additional award made by the court to the successful party in a lawsuit to compensate him for the reasonable value of the services of his attorney.

ATTRACTIVE NUISANCE the doctrine in **tort** law which holds that one who maintains something dangerous on his premises that is likely to attract children is required to reasonably protect the children against the dangers of that attraction. Thus, one has a duty to fence swimming pools, to remove doors from discarded refrigerators, to enclose partially constructed buildings and to be sensitive to other potentially dangerous conditions that attract curious children.

AUCTION see **sale [AUCTION SALE].**

AUDIT an inspection of the accounting records and procedures of a business, government unit or other reporting entity by a trained accountant, for the purpose of verifying the accuracy and completeness of the records. It may be conducted by a member of the organization (internal audit) or by an outsider (independent audit).

EXAMPLE: Since its inception, the welfare agency has been criticized for mismanagement of federal money by the agency directors and for allowing people to file double and sometimes triple claims. The General Accounting Office, an agency of the federal government, agrees to conduct an *audit* to determine if these allegations are true and to trace where the money had been spent.

See **audit of return.**

AUDIT OF RETURN a review by an agent of the **Internal Revenue Service** of the tax return filed by the taxpayer and of the books and records supporting the information contained on the tax return. See **return, income tax.**

AUDITOR 1. a public officer charged by law with the duty of examining and verifying the expenditure of public funds; 2. an accountant who performs a similar function for private parties.

AUTHORIZED ISSUE the total number of shares of capital stock that a corporation may issue under its charter.

AUTOMOBILE GUEST STATUTE see **guest statute.**

AUTOPSY the dissection of a body to determine the cause of death. It may involve the inspection of important organs in order to determine the nature of a disease or abnormality.

AVERMENT a positive statement or **allegation** of facts in a **pleading,** as distinguished from one based on reasoning or on inference.

AVOID to cancel or make void; to prevent a certain result.

AVOIDANCE see **confession and avoidance.**

AVOIDANCE OF TAX the method by which a taxpayer reduces his tax liability without committing **fraud**—e.g., by investing in a **tax shelter.** Compare **evasion of tax.**

AVULSION an abrupt change in the course or channel of a stream that forms the boundary between two parcels of land, resulting in an apparent loss of part of the land of one **riparian** landowner and an apparent increase in the land of the other. The sudden and perceptible nature of this change distinguishes avulsion from **accretion:** when the change is abrupt, as in avulsion, the boundary between the two properties remains unaltered. When the changes are brought about by accretion—i.e., gradually, as a result of natural causes—the changed boundaries are recognized, and ownership interests are affected.

B

BAD DEBT a **debt** that is not collectible and is therefore worthless to the **creditor;** a debt that becomes uncollectible because the debtor is insolvent. A nonbusiness bad debt is deductible from gross income as a short-term capital loss whereas a business bad debt is allowable as a **deduction** against ordinary income. See **income [GROSS INCOME; ORDINARY INCOME]; capital gains or losses [SHORT-TERM CAPITAL GAINS OR LOSSES].**

BAD DEBT RESERVE rather than take deductions for specific debts that become worthless during the **taxable year,** a businessman may deduct in each year a reasonable percentage of his receivables, which percentage then becomes an addition to the reserve for bad debts. For example, if a taxpayer determines that on the average 3 percent of his **accounts receivable** becomes worthless during the taxable year, the taxpayer may deduct 3 percent and add it to his reserve for bad debts.

BAD FAITH **breach** of faith; a willful failure to respond to plain, well-understood statutory or contractual obligations; dishonesty in fact in the conduct or transaction concerned.

BADGES OF FRAUD facts or circumstances surrounding a transaction that indicate it may be fraudulent, especially in **fraud** of **creditors.** These badges include fictitious **consideration,** false statements as to consideration, transactions different from the usual method of doing business, transfer of all of a debtor's property, **insolvency,** confidential relationship of the parties, and transfers in anticipation of a lawsuit or an **execution** of judgment.

BAD TITLE a purported title that is legally insufficient to **convey** property to the purchaser. A title that is not a **marketable**

title is not necessarily a bad title, but a title that is bad is not marketable and is one that a purchaser ordinarily may not be compelled to accept.

BAIL a monetary or other **security** given to secure the release of a **defendant** until time of trial and to assure his **appearance** at every stage of the **proceedings.** Very often today an accused will be released "R.O.R."(**release on recognizance**) without bail so long as he promises to appear as required.

BAIL BOND the document executed in order to secure the release of an individual in legal **custody.** The **BAIL BONDSMAN,** who acts as **surety,** generally forfeits his security in the event the **defendant** jumps bail—that is, fails to appear as required for court dates.

BAILEE a party who holds the **personal property** of another for a specific purpose agreed to between the parties. See **bailment.**

EXAMPLE: Mike owns a considerable amount of bonds that are payable on a certain date to whoever holds the documents. As a security precaution, Mike delivers the bonds to his bank to hold for him in a custodial capacity. The bank acts as a *bailee* of the bonds; Mike is the **bailor.** If Mike had placed the bonds in a rented safety deposit box, no bailment would have been created.

BAILIFF 1. a court attendant; 2. a person to whom some care, **guardianship** or **jurisdiction** is entrusted: e.g., a steward who has charge of lands, goods and **chattels** to get the best benefit for the owner; a person appointed by private persons to collect rents and manage their estate; or a court-appointed guardian of an **incompetent.**

BAILMENT a delivery of **personal property** to be held in **trust;** the relationship that arises where one person, the **bailor,** delivers property to another, the **bailee,** to hold, with control and **possession** of the property passing to the bailee.

CONSTRUCTIVE BAILMENT one that arises when the person having possession holds it under such circumstances that the law imposes an obligation to deliver to another, even where such person did not come into possession voluntarily, and where therefore no bailment was voluntarily established.

GRATUITOUS BAILMENT one that results when care and custody of the **bailor's** property is accepted by the **bailee** without charge and without any **consideration** or expectation of benefit. In a gratuitous bailment, the bailee is liable to the bailor for the loss of bailed property only if the loss is caused by bailee's gross **negligence.**

INVOLUNTARY BAILMENT one that arises when the owner accidentally and without negligence leaves **personal property** in the **possession** of any person. An involuntary bailment arises if an umbrella is left with the coat check at a restaurant. Compare **abandonment.**

BAILOR a person who delivers **personal property** to another to be held in **bailment.** The bailor need not be the owner of the property involved.

EXAMPLE: A hotel maid finds a necklace in a hallway. She leaves it with the clerk responsible for locking up the guests' jewelry, who will hold it until the rightful owner claims the necklace. The maid is the *bailor* of the necklace. In this instance, the bailment is involuntary and gratuitous. In instances where one pays a fee for another to hold his property (as in a parking lot situation), the bailment is one "for hire."

BAIT AND SWITCH a method of consumer deception practiced by retailers that involves advertising in such an attractive way as to bring the customer in, followed by disparagement of the advertised product (that the seller in truth does not desire to sell) to cause the customer to switch to a more expensive product. This device is also frequently termed **DISPARAGEMENT.** Statutes in many states prohibit this sort of advertising.

BALANCE SHEET a financial statement that gives an accounting picture of property owned by a company and of claims against the property on a specific date. See **assets, liabilities.**

BALLOON NOTE a promissory note repayable in periodic installments of a specified amount, usually representing interest, and a much larger final installment, usually of the entire principal amount.

BANK a corporation formed to maintain savings and checking accounts, issue loans and credit, and deal in negotiable **securities** issued by government agencies and by corporations. Banks are strictly regulated and fall into the following three categories according to the limitations upon their activities:

COMMERCIAL BANK the most common and most unrestricted type of bank, allowed the most latitude in its services and investments. Its major limitation: it must keep on reserve a larger percentage of its deposits than the other two types of banks.

SAVINGS BANK the least common type of bank, prevalent only on the East Coast and in the Midwest. Its major service traditionally has been the time-savings account, from which money could be withdrawn only after a set period or upon thirty days' notice. Its services, however, have been expanded in some instances. By law a savings bank's investments are usually limited to certain corporate and government bonds and securities. Its advantages: it can pay higher interest rates than commercial banks, has certain tax benefits and can keep on reserve a smaller percentage of deposits. Usually, the bank is owned by its depositors as **creditors** whose dividends are paid as interest on their accounts.

SAVINGS AND LOAN ASSOCIATION (or BUILDING AND LOAN ASSOCIATION) similar to a savings bank in history and operation, except that the savings and loan association's primary purpose has been to provide loans for purchasing and building homes. In 1981 these institutions were authorized to offer a variant on checking accounts called a negotiable order of withdrawal **("NOW" account),** which allows depositors to write checks against their interest-bearing savings account.

BANKER'S LIEN the authority enjoyed by a banker to appropriate a depositor's funds or securities that are in the banker's possession and are not dedicated to a special purpose (as a trust) in order to satisfy a debt owed by the depositor to the bank.

BANKRUPTCY popularly defined as **insolvency,** the inability of a **debtor** to pay his **debts** as they become due. Technically, however, it is the legal process under the Federal Bankruptcy Act by which assets of the debtor are **liquidated** as quickly as possible to pay off his creditors and to **discharge** the bankrupt, or free him of his debts, so that he may start anew. In **reorganization,** on the other hand, liquidation may be avoided and the debtor may continue to function, pay his **creditors** and carry on business. At the state level, INSOLVENCY PROCEEDINGS may be brought to obtain more limited relief. See **trustee [TRUSTEE IN BANKRUPTCY].** Compare **receivership.**

BANKRUPTCY COURT a United States district court created specifically to carry out the Federal Bankruptcy Act.

VOLUNTARY PROCEEDING a proceeding under the Federal Bankruptcy Act whereby an insolvent **debtor** may file a **petition** to be declared a voluntary bankrupt.

INVOLUNTARY PROCEEDING a **proceeding** to seize all the insolvent debtor's nonexempt property, to distribute it equally among *creditors* and to release the debtor from liability. Additional qualified creditors have an absolute right to join in the original lawsuit at any time before **judgment** is entered.

CHAPTER 11 REORGANIZATION in addition to voluntary and involuntary proceedings in which a debtor is adjudged bankrupt, under Chapter 11 a debtor is permitted to postpone all payments on debts so that he can reorganize his business. While other **bankruptcy** proceedings seek to have the debtor's assets sold and to have all the creditors paid to the extent possible, Chapter 11 seeks to give the debtor a breathing spell with the hope that his business will recover and all his creditors will be fully repaid. The goal is a plan that specifies how much the creditors will be paid, in what form they will be paid, and other details. See **insolvency; debt.**

BAR 1. in procedure, a barrier to the relitigating of an **issue.** A bar operates to deny a party the right or privilege of rechallenging issues in subsequent litigation. The prevailing party in a lawsuit can use his favorable decision to bar retrial of the action. See **collateral** [COLLATERAL ESTOPPEL]; **res judicata.**

2. a particular position in the courtroom; hence, the defendant standing before the judge is sometimes called the prisoner AT BAR. The complete body of attorneys is called the bar because they are the persons privileged to enter beyond the bar that separates the general courtroom audience from the judge's bench. The CASE AT BAR refers to the particular action before the court.

BARGAIN a mutual voluntary **agreement** between two parties for the **exchange** or purchase of some specified goods. The term also implies negotiation over the terms of an agreement.

EXAMPLE: As a favor to his neighbor, Bob agrees not to erect a swing set in his yard. Two years later, Bob's grandson moves in with him. Bob decides to build the swing set to keep the grandson happy. He is not prevented from building the set even though he had previously told his neighbor he would not erect one. The earlier agreement is not binding on Bob because it was not a *bargained*-for exchange. The neighbor provided nothing in the agreement as **consideration** for Bob's promise; the promise was gratuitous.

BARGAIN AND SALE a **contract,** or **deed** in the form of a contract, that conveys **property** and transfers title to the buyer but lacks any **guarantee** from the seller as to the validity of the title. It is commonly used to convey title to real estate today and in effect transfers to the new owner whatever interest the **grantor** had. It is often combined with a COVENANT AGAINST GRANTOR'S ACTS, an assurance that the grantor has not impaired the title by, for example, conveying the property, or part of it, to someone else. Compare **quitclaim deed; warranty deed.**

BARGAINING UNIT the labor union or other group that represents employees in **collective bargaining.**

BARRATRY in **common law,** the crime of stirring up suits and quarrels, either at law or otherwise. Generally, the statutory crime of barratry is restricted to the practice of instigating groundless lawsuit, to the lawyer's profit.

BARRISTER in England, a legal practitioner whose function is similar to that of an American trial lawyer, although the barrister does not prepare the case from the start. His **SOLICITOR** assembles the materials necessary for presentation to the court and settles cases out of court.

BASIS an amount usually representing the **taxpayer's** cost in acquiring an **asset.** It is used for a variety of tax purposes including computation of gain or loss on the **sale or exchange** of the asset and **depreciation** with respect to the asset.

ADJUSTED BASIS during the time that a taxpayer holds an asset, certain events require that the taxpayer adjust (either up or down) his original basis to reflect the event, thus resulting in an adjusted basis. In general, depreciation deductions allowable in a taxable year with respect to an asset reduce the taxpayer's basis in the asset. On the other hand, if the taxpayer made a **CAPITAL EXPENDITURE** (see **capital**) for the asset, the amount of the expenditure would increase the taxpayer's basis.

CARRYOVER OR SUBSTITUTED BASIS in certain cases a taxpayer's basis is computed by reference to the basis of the property when held by the previous owner or to the basis of the property exchanged for the assets. In both these situations, the taxpayer's basis is said to be a carryover basis. For example, if a taxpayer received a **gift** of property, his basis in the property is the transferor's basis in the property. In other words, the transferor's basis carries over to the taxpayer.

RECOVERY OF BASIS the process by which a taxpayer recovers the basis through **distributions** or payments with respect to the property.

STEP-UP BASIS the process by which a taxpayer's basis is increased to a certain level (usually fair **market value**) as of a certain date. Such a basis is generally available for property received by an **heir** from a decedent.

BASTARD an illegitimate child, one who is not born either in lawful wedlock or within a competent time after its termination; also, a child of a married woman conceived with one other than her husband.

BATTERY the unlawful touching of or use of force on another person **willfully** or in anger. Battery may be considered either a **tort,** giving rise to **civil liability** for damages to the victim, or a crime. Compare **assault.**

BEARER PAPER **commercial paper** that is negotiable upon delivery by any party or that does not designate a specific party by whom it is negotiable. Such commercial paper is said to be **PAYABLE TO BEARER.** The most popular domestic bearer instruments are government securities, such as **treasury bills** and **municipal bonds.** Foreign stocks and bonds are normally in bearer form. A major disadvantage of bearer instruments is that they offer little protection in the event of theft or loss.

EXAMPLE: A thief steals several notes that are payable to bearer and sells them to Tim, who does not know they are stolen. Because the notes are *bearer paper,* Tim can demand payment according to the terms of the notes. The fact that they are stolen has no effect on his ability to collect. Tim is the bearer. The notes are payable to whoever has possession and is therefore the bearer.

See **negotiable instrument.** Compare **order paper.**

BELIEF see **information and belief.**

BENCH 1. the court; the judges composing the court collectively; 2. the place where the trial judge sits.

BENCH WARRANT a court order for the arrest of a person; commonly issued to compel a person's attendance before the court to **answer** a **charge** of **contempt** or if a **witness** or a **defendant** fails to attend after a **subpoena** has been duly served.

EXAMPLE: Wendy was arrested for a traffic violation and ordered to appear in court in two weeks. The order to appear notwithstanding, Wendy continued with her vacation plans and found herself in another state on the required date. As a result of her failure to appear, the court ordered a *bench warrant* for Wendy. On the basis of that order she will be arrested and brought before the court. The issuance of the warrant also subjects Wendy to a penalty for contempt of court.

BENEFICIAL INTEREST the **equitable** interest in a **trust** held by the **beneficiary** of the trust, as distinguished from the interest of the **trustee** who holds legal **title.** Any person who under the terms of a trust instrument has the right to the income or **principal** of the trust fund has a beneficial interest in the trust.

BENEFICIAL USE a right to the use and enjoyment of property that exists where legal title to that property is held by another, in **trust.**

BENEFICIARY 1. a person for whose benefit property is held in **trust.**

EXAMPLE: Grandfather wants to insure that his two granddaughters, Lisa and June, will have sufficient money to pursue a college education. In the trust that Grandfather establishes, the bank is named as trustee and Lisa and June are named as *beneficiaries*. As trustee, the bank holds the money until Lisa and June attend college, at which point the bank pays their education costs. The bank holds the money for the benefit of Lisa and June.

2. a person to whom another is in a **fiduciary** relation, whether the relation is one of **agency,** trust, **guardianship, partnership** or otherwise; 3. a person named to receive the proceeds or benefits of an **insurance** policy; 4. a person named in a **will** to receive certain property.

INCIDENTAL BENEFICIARY a person who may incidentally benefit from the creation of a trust. Such a person has no actual interest in the trust and cannot enforce any right to such incidental benefit.

BENEFIT for tax purposes, a benefit is received by a **taxpayer** whenever anything occurs that results in an economic benefit to the taxpayer. However, not all benefits are included in gross **income** since many benefits are not **realized** in the **taxable year** or are not subject to **tax** under the **Internal Revenue Code** or judicially or administratively developed principles.

FRINGE BENEFITS benefits other than direct salary or compensation (such as parking, health insurance, tuition reimbursement, etc.) received by an employee from his employer as a result of his employment. Generally, fringe benefits are not subject to tax.

BEQUEATH in a will, a **gift** of **personal property,** distinguishing it from a **devise,** a gift of **real property.** The term **disposition** encompasses both a **bequest** of personalty and a devise of realty.

BEQUEST a **gift** of **personal property** by **will.** A **devise** ordinarily passes **real estate,** and a bequest passes personal property. See **legacy.**

CONDITIONAL BEQUEST a bequest that depends upon the occurrence or nonoccurrence of a particular event.

EXECUTORY BEQUEST a bequest of **personalty** or money that does not take effect until the happening of some future event, upon which it is contingent.

RESIDUARY BEQUEST a bequest consisting of the remainder of an **estate** after the payment of **debts** and of general legacies and other specific gifts.

SPECIFIC BEQUEST A bequest of particular items, or of a part of a **testator's** estate that can be distinguished from all others of the same kind, which may be satisfied only by delivery of the particular thing (given by the will) and not merely by a corresponding amount in value or similar property.

BEST EVIDENCE RULE a rule of **evidence** requiring that the most reliable evidence available be used. Thus, where the original of a document is available, a copy will not be accepted as evidence.

BESTIALITY sexual intercourse with an animal. Bestiality constitutes a **crime against nature.**

BEYOND A REASONABLE DOUBT see **reasonable doubt.**

B.F.P. see **bona fide purchaser.**

BID an offer by an intending purchaser to buy goods or services at a stated price, or an offer by an intending seller to sell his goods or services for a stated price. Building **contractors** usually solicit bids based on building specifications from several subcontractors in order to complete a project. Government units are often required by law to construct highways and buildings, and to buy goods and services, through competitive bidding solicited by public advertisement, with the lowest competent bid winning the contract.

BID SHOPPING the practice of a general **contractor** who, before the award of the prime contract, discloses to interested **subcontractors** the current low subbids on certain subcontracts in an effort to obtain lower subbids.

BIGAMY the criminal offense of having two or more wives or husbands at the same time. A bigamous marriage is **void.**

BILATERAL CONTRACT see **contract.**

BILATERAL MISTAKE see **mistake** [**MUTUAL (BILATERAL) MISTAKE**].

BILL 1. an order drawn by one person on another to pay a certain sum of money; 2. in commercial law, an account for goods sold, services rendered and work done; 3. in the law of **negotiable instruments,** any form of paper money; 4. in legislation, a draft of a proposed statute submitted to the legislature for enactment; 5. in **equity pleadings,** the name of the pleading by which the complainant sets out his cause of action.

BILL FOR A NEW TRIAL a bill submitted to a **court of equity** stating **equitable** grounds for suspending **execution** of a **judgment** rendered in a **court of law** and proposing a new suit in **equity.**

BILL OF CERTIORARI a **petition** for **writ** of **certiorari.**

BILL OF DISCOVERY see **discovery.**

BILL OF EXCEPTIONS a writing submitted to a trial court stating for the **record** objections to rulings made and instructions given by the trial judge.

BILL OF EXCHANGE a written order directing another party to pay a certain sum to a third party. See **draft.**

BILL OF INTERPLEADER see **interpleader.**

BILL OF REVIEW a form of equitable proceeding brought to secure an explanation, alteration or reversal of a final **decree** by the court that rendered it, because of errors on the face of the record, or new evidence or new matters that have appeared after entry of that decree.

BILL OF SALE a written agreement under which **title** to personal **chattels** is transferred.

CROSS BILL a pleading in a court of equity by the defendant against the plaintiff or against another defendant in the suit; similar to **counterclaim** and **cross-claim** at law.

TREASURY BILL a promissory note, having maturity of no longer than one year, issued by the Treasury Department of the U.S. government. See **treasury bill.**

BILL OF ATTAINDER a legislative act that applied either to individuals or to members of a group in such a way as to pronounce sentence on them without a trial. Such acts are prohibited by the Constitution because they are, in effect, a legislative judgment of conviction without a hearing. See **attainder.**

BILL OF EXCHANGE see **bill; draft.**

BILL OF LADING in commercial law, the receipt a **carrier** gives to a shipper for goods given to the carrier for transportation. The bill evidences the contract between the shipper and the carrier, and can also serve as a document of *title* creating in the person possessing the bill ownership of the goods shipped.

EXAMPLE: Worldwide Ski Company agrees to ship goods to Stanley's Sport Centers but wants to be sure that it is paid before Stanley's takes possession of the goods. When Worldwide leaves the goods with Carrier, the transportation company, Carrier issues Worldwide a *bill of lading*. Carrier will not release the goods to Stanley's unless he presents the bill of lading. Worldwide is therefore protected since it will not give Stanley's the document until Stanley's pays for the goods.

ORDER BILL OF LADING a negotiable bill of lading that can be negotiated like any other **negotiable instrument,** so that the shipper can sell it to anyone, not just the intended recipient of the goods. The bill not only states that the carrier is to deliver the goods to a specified person at a specified place, but also requires the carrier to release the goods only when the bill of lading is given him by the recipient. An order bill operates as a document of title and must be presented by the recipient before possession of goods will be delivered. Under this arrangement, the shipper can withhold the bill of lading, and thus the goods themselves, until the intended recipient pays for them.

STRAIGHT BILL OF LADING a nonnegotiable bill of lading, which merely states that the carrier is to deliver the goods to a specified person at a specified place.

BILL OF PARTICULARS a detailed statement provided in a criminal case, as an amplification of the **pleading** to which it relates, in order to advise the court, and, more particularly, the defendant, of the specific facts or allegations he will be required to respond to.

BILL OF RIGHTS the first ten amendments to the United States Constitution; that part of any constitution that sets forth the fundamental rights of citizenship. It is a declaration of rights that are substantially immune from government interference. See **Fourteenth Amendment.**

BINDER 1. a written memorandum of the most important items of a preliminary **contract;** 2. an insurer's acknowledgment of its contract to protect the insured against accidents of a specified kind until a formal policy can be issued or until insurer gives notice of its election to terminate.

BINDER RECEIPT a memorandum that serves as evidence of an approved application for **insurance** and is intended to take the place of an ordinary policy until the policy can be issued.

BINDING obligatory.

BINDING AGREEMENT a conclusive agreement.

BINDING INSTRUCTION an instruction that directs the jury how to determine an issue in the case if certain conditions stated in that instruction are shown to exist.

BIND OVER to order that a defendant be placed in **custody** pending the outcome of a **proceeding** (usually criminal) against him. He may thereafter be released on **bail** or on other conditions of release.

BLACKMAIL the demanding of money either for performing an existing duty, or for preventing an injury or for exercising an influence; the **extortion** of things of value from a person by threats of personal injury, or by threatening to accuse him of crime or immoral conduct, which, if true, would tend to disgrace him.

EXAMPLE: As a child, Evan had once been caught shoplifting. Now, Evan occupies a position of high standing in the community and enjoys an untarnished reputation. Tom wants Evan to lend him a considerable amount of money. To persuade Evan to advance the loan, Tom *blackmails* Evan by threatening to reveal the childhood incident, which would discredit Evan. The criminal nature of Tom's attempt to blackmail is not affected by the truthfulness underlying the threat.

BLANK INDORSEMENT see **indorsement.**

BLASPHEMY in common law, the **misdemeanor** of reviling or ridiculing the established religion (Christianity) and the existence of God.

BLUE CHIP STOCK the common stock of a company known nationally for the quality and wide acceptance of its products or services, and for its ability to generate consistent profits and pay increased dividends. The term probably evolved from its use in gambling casinos, where blue chips are valued at $100, since common stocks of leading companies were offered at $100 per share around the turn of the last century.

BLUE LAWS strict statutes or local ordinances most frequently enacted to preserve observance of the sabbath by prohibiting commercial activity on Sundays.

EXAMPLE: In Ewing Township, local *blue laws* prevent a merchant from selling automobile tires on Sunday but permit him to sell toothpaste and soap. The difference is rationalized by the belief that selling tires promotes working on a car instead of attending church. Toothpaste sales will have no such effect.

With increasing frequency, blue laws are being abolished so that people may freely choose activities without regard to societal notions as to appropriate Sunday conduct.

BLUE RIBBON JURY see **jury [BLUE RIBBON JURY].**

BLUE SKY LAWS state laws regulating the sale of corporate **securities** through investment companies, enacted to prevent the sale of securities of fraudulent enterprises. See also **Securities and Exchange Commission [SEC].**

BOARD OF DIRECTORS a group elected by **shareholders** to set company policy and appoint the chief executives and operating officers.

BOARD ROOM a stockbroker's office where **registered representatives** (that is, securities salespersons registered with the SEC) work and where the public is allowed to visit and obtain stock price quotations throughout the market day. Offices are equipped with electronic machines that provide information on trading in **listed stocks,** and **over-the-counter markets** and also provide business news.

BOILERPLATE 1. any standardized or preprinted form for agreements.

EXAMPLE: Scott is a rental agent and rents apartments for many landlords throughout the city. Although both the apartments and the landlords' requirements differ greatly, each rental agreement includes, in addition to clauses related to each particular group of apartments, nineteen *boilerplate* provisions covering liability of the various parties, damage deposits, security arrangements and other matters common to such agreement.

2. also, standardized language, as on a printed form containing the terms of a lease or sales contract, often phrased to the advantage of the party furnishing the form, with the expectation that the contract will be signed without being carefully examined. See **adhesion contract; unconscionable.**

BOILER ROOM [OR SHOP] a place devoted to high-pressure promotion by telephone of stocks, bonds, diamonds, commodities, contracts, etc., which are of very questionable value. Extensive **fraud** is usually involved, but successful prosecution may be difficult since operations often disband before detection and since little tangible evidence is obtainable.

BONA *(bō'-nȧ)* Lat.: good, virtuous; also, goods, property.

BONA FIDE *(bō'-nȧ fīd)* Lat.: in *good faith*. Without fraud or deceit; genuine.

BONA FIDE PURCHASER [B.F.P.] one who pays a valuable **consideration,** has no notice of outstanding rights of others and acts in **good faith** concerning the purchase. In commercial law, the phrase **holder in due course** signifies the same thing. See **buyer in ordinary course of business.**

EXAMPLE: George owns a textile mill and stores his products in a warehouse. The owner of the warehouse sells several boxes of shirts to Jerry without George's permission. Jerry suspects no wrongdoing because he has frequently dealt with the warehouse in a similar manner without any trouble. Since George left the goods with the warehouse, the subsequent sale to Jerry for value makes Jerry a *bona fide purchaser* who is legally entitled to own the goods. Jerry even has superior claim to the goods over George, so that in order to be compensated for his loss, George must pursue his claim against the warehouse owner.

BOND evidence of a long-term debt that is legally guaranteed as to the principal and interest specified on the face of the bond certificate. The rights of the holder are specified in the bond **indenture,** which contains the legal terms and conditions under which the bond was issued. Bond debt is secured or guaranteed primarily by the ability of the issuer (borrower) to pay the interest when due and to repay the principal at maturity.

Bonds are available in two forms. **REGISTERED BONDS** are recorded on the books of the issuer by the trustee, and interest is paid by mail to the **holder** of record. **BEARER BONDS** are **negotiable instruments** that must be safeguarded by the owner to prevent loss. Interest is paid by **coupon** redemptions.

BONDED DEBT that part of the entire indebtedness of a **corporation** or state that is represented by bonds it has issued; a debt contracted under the obligation of a bond.

BOND FOR DEED [TITLE] a document given by the owner of **real estate** to **convey** the property upon being paid money; an agreement to convey **title** in the future that, so long as it remains **executory** (not yet performed), allows title to remain **vested** in the original owner.

BOND DISCOUNT a reduction from the face amount of a bond that occurs where bonds are sold on the market for cash at a price less than the face amount. Since bonds **mature** (become due) years after issue, they are discounted to reflect present value.

BOND FOR GENERAL PURPOSES government bonds that are a charge against the taxpayers generally, as distinguished from bonds for improvements, the cost of which is charged to the property specially benefited.

BOND ISSUE the offering of bonds for sale to investors.

BOND PREMIUM the amount that the purchaser pays in buying a bond that exceeds the face or call value of the bond.

BOND YIELD see **yield.**

PERFORMANCE BOND a contractor's bond, guaranteeing that the contractor will perform the contract and providing that, in the event of a default, the surety may complete the contract or pay damages up to the bond limit.

SERIAL [SERIES] BONDS bonds issued in a series by a public entity that are payable at different times.

SURETY BOND a bond issued by one party, the **surety,** guaranteeing that he will perform certain acts promised by another or pay a stipulated sum, up to the bond limit, in lieu of performance, should the principal fail to perform. In a criminal case, the surety bond assures the appearance of the **defendant** or the repayment of bail forfeited upon the defendant's failure to appear in court.

BONDSMAN a **surety;** one who serves as security for another; a person who obtains surety bonds for others for a fee; also, the individual who arranges for the defendant in a criminal case to be released from jail by posting a **bail bond.** Compare **underwriter.**

BONUS STOCK **common stock** offered as an additional incentive to **underwriters** or buyers of a **bond** or **preferred stock issue.**

BOOK VALUE the value of individual **assets,** calculated as actual cost less allowances for any **amortization** such as **depreciation.** It may be quite different from **market value,** giving rise to hidden assets. Book value on an overall **balance sheet** basis is **net asset value;** that is, total assets less all **liabilities.** In reports to shareholders of publicly held corporations, common shareholders' per-share **equity** or book value is obtained by dividing book value less any **liquidation** price for preferred issues by the outstanding issue of **common stock.**

EXAMPLE: A corporation decides to close ten of its branch offices located throughout the country. As part of the closing, it makes a deal with another company to sell the buildings in which the offices were located. The original cost of the buildings was $6 million, and their *book value* has been reduced to $4 million through depreciation. The actual market value is $8 million since in fact the buildings have appreciated in value.

Companies that invest in stock of other companies usually carry the investment at its original cost as book value. The true market value may be many times the cost if the stock has been held a long time.

BOYCOTT to refrain from commercial dealing with someone by concerted effort; to persuade someone to refrain from doing business with another.

BRAIN DEATH the irreversible cessation of brain function; statutory or case law definitions of death are being expanded in many jurisdictions to include this. Among the factors considered are the failure to respond to external stimuli, the absence of breathing or spontaneous movement, the absence of reflex movement, and a flat electroencephalograph reading following a 24-hour observation period.

BREACH failure to perform some contracted-for or agreed-upon act, or to comply with a legal duty owed to another or to society.

ANTICIPATORY BREACH see **anticipatory breach.**

BREACH OF CONTRACT a wrongful nonperformance of any contractual duty of immediate performance; failing to perform acts promised, by hindering or preventing such performance or by repudiating the duty to perform.

BREACH OF THE PEACE conduct that destroys or menaces public order and tranquillity, including violent acts or acts and words likely to produce violence in others. In its broadest sense the term refers to any criminal offense.

BREACH OF PROMISE failure to fulfill a promise; often used as a short form for breach of the promise of marriage.

BREACH OF TRUST a **trustee's** violation, whether willful and **fraudulent,** or because of **negligence,** oversight or forgetfulness, of a **duty** that **equity** places upon him.

BREACH OF WARRANTY infraction of an express or implied agreement as to the **title,** quality, content or condition of a thing sold.

MATERIAL BREACH see **material.**

PARTIAL BREACH see **partial breach.**

BREAKING AND ENTERING two of the elements necessary to constitute a **burglary,** consisting of the use of physical force, however slight, to remove an obstruction to an entrance. For example, pushing open a door that is ajar, followed by unauthorized entry into a building, is sufficient to constitute the breaking and entering elements of burglary.

BRIBERY the voluntary giving of something of value to influence the performance of an official duty.

EXAMPLE: Frank wants to build a shopping center in town, but for years his requests for building permits have been turned down. Another company is then granted the permits after one request. When Frank inquires why that company is treated differently, he is informed that they "make sure" their requests are granted. Frank understands that to mean he needs to pay money to town council members. If Frank pays the money, he is guilty of *bribery* even though payment is the only means to secure permits.

COMMERCIAL BRIBERY includes the breach of duty by an employee in accepting secret compensation from another in exchange for the exercise of some **discretion** conferred upon the employee by his employer, as in the approval of a contract.

BRIEF a written argument concentrating upon legal points and authorities (i.e., **precedents**) used by the lawyer to convey to the court (trial or **appellate**) the essential facts of his client's case, a statement of the questions of law involved, the law that should be applied and the application that he desires made of that law by the court. The brief is submitted in connection with an application, **motion, trial** or **appeal.** Compare **memorandum [MEMORANDUM OF LAW].**

BROKER one who for a commission or fee brings parties together and assists in negotiating **contracts** between them; a person whose business it is to bring buyer and seller together.

BRUTUM FULMEN *(brū'-tŭm fŭl'-mĕn)* Lat.: inert thunder. An empty threat or charge, or a void **judgment** that is in legal effect no judgment at all. A brutum fulmen is any potentially powerful and effective **order,** document, **decree** or judgment that is powerless due to some imperfection causing it to be unenforceable.

BULK SALES ACTS statutes designed to prevent the defrauding of **creditors** by the secret sale in bulk of substantially all of a merchant's goods. These laws generally require that notice be given to creditors before any sale of **debtor's** goods. See **bulk transfer.**

BULK TRANSFER a type of commercial **fraud** in which a merchant (or the owner of a business) transfers the business or a major part of it for **consideration** and then fails to pay his **creditors** with the proceeds. Any transfer in bulk of a major part of the materials, supplies, merchandise or other inventory, not in the ordinary course of the retailer's business, is subject to the provisions of the **Uniform Commercial Code [UCC].**

BUNCHING the concentration of gross **income** in one or more **taxable years.** This results in adverse tax consequences because, under the progressive **tax rate** structure, in the years that have the larger amount of income there is a higher effective rate of tax. These adverse effects are minimized by **income averaging** and by the preferential tax treatment afforded to **capital gains.**

BURDEN anything that is grievous, wearisome or oppressive; in property law, any restriction on the use of land, such as a **zoning ordinance** or **covenants running with the land.**

BURDEN OF PROOF 1. the duty of a party to substantiate an **allegation** or **issue,** either to avoid **dismissal** of that issue early in the trial or to convince the court the of truth of that claim and hence to prevail in a civil or criminal **suit.**

EXAMPLE: Jean files a lawsuit claiming that Don fraudulently induced her to buy a vacuum cleaner. Don replies that he has never met Jean and that he has never sold vacuum cleaners in Jean's section of town. Jean has a *burden of proof* to show facts that Don sold her a vacuum cleaner and did so by fraudulent means.

2. the duty of a **plaintiff,** at the beginning of a trial, to make a **prima facie** showing of each fact necessary to establish the existence of a **cause of action;** referred to as the **DUTY OF PRODUCING EVIDENCE** (also **BURDEN OF EVIDENCE** or **PRODUCTION BURDEN**). 3. the obligation to plead each element of a cause of action or **AFFIRMATIVE DEFENSE** (see **defense**) or suffer a dismissal; referred to as the **PLEADING BURDEN.**

BURGLARY in common law, an actual breaking into a dwelling, at night, with intent to commit a **felony.** Some statutes have expanded burglary to include any unlawful entry into or remaining in a building or vehicle with intent to commit a crime.

BUSINESS CYCLE the periodic expansion and contraction of economic activity. Economic researchers have identified three overlapping cycles of approximately 4 years', 10 to 20 years', and 45 to 60 years' duration. Causes of the short-term cycles (average duration: 52 months, as measured by the U.S. National Bureau of Economic Research) are believed to be a combination of money expansion and contraction (monetary theory), alternate savings and spending patterns of consumers (consumer confidence theory), and alternate expansion and contraction patterns of business inventory and business capital investment. It has also been suggested that the attitudes and perceptions of consumers and business managers guide their spending decisions and thus determine the business cycle (psychological theory). The longer-term economic cycles are dependent on more fundamental forces such as growth in labor force and productivity, capital investments, technological innovation and long-term weather cycles.

BUSINESS TRUST see **Massachusetts trust.**

BUT FOR in **tort** and in criminal law, a test of whether an individual's action caused a particular event. The test is applied by asking whether an accident or injury would have occurred ''but for'' (or in the absence of) the individual's act. See **cause [PROXIMATE CAUSE].** See also **causa [CAUSA SINE QUA NON].**

BUYER IN ORDINARY COURSE OF BUSINESS a person who, in **good faith** and without knowledge that the sale to him violates a third party's ownership rights or **security interest** in the **goods,** buys in the usual manner from a person in the business of selling goods of that kind. The buyer acquires the goods free of any security interest created by the seller. See **bona fide purchaser; holder in due course.**

EXAMPLE: Rich, a truck driver, fraudulently obtains a truckload of computer parts from a manufacturing company and sells them to a parts supplier. Unless the supplier frequently buys large amounts of new parts from truck drivers, the supplier cannot be a *buyer in the ordinary course of business* and therefore cannot claim ownership of the parts over the manufacturing company. If the supplier had bought the parts from a normal dealer in computer parts, the supplier would have ownership rights superior to the manufacturing company. The buyer should have suspected that the truck driver was not in legitimate possession of the goods. In purchasing goods from him, the buyer assumed the risk that the truck driver might later be exposed as a thief.

BYLAWS rules adopted for the regulation of an **association's** or **corporation's** own actions. In corporation law, bylaws are self-imposed rules that constitute an agreement or contract between a corporation and its members to conduct the corporate business in a particular way. In the absence of law to the contrary, under **common law** the power to make bylaws resides in the members or **shareholders** of the corporation. When used by corporations, the term bylaws deals with matters of corporate structure and machinery as distinguished from regulations, which are imposed by a board of directors to deal with problems relating to the day-to-day management.

BY OPERATION OF LAW see **operation of law.**

BY THE ENTIRETY see **tenancy** [TENANCY BY THE ENTIRETY].

C

CAB see **Civil Aeronautics Board [CAB].**

CALENDAR CALL a hearing in court in a pending cause to ascertain the status of the matter and to establish a date for trial.

CALL 1. a demand by a **corporation** on a **shareholder** to pay an additional sum to the corporation proportionate to his share of **stock;** also, an obligation of a corporation to issue stock at a certain price on demand, in which case the privilege of calling for the stock belongs to the buyer; 2. in property law, an identifiable natural object designated in a **deed** or other **instrument** of **conveyance** as a landmark, to mark the boundary of the land conveyed.

CALL OPTION see **stock option** [CALL OPTION].

CALUMNY **slander, defamation;** false prosecution or accusation.

CAMERA see **in camera.**

CANON 1. a rule of **ecclesiastical law,** primarily concerning the clergy, but also at times embracing lay members of a congregation. 2. a rule of **construction.** One of a body of rules to guide the interpretation of statutes, ordinances, etc. A PROFESSIONAL CANON is a rule or standard of conduct adopted by a professional group to guide the professional conduct of its members.

CAPIAS *(kā'-pē-ăs)* Lat.: that you take. In common law, a **writ** executed by seizing either the property or the person of the **defendant** to compel his answering a particular **charge**

in court. The term describes several types of judicial writs or **process,** by which **actions** in a court of law were commenced. The writs have been largely replaced by service of process.

CAPIAS AD AUDIENDUM JUDICIUM *(ăd ô-dē-ĕn'-dŭm jū-dŭ'-shē-ŭm)* Lat.: that you take to hear judgment. A writ to bring to court a defendant who has **appeared** and been found **guilty** of a **misdemeanor,** to receive the court's judgment.

CAPIAS AD RESPONDENDUM *(ăd rĕs-pŏn-dĕn'-dŭm)* Lat.: that you take to answer. A writ directing the arrest and production of a defendant before **judgment.** It not only notifies a defendant to defend **suit,** like a **summons,** but also enables his **arrest** as security for the **plaintiff's** claim.

CAPIAS AD SATISFACIENDUM *(ăd să-tĭs-fă-shē-ĕn'-dŭm)* Lat.: that you take to satisfy. A writ for the arrest of a judgment **debtor** until the **debt claim** is satisfied. See also **service of process.**

CAPITAL the money and other property of a corporation or other enterprise used in transacting its business. Compare **capitalization.**

CAPITAL ASSETS property with a relatively long life, or the fixed **assets** in a trade or business. In U.S. tax law, the term refers to property held for investment by the taxpayer which when sold is subject to special tax treatment (as **capital gains** and **losses**). Property that is part of one's stock in trade does not qualify as a capital asset.

CAPITAL EXPENDITURE expenditure made for the acquisition, repair or improvement of a capital asset.

EXAMPLE: Aerospace Corporation, a thriving industry, wants to expand its production capabilities to meet the increase in demand for its products. Its minimum needs are two new plants and four new office buildings in various parts of the country. Regardless of where Aerospace obtains the money for the new construction, whether from a bank or from profits the corporation has retained, the money spent to acquire these buildings represents a *capital expenditure*.

CAPITAL INVESTMENT (money paid out to acquire something for permanent use or value in a business or home; also, moneys paid out for an interest in a business, as in a **stock** purchase.

CAPITAL STOCK the amount of money or property contributed by **shareholders** to be used as the financial foundation for the **corporation.** The total of a corporation's capital stock is divided into **shares.**

CAPITAL ACCOUNT the group of accounting records that involves transactions in the **equity** or ownership of the business.

CAPITAL GAINS OR LOSSES gains or losses **realized** from the **sale or exchange** of CAPITAL ASSETS (see **capital**) and calculated as the difference between the amount realized on the sale or exchange and the taxpayer's **basis** in the assets.

LONG-TERM CAPITAL GAIN OR LOSS a capital gain or loss from the sale or exchange of capital assets held for the required holding period (generally, one year for the **taxable years** beginning after 1977).

SHORT-TERM CAPITAL GAIN OR LOSS a gain or loss from the sale or exchange of capital assets held for a period shorter than the required holding period.

CAPITAL INTENSIVE an industry or economic sector that requires a large amount of machinery, equipment, etc., relative to the quantity of labor or land required. The energy industries—oil production and refining, coal mining and electric power generation—require large amounts of capital equipment per unit of output. Historically, coal mining was a labor intensive industry requiring a large labor force to dig the product using hand tools. Today, however, this is no longer the case, as modern strip-mining machinery can dig more coal per hour than fifty miners using hand tools could dig in a shift.

CAPITAL INVESTMENT see **capital** [CAPITAL INVESTMENT].

CAPITALIZATION 1. for accounting purposes, the process of converting expected earnings or an expense item into an **asset;** 2. the total of long-term **capital,** such as long-term loans and notes, bonds, mortgages, and stock, used by a business to purchase assets.

CAPITALIZED VALUE the current worth of money expected to be earned or received in the future, calculated by using an appropriate discount rate to accurately express current value.

CAPITAL MARKET the organized buying and selling of long-term fixed-income securities such as **bonds** or **mortgages,** proceeds from the sale of which are used to finance **capital expenditures.** In contrast to the capital market, the money market is used to raise short-term funds and the EQUITY MARKET (see **equity**) is used to obtain permanent **capital** through the sale of stock.

CAPITAL OFFENSE a criminal offense punishable by death, for which **bail** is generally unavailable to the **defendant.**

CAPITAL PUNISHMENT imposition of the death penalty.

CAPITAL STOCK see **capital** [CAPITAL STOCK].

CAPTION 1. the heading of a legal document containing the names of the **parties,** the court, the index or **docket** number of the case, etc.; 2. the act of seizing, which, together with ASPORTATION (the act of carrying away), was a necessary element of common law **larceny.**

CARNAL KNOWLEDGE sexual intercourse; the slightest penetration of the female sexual organ by the male sexual organ; does not require rupture of the hymen. Popularly known as "statutory rape" when conducted with a female child under the age of consent. See **rape.**

CARRIER [COMMON CARRIER] one who is in the business of transporting goods or persons for hire, as a public utility. A private carrier, in contrast, is not in the business of transporting as public employment, but hires out to deliver goods in particular cases.

CARRYBACK a process by which the **deductions** or **credits** of one **taxable year** that cannot be used to reduce tax liability in that year are applied against tax liability in an earlier year or years. Carrybacks are available, for example, with respect to operating losses of businesses, **charitable deductions** and investment tax credits. Compare **carryover.**

CARRYOVER a process by which the **deductions** and **credits** of one **taxable year** that cannot be used to reduce tax liability in that year are applied against tax liability in subsequent years. Compare **carryback.**

CARTEL a group of independent industrial **corporations,** usually operating internationally, which agree to restrict trade to their mutual benefit.

CARVE OUT the process by which a **taxpayer** separates the present **income** stream of property from the property itself. For example, if an owner of mineral property sells for a certain number of years a portion of the future mineral production from such property, the sale of such future production is a "carved out" interest in the mineral property.

CASE an **action,** cause, **suit,** or **controversy, at law** or in **equity.**

CASE AT BAR see **bar.**

CASE LAW see **common law.**

CASE OF FIRST IMPRESSION see **first impression.**

CASE, ON THE see **trespass [TRESPASS ON THE CASE].**

CASE OR CONTROVERSY see **controversy.**

CASHIER'S CHECK see **check.**

CASH SURRENDER VALUE the amount the insurance company will pay on a given life insurance policy if the policy is cancelled prior to the death of the insured.

CASH VALUE see **market value.** Compare **book value.**

CASUALTY LOSS a loss of property due to fire, storm, shipwreck or other casualty, which is allowable as a **deduction** in computing TAXABLE INCOME (see **income**). For a loss to qualify as a casualty loss it must be due to a sudden, unexpected or unusual event. Thus, while property damage due to a storm would normally qualify as a casualty loss, gradual erosion by wind or water would not.

CAUSA *(kaw'-zà)* Lat.: **cause,** motive, reason. A lawsuit or case.

CAUSA MORTIS *(môr'-tĭs)* Lat.: in anticipation of approaching death.

CAUSA PROXIMA *(prŏk'-sĭ-mà)* Lat.: proximate cause; most closely related cause. A cause sufficiently related to the result to justify imposing legal liability on the actor who produces the cause. See **cause** [PROXIMATE CAUSE]; see also **cause** [DIRECT CAUSE].

CAUSA SINE QUA NON *(se'-nà kwä nŏn)* Lat.: a cause without which it would not have occurred. Used most often in connection with the "**but for**" test of causation. See **cause.**

CAUSE that which effects a result.

DIRECT CAUSE the active cause that sets in motion a train of events that brings about a result without the intervention of any other source; often used interchangeably with PROXIMATE CAUSE.

IMMEDIATE CAUSE the nearest cause in time and space.

INTERVENING [SUPERVENING] CAUSE the cause that actively produces the result *after* the **negligence** or **breach** or **culpable** act of the defendant.

PROXIMATE CAUSE that which in natural and continuous sequence, unbroken by any new independent cause, produces an event, and without which the injury would not have occurred.

SUPERSEDING CAUSE an intervening cause so substantially responsible for the ultimate injury that it cuts off the liability of preceding actors regardless of whether their prior negligence was a substantial factor in bringing about the injury.

EXAMPLE: June pulls into a gasoline station and asks the attendant to fill up her car. In the process, the attendant accidentally squeezes the handle, and gas spills on the pavement, something that is not uncommon. Sal, who is near the car and unaware of what happened, lights a cigarette and tosses the match in the puddle of gas. June's car is destroyed. Courts would find that, although the attendant may have been negligent in spilling gasoline, Sal's action is the *superseding cause* of the fire. The gas on the pavement would not have created a problem had Sal never lit a cigarette near the pumps.

SUPERVENING CAUSE see **INTERVENING CAUSE.**

CAUSE OF ACTION a claim in law and fact sufficient to form the basis of a valid lawsuit, as a **BREACH OF CONTRACT.** A **RIGHT OF ACTION** is the legal right to sue; a cause of action is the composite of facts that gives rise to a right of action.

CAVEAT *(kä'-vē-ät)* Lat.: let him beware. 1. A warning or caution; a suggestion to a judicial officer that he ought to take care how he acts in a particular matter and should suspend the proceeding until the merits of the issue thus raised (the caveat) are determined; 2. an **in rem** proceding attacking the validity of an **instrument** purporting to be a **will,** or a remedy given to prevent a **patent** from being issued in cases where the directions of the law have been violated.

CAVEAT EMPTOR *(kä'-vē-ät ĕmp'-tŏr)* Lat.: let the buyer beware. This phrase expresses the rule of law that the purchaser buys at his own risk.

CD see **certificate of deposit.**

CEASE AND DESIST ORDER an order of a court or other body having judicial authority prohibiting the person or entity to which it is directed from undertaking or continuing a particular activity or course of conduct. Such an order may be issued upon a showing, to a degree of certainty or probability, that the conduct is unlawful or likely to be found unlawful.

EXAMPLE: Timber Company had received permission from the Interior Department to cut wood in a section of one of California's giant redwood forests. Several environmental groups brought a court action to stop Timber, claiming that any lumbering activities in the forests would violate the express purpose of Congress in establishing the forests and would result in irreparable harm. The court agreed and issued a *cease and desist order* requiring Timber to stop cutting wood.

CENSURE a reproach or reprimand, especially when delivered by a judicial or other official body; 2. the act of pronouncing such a reproach or reprimand.

CERTIFICATE OF DEPOSIT an acknowledgment by a bank of receipt of money with an agreement to repay within a specified time.

CERTIFICATE OF INCORPORATION similar to **articles of incorporation.** In some states the certificate is issued by a state agency after the articles of incorporation have been properly filed; the corporation's existence begins upon the issuance of the certificate.

CERTIFICATE OF OCCUPANCY a document by a local government agency signifying that a building or dwelling conforms to local building code regulations. Generally, entry or transfer of title requires a valid certificate of occupancy.

CERTIFICATE OF TITLE a document indicating ownership, similar to a BILL OF SALE (see **bill**) and usually associated with the sale of new motor vehicles.

CERTIFICATION see **certiorari.**

CERTIFIED CHECK see **check.**

CERTIORARI *(sėr-shē-ô-rä'-rē)* Lat.: to be informed of. A means of gaining **appellate** review; a **common law writ,** issued by a superior court to a lower court, commanding the latter to certify and return to the former a particular case record so that the higher court may inspect the proceedings for irregularities or errors.

CESTUI QUE *(sĕs'-tĭ kā* or *sĕs'-twē kā;* pl.: **CESTUIS QUE***)* Old Fr.: the one who; the person who. Used only in the following phrases:

CESTUI QUE TRUST *(trŭst)* Old Fr.: the one who trusts. The beneficiary. See *trust.*

CESTUI QUE USE *(ūz)* Old Fr.: the one who has the use. The person for whose use the property is held by another. Cestui que use enjoys the equitable and beneficial rights to the profits and income of the estate, while the legal title and obligations remain in the **trustee.**

CESTUI QUE VIE *(vē)* Old Fr.: the one who lives. The person by whose life the duration of an estate is measured.

CHAIN OF TITLE the succession of **conveyances** of **title** to property, commencing with the **patent** from the government (or other original source) down to and including the conveyance to the present holder. The **recorded** chain of title consists only of the documents affecting title that have been recorded in a manner that makes their existence readily discoverable by a **bona fide purchaser.** Of the two systems for recording such documents, the TRACT INDEX records in the same place all **instruments** relating to a particular property, while the GRANTOR-GRANTEE INDEX indexes all such instruments under the names of the various grantors or grantees of the property. See **title search; recording acts.**

CHALLENGE an objection by a party (or his lawyer) to the inclusion of a particular prospective juror as a member of the jury that is to hear that party's cause or trial, with the result that the prospective juror is disqualified from the case.

CHALLENGE FOR CAUSE a challenge based upon a particular reason (such as bias) specified by law or procedure as a reason that a party (or his lawyer) may use to disqualify a prospective juror.

PEREMPTORY CHALLENGE a right given to attorneys at trial to dismiss a prospective juror for no particular reason; the number of times an attorney can invoke this right is usually limited. If a specific reason exists why a particular juror may not fairly decide a matter, the juror may be **CHALLENGED FOR CAUSE.** This conserves the peremptory challenges. Even the government can use these challenges.

CHAMPERTY in common law, an unlawful agreement between an attorney and his client that the attorney will sue and pay the costs of the client's suit in return for a portion of the damages rewarded. Today the prohibition against champerty survives only in a few jurisdictions and only in modified form. See also **criminal maintenance.** Compare **barratry.**

CHANCELLOR 1. in early English law, the King's minister who would dispense justice in the King's name by extraordinary **equitable relief** where the remedy **at law** was inadequate; later, the name of the chief judge of the court of **chancery.** 2. in American law, a judge in a court of chancery.

CHANCERY the jurisprudence that is exercised in a **court of equity;** synonymous with **equity** or equitable jurisdiction.

CHAPTER 11 see **bankruptcy court.**

CHARACTER WITNESS see **witness.**

CHARGE 1. in criminal law, a description of the underlying offense in an **accusation** or **indictment**; 2. in trial practice, an address delivered by the court to the **jury** at the close of the **case,** telling them the principles of law they are to apply in reaching a decision.

EXAMPLE: At the end of the trial for assault and robbery, the judge *charged* the jury with (i.e., explained to them) the necessary elements of law that must be proved in order to convict the defendant. As in all criminal trials, the judge also charged the jury that they are the sole deciders (triers) of fact and should not be influenced by impressions from the judge or any attorney. Finally, the jurors were instructed to apply the law only as charged by the judge and not to base their decision on their own conception of the law.

The charge may also include instructions given during the trial for the jury's guidance.

See also *complaint*.

CHARITY a nonprofit institution organized and operated exclusively for charitable, religious, scientific, literary, educational or like purposes, whose income is exempt from federal income tax. Contributions to such organizations are allowable, with limitations, as a **deduction** in computing one's **TAXABLE INCOME** (see income).

PUBLIC CHARITY a charity that, under certain tests, is deemed to receive the major portion of its support from the public rather than from a small group of individuals.

PRIVATE FOUNDATIONS organizations that, although charities, are deemed to receive a substantial portion of their support from nonpublic sources, usually from small groups of individuals. A private foundation is subject to additional restrictions on its activities and its financial dealings, including accumulation of income.

CHARTER a document issued by the government establishing a corporate entity. See **articles of incorporation; certificate of incorporation.**

CHATTEL any tangible, movable thing; **personal property** as opposed to **real property; goods.**

CHATTEL MORTGAGE a mortgage on personal property created to secure the payment of moneys owed or the performance of some other obligation. This security device has for the most part been replaced by the security agreements available under the **Uniform Commercial Code.**

CHATTEL PAPER a document that shows both a debt and a **security interest** in or a **lease** of specific goods.

CHECK a **draft** upon a bank, payable on **demand,** and by the **maker** or **drawer,** containing a promise to pay an amount of money to the **payee.**

CASHIER'S CHECK a check issued by an officer of a bank to another person, authorizing the **payee** to receive upon demand the amount of the check. It is drawn on the bank's own account, not that of a private person, and is therefore accepted for many transactions where a personal check would not be.

CERTIFIED CHECK a check containing a certification that the drawer of the check has sufficient funds in the bank to cover payment.

MEMORANDUM CHECK a bank check with the word ''memorandum'' written across its face, which is not intended for immediate presentation, but simply as evidence of an indebtedness by the **drawer** to the **holder.**

CHECK-KITING an illegal scheme that establishes a false line of credit by the exchange of worthless checks between two banks. For instance, a check-kiter might have empty checking accounts at two different banks, *A* and *B*. The kiter writes a check for $50,000 on the Bank *A* account and deposits it in the Bank *B* account. If the kiter has good credit at Bank *B*, he will be able to draw funds against the deposited check before it clears (i.e., is forwarded to Bank *A* for payment and paid by Bank *A*.) Since the clearing process usually takes a few days, the kiter can use the $50,000 for a few days, and then deposit it in the Bank *A* account before the $50,000 check drawn on that account clears.

CHIEF JUSTICE the presiding member of certain courts with more than one judge; especially, the presiding member of the U.S. Supreme Court, who is the principal administrative officer of the federal judiciary.

CHILD AND DEPENDENT CARE CREDIT a **tax credit** allowed for 20 percent of the expenses incurred for household services or for care of a child or other dependent where a **taxpayer** maintains a household that includes one or more **dependents** who are under 15 years of age or mentally or physically incapacitated.

CHILD SUPPORT see **alimony.**

CHILL [CHILLING EFFECT] limitations on the exercise of First Amendment rights imposed not by law but by individuals who, fearful of the possible application of laws and sanctions, choose not to exercise their legitimate rights rather than risk prosecution.

EXAMPLE: A protest group schedules a weekend march to show support for that group's position. Even though the group has a permit, word is spread that the police plan to use tear gas and arrest marchers. The rumor has a *chilling effect* and keeps some people home who would otherwise have joined the protest.

CHOSE *(shōz)* Fr.: a thing.

CHOSE IN ACTION a **claim** or **debt** upon which recovery may be made in a lawsuit; not a present possession, but merely a right to sue, becoming a possessary thing only upon successful completion of a lawsuit.

CHOSE IN POSSESSION a thing actually possessed or possessable.

CHURNING excessive trading in a stock investment account. If the pattern of activity is inappropriate for the customer and if the prime result is excessive brokerage commissions for the **registered representative,** then the practice is unethical and recovery of damages by the customer is possible.

C.I.F. cost, insurance and freight; also written C.F.I. In a **contract** of sale it means that the cost of the goods, the insurance and the freight to the destination is included in the contract price, and unless there is something in a C.I.F. contract to indicate to the contrary, the seller completes his contract when he delivers the merchandise to the shipper, pays the freight to point of destination and forwards to the buyer the **bill of lading,** invoice, insurance policy and receipt showing payment of freight.

CIRCUIT COURT one of several courts in a given jurisdiction; a part of a system of federal courts extending over one or more counties or districts; formerly applied to the U.S. courts of appeals. Compare **district court.**

CIRCUMSTANTIAL EVIDENCE indirect evidence; secondary facts by which a principal fact may be reasonably inferred.

EXAMPLE: There are no eyewitnesses to place Steve at the site of the car accident, but there is a variety of *circumstantial evidence* to suggest that Steve was involved. The prints at the scene of the accident match the tires on his car, the color of several scratches on the other person's car is the same as the color of Steve's car, and his car is dented precisely where the other driver said it would be. That evidence could be used to implicate Steve in the collision.

CITATION 1. a reference to a legal authority—for example, a citation to a statute or case; 2. a writ similar to a **summons,** in that it commands the appearance of a party in a **proceeding.** The object of a citation is to give the court proper **jurisdiction** and to notify the **defendant** that a **suit** has been filed.

CITE 1. to summon; to order to appear, as before a tribunal; 2. to make reference to a text, statute, case or other legal authority in support of a proposition or argument; also the reference thus made.

CIVIL 1. the branch of law that pertains to suits other than criminal practice and is concerned with the rights and duties of persons in **contract, tort,** etc.; 2. **civil law** as opposed to **common law.**

CIVIL ACTION an action to protect a private right or to compel a civil remedy in a dispute between private parties, as distinguished from a criminal **prosecution.**

CIVIL AERONAUTICS BOARD [CAB] an independent federal agency established by Congress in 1938 to regulate commercial aviation and provide public air safety and navigation facilities. In 1958, Congress transferred all the functions except economic regulation of air carriers, aircraft registration, pilot licensing, and accident investigation to the **Federal Aviation Administration [FAA].**

CIVIL CONTEMPT see **contempt of court.**

CIVIL LAW 1. Roman law embodied in the Justinian Code and presently prevailing in most Western European states; it is also the foundation of the law of Louisiana. 2. the law concerned with noncriminal matters. 3. the body of laws established by a state or nation, as distinguished from **natural law.**

CIVIL LIABILITY amenability to **civil action** as distinguished from criminal action; a liability to actions seeking private remedies or the enforcement of personal rights, based on **contract, tort,** etc.

CIVIL LIBERTIES see **civil rights.**

CIVIL PENALTIES fines or money damages imposed by a regulatory scheme. Civil penalties are imposed as punishment for a certain activity and act as a criminal sanction, while civil remedies redress wrongs between private parties.

CIVIL PROCEDURE the body of rules of **practice** to be adhered to in adjudicating a controversy before a court of **civil,** as opposed to criminal, **jurisdiction.** The term refers to matters of form rather than to the principles of **substantive law** that must be applied to determine the rights of the parties.

CIVIL RIGHTS the nonpolitical rights of all citizens, especially those rights relating to personal liberty. Civil rights differ from **CIVIL LIBERTIES** in that civil rights are positive in nature, and civil liberties, negative; that is, civil liberties are immunities from governmental interference or limitations on governmental action (as in the First Amendment) that have the effect of reserving rights to individuals.

EXAMPLE: Neal is harassed as he enters a building designated as a polling place. The purpose is to prevent Neal from voting. The harassment violates Neal's *civil rights,* since he is guaranteed his right to vote.

CLAIM 1. the assertion of a right to money or **property;** 2. in pleading, the facts giving rise to a right enforceable in the courts, which must show the existence of a right, an injury and **damages.** One who makes a claim is the claimant.

CLAIM FOR REFUND a claim by a **taxpayer** to the **Internal Revenue Service** that he is entitled to a refund of all or part of the **taxes** paid by him in earlier years; such a claim must be made in writing within a specified time from the filing date of the **return** to which it relates and is a necessary prerequisite to any allowance of a refund by the IRS or to any suit by the taxpayer against the IRS for disallowance of a claimed refund.

CLAIM OF RIGHT a doctrine that requires a **taxpayer** to include in his gross **income** all amounts received by him under claim that he is entitled to the amounts, whether or not he is legally entitled to keep them and whether he is required to repay them in a subsequent year. When repayment occurs, a **deduction** is allowed under a special section of the **Internal Revenue Code** designed to minimize the tax distortion caused by the inclusion of such amounts in the wrong tax years.

CLASS ACTION a **suit** brought by one or more members of a large group of persons on behalf of all members of the group. If the court permits the class action, all members must receive notice of the action and must be given an opportunity to exclude themselves. Members who do not exclude themselves are bound by the **judgment,** whether favorable or not.

EXAMPLE: In accordance with securities law, a corporation files a registration statement with the Securities and Exchange Commission concerning a stock sale. After investors buy several million shares of stock and a few years pass, the corporation files for bankruptcy. At that point, a few of the investors realize the statement was false and misleading. Those investors, on behalf of all investors of the corporation, file a *class action* lawsuit seeking to recover the money they originally paid for the stock.

CLASSIFIED STOCK common stock divided into two or more classes. A typical approach is for a company to issue Class A **stock** to raise the bulk of **equity** capital while vesting voting rights in Class B stock, which is retained by management and/or founders. The practice is usually confined to promotional ventures, and very few publicly held companies have classified stock as part of their **capitalization.**

CLEAN HANDS the concept in **equity** that a **claimant** who seeks **equitable relief** must not himself have acted unfairly or unjustly in the transaction in which relief is sought.

CLEAR AND CONVINCING as a standard of proof, the amount of evidence that is beyond mere **preponderance** but is not "beyond **reasonable doubt,**" which will convince the trier of fact (**fact finder**) as to the facts sought to be established.

CLEAR AND PRESENT DANGER in constitutional law, a standard used to determine if one's First Amendment right to speak may be curtailed or punished. If the words are spoken in such circumstances and are of such a nature as to create a clear and present danger that they will bring about certain evils that government has a right to prevent, the government may prohibit or punish the use of those words.

CLEARINGHOUSE 1. an association, usually formed voluntarily by banks, to exchange checks, drafts or other forms of indebtedness held by one member and owed to another. Its object is to effect at one time and place the daily settlement of balances between the banks of a city or region with a minimum of inconvenience and labor. 2. in a stock or commodities exchange, an organization to facilitate settlement of the debits and credits of its members with each other. In essence, it operates on the same principles of centrality and convenience as does the clearinghouse association for banks. For example, if broker *A* is obligated to deliver 5,000 shares of *XYZ* stock and is entitled to receive 4,500 such shares from brokers *B, C* and *D,* at the end of the day he would deliver to the clearinghouse only 500 shares.

CLEAR TITLE **title** free from any **encumbrance,** obstruction, **burden** or limitation that presents a doubtful or even a reasonable question of law or fact as to its validity. See **good title; marketable title.**

CLEMENCY see **executive clemency.**

CLERICAL ERROR a mistake made while copying or transmitting legal documents as distinguished from a **JUDICIAL ERROR,** which is an error made in the exercise of judgment or discretion.

CLERK an assistant or a subordinate. A **COURT CLERK** is an officer whose duties include keeping records, issuing process and entering judgment. A **LAW CLERK** is an assistant to a lawyer or a judge, whose primary job is to aid in the research and writing of briefs or opinions and the handling of cases.

CLOSE see **enclosure.**

CLOSE CORPORATION see **corporation.**

CLOSED SHOP an enterprise in which, because it is required by the terms of a collective bargaining agreement between a labor union and the owners/managers of the enterprise, all workers must be union members, as a condition of their employment.

CLOSING the consummation of a transaction involving the sale of real estate or of an interest in real estate, usually by payment of the purchase price (or some agreed portion), delivery of the **deed** or other **instrument** of **title,** and finalizing of collateral matters.

CLOSING AGREEMENT a written agreement between a **taxpayer** and the **Internal Revenue Service** that conclusively settles his tax liability for the **taxable year** ending prior to the agreement date or settles one or more issues affecting his tax liability. The agreement is binding on both the taxpayer and the IRS unless **fraud** or misrepresentation of a **material** fact is demonstrated.

CLOTURE in legislative assemblies that permit unlimited debate (**FILIBUSTER**), a procedure or rule by which debate is ended so that a vote may be taken on the matter. In the U.S. Senate, a two-thirds majority vote of the body is required to invoke cloture and terminate debate.

CLOUD ON TITLE any matter appearing in the record of a **title** to real estate that on its face appears to reflect the existence of an outstanding **claim** or **encumbrance** that, if valid, would defeat or impair title, but that might be proven invalid by evidence outside the title record.

EXAMPLE: Julie locates a house she wants to buy but demands an abstract of title to be sure that no one else may have a claim to the land or house. The abstract shows a *cloud on the title* from about sixty years ago concerning a transfer of the land wherein a joint owner did not sign the deed transferring title. Julie may not want to purchase the house, or she may want title insurance to cover a problem if one arises. Where a cloud on a title exists, the seller ordinarily gives the purchaser a **quitclaim deed,** which transfers all of the interest the seller owns and no more. Title companies usually will not insure a clouded title or will insure it subject to that cloud which is listed in the policy as an exception.

CODE a systematic compilation of laws, for example, the Criminal Code (referring to penal laws) and the Motor Vehicle Code (referring to laws relating to motor vehicles).

CODEFENDANT a **defendant** who is joined together with one or more other defendants in a single **action.** See **joinder.**

CODE OF PROFESSIONAL RESPONSIBILITY a set of rules based on ethical considerations that govern the conduct of lawyers; passed by the American Bar Association and **adopted** by most states; enforced by state disciplinary boards. Some states require lawyers to prove their knowledge of the Code by passage of a course or test before being allowed to practice in that state.

CODE PLEADING the term applied to the system of **pleading,** now abandoned, which was developed in this country through practice codes enacted in a majority of the states, to consolidate and improve the **common law** and **equity** systems of pleading previously used.

CODICIL a supplement to a **will,** whose purpose is to add to, subtract from, or qualify, modify or revoke the provisions of a prior will.

EXAMPLE: Larry executed his will at a time when his relationship with his brother was at a low point. As the relationship improves, Larry writes a *codicil* to his will providing that a certain amount of money pass to the brother. The codicil also revokes any statement in the will that specifically denies the brother anything.

COGNIZABLE within the **jurisdiction** of the court. An interest is cognizable in a court of law when that court has the power to decide the controversy.

COHABITATION 1. the act of living together; often statutorily expanded to include living together publicly, as husband and wife; 2. having sexual intercourse.

COHEIR one who inherits a property with another.

COINSURANCE an **insurance** plan in which the insurer provides **indemnity** for only a certain percentage of the insured's loss, reflecting the relative division of risk between insurer and **insured.**

COLLATERAL 1. secondary; on the side; 2. in commercial transactions, the property offered as **security,** usually as an inducement to another party to lend money or extend credit.

COLLATERAL ATTACK a separate **action** brought to challenge the integrity of a **judgment,** as distinguished from a DIRECT ATTACK, brought to void a judgment within the same action (through an appeal or request for a new trial, etc.).

COLLATERAL ESTOPPEL the doctrine that recognizes that the determination of facts **litigated** between two **parties** in a **proceeding** is binding on those parties in all future proceedings against each other. See **estoppel.** See also **bar; res judicata.**

EXAMPLE: Flip Corporation files a suit in federal court claiming that another company infringed upon a patent that Flip owned. Flip loses the case after the court determines that the patent is invalid. While that suit is pending, Flip files another suit against Ace Corporation claiming the same patent infringement. Ace Corporation can use the doctrine of *collateral estoppel,* which allows Ace to introduce the first court's finding that no patent exists, and ask for a dismissal of this suit based on the earlier court holding. Ace will generally win on those grounds, unless Flip can show that it did not have a full and fair opportunity to litigate the issue at the first trial.

COLLATERAL FRAUD see **fraud** [EXTRINSIC FRAUD].

COLLATION the preparation of an estimate of the value of **advancements** made by an **intestate** [person who dies without a **will**] to his or her children, in order that the whole of the **estate** may be divided in accordance with law.

COLLECTIVE BARGAINING the process of settling labor disputes by negotiation between the employer and representatives of employees. Compare **arbitration.**

COLLUSION 1. the making of a secret agreement with another to commit **fraud** or engage in other illegal activity, or in legal activity with an illegal end in mind; 2. an agreement between husband and wife to suppress facts or to make up **evidence** important to the existence of lawful grounds for divorce.

COLLUSIVE ACTION an **action** brought by **parties** not actually **adversaries** to determine a hypothetical point of law or to produce a desired legal **precedent.** Because such a suit does not involve a genuine **controversy,** it will not be entertained by a court.

COLOR deceptive appearance or disguise; designates hiding a set of facts behind a false, but technically proper, legal theory. See **color of law; color of title.**

COLOR OF LAW the semblance of legal right. An action under color of law has the apparent authority of law but is actually contrary to law.

COLOR OF TITLE an **instrument** that appears to pass title, and on which one relies as passing title, but that is not valid, either because title is lacking in the person conveying or because the **conveyance** itself is defective.

COMITY [COMITAS] a rule of courtesy by which one court defers to the concomitant **jurisdiction** of another; most often used in reference to the longstanding public policy against federal court interference with state criminal proceedings.

EXAMPLE: Jack kidnaps a young girl and takes her across state lines, a crime that violates both federal and state laws. Although Jack could be prosecuted by both jurisdictions or either of them, under principles of *comity* the federal prosecutor allows the state to proceed first, because of the anger of the community and their desire to try Jack in a local setting.

COMMENT statements made by a judge or counsel concerning a defendant, where such statements are not based on fact, but rather on alleged facts.

COMMERCIAL BRIBERY see **bribery.**

COMMERCIAL FRUSTRATION see **frustration of purpose.**

COMMERCIAL LAW the body of law that concerns the rights and obligations of persons in their commercial dealings with one another (such as the **Uniform Commercial Code,** laws prohibiting unfair trade practices, etc). See **law merchant; mercantile law; Uniform Commercial Code.**

COMMERCIAL PAPER a **negotiable instrument,** that is, a writing **indorsed** by the **maker** or **drawer,** containing an unconditional promise or order to pay a certain sum on demand or at a specified time, and payable to order or to bearer. See also **order paper.**

COMMERCIAL PREFERENCE see **preference.**

COMMERCIAL UNIT a unit considered by trade or usage to be a whole that cannot be divided without materially impairing its value, character or use; for example, a machine or a suite of furniture. Since acceptance of any part of a commercial unit constitutes acceptance of the whole, the term becomes significant when a buyer attempts to reject part of a **contract** for nonconformance. If the item rejected is part of a commercial unit, the rejection will not be allowed.

COMMINGLING OF FUNDS the act of a **fiduciary** or **trustee,** including a lawyer, in mixing his or her own funds with those belonging to a client or customer; generally prohibited unless the fiduciary maintains an exact accounting of the client's funds and how they have been used.

EXAMPLE: The bank trustee felt he had an excellent tip on a stock, so he *commingled the funds* of one of the bank trusts with his own funds. The investment is successful, but the trustee is still disciplined because he never made an exact accounting of the stock purchased with trust money.

COMMISSION a fee paid to an employee or agent for services performed—especially, a percentage of a total amount received in a transaction—as distinguished from salary, which is a fixed amount payable periodically.

COMMITMENT 1. a judge's order directing that a person be taken to prison or jail, either to await trial or following an imposition of sentence; 2. an order mandating a person to confinement in a medical institution.

COMMITTEE 1. in legislative practice, a group appointed to investigate some special matter or area of interest and report its findings and recommendations to the legislative body; 2. a person appointed by the court to manage the affairs of a legally **incompetent** person. See **guardian; ward.**

COMMODITY any tangible **good;** a product that is the subject of **sale** or barter. See also **futures.**

COMMON CARRIER see **carrier [COMMON CARRIER].**

COMMON LAW the system of **jurisprudence,** which originated in England and was later applied in the United States, that is based on judicial **precedent** (court decisions) rather than legislative enactment (statutes) and is therefore derived from principles rather than rules.

In the absence of statutory law regarding a particular subject, the judge-made rules of **common law** are the law on that subject. Thus the traditional phrase "at common law" refers to the state of the law in a particular field prior to the enactment of legislation in that field.

COMMON-LAW COPYRIGHT see **copyright.**

COMMON-LAW MARRIAGE one based not upon ceremony and compliance with legal formalities, but upon the agreement of two persons, legally competent to marry, to **cohabit** with the intention of being husband and wife, usually for a minimum period of seven years.

COMMON-LAW TRUST see **Massachusetts trust.**

COMMON NUISANCE see **nuisance [PUBLIC (COMMON) NUISANCE].**

COMMON PROPERTY see **property.**

COMMONS 1. land set aside for public use, for example, public parks; 2. the untitled class of Great Britain, represented in Parliament by the House of Commons.

COMMON STOCK a security representing an ownership interest in a corporation. Ownership may also be shared with **preferred stock,** which has prior claim on any **dividends** to be paid and, in the event of liquidation, prior claim to the distribution of the corporation's **assets.** As owners of the corporation, common stockholders **(shareholders)** assume the primary risk if business is poor, realize the greater return in the event of success and elect the **board of directors** that controls the company.

COMMUNITY PROPERTY all property that a husband and wife acquire by joint effort during marriage. Property owned prior to marriage or acquired by gift or inheritance is considered **SEPARATE PROPERTY.**

EXAMPLE: As a result of hard work and prudent investing, a wife has acquired a great deal of property during her marriage. If the marriage fails, her husband is entitled to one-half of whatever property she has acquired in her work if the couple reside in a state that follows *community property* law. That law applies regardless of the fact that the wife's efforts alone resulted in accumulation of the property.

Currently, eight states have adopted the community property doctrine. Other states have instead adopted **EQUITABLE**

DISTRIBUTION statutes to achieve a similar distribution of the marital estate upon dissolution of a marriage.

Community property is similar to, but should be distinguished from, TENANCY BY THE ENTIRETY and JOINT TENANCY. (see **tenancy**).

COMMUTATION change; in criminal law, substituting a lesser punishment for a greater one, such as life imprisonment for a death sentence, a shorter term for a longer one. Commutation is the prerogative of the chief executive (president or governor), who possess the power of **executive clemency.** A commutation can be granted only after a conviction, whereas other forms of clemency, such as a **pardon,** can be granted at any time. Also, a commutation merely lessens punishment, while a pardon removes all legal disabilities of a conviction. Compare **reprieve.**

EXAMPLE: Several years ago, eight persons were sentenced to fifteen years' imprisonment for possession of a small quantity of marijuana. In light of the new attitude towards personal use of the drug and the recent decriminalization of many marijuana laws, the governor *commuted* (reduced) the prisoners' sentences to time already served, allowing the prisoners to be released immediately.

COMPANY a group of people organized to perform an activity, business or industrial enterprise.

HOLDING COMPANY see **holding company.**

JOINT STOCK COMPANY a company or association, usually unincorporated, that has the capital of its members pooled in a common fund; the CAPITAL STOCK (see **capital**) is divided into **shares** and distributed to represent ownership **interest** in the company. A form of partnership, it is distinguished from a partnership in that the membership of a joint stock company is changeable, its shares are transferable, its members can be many and not necessarily known to each other, and its members cannot act or speak for the company.

COMPARATIVE NEGLIGENCE see **negligence.**

COMPENSATION payment for work done or for an injury.

COMPENSATORY DAMAGES see **damages** [ACTUAL DAMAGES].

COMPETENT properly or legally qualified; able; capable of understanding or of acting reasonably. COMPETENT EVIDENCE is both relevant and proper to the issue being **litigated.** A COMPETENT COURT has proper jurisdiction over the person or property at issue. A criminal defendant is competent to stand trial if he is able to consult with his lawyer with a reasonable degree of rational understanding and has a rational as well as a factual understanding of the **proceedings** against him. An individual is competent to make a **will** if he understands the extent of his **property,** the identity of the natural objects of his bounty, and the consequences of making a will.

EXAMPLE: Upon their father's death, his children learned that his will left all his property to his mistress. The children brought a lawsuit to invalidate the will, claiming the father was not *competent* to understand what he was signing or to whom he was leaving his property. The children's evidence included examples of frequent outbursts of rage and depression by the father, as well as occasional stays at a nearby sanitarium.

COMPLAINANT the party who initiates the **complaint** in an **action** or **proceeding;** practically synonymous with **petitioner** and **plaintiff.** The appropriate term to use is determined by the nature of the proceeding and the court in which it is instituted. Compare **accused; defendant; respondent.**

COMPLAINT 1. in a civil action, the first **pleading** of the **plaintiff** setting out the facts on which the claim is based; the purpose is to give notice to the adversary of the nature and basis of the claim asserted. 2. in criminal law, the preliminary **charge** or accusation made by one person against another to the appropriate court or officer, usually a magistrate. However, court proceedings, such as a trial, cannot be instituted until an **indictment** or **information** has been handed down against the defendant.

COMPOS MENTIS *(kŏm'-pōs mĕn'-tĭs)* Lat.: mentally competent. Compare **non compos mentis.**

COMPOUNDING A FELONY the refusal by one injured by a **felony** to **prosecute** the felon, in exchange for which the injured party receives a bribe or reparation.

COMPOUND INTEREST see **interest.**

COMPULSORY PROCESS the right of a **defendant** to have the **subpoena** power of the court used on his behalf to compel the **appearance** of **witnesses.** In civil actions, the right to compulsory process is often secured through state constitutional or statutory provisions. In a criminal proceeding, this right is guaranteed to the defendant by the Sixth Amendment to the United States Constitution. The right extends only to competent, **material** witnesses who are subject to the court's process and whose expected testimony will be **admissible.**

CONCEALMENT an act making more difficult the discovery of that which one is legally obligated to reveal or not to withhold, such as the failure of a **bankrupt** to schedule all his **assets,** or the failure of an applicant for an insurance policy to disclose information relevant to the insurer's decision to insure the risk.

CONCERTED ACTION [CONCERT OF ACTION] 1. action that has been arranged and agreed upon between parties, in pursuance of some common design or in accordance with some scheme. In criminal law, concerted action is found only where there has been a **conspiracy** to commit an illegal act—that is, all share the criminal intent of the actual perpetrator. 2. The term also applies to **joint tortfeasors** where there is **tort** liability for conspiracy.

CONCLUSION OF FACT a conclusion as to a factual matter,

reached solely through the use of facts and natural reasoning, rather than rules of law.

EXAMPLE: The legal issue before the judge is simple; if the manufacturer does not provide necessary safeguards, he is liable for the workman's injury. The only issue is a question of fact: Did the manufacturer provide the safeguards which the workman subsequently disregarded or were the safeguards never provided? After hearing the evidence, the judge ruled as a *conclusion of fact* that the safeguards had been disregarded by the workman.

CONCLUSION OF LAW a conclusion as to a legal issue, reached by applying the rules of law.

EXAMPLE: In a particular case, the facts were not in question; but the defense counsel had never called a witness who might have been crucial to the defendant's case. A few years later, when the defendant attempts to have the conviction reversed, the legal issue concerns the standard to be used when a lawyer's incompetent advice results in a conviction. As a *conclusion of law,* the judge finds that, in his particular state, the law requires a stronger showing of incompetence than the one made in this case and therefore refuses to reverse the conviction.

CONCLUSIVE PRESUMPTION see **presumption.**

CONCUR to agree. A concurring opinion agrees with the conclusion of the majority but may state different reasons why such a conclusion is reached.

CONCURRENT existing together; in conjunction with. In criminal law, CONCURRENT SENTENCE describes multiple sentences that a convicted defendant is to serve at the same time.

CONDEMN 1. to take private property for public use, such as the building of a highway, with or without consent but for **just compensation;** 2. to declare legally useless or unfit for habitation, as an unsafe building; . . . to sentence to death a person convicted of a **capital offense.**

CONDITION 1. a prerequisite or requirement; 2. a possible future event, which will trigger the duty to perform a legal obligation or will cause a **real property** interest to arise, vest or be extinguished.

CONDITION PRECEDENT an act or event that must occur before a duty of immediate performance of a promise arises, or before a real property interest will arise or vest.

CONDITION SUBSEQUENT a fact that will extinguish a duty to make compensation for **BREACH OF CONTRACT** after the breach has occurred, or whose occurrence will result in the extinguishment of an interest in real property.

CONCURRENT CONDITION a condition precedent that exists only when parties to a contract are obligated to perform at the same time.

CONDITIONAL FEE [OR ESTATE] a limited **fee simple** that must eventually pass from the **donee** to certain **heirs** or to the **issue** (children) of the donee (**heirs of the body**). Should the designated heir fail to be alive at the time of the donee's death, the property **reverts** to the **donor** or his **estate.** However, the entire estate remains with the donee until his death, the donor having the mere **possibility of a reverter.**

EXAMPLE: The mother gave Kim, her daughter, title to a home and instructed Kim to pass the home to Kim's daughter or, if she did not have a daughter, to Kim's son, upon Kim's death. This gift to Kim was a *conditional fee,* since if Kim died without a daughter or son, title to the home returned to the mother. If the mother predeceased Kim, the home would return to the mother's estate and pass under the mother's will.

CONDOMINIUM a type of ownership associated with multiunit projects, which consists of individual ownership (in **fee**) of a single unit and shared ownership (**tenancy** in common) of the common areas (such as elevators, grounds, etc.). A condominium is distinguished from a **COOPERATIVE,** in which a corporate or business **trust** entity holds **title** to the **premises** and grants rights of occupancy to apartments through proprietary **leases** or similar arrangements.

CONFESSION an admission of guilt or other incriminating statement by the **accused;** not admissible at trial unless voluntarily made. See **Miranda Rule.**

CONFESSION AND AVOIDANCE a **pleading** by which a **party** admits the **allegations** against him, either expressly or by implication, but presents **new matter** that **avoids** or annuls, the effect of his admitting those allegations. See **defense [AFFIRMATIVE DEFENSE].**

CONFESSION OF JUDGMENT the entry of a **judgment** upon the written **admission** or **confession** of a **debtor,** without a legal **proceeding.** It is accomplished through an advance, voluntary submission to the **jurisdiction** of the court, as when a buyer of goods on **credit** agrees in his purchase **contract** that if he fails to pay on time the amounts due he will consent to the entry of a judgment against him for the amount outstanding (and, often, reasonable **attorney's fees** not exceeding a fixed percentage).

CONFIDENCE GAME a scheme by which a swindler wins the confidence of his victim and then cheats him of his money by taking advantage of the confidence reposed in him.

CONFISCATE 1. with regard to acts by a government entity, to take private property without **just compensation;** 2. to seize goods or property and divest the owner of his proprietary rights, usually as a result of some violation of the law involving the goods or property seized. Compare **condemn.**

CONFLICT OF INTERESTS an inconsistency between the public interest and the personal interest of a public official, which arises in connection with the performance of his official duties.

CONFLICT OF LAWS [CHOICE OF LAW] the body of law that contains the rules by which the court in which an **action** is brought chooses between the applicable law of the court's state (the "forum state") and the differing applicable law of another **jurisdiction** connected with the controversy.

EXAMPLE: Mary died intestate (i.e., without a will). At her death, she lived and owned property in Florida but had set up a trust in Delaware for her children and grandchildren. Florida claims that, because Mary was a resident of Florida, that state's intestate laws should apply to all of Mary's property. Delaware feels that its intestate laws should apply to the trust accounts since she purposefully set up the account in Delaware. A court will consider the rules concerning *conflict of laws* to determine which state's law applies to the trust.

CONFUSION OF GOODS a mixing together of **personal property** belonging to two or more owners so the property of any of them no longer can be identified except as part of a mass of like goods.

CONGLOMERATE a group of **corporations** engaged in unrelated businesses and controlled by a single corporate entity.

CONGRESS 1. a formal body of delegates or representatives; 2. in the United States, the national legislative body consisting of the Senate and the House of Representatives. The lawmaking power of the United States vests in this body.

CONJUGAL RIGHTS the rights of married persons, which include companionship, domestic happiness, the comforts of dwelling together, joint property rights, and the intimacies of domestic relations. In prison, a **CONJUGAL VISITATION** permits an opportunity for sexual intimacy between the inmate and his or her spouse.

CONSCIENTIOUS OBJECTOR a status recognized by U.S. Selective Service (''draft'') laws and accorded to one who, in good conscience, because of religious belief, is opposed to war. Such a person may be excused from participation in military service otherwise required by law and may be permitted to substitute community service.

CONSCIOUS PARALLELISM in **antitrust law,** an independent decision by one party, aware that a particular course of conduct has been followed by a competitor, to follow the same course; distinguished from **conspiracy,** which requires an agreement, either implied or express, between the parties engaged in the parallel conduct.

EXAMPLE: Shopper Supermarkets decides to end its three-month promotion of offering double coupons. Because of Shopper's action, other area supermarkets end similar promotions. When complaints arise against the supermarkets for acting together to raise prices by ending the discounts, in violation of antitrust laws, the supermarkets reply that their action was not unlawful but represented *conscious parallelism*—when Shopper ended the discounts, the other supermarkets felt they could do the same without losing business but they did not act together in an anticompetitive and illegal way.

CONSENT DECREE see **consent judgment.**

CONSENT JUDGMENT recorded agreement of parties to a lawsuit concerning the form the **judgment** should take. Such a contract cannot be nullified without consent of the parties, except for **fraud** or **mistake.** Consent judgments have the same force as any other judgment. Because the agreement of the parties waives exception to irregularities before agreement, **appeal** from a consent judgment is limited to attack for mistake, fraud or lack of **jurisdiction.**

CONSENT ORDER any court **order** to which the opposing party agrees; in **antitrust law,** an agreement between the **Federal Trade Commission** and a party being investigated; the party consents to cease activities that could be subject of antitrust action and the FTC refrains from initiating suit.

CONSENT DECREE the counterpart of a consent judgment issued in a **court of equity;** only as binding as any other **equitable** remedy. For instance, in antitrust cases, the court can modify a consent decree according to changed circumstances.

CONSEQUENTIAL DAMAGES see **damages.**

CONSERVATOR temporary court-appointed **guardian** or custodian of **property.**

CONSIDERATION something of value given in return for performance or promise of performance for the purpose of forming a **contract;** generally required to make a promise binding and to make agreement of the parties enforceable as a contract. Consideration distinguishes a contract from a **gift.**

FAILURE OF CONSIDERATION or **WANT OF CONSIDERATION** refers to the circumstance in which consideration was bargained for but either has become worthless, has ceased to exist or has not been provided as promised.

EXAMPLE: Although Paula ran a prosperous business on the West Coast and was enjoying life as a "single," she agreed to return East to care for her aging mother. As a demonstration of her gratitude, the mother promised Paula the money located in a bank account. Nothing was ever signed, and upon the mother's death, the other children contested Paula's claim to the whole account. They felt that there was no contract between the mother and Paula because Paula gave no *consideration* in return for the money in the account. A court would probably find that Paula's care for the mother at the mother's request, as well as the giving up of a prosperous business, constituted consideration and hence the promise is enforceable.

CONSIGNMENT **bailment** for care or sale. A delivery of goods, without **sale,** to a dealer, who must sell the goods and remit the price to the person making delivery; or if the goods are not sold, the dealer must return them to the owner.

CONSIGNEE 1. a person to whom goods are shipped for sale under a consignment contract; 2. the person named in a **bill of lading** to whom the bill promises delivery; 3. one to whom a carrier may lawfully make delivery in accordance with his contract of carriage. See **carrier [common carrier].**

CONSIGNOR one who sends a consignment; a shipper of goods; the person calling upon a common carrier for transportation service, who is not necessarily the person in whose name a bill of lading is made.

CONSOLIDATION see **merger.**

CONSORTIUM the conjugal fellowship of husband and wife, and the right of each to the aid of the other in every conjugal relation. A person willfully interfering with this relation, depriving one spouse of the consortium of the other, is liable in **damages** and may give rise to action for **alienation of affection.** Loss of consortium can figure in action for injury or **wrongful death** of a spouse. See also **conjugal rights.**

CONSPIRACY a combination of two or more persons to commit an unlawful act, or to commit a lawful act by unlawful means. A conspiracy to injure another is an actionable **tort;** it may also be a criminal offense. Compare **accomplice.**

CONSPIRATOR [COCONSPIRATOR] one involved in a **conspiracy;** one who acts with another, or others, in furtherance of an unlawful transaction. See also **accessory.** Compare **principal.**

CONSTITUTION the fundamental principles of **law** by which a government is created and a country is administered. In Western democratic theory, a **mandate** from the people in their **sovereign** capacity, concerning how they shall be governed. Distinguished from a **statute,** which is a rule decided by legislative representatives and is subject to limitations of the Constitution.

CONSTITUTIONAL RIGHTS individual liberties granted by the State or Federal **Constitutions** and protected from governmental interference.

CONSTRUCTION an interpretation of something not totally clear. To determine construction of a **statute** or **constitution** is to decide the meaning of an ambiguous part of it.

STRICT CONSTRUCTION a conservative or literal interpretation of statutes, stressing rigid adherence to terms specified.

CONSTRUCTIVE not actual, but accepted in law as a substitute for whatever is otherwise required. Thus, anything the law finds to exist constructively will be treated by the law as though it were actually so.

[For the meaning of constructive as applied to various legal concepts, refer to those specific entries.]

CONSUMER PROTECTION refers to laws designed to aid retail consumers of goods and services that have been improperly manufactured, delivered, performed, handled, or described. Such laws provide the retail consumer with additional protections and remedies not generally provided to merchants and others who engage in business transactions, on the premise that consumers do not enjoy an "**arm's-length**" bargaining position with respect to the businessmen with whom they deal and therefore should not be strictly limited by the legal rules that govern **recovery** for **damages** among businessmen.

EXAMPLE: John contracted with a company to put aluminum siding on his house. The company transfers the contract to a finance agency and receives the amount John had agreed to pay the company, less a small discount so that the finance agency can make a profit on the transfer. Under basic commercial law, if the company does not perform the work satisfactorily, John will still have to pay the finance agency, because that area of law protects the agency [as a **holder in due course**] from claims against the company once the agency assumes the contract. But under some states' *consumer protection* laws, the finance agency must take responsibility for the company work in most instances.

CONTEMPT OF COURT an act or omission tending to interfere with orderly administration of justice, or to impair the dignity of the court or respect for its authority. **DIRECT CONTEMPT** takes place openly and in the presence of the court. **CONSTRUCTIVE CONTEMPT** occurs outside the court; an example is failure to comply with court orders.

CIVIL CONTEMPT consists of failure to do something ordered by the court for the benefit of another party to the proceedings (sometimes called **RELIEF TO LITIGANTS**); **CRIMINAL CONTEMPT** includes acts disrespectful of the court or its processes that obstruct administration of justice.

EXAMPLE: A judge orders a litigant to disclose several important documents to his adversary. The litigant refuses because he feels that the documents will give away trade secrets. The court has certain formulas and designs deleted, and orders that the documents be relinquished. If the litigant still refuses, he can be held in *contempt of court,* resulting in a jail sentence and/or a fine. The nature of the sanction is within the trial judge's discretion. As a general legal proposition, an order of a court must be obeyed or appealed. It may not be disregarded.

CONTIGUOUS adjacent, connected.

CONTINGENT BENEFICIARY one who will receive the benefit or proceeds of an **estate, trust,** life insurance policy or the like but only if some particular event or circumstance, whose happening or outcome is not presently known or assured, does in fact occur.

EXAMPLE: A husband establishes a trust to take effect at his death and names his wife as beneficiary. The trust instrument also provides that if the wife should remarry, the husband's son and daughter become the beneficiaries and the wife is no longer eligible to take under the trust. Since there is no assurance that the wife will ever remarry, the son and daughter are considered *contingent beneficiaries*.

CONTINGENT ESTATE [OR INTEREST] an **interest** or **estate** in land that might or might not begin in the future, depending upon occurrence of a specific but uncertain event or depending on the determination or existence of the person[s] to whom the estate is limited. Compare **conditional fee; future interest.**

EXAMPLE: The brother grants land to Jane until she dies and then provides that the land go to Paul's children. Paul has no children at this time, so the grant of the land to them following Jane's death is a *contingent estate*. If Paul has no children when Jane dies, the title to the land reverts back to the brother (who first granted it).

CONTINGENT FEE a charge made by an attorney for services rendered to his client, recovery of which depends upon a successful outcome of the case. The amount is often agreed to be a percentage of the client's recovery. Such fee arrangements are often used in **negligence** cases, but it is unethical for an attorney to charge a criminal defendant a fee contingent upon the result.

CONTINUANCE the adjournment or postponement, to a specified subsequent date, of an **action** pending in a court.

CONTRA *(kôn'-tră)* Lat.: against. In opposition to; in violation of; the reverse of.

CONTRA BONOS MORES *(kôn'-trȧ bō'-nōs mô'-rāz)* Lat.: against good morals. Refers to conduct that offends the average conscience and commonly accepted standards.

CONTRACT a promise, for the **breach** of which the law provides a **remedy,** or the **performance** of which the law recognizes as a **duty**; a transaction involving two or more individuals whereby each has reciprocal rights to demand performance of what is promised.

BILATERAL CONTRACT one in which there are mutual promises between two parties, each being both a promisor and a promisee.

CONDITIONAL CONTRACT a contract whose performance depends upon a future event; e.g., a contract to purchase a car if it passes a motor vehicle inspection.

EXAMPLE: Glen wants to purchase a large tract of land from seller to build a manufacturing plant but is unsure whether he can get a loan from the bank to finance the construction costs. Therefore, he signs a *conditional contract* with the seller that he will purchase the land only if he obtains a construction loan from the bank.

COST-PLUS CONTRACT one providing that the contractor receives payment of his total costs, plus a stated percentage or profit.

ORAL CONTRACT one that is not in writing or that is not signed by the parties.

OUTPUT CONTRACT one whereby a party promises to deliver his entire output to another and the other promises to accept the entire output supplied.

QUASI CONTRACT see **quasi [QUASI CONTRACT].**

REQUIREMENTS CONTRACT one whereby a party agrees to purchase all his requirements of a particular product from another, and the other agrees to supply the need.

UNILATERAL CONTRACT agreement whereby one makes a promise to do, or refrain from doing, something in return for an actual performance by the other, rather than a mere promise of performance.

CONTRACT OF ADHESION see **adhesion contract.**

CONTRACT OF HAZARD see **sale [SALE IN GROSS].**

CONTRACTOR 1. a party to a **contract;** 2. one who contracts to do work for another. An **INDEPENDENT CONTRACTOR** makes an agreement to do a specific piece of work, retaining control of the means and method of doing the job; neither party has the right to terminate the contract at will. A **GENERAL BUILDING CONTRACTOR** contracts directly with the owner of the property upon which the construction occurs, as distinguished from a **SUBCONTRACTOR,** who would deal only with one of the general contractors.

CONTRACT UNDER SEAL see **sealed instrument.**

CONTRA PACEM *(kŏn'-trȧ pä'-kĕm)* Lat.: against the peace. Used in Latin forms of **indictments,** and also in **actions** for **trespass,** to signify that the alleged offense was committed against the public peace.

CONTRIBUTION 1. sharing, by another person jointly responsible for injury to a third person, of the amount required to compensate the victim. One who is partly responsible for an injury is often entitled to demand contribution from another who is also responsible. The duty generally involves equal sharing of the penalty, but in some **jurisdictions** it may be apportioned among the **joint tortfeasors** according to degree of fault. Compare **indemnity.** 2. In tax law, a tax deductible contribution is a **DONATION.**

CHARITABLE CONTRIBUTION a contribution for the use of a state, the United States, or a **NOT-FOR-PROFIT CORPORATION** (see **corporation**) organized exclusively for religious, charitable, scientific, literary or educational purposes.

CONTRIBUTORY NEGLIGENCE see **negligence.**

CONTROLLED SUBSTANCE a drug whose general availability is restricted; any substance that is strictly regulated or outlawed because of its potential for abuse or addiction. Controlled substances include narcotics, stimulants, depressants, hallucinogens and cannabis.

CONTROVERSY a dispute. In constitutional law, in order to constitute a "case or controversy" sufficient to permit an **adjudication** by the court, a controversy must be real, not one inquiring what the law would be in a hypothetical situation. See **standing.** Compare **declaratory judgment; advisory opinion.**

CONTUMACY willful disobedience to the **summons** or orders of a court; overt defiance of authority. Contumacious conduct may result in a finding of **contempt of court.**

CONVERSION a **tort** consisting of deprivation of another's property without authorization and without **justification.**

EXAMPLE: Ralph steals a check made payable to Overland Corporation and cashes it at his bank. Ralph is guilty of theft, which by definition includes *conversion*. But, in most instances, the bank is also guilty of conversion. It has contributed to the unauthorized taking of the check by giving Ralph cash even though the check was not made out to him. Absent complicity in the theft, the bank is not criminally liable unlike

Ralph. The bank is, however, monetarily liable to Overland Corporation.

CONVERTIBLE SECURITIES **bonds** and **preferred stock** that can be exchanged for **common stock** or other lesser security usually of the same **corporation.** Terms of the exchange specify the exchange ratio and expiration of the right to exchange.

CONVEY in **real property** law, to transfer property from one to another, by means of a written **instrument** and other formalities. Compare **alienation; grant.**

CONVICT 1. one who has been determined by the court to be guilty of the crime charged; 2. to determine such guilt.

CONVICTION the result of a legal **proceeding** in which the guilt of a **party** is ascertained and upon which **sentence** or **judgment** is founded. The **confession** of an **accused** in open court or a **verdict** that ascertains and publishes the fact of guilt are both sufficient to constitute a conviction. See **guilty.**

COOPERATIVE see **condominium.**

COOPERATIVE ASSOCIATION a union of individuals, commonly laborers, farmers or small capitalists, formed for the pursuit in common of a productive enterprise, the profits being shared in proportion to the capital or labor contributed by each.

COPARCENERS persons who, by virtue of **descent,** have become concurrent owners. See **parcener.**

EXAMPLE: Seth and Nathan were left a summer home by their father. As a result of that devise, the two are **coparceners.**

COPARTNER see **partner.**

COPYRIGHT protection by **statute** or by the **common law,** giving authors and artists exclusive right to publish their works or to determine who may so publish. When by statute, copyright is exclusively a matter of federal law.

COMMON-LAW COPYRIGHT a protection that exists before a work is published or otherwise placed in the public domain; protects against unauthorized publication of the unpublished work; also called **RIGHT OF FIRST PUBLICATION.**

COPYRIGHT INFRINGEMENT the offense of unauthorized use of a work protected by copyright. See **plagiarism.**

CORAM NOBIS, WRIT OF see **writ of coram nobis.**

CORONER a public official who investigates the causes and circumstances of suspicious deaths that occur within his jurisdiction and makes a finding in a coroner's **inquest.** See also **post mortem.**

CORPORAL PUNISHMENT punishment inflicted upon the body. The term may or may not include imprisonment; often serves simply to distinguish physical punishment from nonphysical punishment, such as a fine.

CORPORATE OPPORTUNITY the legal doctrine that **directors** or others invested with a **fiduciary duty** toward a corporation may not appropriate for their own benefit a business opportunity properly belonging to the corporation. Persons found guilty of this practice are deemed to hold the property or profits thus obtained in CONSTRUCTIVE TRUST (see **trust**) for the benefit of the corporation, and **injunctive** relief as well as money damages may be available to the victimized shareholders. See **conflict of interests; insider.**

CORPORATION an association of **shareholders** (or a single shareholder) created under law as an ARTIFICIAL PERSON, having a legal entity separate from the individuals who compose it, with the capacity of continuous existence or **succession,** and the capacity of taking, holding and conveying **property,** suing and being sued, and exercising, like a **nat-**

ural person, other powers that are conferred on it by law. A corporation's **liability** is normally limited to its **assets;** the shareholders are thus protected against personal liability for the corporation. The corporation is taxed at special tax rates, and the stockholders must pay an additional tax upon **dividends** or other profits from the corporation. Corporations are subject to regulation by the state of incorporation and by the **jurisdictions** in which they carry on their business.

Special statutes have been enacted in many jurisdictions to permit single individuals or closely knit small groups of individuals to form CLOSE CORPORATIONS to limit their personal liability but to carry on business without the formality of annual meetings and action by boards of directors.

EXAMPLE: Bob runs several clothing shops as a sole proprietor. After speaking with other businessmen, he decides to form a *close corporation*. Under that arrangement, Bob still controls the company, although there may be others, such as a wife and siblings, who hold a nunber of shares of stock in the corporation. He also enjoys the limited liability aspect of a corporation in that, if the corporation owes money, a creditor will be limited to the assets of the corporation.

A small corporation with limited earnings may elect to be taxed as an ordinary **partnership;** its stockholders thus enjoy limited personal liability and only individual (not also corporate) taxation. A corporation electing this federal income tax option is a SUBCHAPTER S CORPORATION.

DE FACTO CORPORATION one existing in fact, but without actual authority of law.

EXAMPLE: Flange Brothers, a partnership, decides to incorporate. After filing what they believe are the necessary papers, the partnership changes it name to Flange Corporation and continues to carry on its business. Several years later, a creditor sues both the corporation and the partners who run it claiming that the partners are not protected from personal liability because they failed to file certain papers for incorporation and a corporation, therefore, was never legally formed. Unless the omission was intentional or under other rare circumstances, a court will generally find that the error was inadvertent, a *de facto corporation* was formed, and the persons running the corporation are protected from liability.

NOT-FOR-PROFIT CORPORATION one organized for some charitable, civil, social or other purpose that does not entail the generating of profit or the distribution of its income to members, principals, shareholders, officers or others affiliated with it. Such corporations are accorded special treatment under the law for some purposes, including federal income taxation.

PUBLIC [OR POLITICAL] CORPORATIONS those created by the state to fulfill certain purposes, such as to form lesser governmental bodies (towns, cities), organize school districts, operate water districts.

PRIVATE CORPORATION the common corporation, created by and for private individuals for nongovernmental purposes.

QUASI CORPORATION a body that exercises certain functions of a corporate character, but that has not been established as a corporation by any statute.

CORPOREAL Having material reality; opposite of **INCORPOREAL,** intangible.

CORPOREAL HEREDITAMENT see **hereditaments.**

CORPUS *(kôr'-pŭs)* Lat.: body. The main substance of a thing. 1. The principal or **res** of an **estate, trust, devise** or **bequest** from which income is derived; can consist of funds, real estate or other tangible or intangible property.

EXAMPLE: Sean creates a trust naming his children as beneficiaries. An office building is stated to be the trust *corpus* in the trust instrument. The rents collected from the [building's] tenants constitute the income that is distributed to the children.

2. In **civil law,** corpus refers to a positive fact as distinguished from a possibility. See **corpus delicti.**

CORPUS DELICTI *(kôr'-pŭs dĕ-lĭk'-tī)* Lat.: body of the crime. The objective proof that a crime has been committed; sometimes refers to the body of the victim of a **homicide,** but the term has a broader meaning. For the state to introduce a **confession** or convict the **accused** it must prove a corpus delicti; i.e., the occurrence of specific injury or loss and a criminal act as the source of the loss. See **moral certainty.**

EXAMPLE: At his trial for murder, Jack asks the court to dismiss his prosecution because no body was ever found. He does not prevail on that theory alone. Although there is no body, the state can still prove a *corpus delicti*. It is possible to prove a murder by showing that the person has not been seen for several years, that items of particular importance which had belonged to the person were found in Jack's house, and that a knife with bloodstains matching the blood type of the person was found in Jack's car. It should be observed that corpus delicti is not related exclusively to homicide. The corpus delicti of a robbery is the stolen money.

CORPUS JURIS *(kôr'-pŭs jūr'-is)* Lat.: body of law. A series of texts containing much of the **civil** and **canon [ecclesiastical]** law.

CORRECTIONAL INSTITUTION a general term used to describe a jail, prison, reformatory or other government-maintained detention facility.

CORRESPONDENT see **adultery.**

COSIGN the act of affixing one's signature in addition to the principal signature of another in order to verify the authenticity of the principal signature.

COST-PLUS CONTRACT see **contract.**

COST OF COMPLETION in **breach of contract,** a measure of **damages** representing the additional expense above the **contract** price that the injured party would incur to obtain substitute **performance** that would place him in the position he would have achieved if the contract had not been breached.

This is often the measure of damages for breaches of construction contracts.

COSTS court expenses of the victorious **party** in a lawsuit, which may be reimbursed by the losing party as part of recovery. Such an allowance is therefore incidental to judgment and compensates for the expense of asserting one's rights in court. Costs may be allowed to the **plaintiff** if the **default** of a **defendant** made it necessary to sue him, and to a defendant if the plaintiff sued without cause. Generally, costs of litigation are recoverable as of right if pursuant to **statute.** If there is no applicable statute, most court rules provide for allowance of costs to be at the discretion of the trial court.

COSTS TO ABIDE THE EVENT court order requiring the losing party to pay legal expenses of the prevailing party up to and including the decision of the court of appeals (see **appellate court**) and sometimes on retrial.

CO-TENANCY possession of and the holding of rights in a unit of property by two or more persons simultaneously. The term does not describe the **estate,** but the relationship between persons who share the property. It encompasses **TENANCY IN COMMON, JOINT TENANCY,** and **TENANCY BY THE ENTIRETY** (see **tenancy**).

COUNSEL 1. attorney or legal adviser; 2. the advice or aid given with respect to a legal matter. 3. In criminal law, the term may refer to the advising or encouraging of another to commit a crime.

COUNT a distinct statement of **plaintiff's cause of action.** In **indictments,** a count, like a **charge,** is an **allegation** of a distinct offense. A **complaint** or indictment may contain one or more counts.

COUNTERCLAIM a counterdemand by **defendant** against the **plaintiff;** it is not a mere **answer** or **denial** of plaintiff's allegation, but asserts an independent **cause of action** in favor of defendant.

EXAMPLE: A retail store owner sues a manufacturer for a shipment of defective clocks. Regardless of the validity of that suit, the manufacturer could *counterclaim* against the store owner if, for example, the owner owed the manufacturer money for past shipments. Both the storeowner's and the manufacturer's claims would then be decided by the courts.

In federal practice, a **COMPULSORY COUNTERCLAIM** arises out of the subject matter of the opposing party's claims, and unless the defendant makes such a counterclaim in the suit that has been brought against him, he may be barred from ever raising that claim again. A **PERMISSIVE COUNTERCLAIM** is any other counterclaim and may be made by the defendant in the action that has been brought against him or in a subsequent suit. See **setoff.** Compare **cross-claim.**

COUNTERFEIT forged; fabricated without right; made in imitation of something else to defraud by passing the false copy for genuine.

COUPONS certificates, usually attached to an **instrument** evidencing a loan, which may be presented separately for payment of a specific sum representing interest on the main instrument.

COURT CALENDAR a schedule of cases awaiting disposition in a given court, also referred to as the **TRIAL LIST** or the **COURT DOCKET.**

COURT-MARTIAL 1. a military or naval tribunal with jurisdiction over offenses against the law of the service in which the offender is engaged; 2. a proceeding in such a court.

GENERAL COURT-MARTIAL one presided over by a law officer and not fewer than five members, having jurisdiction over all members of the armed services of which it is a part, and authorized to try defendants for all military offenses and to prescribe any permitted sanctions.

SPECIAL COURT-MARTIAL one presided over by three members, that may try all noncapital offenses and that is limited in its authority to prescribe sanctions such as dismissal, hard labor and extended confinement, but may not authorize execution.

SUMMARY COURT-MARTIAL one presided over by a single commissioned officer, and limited in respect to the military personnel over whom it has jurisdiction and the sanctions it may prescribe. The accused may refuse trial by a summary court-martial, but the charges may then be referred to a higher level court-martial.

COURT OF APPEALS see **appellate court.**

COURT OF CLAIMS the court of the United States, created to determine all presented claims founded upon any law of Congress, upon any regulation of an executive department, or upon any **contract,** express or implied, with the government of the United States, and also all claims that may be referred to the court by either house of Congress. It has no power over matters in **equity.**

COURT OF CUSTOMS AND PATENT APPEALS see **federal courts.**

COURT OF EQUITY a court having **jurisdiction** in cases where an adequate and complete remedy cannot be had at law. Courts of equity in **common law** developed their own principles and unique remedies (e.g., **injunction, specific performance**). Actions were brought either equitably in **chancery** or legally **at law.** Today, courts that are guided primarily by equitable doctrine are still said to be courts of equity. Thus, a **bankruptcy court** is a court of equity. Courts of equity, which arose independent of courts of law in England, have merged with the latter in most jurisdictions of the United States. See **equity.**

COURT OF KING'S [QUEEN'S] BENCH see **King's Bench.**

COURT OF LAW a **tribunal** with **jurisdiction** over cases at **law.** The term applies to courts that administer justice according to federal or state law or **common law,** as distinguished from courts that follow the principles of **equity** and are called **chancery** courts. Law courts and equity courts, however, are generally no longer distinguished, and a court of law is any tribunal administering the law.

COURT OF RECORD a court that, like most modern courts, is required by law to keep a record of its proceedings, including the orders and judgments it enters, and that has the authority to imprison and to levy fines.

COVENANT 1. to enter a formal agreement; to bind oneself in **contract;** to make a stipulation; 2. an agreement to do or not to do a particular thing; 3. a promise incidental to a **deed** or contract, either express or implied.

EXAMPLE: Rita wants to sell a large tract of land adjacent to her home. As an inducement to Jim, the buyer, Rita is willing to *covenant* with (i.e., promise) him that he has access to and use of her driveway so that he will not have to build one.

CONCURRENT COVENANTS those that require the performance of obligation by one party when the other party is ready and offers performance.

COVENANT NOT TO COMPETE see **covenant not to compete.**

DEPENDENT COVENANTS those in which the obligation to perform one covenant arises only upon the prior **performance** of another; therefore, until the prior **condition** of performance has been met, the other party is not liable in an **action** on his covenant.

INDEPENDENT [OR MUTUAL] COVENANTS those that must be performed by one party without reference to the obligations of the other party.

In deeds, the usual COVENANTS OF TITLE, which may be deemed by law to be a part of certain kinds of real property conveyances, include:

COVENANT AGAINST ACTS OF THE GRANTOR one often inserted into a **bargain and sale** deed to assure that the grantor has not done, nor caused to be done, any act by means of which the premises or any part thereof may be encumbered in any way.

COVENANT AGAINST ENCUMBRANCES a guarantee given to the grantee of an estate that the estate is without **encumbrances.** Compare **run with the land.**

COVENANT OF FURTHER ASSURANCE one that obligates the covenantor to perform whatever acts are reasonably demanded by the covenantee for the purpose of perfecting or assuring the **title** that is conveyed. This type of covenant is no longer in general use.

COVENANT OF QUIET ENJOYMENT see **quiet enjoyment.**

COVENANT OF SEISIN AND RIGHT TO CONVEY covenant that the grantor has an **estate,** or the right to **convey** an estate, of the quality and quantity that he purports to convey (which, in the case of a covenant of **seisin,** is a **fee simple**).

COVENANT OF WARRANTY AND QUIET ENJOYMENT one that obligates the covenantor to protect the estate against the existence of lawful claims of ownership by third parties. A cause of action arises only when there is **eviction,** actual or constructive.

RESTRICTIVE COVENANT see **restrictive covenant.**

COVENANT NOT TO COMPETE a contractual promise to refrain from conducting business or professional activities similar to those of another party. These covenants are encountered principally in contracts of employment, partnership, or sale of a business.

EXAMPLE: A chain of discount appliance stores is bought by a large corporation. The corporation offers to hire Frank, the owner of the chain, and to allow him to organize a separate business if he wants. The only condition on the offer is that Frank sign a *covenant not to compete,* which would prohibit Frank from organizing another chain of discount appliance stores or selling any other merchandise this corporation distributes. Ordinarily, such covenants have geographic and duration limits, i.e., that for a period of three years Frank may not open a competitive store within fifty miles of the chain he sold.

The protection of **trade secrets,** customer lists, business methods specific to a particular employer, and the unique qualifications of the employee have been held to constitute legitimate interests for protection by covenants not to compete.

COVER in commercial law, refers to a buyer's purchase on the open market of **goods** similar or identical to the goods contracted for after a seller has **breached** a contract of sale by failure to deliver the goods contracted for. Under the **Uniform Commercial Code,** after a seller breaches and the buyer covers, the buyer is entitled to the difference between the cost of the substitute goods and the original contract price, provided the buyer has acted in good faith and without unreasonable delay in effecting such cover.

EXAMPLE: Phil contracts with the Prime Leather Company to supply him with raw leather hides at a certain price. By the delivery date, the cost of hides has risen so sharply that Prime would lose a considerable amount of money if it ships the hides to Phil. Prime decides to breach the contract. If Phil *covers* on this contract by purchasing the hides from another company, he can sue Prime for the difference between his purchase price with the new company and the price agreed to in the contract with Prime.

COVERTURE in **common law,** the state of a married woman whereby the existence of the wife was for many civil purposes merged with that of her husband, particularly with regard to ownership of property.

CREDIT 1. a privilege of delayed payment extended to a buyer or borrower on the seller's or lender's belief that what is given will be repaid.
2. In accounting, a credit represents money due.

CREDIT CARD an indication to sellers of commodities that the person who received the card from the issuer has a satisfactory credit rating and that if **credit** is extended, the issuer of the card will pay (or see to it that seller receives payment) for the merchandise delivered.

CREDITOR one to whom money is owed by the **debtor;** one to whom an obligation exists. In its strict legal sense, a creditor is one who voluntarily gives credit to another for money or other property; in its more general sense it is one who has a right by law to demand and recover of another a sum of money on any account.

CREDITOR'S BILL (OR SUIT) a **proceeding** in **equity** in which a **judgment creditor** (a **creditor** who has secured **judgment** against a **debtor** and whose **claim** has not been satisfied) attempts to gain a **discovery,** accounting and delivery of **property** owed to him by the **judgment debtor,** which property cannot be reached by execution (seizure and forced sale) at law.

CRIME a wrong that the government has determined is injurious to the public and that may therefore be prosecuted in a **criminal proceeding.** Crimes include **felonies** and **misdemeanors.** A common law crime was one declared to be an offense by the developed case law of the **common law** courts. Today all criminal offenses are exclusively statutory in nearly every American jurisdiction. See **infamous crime.**

CRIME AGAINST NATURE sexual deviation, including **sodomy** and **bestiality,** considered a crime in common law and carried over into statutory law.

CRIMEN FALSI *(krĭ' -mĕn fäl' -sē)* Lat.: a **crime** of **deceit.** In **common law** a crime involving falsehood and **fraud.** Having committed such a crime generally disqualified a person as a **witness** in a judicial **proceeding.** Examples of crimen falsi include **forgery, perjury, subornation of perjury,** suppression of **testimony, conspiracy** in the absence of a **witness** and fraudulent making or alteration of a document.

CRIME OF PASSION a crime committed under the influence of sudden or extreme passion. That an act was committed in the heat of passion may provide a defense to a charge of murder, since it negates the element of **premeditation,** a necessary element of murder. See **manslaughter.**

EXAMPLE: Nancy comes home and finds her husband in bed with another lover. In a fit of rage she shoots both of them. Although Nancy is charged with murder, she claims that the shootings were a *crime of passion.* As part of her proof, she states that her act resulted from seeing her husband in bed with someone else and not from a rational or premeditated plan to kill, which would be required to support a first degree murder conviction.

CRIMINAL 1. done with **malicious intent,** with a disposition to injure persons or property; 2. one who has been convicted of a violation of the criminal laws. A **HABITUAL OFFENDER** has been repeatedly convicted of crimes and therefore is subject to extended imprisonment under the habitual offender laws of many **jurisdictions.**

CRIMINAL CODE see **code.**

CRIMINAL CONTEMPT see **contempt of court.**

CRIMINAL CONVERSATION see **alienation of affections.**

CRIMINAL MAINTENANCE unauthorized interference in a lawsuit by helping one party, with money or otherwise, to prosecute or defend a **cause of action** so as to obstruct justice, promote unnecessary litigation or unsettle community peace. Unlike **champerty,** criminal maintenance does not necessarily involve personal profit. See also **barratry.**

CRIMINAL NEGLIGENCE see **negligence.**

CRIMINAL POSSESSION see **possession.**

CROSS-CLAIM a claim **litigated** by co**defendants** or co**plaintiffs** against each other, and not against a party on the opposite side of the litigation. Compare **counterclaim.**

CROSS-EXAMINATION the questioning of a witness, by a party or lawyer other than the one who called the witness, concerning matters about which the witness has testified during DIRECT EXAMINATION. The purpose is to discredit or clarify testimony already given so as to neutralize damaging testimony or present facts in a light more favorable to the party against whom the direct testimony was offered.

DIRECT EXAMINATION the initial questioning of a witness by the party who called the witness. The purpose is to present testimony containing the factual argument the party is making.

REDIRECT EXAMINATION the questioning of a witness by a party who called the witness, which occurs after that witness has been subjected to cross-examination. The purpose of redirect examination is to rebut or to clarify any damaging testimony elicited on cross-examination.

CRUEL AND UNUSUAL PUNISHMENT a penalty tantamount to torture, or excessive in proportion to the offense for which it is imposed, or inherently unfair, or by contemporary standards shocking to people of reasonable sensitivity. A punishment not inherently cruel and unusual may become so by the manner in which it is inflicted. Such punishment is prohibited by the Eighth Amendment to the U.S. Constitution.

CULPABLE deserving of moral blame or punishment; at fault; having acted with indifference to consequences and to the rights of others.

CULPABLE MENTAL STATE the state of mind necessary to commit a crime. In common law, both intent to commit a crime, called **mens rea,** and the acts that constitute the crime were required to establish guilt.

EXAMPLE: After a long night drinking, Rod stumbles into what he believes is his car and attempts to start the car with his own set of keys. As it turns out, the car is not his, and the rightful owner, who comes out seconds later, sees Rod and has him arrested for attempting to steal a car. Rod argues that he did not have the *culpable mental state* required for theft since he had no intention to steal the car.

See also **negligence** [CRIMINAL (CULPABLE) NEGLIGENCE].

CUMULATIVE DIVIDEND see **dividend.**

CUMULATIVE VOTING a system of **shareholder** voting for a board of **directors,** that allows all the votes an individual is eligible to cast to be cast for a single candidate. The system is designed to give minority shareholders representation on the board. For example, the owner of a single share of stock voting in an election for five directors would be able to cast one vote for each position under a straight voting system, but would be able to cast all five votes for a single position or distribute them in any manner desired under a cumulative voting system.

CURIA REGIS *(kū'-rē-ȧ rā'-gĭs)* Lat.: the king's court. See **King's Bench.**

CURRENT ASSETS see **asset; balance sheet.**

CURRENT LIABILITIES debts incurred by the reporting entity as part of normal operations and that are expected to be repaid during the following twelve months. Examples are **accounts payable,** short-term loans and that portion of long-term loans due in one year. See **balance sheet.**

CURTESY the husband's right in **common law,** upon the death of his wife, to a **life estate** in all lands of which his wife was **seised** in **fee simple** or in **fee tail** at any time during the marriage, provided that there was **issue** born of the marriage capable of inheriting the estate. Compare **dower.**

CURTILAGE in **common law** the land around the **dwelling house.**

CUSTODY 1. as applied to property, the condition of holding a thing within one's personal care and control; 2. as applied to persons, such control over a person as will insure his presence at a **hearing,** or the actual imprisonment of a person resulting from a criminal **conviction.** 3. **Custody of children** is legal **guardianship.**

CUSTODY OF CHILDREN the care and control of minor children awarded by the court to one parent in a divorce proceeding. Where parents both make application for **JOINT CUSTODY,** and circumstances render the arrangement feasible, some courts have awarded custody to both parents so that responsibility for the children is shared. Under a joint custody order, each parent would assume custody of the children for a fixed period, such as for six months or for the school year or for the summer vacation.

CUSTOMS COURT see **federal courts.**

CY-PRÈS *(sī'-prĕ)* Fr.: so near, as near. In the law of **trusts** and **wills,** the principle that a court of **equity** will, when a charity bequest is illegal or becomes impossible or impracticable, substitute another charitable object that is believed to approach closely the original purpose of the **testator** or **settlor.**

EXAMPLE: In her will, Ruth provided that $10,000 go to the Animal Humanitarian Society for their work in placing lost or abandoned pets and for running an animal hospital. At her death, the society no longer existed. Under the doctrine of *cy-près,* the court awarded the $10,000 to the American Society for the Prevention of Cruelty to Animals.

D

DAMAGES monetary compensation that the law awards to one who has been injured by the action of another; monetary recompense for a legal wrong such as a **breach of contract** or a **tortious** act.

ACTUAL DAMAGES losses directly referrable to the breach or tortious act; losses that can readily be proven to have been sustained, and for which the injured party should be compensated as a matter of right.

CONSEQUENTIAL [SPECIAL] DAMAGES indirect loss or injury. In contract law, consequential damages are recoverable if it was reasonably foreseeable at the time of contract that the injury would probably result if the contract were broken. The availability of award of such damages depends upon the defaulting party's actual or **constructive** knowledge of conditions that make likely some special injury upon default.

EXAMPLE: Crystal Lighting contracts with a construction company to install light fixtures throughout a new building. On the basis of that contract, Crystal also contracts with one of its suppliers to have several hundred fixtures delivered to Crystal. Since this is not a normal order for Crystal, Crystal explains what all the fixtures are for. The supplier then breaches his contract. Any damages in the contract between Crystal and the construction company that result from the breach are the direct foreseeable result of the supplier's breach. As such, those damages are called *consequential damages*.

DOUBLE [TREBLE] DAMAGES twice [or three times] the amount of damages that a court or jury would normally award, recoverable for certain kinds of injuries pursuant to a statute authorizing the double [or treble] recovery. These damages are intended in certain instances as punishment for improper behavior. Treble damages is a statutory remedy most often awarded in antitrust violations.

EXEMPLARY [PUNITIVE] DAMAGES compensation in excess of actual damages that is a form of punishment to the wrongdoer and reparation to the injured. Exemplary damages are awarded only in rare instances of **malicious** and **willful** misconduct.

EXAMPLE: Several corporations are found guilty of fixing the price of milk over a nine-year period. In addition to assessing a fine on the corporations, a judge awards an additional amount as *punitive damages*. Since all purchases of milk were affected by the price-fixing, the judge might order that the amount of the punitive damages be repaid to consumers by a coupon offering.

EXPECTATION DAMAGES a measure of the money damages available to **plaintiff** in an action for breach of contract, based on the value of the benefit he would have received from the contract if the **defendant** had not breached, but had completed **performance** as agreed. The amount is generally the monetary value of full performance of the contract to the plaintiff minus costs plaintiff avoided by not performing his own part of the contract.

INCIDENTAL DAMAGES losses reasonably incident to conduct giving rise to a claim for actual damages.

LIQUIDATED DAMAGES see **liquidated damages.**

NOMINAL DAMAGES a trivial sum awarded as recognition that a legal injury was sustained, though slight. Nominal damages will be awarded for a breach of contract or for an intentional tort to vindicate the plaintiff's claim where no recoverable loss can be established.

DAMNUM ABSQUE INJURIA *(dăm' nūm ăb'-skwā ĭn-jū'-rē-ä)* Lat.: harm without **injury.** Refers to damage without violation of law, or to damage caused by nature, where the law provides no **cause of action** to recover for the loss. Compare **compensation.**

DANGEROUS WEAPON [OR INSTRUMENTALITY] almost any device that has the potential to cause serious bodily injury or endanger life.

DAY IN COURT refers broadly to the opportunity afforded a party to a lawsuit to be heard by the court. See also **appearance; due process of law.**

DEADLY WEAPON any device capable of causing death or serious bodily injury. An instrument may be intrinsically deadly, as a knife or pistol, or deadly because of the way it is used, as a wrench or hammer.

DEALER one who produces or acquires something in order to sell it. One is a dealer if he has structured his business so that he can, upon reasonable **notice, deliver** his commodity once a sale has been made.

DEATH the point at which life ceases; permanent and irreversible termination of vital signs. Several states have adopted **statutes** defining death to include brain criteria. See **brain death.**

DEATH PENALTY the ultimate punishment imposed for murder or other capital offenses. The U.S. Supreme Court has determined that the death penalty is not in every instance to be considered unconstitutional, as cruel and unusual punishment.

DE BENE ESSE *(dĕ bĕ'-nĕ ĕs'-sĕ)* Lat.: conditionally; provisionally.

APPEARANCE DE BENE ESSE a conditional **appearance,** by which one appearing in the jurisdiction intends not to thereby subject himself to the authority of the court for all purposes.

DEPOSITIONS DE BENE ESSE conditional **depositions** that cannot be introduced in evidence if the **witness** is available at the trial.

EVIDENCE DE BENE ESSE **evidence** whose **admissibility** is conditioned upon a subsequent showing of facts necessary to support its admission.

DEBENTURE written acknowledgement of a **debt** secured only by the general **credit** or promise to pay of the issuer. Debentures are the common type of **bond** issued by large, well-established corporations with adequate credit ratings. The written agreement under which the debentures are sold, the **indenture,** is specific as to maturity date, interest rate, **call** features and **convertibility.** Holders of debentures representing corporate indebtedness are creditors of the corporation and entitled to payment before **shareholders** upon **dissolution** of the corporation.

DEBT any obligation of one person to pay or compensate another.

DEBTOR one who owes another anything, or is under obligation, arising from express agreement, implication of law, or principles of natural justice, to pay money or to fulfill some other obligation; in **bankruptcy** or similar proceedings, the person who is the subject of the proceeding.

DECEASED one who has died. In property law, the alternate term **DECEDENT** is generally used. In criminal law, "the deceased" refers to the victim of a **homicide.**

DECEDENT see **deceased.**

DECEIT the **tort** or **fraudulent** representation of a **material** fact made with knowledge of its falsity, or recklessly, or without reasonable grounds for believing its truth and with intent to induce **reliance** on it; the **plaintiff** justifiably relies on the deception, to his **injury.**

DECISION ON THE MERITS see **judgment [JUDGMENT ON THE MERITS].**

DECLARATION in common law, the formal document specifying plaintiff's **cause of action,** including the facts necessary to sustain a proper cause of action and to advise **defendant** of the grounds upon which he is being sued. See **complaint.**

DECLARATORY JUDGMENT a **judgment** of the court to establish the rights of the parties or express the opinion of the court on a question of law, without ordering anything to be done or granting any remedy.

EXAMPLE: A state legislature passes a taxing measure that will have a widespread effect on corporations doing interstate business within that state. A payment of the tax with a subsequent refund if the tax is found invalid would result in administrative difficulties. Therefore, one of the affected corporations asks a court for a *declaratory judgment* on the validity of the tax.

Compare **advisory opinion; injunction.**

DECLARATORY STATUTE a statute that merely declares the existing law without proposing changes, for the purpose of resolving conflicts concerning the meaning of a previous statute or portion of the **common law.**

DECREE 1. the judicial decision in a **litigated** cause rendered by a **court of equity;** 2. the determination of a cause in courts of **admiralty** and **probate.** It is accurate to use the word **judgment** for a decision of a **court of law,** and decree from a court of equity, although the former term now includes both.

CONSENT DECREE an agreement of the parties made under sanction of the court, not the result of a judicial determination, but merely agreement to be bound by certain stipulated facts.

DECREE NISI in English law, a provisional decree of divorce, which becomes absolute only after a specified interval, usually six months, during which parties have the opportunity to show cause why the decree should not become absolute.

FINAL DECREE one that ultimately disposes of every matter of contention between the parties and constitutes a bar to another action on the same subject matter between the same parties.

INTERLOCUTORY DECREE one made upon some point arising

during the progress of the suit that does not determine finally the **merits** of the entire suit.

DECRIMINALIZATION the adoption or repeal of legislation, the effect of which is that acts or omissions formerly considered criminal are no longer so characterized, and penal sanctions for such acts or omissions are removed.

DEDICATION a **conveyance** of land as a **grant** to the public by a private owner and an acceptance of that land on behalf of the public.

EXAMPLE: A company buys a large area of land, on which it plans to locate its national headquarters. To promote goodwill between the company and the surrounding communities, the company *dedicates* a portion of land to the county parks committee, who accept permanent ownership of the land.

DEDUCTIONS amounts allowed to taxpayers under the **Internal Revenue Code** as offsets against **GROSS INCOME** or **ADJUSTED GROSS INCOME** (see **income**).

ITEMIZED DEDUCTIONS specific individualized deductions, allowed under provisions of the Code for specific expenses incurred by the **taxpayer** during the **taxable year.** These deductions are allowed in computing **TAXABLE INCOME** (see **income**) to the extent they exceed the **ZERO BRACKET AMOUNT.**

MARITAL DEDUCTION a deductible amount under the unified estate and gift tax for certain interests in property transferred to a spouse.

PERSONAL EXPENSES DEDUCTION personal expenses as opposed to expenses for income-producing or business expenses. Personal expenses are not allowed as deductions except as specifically enumerated in the Internal Revenue Code.

STANDARD DEDUCTION a provision allowing a taxpayer to deduct, in lieu of itemized deductions, a percentage of gross income up to certain specified amounts, repealed and replaced by the **ZERO BRACKET AMOUNT.**

ZERO BRACKET AMOUNT DEDUCTION an amount of income below the amounts at which, according to the tax tables, income taxes must be paid.

DEED an **instrument** in writing that **conveys** an **interest** in land (**realty**) from the grantor to the grantee. Its main function is to pass **title** to land. See **bargain and sale; quitclaim deed; warranty.**

DEED OF TRUST a transfer of legal **title** to property from owner to a **trustee,** so that the trustee may hold the title as security for the **performance** of certain obligations, monetary or otherwise, by the owner of a third party. Compare **mortgage.**

DEED POLL a **deed** made by and obligatory upon one **party** alone.

DEEP ROCK DOCTRINE a doctrine that makes available a **remedy** for improper conduct in connection with a loan to a corporation by a controlling **shareholder.** Though generally loans to a corporation by a shareholder are entitled to equal priority with loans made by outside **creditors,** the doctrine allows, when there are **bankruptcy** proceedings involving the corporation, subordination of the shareholder loans to the claims of other creditors where it would be manifestly unfair to permit a controlling shareholder to participate equally with these other creditors.

The unfairness occurs most commonly where the corporation is undercapitalized and frequently involves a parent corporation as the controlling shareholder of a **subsidiary.**

DE FACTO *(dĕ făk'-tō)* Lat.: in fact. By virtue of the deed or accomplishment; actually. Used to refer to a situation in which a condition or institution is operating as though it were official or pursuant to law, but which is not legally authorized. Such situations may arise where, for example, an authorizing law is declared invalid, or because required legal formalities have not been satisfied.

EXAMPLE: Nursing homes were established throughout a particular state under the authority of a newly enacted state law. Now, two years later, portions of the law are found to be unconstitutional. Instead of closing all the homes that were set up, the state permits them to continue to operate under its *de facto* authority until the law is amended and legal.

The de facto acts of a person or entity may for some purposes be regarded as legally binding. Compare **de jure.**

DEFALCATION failure of one entrusted with money to pay over the money when it is due to another. The term is like misappropriation and **embezzlement,** but is wider in scope because it does not imply criminal **fraud.**

DEFAMATION the publication of anything injurious to the reputation of another. Defamation designed to be read is **libel;** oral defamation is **slander.**

EXAMPLE: A reporter publishes an article that Ryan is being investigated for misapplication of public funds. The article has no basis in fact, but, as a result of it, Ryan is forced to temporarily leave his position as director. Ryan has been **libeled** and probably has a *defamation* action against the reporter.

DEFAULT failure to discharge a duty. The term is often used in the context of **mortgages** to describe failure of the mortgagor to pay **installments** when due, and in the context of judicial **proceedings** to describe failure of one of the parties to take **procedural** steps to prevent entry of a **judgment** against him (called a **default judgment**). See **delict.**

DEFAULT JUDGMENT 1. a **judgment** against **defendant** who has failed to respond to **plaintiff's action** or to appear at the **trial** or hearing.

EXAMPLE: A carpenter files a suit against a homeowner, claiming that the homeowner failed to pay the carpenter for work performed six months ago. Under the state's court rules, the homeowner has twenty days to file an answer to the carpenter's claim. If the homeowner fails to do so within twenty days, the court will enter a *default judgment* against him declaring that the homeowner must pay the carpenter what is claimed.

2. judgment given without the defendant's being heard in his own defense. Compare **confession of judgment; ex parte.**

DEFEASANCE an **instrument** that negates the effectiveness of a **deed** or of a **will;** a **collateral** deed that defeats the force of another deed upon the performance of certain conditions.

DEFEASIBLE subject to revocation if certain **conditions** are not met; capable of being avoided or annulled, or liable to such avoidance or annulment.

DEFECTIVE 1. incomplete, faulty; 2. not reasonably safe for a use that can be reasonably anticipated. See also **products liability; warranty.**

DEFECTIVE TITLE unmarketable right of ownership. 1. With reference to land, it means that the **title** held by the person making the **conveyance,** claiming to own **good title,** is or might be subject to partial or complete **ownership** by someone else.

EXAMPLE: Ruth wants to sell her house to a friend who is moving into the state. Prior to purchasing the house, the friend has a title search done to determine if anyone else has claimed ownership of the house besides Ruth. That search discloses a bank note that has never been paid but which the bank has never acted upon. Still, the outstanding bank note gives rise to a *defective title,* which now makes the friend reluctant to buy the house.

2. As to **negotiable instruments,** the term denotes title obtained through **fraud** or other illegal means.

DEFENDANT 1. in **civil proceedings,** the **party** responding to the **complaint;** one who is sued and called upon to make satisfaction for a wrong complained of by another; 2. in criminal proceedings, the **accused.** See also **respondent.**

DEFENDANT IN ERROR the prevailing party in the lower court who is the adverse party in the appellate proceeding where review has been sought on a writ of error. The person who brings the **action** at the **appellate** level is called the PLAINTIFF IN ERROR. See also **appellee.**

DEFENSE a denial, answer or plea disputing the validity of plaintiff's case, or making some further contention that renders the defendant not liable upon the facts alleged by the plaintiff.

AFFIRMATIVE DEFENSE one that serves as a basis for proving some new fact, whereby defendant does not simply **deny** a **charge** but offers new **evidence** to avoid **judgment** against him.

EQUITABLE DEFENSE a defense that is recognized by **courts of equity** acting solely upon rules of **equity.** Such defenses can now be asserted in **courts of law** as well.

DEFERRED PAYMENTS payments extended over a period of time or put off to a future date.

DEFICIENCY the excess of a **taxpayer's** correct tax liability for the **taxable year** over the amount of **taxes** previously paid for such year. The **Internal Revenue Service** is authorized to assess deficiencies during an **audit** of the taxpayer's return, and a deficiency may be used to assess penalties for the underpayment of tax, such as for **negligence** or **fraud** in filing the return.

DEFICIT insufficiency in an account or number, whether as the result of **defaults** and misappropriations or of mistake or shrinkage in value.

DEFRAUD to deprive a person of **property** or **interest, estate** or right by **fraud** or **deceit.**

DE JURE *(dĕ ju'-rā)* Lat.: by right; lawful; legitimate.

EXAMPLE: a new corporation is set up exactly according to both state and federal incorporation laws. The corporation is therefore a *de jure* (i.e., legal) corporation.

Generally used in contrast to **de facto;** de jure connotes "as a matter of law," whereas de facto connotes "as a matter of practice not founded upon law."

DELEGATE 1. to appoint, authorize or commission; the **transfer** of authority by one person to another. 2. a person commissioned to act instead of another.

DELEGATED POWER power conferred by one person on another who will act for his benefit.

DELIBERATION the process by which the reasons for and against a **verdict** are weighed by **jurors.** While such verdict should be the consensus of the judgments of each juror, the purpose of deliberation is to allow opinions to be changed by conference in the **jury** room.

DELICT a **tort;** a wrong or injury; any statutory violation; sometimes used in the sense of a **default** on a monetary obligation.

DELICTUM Latin for tort. An action **EX DELICTO** is an action in tort as distinguished from one **EX CONTRACTU,** in **contract.**

DELINQUENT in a monetary context, payable but overdue and unpaid. See **default.** See also **juvenile delinquent.**

DELISTING removal of an issue from trading on an organized exchange such as the **New York Stock Exchange.** Organized exchanges have minimum listing requirements that must be met before listed trading is allowed. If the issuer fails to maintain the minimum requirements, trading in its listed securities can be suspended or eliminated.

DELIVERY a voluntary transfer of **title** or **possession** from one **party** to another; a legally recognized handing over to another one's possessory rights. Where actual delivery is cumbersome or impossible, the courts may find **constructive** delivery sufficient if the intention is clearly to transfer title. Thus, one may deliver the contents of a safety deposit box by handing over the key together with any necessary authorization. Such action is also called **SYMBOLIC DELIVERY**. Compare **bailment.**

DEMAND NOTE 1. an **instrument** that by its express terms is payable immediately on an agreed-upon date of **maturity** without further demand for payment; 2. an instrument payable at sight, or upon presentation, or one in which no time for payment is stated.

DE MINIMIS *(dĕ mĭ′-nĭ-mĭs)* Lat.: trifling. Of insufficient significance to warrant judicial attention.

DE MINIMIS NON CURAT LEX *(nŏn kū′-rät lĕx)* Lat.: the law does not care for small things; the law does not bother with trifles.

EXAMPLE: Tom is arrested for possession of one marijuana cigarette. Although marijuana possession has not been decriminalized in the state where Tom is arrested, the prosecutor decides not to prosecute Tom for the possession since it is only a *de minimis* infraction.

DEMISE term used to describe a **conveyance** of an **estate** in **real property;** to let, especially pursuant to a **lease** for a term of years.

DEMONSTRATIVE EVIDENCE **evidence** consisting of an object or thing, such as a weapon used in a crime, a stolen item, or a photograph or x-ray, that may aid the jury in understanding the crime before it but has no effect on the question of guilt; evidence other than a person's oral testimony but which may help to explain that testimony.

DEMURRER formal **allegation** that facts as stated in the **pleadings,** even if true, are not legally sufficient for the case to proceed further. It does not admit anything but tests whether the **complaint** is sufficient to state a **cause of action.** In modern **procedure,** a **motion** to **dismiss** for failure to state a **claim** upon which relief may be granted replaces the demurrer. Compare **summary judgment.**

DENIAL a contradiction or **traverse;** in practice, a refutation of affirmative **allegations** contained in the **pleading** of an adversary. A defendant in his **answer** must admit, deny or state he has insufficient information upon which to admit or deny the allegations.

DE NOVO *(dĕ nō'-vō)* Lat.: anew. A second time, as though the first had never taken place.

DE NOVO HEARING a new hearing, in which the **judgment** of the first hearing is suspended and the case proceeds as if it had originated in the reviewing **tribunal.**

EXAMPLE: A state statute gives a defendant convicted in a municipal court the right to appeal that conviction *de novo* in a higher court. That right means that the defendant will have a new trial in which the facts and issues will be retried as though the first trial never took place.

DEPENDENT any person with respect to whom a **taxpayer** can claim a dependency **exemption;** defined by the **Internal Revenue Code** as any individual supported by the taxpayer who is related to the taxpayer in specified ways or who makes his principal abode in the taxpayer's household.

DEPLETION the exhaustion of a natural resource, the amount of the original deposit being hidden and thus necessarily unknown. Depletion is most often referred to in federal income **tax deduction** provisions that deal with exhaustion of natural resources.

The **DEPLETION ALLOWANCE** is a formula for computing and excluding from the proceeds of natural resource operations that part of the operations' proceeds that is in effect a return of **capital.**

EXAMPLE: Petro Corporation purchases several leases of land on which it plans to drill oil. If oil is extracted from any of those leased lands, the value of the lease is reduced. The *depletion allowance* determines a figure based on that reduction in value. Petro then uses that figure to reduce its tax obligation.

Depletion allowance should be contrasted with **depreciation** deduction provisions that deal with deterioration of tangible physical **property** incident to its use that shortens its period of service.

DEPONENT a **witness;** especially one who gives information under oath, in a **deposition** concerning facts known to him.

DEPORTATION the transfer of an **alien** to a foreign country because the deporting government refuses to harbor a person whose presence is deemed inconsistent with the public welfare. Compare **extradition.**

DEPOSE 1. to give **evidence** or **testimony,** especially in response to interrogation during a **deposition.** 2. the act of interrogating and eliciting testimony during a deposition, typically conducted by a lawyer.

DEPOSITION a method of pretrial **discovery** that consists of a stenographically transcribed statement of a **witness** under oath, in response to an attorney's questions, with opportunity for the opposing party or his attorney to be present and to cross-examine. Such a statement is the most common form of discovery and may be taken of any witness (whether or not a **party** to the **action**). When taken in the form described, it is called an oral deposition. Depositions may also be taken upon written **interrogatories,** where the questions are read to the witness by the officer who is taking the deposition.

DEPOSITION DE BENE ESSE see **de bene esse.**

DEPRECIATION a **deduction** allowed to a **taxpayer** representing a reasonable allowance for the exhaustion of property used in a trade or business, or property held for the production of income. The purpose of charging depreciation against equipment is to generate a tax-free stream of income equal to the portion of the **asset** that has been "used up" and to distinguish the portion of income that is a return of **capital.** Compare **depletion.**

ACCELERATED DEPRECIATION any one of a number of allowed methods of calculating depreciation that permit greater amounts of deductions in earlier years than are permitted under the straight line method, which assumes equal depreciation during each year of the asset's useful life.

STRAIGHT LINE DEPRECIATION a method that calculates the depreciation deduction available by subtracting the asset's SALVAGE VALUE from its total value and dividing the difference by the number of years of the asset's useful life.

SALVAGE VALUE the estimated value of the property when the taxpayer completes his use of the property. In determining the amount of depreciation allowable, salvage value must be subtracted from **basis.**

USEFUL LIFE the reasonable estimate of the term of an asset's usefulness to the taxpayer in his business.

DEPRECIATION RESERVE [ACCUMULATED DEPRECIATION] the total **depreciation** charged against all productive **assets** as stated on the **balance sheet.** The charge is made to allow realistic reduction in the value of productive assets and to allow tax-free recovery of the original investment in assets.

DERELICTION a recession of waters of the sea, a navigable river or other stream, by which land that had been covered with water is left dry. If the alteration is sudden and noticeable, ownership remains according to former bounds; but if recession is gradual and imperceptible, the derelict or dry land belongs to the **riparian** owner from whose shore the water has so receded. The term may also refer to the land that is thus left uncovered. For **contiguous** landowners to gain ownership of the newly uncovered land, the withdrawal of the water must appear permanent, not merely seasonal. Compare **accretion; avulsion.**

DERIVATIVE ACTION 1. an **action** based upon a primary right of a **corporation,** but asserted on its behalf by the

shareholder because of the corporation's failure, deliberate or otherwise, to assert the right; 2. a **cause of action** founded upon an injury to another, as when a husband sues for loss of **consortium** or services of his wife on account of injury to her by the **defendant,** or when a father sues for loss of services of children. See **stockholders' derivative action.**

DERIVATIVE TORT an action in **tort** based on the **criminal** conduct of **defendant** that resulted in **injury** to **plaintiff** for which he seeks **compensation.** The action is distinct from any criminal prosecution that may result from the same conduct by defendant.

DEROGATION partial taking away of the effectiveness of a law; partially repealing or abolishing a law.

DESCENT a method of acquiring **property,** usually **real property,** through the laws of **descent and distribution** from a decedent without the use of a **will;** generally applied to **inheritance** only by **intestate succession.** Compare **devise.** See **worthier title, doctrine of.**

DESCENT AND DISTRIBUTION the transmission of an **intestate's property** to his **heirs.**

DESTRUCTIBILITY refers to a **common-law** rule that when a **contingent remainder** does not **vest** at or before the termination of the preceding freehold estate, the remainder **interest** is destroyed. Thus, the termination of the preceding estate, because of its inherent limitation, or as a result of forfeiture or **merger,** destroys the nonvested contingent remainder.

DESUETUDE a term applied to obsolete laws and practices that may therefore be regarded as no longer in effect.

DETAINER 1. keeping a person from goods or land to which he has a legal right; 2. a **writ** or **instrument,** issued by a competent officer, authorizing a prison warden to keep in his **custody** a person therein named. See also **detention.**

UNLAWFUL DETAINER refusal to deliver on demand, as where the **tenant,** after termination of his lease, refuses to deliver possession to the **landlord.** Compare **tenancy** [**TENANCY AT SUFFERANCE**].

DETENTION holding of a person charged with crime following his arrest on that charge.

DETERMINABLE FEE [FEE SIMPLE DETERMINABLE] an **interest** in **property** that may last forever, but that will automatically terminate upon the happening or nonhappening of a specified event. Also called a **DEFEASIBLE FEE** or a **FEE SIMPLE DEFEASIBLE.**

EXAMPLE: A brother conveys a large office building to his sister provided she remains unmarried. If she is unmarried at her death, she can dispose of it as she pleases in her will. But once she marries, the ownership of the building reverts to the brother. The sister's interest in the building after the brother's conveyance is a *determinable fee*.

DETINUE in **common law,** an **action** for the wrongful detention of **personal property;** a legal claim provided for the recovery of a specific thing, and for obtaining **damages** for its detention. Compare **detainer** [**UNLAWFUL DETAINER**].

DEVISE a gift of **real property** made by **will.** In modern usage, the term may also embrace **testamentary** gifts of **personal property.** Compare **bequest; legacy.**

DEVOLVE to pass property from one person to another by **operation of law,** without any voluntary act of the previous owner.

DICTUM a statement in a judicial **opinion** not necessary for the decision of the case. Dictum differs from the **holding** in that it does not establish a rule binding on the courts in subsequent cases.

EXAMPLE: Sandy claims that the issue of his liability for damage on his sidewalk resulting in injury to another was settled in a previous case. The judge reminds Sandy that the previous case concerned the city's obligation to keep the sidewalks in good repair and the city's liability for injury to a person. The part of the case addressed to a private citizen's liability was not necessary to the decision and hence was only *dictum* and is not binding on this judge.

CONSIDERED DICTUM refers to a discussion of a point of law that, although it is dictum, is nevertheless so well developed that it is later incorporated into an opinion of a court as though it were authority.

DIE WITHOUT ISSUE see **failure of issue.**

DILATORY PLEA (PLEA IN ABATEMENT) in **common law,** a **plea** not responsive to the **merits** of a controversy, but a **defense** that simply delays or defeats the present **action,** leaving the **cause of action** unsettled. If a defendant, by establishing the facts, can defeat the plaintiff's cause of action in whole or in part, or can obtain substantial relief against the plaintiff, the plea is not dilatory, but **on the merits.** This kind of plea has largely disappeared under modern practice. Instead these defenses are now raised by **motion** or in an **answer.**

DIMINISHED CAPACITY in criminal law, the inability to have the state of mind, or **mens rea,** required for the commission of a particular crime. A successful defense of diminished capacity will usually result in conviction of a lesser offense, not an **acquittal.** Compare **insanity.**

DIMINUTION IN VALUE a measure of **damages** for **breach of contract** that reflects a decrease, occasioned by the breach, in the value of property with which the **contract** was concerned. In a building contract, for example, it is the difference between the value of the building as constructed and its value had it been constructed in conformance with the contract. Compare **cost of completion; damages [EXPECTATION DAMAGES].**

DIRECT ATTACK a proceeding instituted to amend, **vacate** or enjoin **execution** of a judgment; an attempt by **appellants**

to **avoid** or correct a **judgment** in a manner provided by law, as by an **appeal.** Compare **collateral** [COLLATERAL ATTACK].

DIRECTED VERDICT a verdict returned by the **jury** at the direction of the trial judge, by whose direction the jury is bound. In **civil proceedings** either party may receive a directed verdict in its favor if the opposing party fails to present a **prima facie case** or a necessary **defense.** In criminal proceedings, there may be a directed verdict of **acquittal,** but not a directed verdict of conviction, which would violate the defendant's constitutional right to a jury determination of his guilt or innocence.

DIRECTOR a member of a board of directors of a **company** or **corporation,** who shares with others directors the legal responsibility of control over the officers and affairs of the company or corporation. A director has a **fiduciary** duty to the corporation and to its **shareholders** to manage the corporation in a manner consistent with their interests.

DISABILITY state of being not fully capable of performing all functions, whether mental or physical; want of legal capacity such as **infancy, insanity** or past criminal conviction that renders a person legally **incompetent;** one person's inability to alter a given legal relation with another person. Compare **Durham Rule.**

DISBAR to rescind an attorney's license to practice law, because of his illegal or unethical conduct.

DISCHARGE 1. to satisfy or dismiss the obligations of **contract** or **debt;** 2. the method by which a legal **duty** is extinguished. Compare **performance; rescission.**

DISCHARGE IN BANKRUPTCY the release of the **bankrupt** from all his provable debts, whether then payable or not, and debts founded on a contract, express or implied; but not a release from debts specifically excepted from discharge by the bankruptcy statute.

3. to release from **custody, acquit.** See **sentence** [SUSPENDED SENTENCE (CONDITIONAL DISCHARGE; UNCONDITIONAL DISCHARGE]. Compare **reprieve.**

DISCLAIMER 1. denial of a person's **claim** to a thing, though previously that person insisted on such a claim or right; 2. renunciation of the right to **possess** and of claim of **title;** 3. denial of a right of another, e.g., where an **insurer** disclaims an allegation of **liability** against its **insured** and thereby refuses to **indemnify** or defend the insured in a law**suit** (DISCLAIMER OF LIABILITY).

DISCONTINUANCE cessation of **proceedings** in an **action** where the **plaintiff** voluntarily puts an end to it, with or without judicial approval. Judicial approval may be required, depending upon each jurisdiction's rules of practice. Compare **dismissal; nonsuit.**

DISCOUNT a deduction from a specified sum; often used with transactions in negotiable **commercial paper** in which the instrument is bought at a price below its face amount to reflect the fact that the debt it represents is not due until a future date.

EXAMPLE: Sidney regularly enters into contracts where he is not to be paid until the work is completed. But Sidney needs the money before he starts the work to purchase work materials and pay other debts. Because the contracts represent obligations to pay by other parties, a bank is willing to give Sidney the money that the contracts call for less a *discount*. That discount mainly covers the difference in the value of the money given to Sidney now versus what the money will be worth when the bank is paid by the other parties, as well as a small profit margin for the bank. The discount will also factor in that percentage of the contracts which are not likely to be collected.

DISCOUNT BOND see **bond** [BOND DISCOUNT].

DISCOUNTED CASH FLOW measure of the present value of a future income stream generated by a **capital** investment.

DISCOVERY modern pretrial procedure by which one **party** gains information held by the adverse party, concerning the case; the disclosure by the adverse party of facts, deeds and documents that are exclusively within his possession or knowledge and that are necessary to support the other party's position. Common types of discovery are **depositions, interrogatories,** production of documents and requests for admissions.

EXAMPLE: Sally gets into an accident when her rear wheels stop for no reason, causing the car to skid into a highway divider. In her lawsuit against the car manufacturer, Sally uses the *discovery* procedure to obtain memos and test-run results that the manufacturer used in designing the car. Without discovery, Sally may not be able to acquire that information.

DISCRETION the freedom of a public officer to make choices, within the limits of his authority, among possible courses of action.

JUDICIAL DISCRETION the reasonable use of judicial power, i.e., the court's freedom to decide within the bounds of law and fact.

EXAMPLE: Jason, a juvenile, is charged with an assault upon another teenager. In Jason's state, the law provides the juvenile judge with the *judicial discretion* to have the case heard in the juvenile court or to transfer the case to an adult court. Previous cases and the law itself establish certain standards to use in determining whether a transfer is appropriate, but the judge has the discretion to make his decision. His decision, though, may be appealed to a higher court.

LEGAL DISCRETION the use of one of several equally satisfactory provisions of law.

PROSECUTORIAL DISCRETION the wide range of alternatives for a **prosecutor** in criminal cases, including decision to prosecute, particular charges to be brought, bargaining, mode of trial conduct, recommendations for sentencing, **parole,** etc.

DISCRETIONARY ACCOUNT in the **securities** trade, one in which the customer gives the **broker** or a third party complete or partial discretion to buy and sell securities. Such discretion typically extends to selection, price, timing, and amount purchased.

DISHONOR to refuse, rightly or wrongly, to make payment on a **negotiable instrument** when such an instrument is duly presented for payment.

DISINHERITANCE the act by the **donor** that dissolves the right of a person to **inherit** that **property** to which he previously had such right.

DISINTERMEDIATION movement of savings from banks and savings and loan associations into money market instruments, such as **treasury bills** and **notes.**

DISJUNCTIVE ALLEGATIONS those that **charge** the **defendant** with either one act or another. The word ''or'' may not leave the **averment** uncertain as to which of two or more things is meant. An **allegation** that charges the commission of a **crime** by one act ''or'' another is **defective** if it does not clearly inform the defendant of the charge against him so that he can prepare a **defense.** The same standard is applied to **pleadings** in **civil** cases, where both disjunctive allegations and disjunctive denials generally constitute defective pleadings and are therefore inadmissible.

DISMISS to terminate a case or some part of it. Before or during the trial of a **civil action,** the suit may be dismissed voluntarily by the **plaintiff,** or involuntarily by the court upon **defendant's motion** to dismiss the **complaint** or any **count** thereof. See **demurrer.**

DISMISSAL a cancellation. Dismissal of a **motion** is a denial of the motion. Dismissal of a **complaint** or a related **count** terminates proceedings on the **claim** asserted in the complaint. Dismissal of an **appeal** places the parties in the condition as if there had been no appeal, confirming the **judgment** of the lower court.

DISMISSAL WITH PREJUDICE usually an adjudication upon the **merits** that operates as a **bar** to future action by preventing plaintiff from making further attempts at a claim based upon the same facts.

EXAMPLE: George brings a lawsuit against a company, claiming that it never refunded his money for an item he returned. The company shows the judge a check made payable to George and cashed by him, with a large notation on the check that it was payment for the return of the item. George then tries to make an additional claim that the company owes him more money for other reasons. The judge will usually **dismiss with prejudice** George's claim for the refund price alone and instruct him to file a separate claim if he is seeking more money. The "with prejudice" aspect of the court's decision means that George can never again sue on the same claim unless he successfully appeals the decision.

DISMISSAL WITHOUT PREJUDICE such a dismissal is not **on the merits** and does not bar a subsequent **suit** on the same **cause of action,** nor affect any right or **remedy** of the parties.

DISORDERLY CONDUCT generic term embracing minor offenses that are generally below the grade of **misdemeanor,** but that nevertheless are somewhat criminal; broadly signifies conduct that tends to **breach** the peace or endanger the morals, safety or health of the community.

DISPARAGEMENT see **bait and switch.**

DISPOSITION 1. the giving up of anything; often used in reference to a testamentary **proceeding,** as in "the disposition of the estate." 2. courts "dispose of" **cases,** i.e., determine the rights of the parties or otherwise terminate the proceedings. 3. In criminal law, the **sentence** of the **defendant** is the disposition.

DISPOSSESS to oust, eject or exclude another from the possession of lands or premises, whether by legal process (as where a landlord lawfully evicts a tenant) or wrongfully. Compare **disseisin.**

DISPUTABLE PRESUMPTION see **presumption [REBUTTABLE PRESUMPTION].**

DISSEISIN 1. the act of wrongfully depriving a person of **seisin** of land; the taking of **possession** of land under claim or **color of title;** 2. any act, with or without the owner's consent, the necessary effect of which is to **divest** him of the **estate.**

DISSENT 1. to disagree; 2. a reasoned **opinion** that differs from that of the majority of the court.

DISSOLUTION in **corporation** law, the end of the legal existence of a corporation, whether by expiration of **charter, decree** of court, act of legislature, vote of **shareholders,** or other means.

DISTRAINT see **distress.**

DISTRESS the act or process of **DISTRAINT**, by which a person (the **DISTRAINER**), without prior court approval, seizes the **personal property** of another in **satisfaction** of a claim, as a pledge for **performance** of a duty or in reparation of an injury. Where goods are seized in satisfaction of a claim, the distrainer may hold the goods until the claim is paid and, failing payment, may sell them in satisfaction. The person whose goods are distrained has recourse against the wrongful distrainer in **replevin.**

EXAMPLE: A warehouseman stores goods for a farmer. When the farmer fails to pay the storage costs for over a year, the warehouseman seizes in *distress* whatever goods the farmer presently has in the warehouse. If the farmer does not then pay for the storage charges that are past due, the warehouseman can sell the goods, take out what he is owed and refund the amount remaining to the farmer.

Originally, distress was a landlord's remedy; see **lien**

[LANDLORD'S LIEN], distinguishable from **attachment,** which is a court-ordered seizure of property. See also **impounding; garnishment.**

DISTRIBUTION a payment of yield in cash or in property to one entitled to such payment.

EXAMPLE: At the end of every three months, a corporation distributes dividends to all of its shareholders. A *distribution* takes place whether the dividends represent checks, an increase in the number of shares each shareholder has, or any other method of payment.

DISTRICT COURT 1. a court, established by the U.S. Constitution, having territorial **jurisdiction** over a district that may include a whole state or part of it. A district court has **original jurisdiction,** exclusive of courts of the individual states, over all offenses against laws of the United States, and is a court of general jurisdiction for **suits** between **litigants** of different states. See **diversity of citizenship; federal question jurisdiction.** 2. an inferior court in several states having limited jurisdiction to try certain minor cases.

DISTURBANCE OF THE PEACE any public act that molests inhabitants or that excites fear among normal persons.

DIVERSITY JURISDICTION see **diversity of citizenship.**

DIVERSITY OF CITIZENSHIP the circumstance that grants to federal courts **original jurisdiction** over **cases** and **controversies** between citizens of different states or between a citizen of a state and an alien, subject to a minimum **jurisdictional amount** (the value in controversy) of $10,000.

DIVESTITURE 1. loss or surrender of a right or title or interest; 2. a **remedy** by which the court orders the offending party to rid itself of assets before the party would normally have done so. Divestiture, like **restitution,** has the purpose of depriving a defendant of the gains of wrongful conduct. It is a remedy sometimes used in the enforcement of the **antitrust laws.**

EXAMPLE: One of the top three oil companies purchases the sixth largest oil company. After a long investigation, the government determines that the purchase will remove gasoline price competition in many states. If a court agrees with the government's position, it will order the larger company to *divest* itself of the smaller company.

DIVIDEND a **corporation's** profits or earnings appropriated for **distribution** among **shareholders.**

CUMULATIVE DIVIDEND a dividend whose unpaid residue is added to the following distribution.

DIVIDEND ADDITION life insurance in addition to the face value of the policy, purchased with dividends of the policy.

EXTRAORDINARY DIVIDENDS dividends of unusual form and amount, paid at unscheduled times from accumulated surplus.

LIQUIDATION DIVIDEND dividend resulting from *winding up* affairs of a business, settling with its **debtors** and **creditors,** and appropriating and distributing to its shareholders a residue proportionate to the profit and loss.

PREFERRED DIVIDEND fund paid to owners of **preferred stock** in priority over that to be paid to another class of shareholders.

SCRIP DIVIDEND a dividend payable not in cash, but in certificates of indebtedness that give the holder certain rights against the corporation.

STOCK DIVIDEND a dividend paid not in cash, but in **stock.**

DIVISIBLE CONTRACT see **severable contract.**

DIVORCE dissolution of the bonds of marriage. Compare **annul.**

NO-FAULT DIVORCE a divorce granted without the necessity of a spouse guilty of marital misconduct. The most common no-fault ground is voluntary separation for a period of time, which creates a statutory presumption of incompatibility or irreconcilable differences. See **community property; equitable distribution.**

SEPARATION [OR DIVORCE A MENSA ET THORO] *(à mĕn'-sà ĕt thô'-rō)* Lat.: from table and bed. A partial divorce decree, usually entered in the course of divorce proceedings, which directs the parties to live separately—indeed, forbids them to **cohabit**—but does not dissolve the marriage.

DOCKET 1. a list of cases on a court's calendar; 2. in **procedure,** a formal **record** of the proceedings in the court whose decision is being appealed.

DOCTRINE OF WORTHIER TITLE see **worthier title, doctrine of.**

DOMAIN land of which one is absolute owner.

DOMICILE an individual's permanent home or principal establishment. Residence is not the same as domicile, since a person can have many transient residences but only one legal domicile, which is the home address to which he always intends to return for prolonged periods.

EXAMPLE: As the result of a long and prosperous business career, Richard has bought houses in Florida, New Jersey, Colorado and California. But Richard spends most of his time at his house in New Jersey because that is only fifteen minutes from his corporation's headquarters. Richard's *domicile* is New Jersey and would remain so even if in one particular year he spent more time at one of his other homes. Should he sell his business and leave New Jersey to permanently live in California, his domicile would then change.

The domicile of a business is the address where the establishment is maintained or where the governing power of the enterprise is exercised. For purposes of taxation, it is often a principal place of business.

DOMINANT ESTATE [OR TENEMENT] **property** retained by an original grantor when a particular tract is subdivided and a portion is **conveyed,** and to which there attaches a right to some beneficial use of the conveyed or **servient estate** or a portion of it. The owner of the retained land (dominant estate) is said to have a right of **easement** in the servient estate.

DONATIO *(dō-nä'-shē-ō)* Lat.: a **gift;** donation.

DONATION see **contribution.**

DONATIVE INTENT voluntary intent on the part of a **donor** to make a **gift.**

DONEE the recipient of a **gift** or **trust;** one who takes without first giving **consideration;** one who is given a power, right or interest. Compare **bailee; trustee.**

DONOR one who gives a **gift;** creator of a **trust;** the party conferring a power, right or interest.

DOUBLE JEOPARDY prosecution or punishment twice for the same offense, which is prohibited by the U.S. Constitution and by many state constitutions.

EXAMPLE: Ray is charged with destroying government property. After a long trial, a jury finds Ray not guilty. Immediately after the trial, new evidence is discovered that unquestionably links Ray to the destruction. Under principles of *double jeopardy,* the prosecutor cannot retry Ray for the crime even with the new evidence.

See also **collateral** [COLLATERAL ESTOPPEL].

DOWER a surviving wife's **life estate** in one third of all the property of which her husband was **seised** in **fee** at any time during the marriage, to which she was entitled in **common law** upon the death of her husband.

Dower rights have been abrogated in many jurisdictions or limited to interests that the husband holds at his death. Where dower still exists, a wife can join in a **conveyance** and thereby give up her dower rights. See **widow's election.** Compare **curtesy.**

DOWRY the money and personal property that a wife brings to her husband in marriage.

DRAFT 1. an order in writing directing a person other than the **maker** to pay a specified sum to a named person. Drafts may or may not be **negotiable instruments,** depending upon whether the elements of negotiability are satisfied. Draft is synonymous with **BILL OF EXCHANGE**. 2. the preliminary form of a legal document (e.g., the draft of a contract—often called "rough draft"); 3. the process of preparing or **DRAWING** a legal document (e.g., drafting a will) or piece of proposed legislation; 4. in a military context, conscription of citizens into the military service.

SIGHT DRAFT one that is payable on demand; a **bill** of exchange for immediate collection.

DRAM SHOP ACT a legislative enactment imposing **strict liability** upon the seller of intoxicating beverages when the sale results in the harm of a third party's person, **property** or means of support.

EXAMPLE: Jake left a tavern after consuming an excessive amount of alcohol. His drinking caused an accident. The victim of the accident sues the tavern owner under that state's *Dram Shop Act*. Since the act imposes strict liability on the owner, he is liable even if he did not realize or had no way of realizing that Jake was drunk.

DRAW 1. to withdraw money from an account in a bank or other depository; 2. to execute a check or **draft** for the withdrawal of money; 3. to prepare a draft of a legal document, such as a **complaint,** a **deed** or a **will.**

DRAWEE one whom a **BILL OF EXCHANGE** (see **bill; draft**) or a **check** directs to pay to another a specified sum of money. In the typical checking account situation, the bank is the drawee, the person writing the check is the **maker** or **drawer,** and the person to whom the check is written is the **payee.**

DRAWER person by whom a **check** or **BILL OF EXCHANGE**

(see **bill**) is drawn; person directing payment by another by way of a **draft.**

DRIVING WHILE INTOXICATED [D.W.I.] the criminal offense of operating a motor vehicle while under the influence of alcohol or drugs. State law controls both the definition of "operating," such as whether it includes the actual driving of the car or merely sitting in the car, and the level of intoxication needed in order to be found in violation of the law.

DROIT *(drwäh)* Fr.: a right; law; the whole body of the law.

DUCES TECUM *(dū'-chĕs tā'-kūm)* Lat.: bring with you. See **subpoena [SUBPOENA DUCES TECUM].**

DUE CARE the degree of care that a person of ordinary prudence and reason (a **reasonable man**) would exercise under given circumstances. The concept is used in **tort** law to indicate the standard of care or the legal **duty** one normally owes to others. **Negligence** is the failure to use due care.

EXAMPLE: Basic construction trade usage mandates that a certain size beam be used to support a certain amount of weight. In its hurry, a construction company uses a smaller beam because it is all that is available. The floor supported by that beam collapses, and three workers are injured. The use of the smaller beam represents a failure on the part of the company to use *due care*.

DUE DATE time fixed for payment of **debt, tax, interest,** etc.

DUE PROCESS OF LAW a phrase introduced into American jurisprudence in the Fifth and Fourteenth Amendments to the U.S. Constitution; the principle that the government may not deprive an individual of life, liberty or property unless certain rules and procedures required by law are followed. The phrase does not have a fixed meaning, but embodies society's fundamental notions of legal fairness. Specifically, the constitutional safeguard of **SUBSTANTIVE DUE PROCESS** requires that all legislation, state or federal, must be reasonably related to a legitimate government objective. The concept of **PROCEDURAL DUE PROCESS** guarantees procedural fairness where the government attempts to deprive one of his property or liberty; this requires notice and a fair hearing prior to a deprivation of life, liberty or property.

EXAMPLE: Police in a municipality devise a scheme to produce a confession from Randy, who was accused of murder. The trial judge permits the prosecution to use the confession, and Randy is convicted. On appeal, a judge could find that the scheme violates *procedural due process of law,* based on the nature of the police scheme and the general nature of the American judicial system, which looks to produce convictions based on evidence acquired from sources other than the accused. In essence, due process is that level of process which is deemed fair based on a balancing of all interests.

DUPLICITY the technical invalidity resulting from uniting two or more **causes of action** in one **count** of a **pleading,** or multiple defenses in one plea, or multiple **crimes** in one count of an **indictment,** or two or more incongruous subjects in one legislative act, all contrary to proper **procedural** or constitutional requirements. See also **joinder; misjoinder.**

DURESS refers to conduct that has the effect of compelling another person to do what he need not otherwise do. It is a recognized **defense** to any act, such as a **crime,** contractual **breach** or **tort,** all of which must be voluntary to create **liability.** See **involuntary.**

EXAMPLE: Marcy is held at gunpoint until she agrees to help some people rob a bank. At her trial for the robbery, Marcy pleads *duress* and explains what happened. If her version of the facts is accepted, her defense of duress prevents a finding of guilty against her.

DURHAM RULE a test of criminal responsibility that states that an accused is not criminally responsible if his unlawful act was the product of mental defect. The Durham Rule was the first major modification of the **common law M'Naghten Rule** but is no longer in force in the District of Columbia (where it was adopted), having been superseded by the American Law Institute's Model Penal Code test. This new test asks whether the defendant lacks substantial capacity to conform his conduct to the requirements of law, and is now used by a number of jurisdictions. See **insanity.**

DUTY 1. obligation of one person to another. 2. In **tort** law, duty is a legally sanctioned obligation the **breach** of which results in the **liability** of the actor. Thus, an individual owes a DUTY OF CARE to conduct himself to avoid **negligent** injury to others. See **due care.** 3. In tax law, a duty is a levy [tax] on **imports** and exports.

DELEGABLE DUTY a duty that the person under legal obligation is able to transfer to another.

DWELLING HOUSE one's residence; a structure or apartment used as a home for a family unit; a house in which the occupier and his family usually reside. In the law of real property, it includes everything attached to or considered an accessory to the main building, such as a garage or barn, and may consist of a cluster of buildings.

D.W.I. see **driving while intoxicated.**

E

EARNEST in **civil law,** something of value given by one party to another to bind a **contract,** usually a sales agreement; serves both as part payment or **performance** and as a method of predetermining **liquidated damages** for **breach** of the contract. On breach by buyer, seller retains the earnest, while in seller's breach, buyer is entitled to twice the value of the earnest.

In **common law,** earnest often denotes a down payment, but unlike a down payment, earnest is by definition forfeited on breach of contract.

EARNINGS AND PROFITS a tax term referring to the income of the **corporation** that, if distributed to its **shareholders,** would constitute a **dividend** to each shareholder.

ACCUMULATED EARNINGS AND PROFITS the amount of earnings and profits from prior years earned by a corporation but not yet distributed to its shareholders.

CURRENT EARNINGS AND PROFITS the earnings and profits of a corporation earned during the current taxable year. For dividend purposes, **distributions** to shareholders are deemed paid first out of current earnings and profits.

EASEMENT a right, created by an express or implied agreement, to make lawful and **beneficial use** of the land of another. Such use must not be inconsistent with any other uses already being made of the land. An easement is a privilege connected with the land and is therefore not a **possessory interest** or **fee.**

EASEMENT APPURTENANT a pure easement, or easement proper, that is, one that belongs to whomever owns the **dominant estate** to which the benefit of the easement attaches. In contrast to an EASEMENT IN GROSS (definition follows), an easement appurtenant passes with the dominant estate to all subsequent **grantees** and is **inheritable.** See **appurtenant.**

EASEMENT IN GROSS a personal privilege to make use of another's land. It is not appurtenant to a dominant estate and is therefore not **assignable** or **inheritable.** See **license.**

EASEMENT OF NECESSITY one necessary for the continued use of the land when a larger tract of land has been subdivided. If without the easement either the grantee or grantor cannot make use of his property, the existence of an easement of necessity is implied by **operation of law.**

IMPLIED EASEMENT one created by operation of law from the particular circumstances involved rather than by a written instrument. A QUASI EASEMENT will be implied where at the time of the grant there existed an apparent, permanent, continuous and necessary use of the land from which it can be inferred that an easement permitting its continuation was intended, as, for example, where a lot containing a driveway is severed from the lot containing the house.

NEGATIVE EASEMENT an easement that restricts a landowner from doing certain acts he would normally be permitted to do in connection with his own land. See **restrictive covenant.**

PRESCRIPTIVE EASEMENT [EASEMENT BY PRESCRIPTION] an easement that is acquired through the uninterrupted use of another's land for a period of time that would be sufficient to acquire title to the land by **adverse possession.**

PUBLIC EASEMENT see **public easement.**

RECIPROCAL NEGATIVE EASEMENTS an implied restriction upon the use of property that can arise where a common grantor of several adjoining parcels (especially a subdivision) has failed to insert the restrictions from prior deeds into deeds to parcels conveyed later. See **license.** Compare **run with the land.**

EXAMPLE: When Sunbelt Housing Cooperative sold the first half of a housing complex, they included a provision that no commercial establishments would be allowed on any property owned by Sunbelt. The contracts for sale on the second half of the complex included no such provision. Still, a purchaser of a lot on the second half cannot set up a psychologist's clinic in his home. A court will usually imply a *reciprocal negative easement* based on the sales contracts of the first half of the complex, thereby limiting all structures throughout Sunbelt to residental use.

ECU see **Eurodollar.**

EGRESS see **ingress and egress.**

EJECTMENT a legal action brought by one claiming a right to possess **real property** against another who has **adverse possession** of the premises or who is a **holdover (tenant** who remains beyond the termination of a **lease).** In **common law** the action was originally commenced by a **lessee** against an intruder. Later it became a possessory action brought by the holder of legal **title** to recover possession from one holding under an invalid title. Compare **eviction.**

EJUSDEM GENERIS *(ĕ-yūs'-dĕm jĕn'-ĕr-ĭs)* Lat.: of the same class. A rule of statutory **construction,** generally accepted by both state and federal courts, providing that where general words follow enumerations of particular classes of persons or things, the general words shall be construed as applicable only to persons or things of the same general kind as those enumerated.

EXAMPLE: A state law forbids concealing on one's person "pistols, revolvers, derringers, or other dangerous weapons." Jed is arrested under that law for concealling a long-blade knife. Under the rule of *ejusdem generis,* the law will probably not apply to Jed since "other dangerous weapons" as used here implies firearms or, perhaps even more narrowly, handguns.

Compare **sui generis.**

ELECTION OF REMEDIES a choice of possible **remedies** permitted by law for an injury suffered; a rule of **procedure** that requires the party to make a choice among alternative and inconsistent remedies all of which are allowed by law on the same facts. Once a choice is made, the alternatives not chosen are **waived.** Thus, while the plaintiff may seek the alternative remedies of **specific performance** or **damages** for a **breach** of **contract,** he may not ask for alternative inconsistent remedies such as **rescission** and damages, since rescission elects to treat the contract as **void** and the request for damages seeks to enforce a valid contract. Many jurisdictions do not require election of remedies until late in the proceedings.

ELECTION UNDER THE WILL the principle that to take under a **will** is to submit to all its provisions. Specifically, it consists of the choice of accepting the benefit given under the will and relinquishing a claim, such as **dower,** that one may have to a portion of the **estate** of another, or retaining that claim and rejecting the request provided by the will.

ELEMENT an ingredient or factor, as the elements of an offense.

EMANCIPATION 1. freeing of someone from control of another; 2. express or implied relinquishing by a parent of rights in, or authority and control over, a **minor** child.

EMBEZZLEMENT **fraudulent** appropriation for one's own use of property lawfully in his **possession,** a type of **larceny** that did not exist in **common law** because it does not involve a **trespassory** taking; thus it is a crime created by statute. Embezzlement is often associated with bank employees, public officials or officers of organizations, who may in the course of their lawful activities come into possession of property, such as money, actually owned by others.

EXAMPLE: A bank teller finds herself short of cash one month, so she takes some money out of the deposits she receives, with the full intention of returning it in a few weeks. Her intent to return the money, though, has no relevance to the fact that she *embezzled* money. Her only defense in this instance would be that she thought the money was hers or that she had the owner's consent to borrow the money.

Compare **defalcation; misapplication [misappropriation] of property.**

EMBLEMENTS 1. the right of a **tenant** of agricultural land to remove crops that he has planted, even if the tenancy has expired before harvest; 2. vegetable **chattels** such as corn, produced annually as the result of one's labor and deemed **personal property** in the event of the death of the farmer before the harvest.

EMBRACERY the common-law **misdemeanor** of attempting to bribe or corruptly influence a **juror;** also called JURY TAMPERING. See **obstruction of justice.**

EMINENT DOMAIN the inherent right of the state to take private property for **public use,** without the individual property owner's consent; but just compensation must be paid to the property owner. See **expropriation.** Compare **public domain; public easement.**

EMOLUMENT profit derived from office, rank, employment, or labor, including salary, fees and other **compensation.**

EMPLOYEE STOCK OPTION see **stock option [employee stock option].**

EMPLOYER'S LIABILITY ACTS statutes specifying the extent to which employers shall be **liable** to make **compensation** for **injuries** sustained by their employees in the course of employment. Unlike in **workers' compensation** laws, which have replaced these acts in many states, the employer is made liable only for injuries resulting from his **breach** of a **duty** owed the employee, i.e., his **negligence.** See **assumption of risk; fellow servants.**

ENABLING CLAUSE a provision in most new laws or statutes that gives appropriate officials the power to implement and enforce the law.

EXAMPLE: A statute that provides extra money for public housing is passed. The statute will include an *enabling clause* permitting the Department of Housing and Urban Development to spend the money accordingly.

ENACTING CLAUSE generally, the **preamble** of a **statute,** or the part that identifies the statute as a legislative act and authorizes it as law. Thus, "Be it enacted by the Senate and House of Representatives of the United States in Congress assembled," etc., is the enacting clause used in Congressional legislation.

EN BANC *(än bänk)* Fr.: by the full court. Many **appellate courts** sit in divisions of three or more judges from among a larger number on the full court. Sometimes either on the court's **motion** or at the request of a **litigant** the court will consider a case by the full court rather than by only a part of it. A matter reconsidered by the whole court after a part of it has rendered its decision is called a **REHEARING EN BANC,** sometimes spelled "en bank."

ENCLOSURE land enclosed by something other than an imaginary boundary line, i.e., a wall, hedge, fence, ditch or other actual obstruction; also called a **CLOSE.**

ENCROACH to intrude gradually upon the rights or property of another. An encroachment is any infringement on the property or authority of another.

ENCUMBRANCE any right to, interest in or legal **liability** upon **real property** that does not prohibit passing **title** to the land but that diminishes its value. Encumbrances include **easements, licenses, leases,** timber privileges, **homestead** privileges, **mortgages,** judgment **liens,** etc.

EXAMPLE: A piece of land Seth wants is *encumbered* by a mortgage that is greater than the stated value of the land. He purchases the property anyway, believing that the value is understated and that one day he will be able to sell the land at a great profit.

ENDORSEMENT see **indorsement.**

ENDOWMENT a permanent fund of **property** or money bestowed upon an institution or a person, the income from which is used to serve the specific purpose for which the gift was intended.

ENFEOFF to create a **feoffment.** The term refers to an early common law means of conveying **freehold** estates and has been used in some modern **deeds** to signify a conveyance of **title.**

EN GROS *(än grō)* Fr.: in gross (large) amount; total; by wholesale.

ENJOIN to command or instruct with authority; to suspend or restrain. One may be enjoined or commanded by a court either to do a specific act or to refrain from doing a certain act. See **injunction.**

EXAMPLE: Southwest Plastics has been disposing of its waste products in an adjacent river for over a decade. Environmentalists finally determine that some of the liquid waste contains a deadly carcinogen. A court *enjoins* (i.e., forbids) Southwest from using the river for disposal based on the environmentalists' proofs.

ENJOYMENT substantial present economic benefit; **beneficial use** and purpose to which **real** or **personal property** may be put; implies right to use and to profits and income from use, rather than mere technical ownership. In common usage, synonymous with use and occupancy; usually infers **possession.**

COVENANT OF QUIET ENJOYMENT see **quiet enjoyment.**

ENTAIL to create a **fee tail;** to create a fee tail from a **fee simple.**

ENTIRETY see **tenancy** [TENANCY BY THE ENTIRETY].

ENTRAPMENT in criminal law, an AFFIRMATIVE DEFENSE (see **defense**) created either by statute or by court decision in the given jurisdiction that excuses a **defendant** from criminal liability for **crimes** induced by trickery on the part of law enforcement officers or other agents of the government.

To sustain the defense, the defendant must demonstrate that but for the objectionable police conduct, he would not have committed the crime, or that an ordinary, law-abiding citizen would have been persuaded, under the same circumstances, to commit the crime.

EXAMPLE: Larry does not touch or go near anything related to drugs since his conviction for drug dealing six years ago. One day, an undercover police officer asks Larry to buy some drugs. He refuses, but the officer continues his request over several days and even offers to provide the narcotics to Larry on credit. Low on cash, Larry accepts, acquires the drugs and is then arrested. The officer's conduct in continually pressing Larry after he refused on several occasions may constitute *entrapment*.

ENTRY, FORCIBLE see **forcible entry.**

ENVIRONMENTAL PROTECTION AGENCY [EPA] an agency of the federal government charged with a variety of responsibilities relating to protection of the quality of the natural environment, including research and monitoring, promulgation of standards for air and water quality, control of the introduction of pesticides and other hazardous materials into the environment, and the like. See **police power.**

EQUAL EMPLOYMENT OPPORTUNITY COMMISSION [EEOC] see **equal opportunity.**

EQUAL OPPORTUNITY a term to signify an employer's adoption of employment practices that do not discriminate on the basis of race, color, religion, sex or national origin. Such discrimination was outlawed by Title VII of the Civil Rights Act of 1964.

Title VII also created the EQUAL EMPLOYMENT OPPORTUNITY COMMISSION [EEOC] to implement equal opportunity policy by working with local agencies.

EQUAL PROTECTION OF THE LAWS constitutional guarantee embodied in the **Fourteenth Amendment** to the U.S. Constitution, which states in relevant part that "No State shall . . . deny to any person within its jurisdiction the equal protection of the laws.'' The essential purpose of this constitutional doctrine is to ensure that the laws and the government treat all persons alike, unless there is some substantial reason why certain persons or classes of persons should be treated differently.

EXAMPLE: Women and men who perform equal tasks in their jobs for the state receive unequal pay. In a lawsuit seeking equal pay, the fact that a question based on gender is raised forces the state to demonstrate a compelling government interest to justify the distinction.

EQUAL RIGHTS AMENDMENT [E.R.A.] a proposed amendment hoping to eliminate sex as a basis for any decisions made by a state of the United States. This amendment was never ratified by a sufficient number of states to qualify as a constitutional amendment, but the basic premise underlying the proposal has become an accepted standard in many statutes and court decisions.

EQUITABLE according to natural right or natural justice; marked by due consideration for what is fair and impartial, unhampered by technical rules the law may have devised that limit **recovery** or **defense.**

EQUITABLE DISTRIBUTION see **equitable distribution.**

See **equity.**

EQUITABLE DEFENSE see **defense.**

EQUITABLE DISTRIBUTION 1. a just division of property among interested parties; 2. the process by which, as part of a dissolution of marriage proceeding under a no-fault **divorce** statute, the court apportions between husband and wife all **assets** acquired by either or both of them, whether owned jointly or individually, during the marriage. See **alimony, community property.**

EQUITABLE EASEMENT see **equitable servitude.**

EQUITABLE ESTATE see **estate.**

EQUITABLE ESTOPPEL see **estoppel** [**ESTOPPEL IN PAIS**].

EQUITABLE RECOUPMENT in certain situations in which a **taxpayer** erroneously pays taxes in one **taxable year** when they are properly payable in a later year, this doctrine allows the taxpayer to recoup the additional taxes paid by reducing his taxes payable in the later year.

EQUITABLE SERVITUDE a **covenant** that is enforceable only in **equity.** For a covenant to be valid at law, as to remote grantees of the affected property there must exist **PRIVITY OF ESTATE** (see **privity**) between the covenantor and covenantee, but such a relationship is not necessary to create an enforceable equitable servitude so long as the subsequent grantee has either actual or **CONSTRUCTIVE NOTICE** (see **notice**) of the covenant.

EQUITABLE TITLE see **title.**

EQUITY generally, justice or fairness. Historically, equity refers to a separate body of law developed in England in reaction to the inability of the **common law** courts, in their strict adherence to rigid **writs** and **forms of action,** to consider or provide a **remedy** for every injury. The king therefore established the court of **chancery,** to do justice between **parties** in cases where the common law would give inadequate redress. The principle of this jurisprudence is that equity will find a way to achieve a lawful result when legal procedure is inadequate. Equity and **law** courts are now merged in most jurisdictions, though equity **jurisprudence** and equitable doctrines are still independently viable.

Equity also refers to the value of **property** minus **liens** or other **encumbrances.** For example, one's equity in a home with a **mortgage** is the value of the property beyond the amount of the mortgage debt.

In accounting, equity refers to the ownership interest in a company as determined by subtracting **liabilities** from **assets.** See **balance sheet.** For incorporated business enterprises, equity is owned by the common and preferred **shareholders.**

If the corporation is publicly held, the shares will be traded on a **stock exchange** or **over-the-counter market** which together comprise the EQUITY MARKET.

EQUITY OF REDEMPTION right of mortgagor to redeem his property (save it from **foreclosure**) after **default** in the payment of the **mortgage debt,** by subsequent payment of all costs and interest, in addition to the mortgage debt, to the mortgagee.

ERGO *(ĕr'-gō)* Lat.: therefore; consequently; hence; because.

ERRONEOUS involving a mistake; signifies a deviation from the requirements of the law, but it does not connote a lack of legal authority, and is thus distinguished from illegal. If, while having the power to act, one commits error in the exercise of that power, he acts erroneously.

ERRONEOUS JUDGMENT one rendered according to practice of court, but contrary to law, upon a mistaken view of law, or upon erroneous application of legal principles.

ERROR a mistake; an act involving a departure from truth or accuracy. In a legal proceeding such as a trial, an ERROR OF LAW furnishes grounds for the **appellate court** to **reverse** a **judgment.**

ESCALATOR CLAUSE that part of a **lease** or **contract** that provides for an increase in the rent or contract price upon the occurrence of certain conditions beyond the parties' control, such as an increase in the cost of labor or of a necessary commodity, or the fixing of maximum prices by a government agency. Escalator clauses in leases may permit an increase in rent whenever real estate taxes or interest rates rise. In a divorce decree one's **alimony** payments may increase as the cost of living rises or when the ex-spouse who is paying alimony has a higher income.

ESCAPE CLAUSE a clause in a contract permitting a party to renege on its obligations under certain conditions without incurring a penalty or other liability.

EXAMPLE: Stilton Harvest Corporation agrees to provide a bread company with all the wheat it needs for one year. The agreement includes a provision that, if the annual harvest for a group of states falls below an established level, Stilton is relieved of its obligation.

ESCHEAT assignment of **property** to the state because there is no verifiable legal owner.

ESCROW a written **instrument,** such as a **deed,** temporarily deposited with a neutral third party (the **ESCROW AGENT**), by the agreement of two parties to a valid **contract.** The escrow agent will deliver the document to the benefited party when the conditions of the contract have been met. The depositor has no control over the instrument in escrow. In **common law,** escrow applied to the deposits only of instruments for **conveyance** of land, but it now applies to all instruments so deposited. Money or other property so deposited is also loosely referred to as escrow.

ESQUIRE [ESQ.] a title for lawyers.

ESTABLISHMENT CLAUSE provision in the First Amendment of the U.S. Constitution prohibiting enactment of laws pertaining to "the establishment of religion." It has been said that the establishment clause means that neither a state nor the federal government may set up a church; neither may pass laws that aid one religion, aid all religions or prefer one religion over another. In the words of Jefferson, the clause was intended to erect a "wall of separation between church and state."

ESTATE 1. technically, the nature and extent of a person's **interest** in or ownership of land; 2. broadly, estate applies to all that a person owns, whether **real** or **personal property.**

CONTINGENT ESTATE see **contingent estate.**

DOMINANT ESTATE see **dominant estate.**

EQUITABLE ESTATE an estate or interest that can be enforced only in **equity;** applies especially to every **trust,** express or implied, that is not converted to a legal estate by the **Statute of Uses.**

FUTURE ESTATE an estate in land that is not **possessory** but that will or may become so in the future. Future estates are either **vested** or **contingent,** and include **remainders** and **reversions.**

LEGAL ESTATE originally, an interest in land that was enforced by courts of **common law,** as opposed to an equitable estate, enforced by **courts of equity.**

PRECEDING ESTATE see **preceding estate.**

SERVIENT ESTATE see **servient estate.**

VESTED ESTATE one either presently in **possession** or owned by a presently existing person to whom (or to whose successors in interest) the property interest will automatically accrue upon the termination of a PRECEDING ESTATE. Such an estate thus represents a present interest and as such is neither subject to any contingency nor otherwise capable of being defeated.

ESTATE AT SUFFERANCE see **tenancy** [TENANCY AT SUFFERANCE].

ESTATE AT WILL see **tenancy** [TENANCY AT WILL].

ESTATE BY THE ENTIRETY see **tenancy** [TENANCY BY THE ENTIRETY].

ESTATE FOR LIFE see **life estate.**

ESTATE FOR YEARS see **tenancy** [TENANCY FOR YEARS].

ESTATE FROM YEAR TO YEAR see **tenancy** [PERIODIC TENANCY].

ESTATE IN COMMON see **tenancy** [TENANCY IN COMMON].

ESTATE OF INHERITANCE a **common law** species of land ownership that could descend to **heirs;** a type of **freehold estate** that the owner can both enjoy during his life and **bequeath** according to an established order of **descent.** Estates of inheritance include estates in **fee simple** absolute, fee simple conditional, fee simple determinable and estates in **fee tail.**

ESTATE PER AUTRE VIE see **per autre vie.**

ESTATE TAX see *tax.*

ESTOPPEL a restraint; a bar; arises where a person has done some act that the policy of the law will not permit him to deny, or where circumstances are such that the law will not permit a certain argument because it would lead to an unjust result. In the context of **contract** law, for example, one is estopped from denying existence of a binding contract where he has done something intending that another rely on his conduct, and the result of the reliance is detrimental to that other person. Compare **waiver.**

EXAMPLE: Nelson convinces an associate to sign what appears to be a valid contract which gives the associate the right to buy certain items from Nelson. When the contract turns out to harm Nelson more than the associate, Nelson tries to deny the validity of the instrument. A court will find that Nelson is *estopped* (i.e., prevented) from raising that claim since it was Nelson who initiated the offer.

COLLATERAL ESTOPPEL see **collateral.**

ESTOPPEL BY DEED a bar that precludes a party from denying the truth and legitimacy of the conveyance represented by a **deed** he has given. It may be invoked only in a suit on the deed or concerning a right arising out of it.

ESTOPPEL BY JUDGMENT see **judgment.**

ESTOPPEL BY LACHES see **laches.**

ESTOPPEL IN PAIS [*pá'-ēs*] Old Fr: the country, the neighborhood. An estoppel that arises out of a person's statement of fact, or out of his silence, acts or omissions, rather than from a **deed** or record or written contract; also called an EQUITABLE ESTOPPEL.

PROMISSORY ESTOPPEL see **promissory estoppel.**

ESTOVERS the right of the **tenant,** during the period of his **lease,** to use timber on the leased premises for proper maintenance of the property.

ET AL. *(ĕt äl)* Lat.: and others; abbreviation of et allii.

ET NON *(ĕt nŏn)* Lat.: and not.

ET SEQ. *(ĕt sĕk)* Lat.: and the following; abbreviation of et sequentes or et sequentia. Most commonly used in denominating page reference numbers: page 13 et seq.

ET UX. *(ĕt ŭks)* Lat.: and wife; abbreviation of et uxor. Used in old legal documents such as **wills** or deeds; for example, "This will made by John Doe *et ux*."

EURODOLLAR a U.S. dollar held as a deposit in a European commercial bank. Eurodollars were created after World War II by United States foreign defense and aid expenditures. Since the dollar was backed by gold, it became a popular reserve currency in Europe and among all the trading partners of the United States.

EUTHANASIA the putting to death, as an act of mercy, of someone in considerable pain as the result of disease or other physical malady, for whom there is no hope of recovery. While routinely permitted for animals, it has not been permitted in this country for human beings, although some states have authorized removal of extraordinary life support systems in individual cases. See **brain death.**

EVASION OF TAX generally applied to any of various fraudulent methods by which a **taxpayer** may pay less than his proper tax **liability.**

EXAMPLE: As an independent consultant, Julie works for many different companies. Her scheme has each company pay her under a different fictitious name. She then sets up bank accounts in each name to facilitate cashing the checks. By that method, she *evades her taxes* because the Internal Revenue Service is unable to locate any of the fictitious individuals.

Evasion is to be distinguished from **avoidance of tax,** which denotes the legal interpretation of relevant tax law to minimize tax liability.

EVICTION originally, the physical expulsion of someone from land by the assertion of **paramount title** or through legal **proceedings.**

CONSTRUCTIVE EVICTION refers to circumstances under the control of the **landlord** that compel the **tenant** to leave the **premises** though he is not asked to do so by the landlord. The tenant may be deemed constructively evicted if the premises are rendered unfit for occupancy, or if the use and enjoyment has been substantially impaired. Where the law of the jurisdiction permits the tenant to claim constructive eviction, he is not responsible for further rent, but he must actually vacate the premises.

PARTIAL ACTUAL EVICTION an eviction that the law may recognize as having occurred when part of the leased premises has been rendered unusable through the fault of the landlord. If the lease rental is not apportioned by room, nor the premises partitioned in the lease agreement, the tenant may not be responsible for any part of the lease rental while actually evicted from a part of the leased premises, and he need not vacate the habitable part of the premises.

EVIDENCE all the means by which any alleged matter of fact, the truth of which is submitted to investigation at judicial **trial,** is established or disproved. Evidence includes the **testimony** of **witnesses,** introduction of records, documents, exhibits or any other relevant matter offered for the purpose of inducing the trier of fact's (**fact finder's**) belief in the party's contention. See **circumstantial evidence; hearsay rule; insufficient evidence; presumption.**

EVIDENCE ALIUNDE see **alliunde.**

EVIDENCE DE BENE ESSE see **de bene esse.**

EXCEPTION an item that ought to be included in a category but that is eliminated. Exceptions arise in numerous contexts in law: 1. statutory exceptions are intended to restrain the **enacting clause** or to exclude something that would otherwise be within it, or to modify it in some manner. 2. an exception to a court's ruling is an objection to such ruling or the act of calling to the attention of a court an error made by the same or a different court. 3. Exception is also used generally to mean the withholding from conveyance of some **estate** or **interest** in the land conveyed.

EXCHANGE to give goods or services and to get goods or services of equal value in return. Generally, a transaction is a **sale** where money is received in return for the goods or services and is an exchange when specific **property** susceptible of valuation is received. Exchange is synonymous with **BARTER**.

EXCISE broadly, any kind of tax not applied to property or the rents or incomes of real estate; a tax upon articles of manufacture or sale and also upon licenses to pursue certain trades or to deal in certain commodities. It is a tax imposed directly and without assessment and is measured by amount of business done, income received, etc.

EXAMPLE: A customer buys a new set of tires for his car, the price of which includes a federal *excise* tax. The money generated by the tax is used for road maintenance and other transportation expenses and is justified by the rationale that anyone who buys tires must be using them on the roads. The tax is a means of ensuring that users pay for related government services.

EXCLUSION an amount that otherwise would constitute a part of **GROSS INCOME** (see **income**) but that under a specific provision of the **Internal Revenue Code** is excluded from gross income.

EXCLUSIONARY RULE a constitutional rule of law that provides that otherwise **admissible evidence** may not be used in a criminal trial if it was obtained as a result of illegal police conduct. See **fruit of the poisonous tree doctrine.**

EXAMPLE: The police unlawfully stop a car, order the driver to wait outside, and proceed to search the vehicle. Twenty pounds of marijuana are discovered in the back seat. Since there was never a lawful reason to stop the car in the first place, the subsequent search of the car is unreasonable and in violation of the Fourth Amendment of the Constitution. The primary remedy today for the violation is to apply the *exclusionary rule,* which bars the prosecutor from using the confiscated marijuana to convict the driver of possession of the drug. In fact, application of the rule will usually end any prosecution based on items that were discovered but now must be excluded.

EX CONTRACTU *(ěks kŏn-trak'-tū)* Lat.: arising out of contract.

EXCULPATORY refers to **evidence** or statements that tend to justify or excuse a **defendant** from alleged fault or **guilt.** Contrast **incriminate; inculpatory.**

EX DELICTO *(ěks dě-lĭk'-tō)* Lat.: arising out of wrongs. See **action ex delicto.**

EXECUTE 1. to complete, as a legal **instrument;** 2. to perform what is required; 3. to give validity to, as by signing and perhaps **sealing** and **delivering.** For example, a **contract** is executed when all acts necessary to complete it and to give it validity as an instrument are carried out, including signing and delivery.

EXECUTED fully accomplished or performed; leaving nothing unfulfilled; opposite of **executory.**

EXECUTED INTEREST see **interest.**

EXECUTION 1. the process of carrying into effect a court's **judgment, decree** or **order.** It gives the successful **party** the fruits of his judgment. For instance, when a party has won a judgment on his **claim,** the **judgment creditor** can enforce or **execute** the judgment by having the sheriff seize and sell the **judgment debtor's** property and then use the proceeds to pay the judgment. 2. in criminal law, the process by which a sentenced **defendant** serves his sentence. For instance, a person sentenced to ten years of imprisonment executes his sentence by spending that amount of time in prison, unless released earlier by **parole.** The term also refers specifically to carrying out a death sentence. See **capital punishment.**

EXECUTIVE AGREEMENT see **treaty.**

EXECUTIVE CLEMENCY the power constitutionally reposed in the President, and by most state constitutions, in the governor, to **pardon** or commute (i.e., reduce) the **sentence** of one convicted by a court within his **jurisdiction.** Compare **reprieve.**

EXECUTOR (OR EXECUTRIX) a person who either expressly or by **implication** is appointed by a **testator** [one who dies leaving a **will**] to carry out the testator's directions concerning the dispositions he makes under his will. When the appointee is a woman, she is the executrix.

EXAMPLE: Frank's will names Nat *executor* of Frank's estate. As executor, Nat must make sure the provisions in Frank's will are carried out, debts against the estate are paid, and any money owed is collected. If there are ambiguities in the will or the will is contested, Nat is responsible for seeing that a lawsuit is either filed or answered. Nat is compensated for his job, although that may be a small amount, and he is reimbursed by Frank's estate for any expenses.

EXECUTORY not fully accomplished or completed, but contingent upon the occurrence of some event or the performance of some act in the future; not **vested;** opposite of **executed.**

an EXECUTORY CONTRACT is one in which some performance remains to be accomplished.

EXECUTORY BEQUEST see **bequest.**

EXECUTORY INTEREST see **interest.**

EXEMPLARY DAMAGES see **damages.**

EXEMPTION a **deduction** allowed to a **taxpayer** because of his status or circumstances rather than because of specific economic costs or expenses during the **taxable year.**

EXAMPLE: Jeff and Lisa are married and have three children. Federal income tax laws allow the couple three *exemptions,* one for each child on the couple's joint tax return. The exemption reduces the amount of income upon which the couple is taxed.

EX GRATIA *(ĕks grä'-shē-ȧ)* Lat.: out of grace; gratuitously. Describes that which is done as a favor rather than as a required task or as of right.

EXILE to force out, or cut off from membership or privileges; the punishment, by a political authority, inflicted upon **criminals** by compelling them to leave a city, place or country for a period of time or for life.

EX OFFICIO *(ĕks ō-fĭ'-shĕ-ō)* Lat.: from the office; by virtue of his office; officially.

EX OFFICIO MEMBER one who is a member of a board, committee or other body by virtue of his title to a certain office, and who does not require further appointment.

EX OFFICIO SERVICES services imposed by law on a public officer by virtue of his office.

EX PARTE *(ĕks pär'-tā)* Lat.: in behalf of or on the application of one party; by or for one party. An ex parte judicial **proceeding** is one brought for the benefit of one party only, without notice to or challenge by an **adverse party.** Therefore, in an ex parte proceeding the adverse party and his **evidence** are excluded. For this reason, such proceedings are not favored, and any **relief** obtained ex parte is subject to speedy review.

EXAMPLE: Applications to install wiretaps on telephones are always made *ex parte,* i.e, without notice to the person whose phone is sought to be electronically surveilled. Otherwise, the person will know his phone is wiretapped and avoid incriminating conversations. Because the application is ex parte, requirements not usually insisted on must be met to protect privacy, and the person who is recorded may challenge the sufficiency of the application at a later opportunity.

EXPECTANCY **future interest** as to **possession** or enjoyment. In the law of **property, estates** may be either in possession or in expectancy; if an expectancy is created by the parties it is a **remainder;** if created by **operation of law** it is a **reversion.** See **contingent estate.** Compare **vested.**

EXPECTATION DAMAGES see **damages.**

EXPENSE any business cost incurred in operating and maintaining property. For purposes of information and in reporting to **shareholders** of publicly held **corporations,** expenses are calculated as the cost of goods and services used in the process of profit-directed business activities.

In tax law, expenses are costs that are currently **deductible,** as opposed to CAPITAL EXPENDITURES (see **capital**), which may not be currently deducted but must be **depreciated** or **amortized** over the useful life of the property.

EXPERT TESTIMONY [OR EVIDENCE] see **expert witness.**

EXPERT WITNESS a **witness** having special knowledge, skill or experience in the subject about which he is to **testify.** Testimony given by such a witness, in his capacity as such, constitutes EXPERT EVIDENCE or EXPERT TESTIMONY.

EXPORT 1. to transport out of one country and into another; 2. the article so transported.

EX POST FACTO *(ěks pōst fak'-tō)* Lat.: after the fact. Refers especially to a law that makes punishable as a crime an act done before the passing of the law and that was innocent when done. An ex post facto law is also one that makes a crime more serious than when it was committed, inflicts a greater punishment, or alters legal rules of **evidence** to require less or different testimony to convict than the law required when the crime was committed. Such laws violate provisions of the Constitution of the United States, which provide that neither Congress nor any state shall pass an ex post facto law.

EXAMPLE: Knowing that he has no money in the bank, Ed writes a check for $150 and is arrested for the crime. At the time of his arrest, the law made it criminal to write bad checks only for amounts over $200. By the time Ed is brought to trial, the amount that is necessary to make the writing of a bad check criminal had been lowered to $100. Ed must be tried under the law as it was at the time he was arrested and is, therefore, not guilty. To prosecute him under the new, lower limit of $100 would violate the *ex post facto* protection of the United States Constitution.

EXPRESS to set forth an **agreement** in words, written or spoken, that unambiguously signify intent. As distinguished from **implied,** the term refers to something that is not left to inference from conduct or circumstances.

EXPRESSIO UNIUS EST EXCLUSIO ALTERIUS *(ěks-prě'-sē-ō ū'-nē-ūs ěst ěks-klū'-sē-ō äl-těr'-ē-ūs)* Lat.: the expression of one thing is the exclusion of another. In construing statutes under this maxim, mention of one thing within the statute is said to imply the exclusion of another thing not mentioned. The maxim is an aid to **construction** and is applicable where the contrast between what is expressed and what is omitted enforces the inference that what is omitted must have been intended to have contrary treatment. Thus a statute granting certain rights to "police, fire, and sanitation employees'' would be interpreted to exclude other public employees not enumerated in the legislation.

EXPROPRIATION the taking of private property for public purpose upon the payment of just compensation, which is recognized as an inherent power of the state over its citizens. See **eminent domain.**

EX REL *(ĕks rĕl)* Lat.: upon relation or report; abbreviation of ex relatione. Legal **proceedings** that are initiated ex rel. are brought in the name of the state but on the information and at the instigation of a private individual with a private interest in the outcome. The **real party in interest** is called the RELATOR. The action will be captioned ''State of X [or United States] ex rel. Y versus Z.''

EX-RIGHTS refers to stock sold without **rights** to purchase stock subsequently offered by the same **corporation.** Rights normally have value, since the new issue is usually priced at a **discount** from the prevailing market price.

EXTENUATING CIRCUMSTANCES unusual factors tending to contribute to the consummation of an illegal act, but over which the actor had little or no control. These factors therefore reduce the responsibility of the actor and serve to mitigate his punishment or his payment of **damages.** Compare **justification.**

EXTINGUISHMENT a **discharge** of an obligation or **contract** by **operation of law** or by express agreement.

EXAMPLE: Phil signs a mortgage with a bank to purchase a new home. After twenty monthly payments, he stops paying the bank. A law in Phil's state provides that if a bank does not sue on a mortgage where no payment has been made for five years, the obligation is *extinguished*. By operation of that law, if the bank does not sue Phil within five years from the first payment date that he fails to meet, Phil is no longer liable on the mortgage.

EXTORTION 1. in common law, the corrupt collection by a public official under **color** of office of an excessive or unauthorized fee; punishable as a **misdemeanor.** 2. under modern statutes the offense includes illegal taking of money by anyone who employs threats, or other illegal use of fear or coercion, to obtain money, and whose conduct falls short of the threat to personal safety required for **robbery.** Extortion is used interchangeably with **blackmail** and is commonly punished as a **felony.**

EXAMPLE: Joe threatens Alice that he will reveal certain aspects of her past that would ruin her career unless she pays him $200 a month. Even if what Joe threatens to say is true, the fact that he has threatened her to obtain money constitutes *extortion.*

Compare **bribery.**

EXTRADITION the surrender by one state to another of an **accused** or convicted person. A state's chief executive has the right to demand from the **asylum** state the return of a person who was accused of crime based on **probable cause.** Extradition prevents the escape of fugitives who seek sanctuary in another state. It enables the state in which the offense occurred to swiftly bring the offender to trial.

EXTRAJUDICIAL beyond a court's **jurisdiction;** not directly connected with a court or its proceedings; e.g., a **confession** or an identification made outside of court.

EXTREMIS see **in extremis.**

EXTRINSIC FRAUD see **fraud.**

EX TURPI CAUSA NON ORITUR ACTIO *(ĕks tūr'-pē kaw'-zȧ nŏn ôr'-ē-tūr äk'-tē-ō)* Lat.: no disgraceful [foul, immoral, obscene] matter can give rise to an **action.**

EYEWITNESS a person who can testify as to what he has experienced by his presence at an event.

F

FAA see **Federal Aviation Administration [FAA].**

FACE VALUE the value indicated in the wording of the **instrument.** For instance, the face value of a bank check is the amount the check is written for. Compare **market value.**

FACILITATION in criminal law, a statutory offense rendering a person guilty when, believing it probable that he is aiding someone who intends to commit a **crime,** he assists the potential criminal in obtaining the means to commit the crime, and in fact such conduct does aid the person to commit the crime.

EXAMPLE: A very irate man walks into a gun store, screaming loudly that he is going to shoot someone for running a red light and destroying his new car. The man demands to purchase a gun, and the owner allows him to do so once the proper forms are filled out, even though the owner is aware of the man's state of mind. If the man then goes out and shoots the person who ran the light, the store owner may be guilty of criminal *facilitation*.

In **common law,** facilitation may give rise to **liability** for **aiding and abetting.** Compare **accomplice; conspiracy.**

FACINUS QUOS INQUINAT AEQUAT *(fä'-sĭ-nŭs kwōs ĭn'-kwĭ-nät ī'-kwät)* Lat.: villainy and guilt make all those whom it contaminates equal in character.

FACTA SUNT POTENTIORI VERBIS *(fäk'-tä sūnt pō-tĕn'-tē-ô' -rē vĕr'-bēs)* Lat.: facts are more powerful than words.

FACT FINDER in a judicial or administrative **proceeding,** the person or group responsible for determining the facts relevant to resolving a controversy. It is the role of a **jury** in a jury trial; in a nonjury trial the judge sits both as a fact finder and as a trier of law; in administrative proceedings it may be a hearing officer or a hearing body. The term TRIER OF FACT generally denotes the same role.

FACTO *(fäk'-tō)* Lat.: in fact; by a deed. See also **de facto.**

FACTOR a person who receives and sells goods for a **commission** (called FACTORAGE). He is entrusted with **possession** of the goods he sells and generally sells them in his own name. The term also refers to a **garnishee** in states where factorizing is the name for **garnishment.** Compare **jobber.**

FACTOR'S ACTS the name of certain English statutes, which have also been enacted in a number of states, whose general effect is to make a **factor's [agent's] possession** of property or documents of **title** stand as evidence of ownership to enable him to do all things the true owner might do with respect to the property or title documents. The owner thus becomes responsible for the factor's actions. The purpose of such statutes is to protect **bona fide purchasers** where the agent has exceeded his authority by giving an appearance that he is the true owner.

FACTUM *(fäk'-tūm)* Lat.: a deed, or accomplishment. With respect to a change in a person's **domicile,** the factum is the person's physical presence in the new domicile. In civil law the word factum distinguishes a matter of fact from a matter of law.

FACTUM PROBANDUM *(fäk'-tūm prō-bän'-dūm)* Lat.: the fact to be proved. See **evidence.**

FAILURE OF CONSIDERATION see **consideration.**

FAILURE OF ISSUE termination of one's bloodline. The words are most often used in a **will** or **deed** to refer to a **condition** that operates in the event either no children be born or no children survive the decedent. These words, or the phrase "die without issue," may fix a condition whereby an estate will, in the event of failure of issue, pass automatically to an alternative person or in an alternative manner designated in the will itself. Unless the **instrument** indicated to the contrary, the common law read the condition as operating ad infinitum. This construction is termed **INDEFINITE FAILURE OF ISSUE**. Thus, if children of the first taker themselves fail to leave children, the estate will still go to the alternative. The first taker is regarded as possessing a **fee tail,** and his descendants continue to hold the same limited estate. A majority of American jurisdictions by statute have reversed this presumption and construe "die without issue" as a **DEFINITE FAILURE OF ISSUE**; i.e., the condition is satisfied fully if the first taker has issue surviving at the time of his death. Alternative expressions include "if he dies before he has any issue," "for want of issue," "without leaving issue."

FAIR COMMENT a **plea** by a **defendant** in a **libel** suit that the statements made, even if untrue, were not intended to create ill will but rather to state the facts as the writer honestly believed them to be. Generally, one will not be held guilty of libel on the basis of honest and unintentional mistakes of fact.

FAIR HEARING a statutorily authorized extrajudicial hearing granted primarily where the normal judicial processes would be inadequate to secure **due process,** either because a judicial **remedy** does not exist, or because one would suffer grievous harm or substantial prejudice to his rights before a judicial remedy became available. Thus, fair hearings have been authorized as forums for the administrative determination of a citizen's rights in a number of contexts.

FAIR MARKET VALUE see **market value.**

FAIRNESS DOCTRINE a requirement that broadcasting stations present contrasting viewpoints on controversial issues of public importance. This doctrine imposes two affirmative responsibilities on the broadcaster: (1) to present adequate coverage of controversial public issues and (2) to ensure that this programming presents differing viewpoints so that the public are fully and fairly informed.

FAIR TRADE LAWS state statutes that permit a manufacturer to establish minimum resale prices that may not be varied by the wholesaler or distributor. Such agreements do not violate the **antitrust laws** when they are entered into under the provisions of state fair trade laws.

FAIR USE in federal **copyright** law, an insubstantial permitted use by another of material protected by copyright.

EXAMPLE: Jenny copyrights an article that she publishes in a medical journal. Although Jenny has the sole right to authorize who may copy the article, the *fair use* doctrine permits a teacher to make as many copies as she needs if the teacher uses the copies for classroom discussion.

FALSE ARREST unlawful **arrest;** unlawful restraint of another's personal liberty or freedom of locomotion. It may be a criminal offense or the basis of a **civil action** for **damages.**

FALSE IMPRISONMENT as a **tort,** the intentional, unjustified detention or confinement of a person. Where the restraint is imposed by virtue of one claiming legal authority to do so and an arrest occurs, it will be a **false arrest** as well as a false imprisonment. Compare **kidnapping.**

FALSE PRETENSE the statutory crime of obtaining money or property by making false representations of fact; also known as **MISREPRESENTATION**.

EXAMPLE: A salesman tells Jackie that the diamond she wants to buy is a perfect cut and therefore very valuable. In reality, the diamond has many flaws and the salesman purposefully made contrary representations. Jackie purchases the diamond based on the salesman's representations since she knows nothing about diamonds. When she learns that the stone is flawed, she can sue the salesman for *false pretense* in the sale.

See **counterfeit; embezzlement; forgery; fraud.**

FALSE RETURN 1. a **return** to a **writ** made by a ministerial officer (such as a sheriff) in which there is a false statement that is injurious to a party having an interest in the writ. For example, if a sheriff is supposed to serve a **summons** and untruthfully claims on his return that he did serve it, this would constitute a false return. 2. an incorrect tax return in which there appears either an intent to deceive on the part of the taxpayer, or at least **negligence** that is sufficiently serious to warrant holding the taxpayer liable for his error.

FALSE SWEARING the giving of a false oath in connection with some proceeding or matter in which an oath is required by law. It is a **common law misdemeanor** and consists of an act that would amount to **perjury** except that it is not committed in a judicial **proceeding.** See **affidavit.**

FALSE VERDICT a manifestly unjust **verdict;** one inconsistent with the **evidence.** When such a verdict is rendered, the court can enter a judgment **n.o.v.** (notwithstanding the verdict).

FALSI CRIMEN see **crimen falsi.**

FAMILY PURPOSE DOCTRINE a doctrine establishing **tort liability** of the owner of a family car when that car is used by another member of the family.

EXAMPLE: A mother explicitly tells her daughter not to use the car at night but leaves a set of keys on the table. The daughter takes the car one night and gets into an accident. The mother is held responsible for any injuries under the *family purpose doctrine,* despite her admonitions to the daughter.

FAMOSUS LIBELLUS *(fă-mō'-sŭs lī-bĕl'-ŭs)* Lat.: a scandalous libel. A **slanderous** or **libelous** letter, handbill, advertisement, petition, written **accusation** or **indictment.**

FAULT generally, **error.** 1. In describing people's conduct, it is the responsibility for or cause of wrongdoing or failure. 2. In describing goods, it is a defect in either the quantity or quality of the goods.

FAVORED BENEFICIARY one who, in a **will,** has been favored over others having equal claim to the **testator's** bounty.

FBI see **Federal Bureau of Investigation [FBI].**

FEALTY in feudal times, loyalty sworn by the **tenant** to his lord.

FEDERAL AVIATION ADMINISTRATION [FAA] an agency of the U.S. Department of Transportation, charged with regulating air commerce, promoting aviation safety and overseeing the operation of airports, including air traffic control.

FEDERAL BUREAU OF INVESTIGATION [FBI] an agency of the U.S. Department of Justice, charged by law with investigating violations of all laws of the U.S. government, except those expressly assigned to other agencies.

FEDERAL COURTS the United States courts (distinguished from the courts of the individual states), including **district courts** (general courts of **original jurisdiction**, which are the federal **trial** courts), courts of appeals (formerly circuit courts of appeals, which are principally **appellate** review **courts**), and the **Supreme Court** (the only court created directly by the constitution, and the court of last resort in the federal system). Other specialized courts in the federal system are **court of claims** (hears suits involving allowable claims against the United States government), **COURT OF CUSTOMS AND PATENT APPEALS** (reviews customs court decisions), and **CUSTOMS COURT** (reviews decisions of the customs collectors).

FEDERALISM a system of government wherein power is constitutionally divided between a central government and local governments.

EXAMPLE: The United States Supreme Court decides that the Constitution does not protect a person's privacy from a certain police tactic. Under the doctrine of *federalism,* though, a state court may nonetheless interpret its state constitution as prohibiting the same police conduct. The federal and state judicial systems are sufficiently separate so that a state court can afford greater protection to its citizens than the federal courts by a more liberal interpretation of its own constitution and laws. The state courts must observe any minimum federal rights, however, under the **Supremacy Clause** to the United States Constitution.

FEDERAL QUESTION JURISDICTION one kind of **original jurisdiction** that allows **federal courts** to hear **cases** wherein the application of something in the Constitution, laws or treaties of the United States is being disputed. See also **diversity of citizenship.**

FEDERAL RESERVE SYSTEM established under the Federal Reserve Act of 1913 to hold cash reserves of member banks and to provide other services, such as furnishing currency for circulation, facilitating clearance and collection of checks, and issuing and redeeming government obligations such as savings bonds. The functions of the agency were expanded in 1933 and 1935 to place greater emphasis on government control of the money supply, the credit structure and the economy in general. Twelve federal reserve banks are located throughout the country. All national banks are member banks; state banks may join at their option.

FEDERAL TORT CLAIMS ACT an act passed in 1946 that confers exclusive **jurisdiction** on United States **district courts** to hear claims against the United States for money **damages,** for injury or loss of property, or personal injury or death, caused by the **negligent** or wrongful act or omission of any employee of the government while acting within the scope of his office or employment, under circumstances where the United States, if a private person, would be liable to the claimant under the laws of the place where the act or omission occurred. The act is a broad waiver of **sovereign immunity,** although there are a number of qualifications on the waiver. Some state governments have enacted similar legislation.

FEDERAL TRADE COMMISSION [FTC] a federal administrative agency established in 1914 to protect consumers against unfair methods of competition and deceptive business practices, including sales frauds and violation of the **antitrust laws.**

FEE in **real property,** an **estate** of complete ownership that can be sold by the owner or **devised** to his **heirs.** Fee, **fee simple** and fee simple absolute are often used as equivalents to signify an estate of absolute ownership; however, the term is used to refer also to ownership that is qualified, as in the case of a **conditional** or **determinable fee,** which are types of estates that might last forever but might terminate upon the happening of a certain event.

EXAMPLE: Nancy conveys land to her brother in fee simple. The brother has absolute ownership of the land and can do with it as he pleases. If she conveys the land to him restricting its use to religious purposes, that conveyance is called a determinable fee. The moment the land is used for some purpose other than a religious one, the land reverts back to Nancy or whomever she designates.

FEE SIMPLE a **freehold estate** of virtually infinite duration and of absolute **inheritance** free of any limitations or restriction to particular heirs; also called FEE SIMPLE ABSOLUTE.

FEE SIMPLE CONDITIONAL see **conditional fee.**

FEE SIMPLE DEFEASIBLE see **determinable fee.**

FEE SIMPLE DETERMINABLE see **determinable fee.**

FEE TAIL the estate created by a **conveyance,** by **deed** or **will,** to a person "and the **heirs of his body.**" A fee tail establishes a fixed line of inheritable **succession** and cuts off the regular succession of **heirs** at law. It is a limited estate in that **inheritance** is through lineal descent only, which, if exclusively through males is called FEE TAIL MALE, and if exclusively through females is called FEE TAIL FEMALE. If the family line runs out (**failure of issue**), the fee **reverts** to the **grantor** or his successors in interest.

FELLOW SERVANTS co-workers: employees engaged in common pursuits under the same general control, serving the same employer, engaged in the same general business and deriving authority and compensation from a common source; defined for the purpose of the **FELLOW SERVENT RULE**, which absolves an employer of **liability** for **injury** to a worker resulting from the **negligence** of a co-worker. Fellow servants were said to assume the risk of each other's negligence. **Employer's Liability Acts** and **Workers' Compensation statutes** have abrogated the fellow servant doctrine.

FELONY generic term employed to distinguish certain high crimes from minor offenses known as **misdemeanors;** crimes declared to be such by statute or to be "true crimes" by the **common law.** Statutes often define felony as an offense punishable by imprisonment for more than one year or by death or imprisonment generally. The original common law felonies were felonious **homicide, mayhem, arson, rape, robbery, burglary, larceny,** prison breach (escape) and rescue of a felon. See also **misprision of felony.**

FELONY MURDER a **homicide** that occurs in the commission or attempted commission of a **felony;** considered first-degree **murder** by operation of this doctrine. In many modern statutes, only homicides that occur in the course of certain specified felonies are felony murders. The **malice** necessary to find someone **guilty** of murder is inferred from the actor's intent to commit a felony.

EXAMPLE: Alan and Mike hold up a liquor store. The owner attempts to trigger an alarm, and Alan fires at him with a pistol, intending only to frighten him but unfortunately killing him. Even though Alan did not intend to kill the owner, both Alan and Mike will be guilty of the owner's murder under the doctrine of *felony murder*.

FEOFFMENT the name given in common law to the means of conveying title to **freehold** estates, which required **livery of seisin.** At the site of the land and in the presence of neighbors, the **vendor** would point out the boundaries of the purchase and hand over to the vendee the appropriate symbol of **seisin.** The method was used until the use of the written **deed** came to be prescribed by statute.

FERAE NATURAE *(fĕr'-ī nä-tūr'-ī)* Lat.: wild beasts of nature. Animals of natural disposition in that, unlike domestic animals, they are untamed.

FERTILE OCTOGENARIAN refers to a legal fiction that, for purposes of the **Rule Against Perpetuities,** every living person is presumed capable of having children as long as he lives, even though it may be biologically impossible. The impact of this fiction under the rule against perpetuities has been modified by statute in many **jurisdictions.**

FIAT JUSTITIA *(fē'-ät jūs-tĭ'-shē-ȧ)* Lat.: let justice be done.

FIDUCIARY a person having a duty, created by his undertaking, to act primarily for the benefit of another in matters connected with his undertaking; one who holds a position of confidence, as, for example, a **trustee.**

FIFO see **first-in, first-out.**

FIFTH AMENDMENT the amendment to the U.S. Constitution, part of the Bill of Rights, that establishes certain protections for citizens from actions of the government by providing (1) that a person shall not be required to answer for a capital or other **infamous crime** unless an **indictment** or **presentment** is first issued by a grand **jury,** (2) that no person will be placed in **double jeopardy,** (3) that no person may be required to testify against himself, (4) that neither life, liberty nor property may be taken without **due process of law,** and (5) that private property may not be taken for public use, without payment of just compensation.

FIGHTING WORDS those that by their very utterance, in the context in which they are spoken, inflict injury or tend to incite an immediate **breach** of the peace.

In **tort** law, one who uses fighting words and thereby creates reasonable apprehension of harm in another person may be guilty of **assault.** See also **defamation.**

EXAMPLE: Dan is very upset with his neighbor's constant exhibitions of wealth. The two are together one day when Dan makes some comments concerning the neighbor's wife's immoral conduct during the husband's absence. Dan's comments are *fighting words* since he expresses them with the sole intention of getting the neighbor to hit Dan first so Dan will have a reason to retaliate.

FINAL DECISION [OR DECREE OR JUDGMENT] a decision that settles the rights of **parties** respecting the subject matter of the **suit** until the decision is **reversed** or set aside; ends the **litigation** on the **merits** and leaves nothing for the court to do but execute the **judgment.** Compare **interlocutory.**

FINAL DECREE see **final decision.**

FINAL JUDGMENT see **final decision; judgment.**

FINAL ORDER see **order.**

FINANCE CHARGES any charge for an extension of credit.

FINANCIAL INTERMEDIARY an organization such as a bank that brings together lenders (in the form of depositors) and borrowers. Other examples include savings and loan associations, credit unions, **real estate investment trusts [REITs]** and various kinds of finance companies.

FINANCIAL STATEMENT see **balance sheet; income statement.**

FINDER OF FACT see **fact finder.**

FINDER'S FEE a fee or commission paid for finding what a customer desires. In **merger** activities, the finder either locates a buyer when the client company wants to sell or locates a seller when the client company is looking for acquisitions. In real estate activities, finder's fees are paid for locating property, for obtaining **mortgage** loans and for referring buyers, sellers and mortgage loans.

FINDING the decision of a court on issues of fact. The decision's purpose is to answer questions raised by the **pleadings** or charges. It is designed to facilitate review by disclosing the grounds on which the **judgment** rests. Findings of fact are made by a **jury** in an **action** at law, or, if there is no jury, they are made by the judge.

FIRM OFFER an offer in writing that states the offer is to be irrevocable for a set time. As long as it is stipulated in a signed writing that the offer is to be held open, it need not be supported by **consideration** to be binding.

EXAMPLE: A new stationery business undertakes an enthusiastic effort to acquire new customers and develop an excellent reputation. Pursuant to that desire, it makes several *firm offers* to other local businesses, guaranteeing that it will supply all the stationery the others need for ninety days at a fixed price. The others can enforce that offer against the new business at any time during the year, even though they provided no consideration in return for the offer.

FIRST DEVISEE the first person who is to receive an **estate devised** by **will.**

FIRST IMPRESSION first discussion or consideration. A case is one of first impression when it presents a **question of law** that has never before been considered by any court, and thus is not influenced by the doctrine of **stare decisis.**

FIRST-IN, FIRST-OUT [FIFO] a method of inventory valuation in which cost of goods sold is charged with the cost of raw materials, semi-furnished goods, and finished goods purchased "first" and in which inventory contains the most recently purchased materials. In times of rapid inflation, FIFO inflates profits, since the least expensive inventory is charged against cost of current sales, resulting in "inventory profits." As a consequence, **LAST-IN, FIRST-OUT [LIFO]** inventory valuation has become a more popular method, since it reduces current taxes by eliminating inventory profits. See **balance sheet.**

FISCAL pertaining to the public finance and financial transactions; belonging to the public treasury (called the FISC).

FISCAL POLICY the use of public finance and financial transactions to achieve desired economic goals.

FISCAL YEAR any 12-month period used by a business as its accounting period.

FIXED ASSETS see **asset.**

FIXTURE something that was once a **chattel** but that is attached to **real property** in such a way that its removal would damage the property, and that is thus considered part of the realty.

EXAMPLE: To install a new chandelier in the house, the occupant had to reinforce the ceiling and attach extra bolts. A few years after the installation, a new room is added that requires construction of a wall near the chandelier. Removal of the chandelier will now require not only a removal of the bolts but destruction of the new wall as well. If the present occupants move, the chandelier must stay behind since it has become a *fixture* of the house.

TRADE FIXTURE see **trade fixture.**

FLIGHT escape; leaving the scene of a crime by one who feels **guilt,** or self-concealment to avoid **arrest** or **prosecution** after arrest. Compare **resisting arrest.** See also **abscond.**

FLOAT checks that are in transit between banks and that have not yet been paid; checks in the process of collection that remain conditional credits in a depositor's checking account until the checks are paid to the bank.

FLOATING DEBT any short-term obligation of a business, such as bank loans due in one year and **commercial paper.**

Government floating debt consists of **treasury bills** and short-term **treasury notes.** Long-term debt, such as **treasury bonds,** is referred to as FUNDED DEBT.

FOOD AND DRUG ADMINISTRATION [FDA] an administrative agency of the Department of Health and Human Services that regulates the safety and quality of foodstuffs, pharmaceuticals, cosmetics and medical devices.

FORBEARANCE the act of declining, usually for a period of time, to enforce a legal right. For purposes of the law of **usury,** the term is often used to refer to a contractual obligation of a **creditor** to refrain for a specific period from claiming a debt that has already become payable; such forbearance is in substance a loan for which a creditor may impose a charge. In **contract** law, forbearance of a valid claim, if bargained for, constitutes **consideration.**

EXAMPLE: A grandfather is so distressed by his grandson Brad's smoking habit that he promises Brad $1,000 if Brad discontinues smoking until his twenty-fifth birthday. The grandfather dies when Brad is twenty-three, but Brad still refrains from smoking. At age twenty-five, he requests the $1,000, but the executor of the estate claims that Brad never promised anything in return for the money. A court will find that Brad's *forbearance* from smoking constitutes consideration to support the contract and will order the executor to pay.

FORCED SALE see **sale.**

FORCIBLE DETAINER see **detainer** [UNLAWFUL DETAINER].

FORCIBLE ENTRY entry on **real property** in the **possession** of another, against his will and without authority of law, by actual force, or with such an array of force and apparent intent to employ it that the occupant, in permitting possession to be taken from him, must be regarded as acting from a well-founded fear that resistance would be perilous or unavailing. In many states a mere **trespass** without any force will be considered forcible. Compare **detainer** [**UNLAWFUL DETAINER**].

FORCIBLE ENTRY AND DETAINER a summary statutory **proceeding** for restoring to the **possession** of land one who has been wrongfully deprived of the possession.

FORECLOSURE generally, the termination of a right to **property;** specifically, an **equitable** action to compel payment of a **mortgage** or other **debt** secured by a **lien.** As to **real property,** foreclosure is precipitated by nonpayment of the debt or other **default** under the loan agreement, and leads to the court's order that the property to which the mortgage or lien is attached be sold to satisfy that debt. As a consequence, the mortgagor's **equity of redemption** is irrevocably destroyed, subject to any statutory **redemption** rights that may survive for a limited time in some jurisdictions. A **security interest** in **personal property** can likewise be foreclosed by a **JUDICIAL SALE** (see **sale** [**FORCED SALE**]) of the **collateral.**

FORENSIC belonging to the courts of justice; indicates the application of a particular subject to the law. For example, **FORENSIC MEDICINE** employs medical technology to assist in solving legal problems.

FORESEEABILITY a concept to limit a party's **liability** for the consequences of his acts to effects that are within the scope of a **FORESEEABLE RISK,** i.e., risks whose consequences a person of ordinary prudence would reasonably expect might occur as a result of his actions.

EXAMPLE: During the refueling of a ship, gasoline spills into the harbor. A spark from a nearby welder ignites when it lands on a piece of highly flammable fabric. The fabric falls into the harbor and a fire develops. Consequently, the whole harbor burns down. Even though no fire would have started had the fueling company been more careful, that company is not responsible for the destruction of the harbor. The damage was an *unforeseeable* consequence of spilling a small amount of fuel oil.

In a contract setting, a party's liability for consequential or special **damages** is limited to damages arising from the foreseeable consequences of his **breach.**

In **tort** law, in most cases, a party's actions may be deemed **negligent** only where the injurious consequences of those actions were foreseeable.

FORFEITURE the permanent loss of **property** for failure to comply with the **law;** the **divestiture** of the **title** of property, without compensation, for a **default** or an offense.

FORGERY 1. **fraudulent** making or altering of a writing with intent to prejudice the rights of another; making of a false **instrument** or the passing of an instrument known to be false. 2. fabrication or **counterfeiting** of **evidence.**

FORM model of a document containing the phrases and **words of art** needed to make the document technically correct for **procedural** purposes; used by lawyers in drafting legal documents.

FORMAL CONTRACT see **sealed instrument.**

FORMS OF ACTION technical categories of personal **actions** developed in **common law,** containing the entire course of legal proceedings peculiar to those actions. The forms of action are no longer in use, but they continue to affect modern **civil procedure** and **tort** law.

Forms of action consisted of proceedings for recovery of debts, and recovery of money **damages** resulting from **breach** of contract, or injury to one's person, property or relations. The forms can be classified as (*a*) actions in form **ex contract,** including **assumpsit,** covenant, debt and account; and (*b*) actions in form **ex delicto** (i.e., those not based on contracts), including **trespass, trover,** case, **detinue** and **replevin.** The result was a highly formal and artificial system of procedure.

FORNICATION generally, sexual intercourse of two unmarried persons of different sexes, punished as a **misdemeanor** by statute in some states. In some states, it refers to illicit sexual intercourse between a man, whether married or single, and an unmarried woman. In some states, illicit intercourse can be fornication for the party who is not married and **adultry** for the party who is married. It is not a **common law** crime and is not part of modern penal codes, though it remains a criminal offense in many **jurisdictions.**

FORUM a court; a place where disputes are heard and decided according to law and justice; a place of **jurisdiction;** a place where **remedies** afforded by the law are pursued. See also **venue.**

FORUM NON CONVENIENS *(fôr'-ŭm nŏn kŏn-vĕ'-nē-ĕns)* Lat.: an inconvenient court. Under this doctrine a court, though it has **jurisdiction** of a case, may decline to exercise it where there is no legitimate reason for the case to be brought there, or where presentation in that court will create a hardship on the **defendants** or on relevant **witnesses** because of the court's distance from them. The court will not **dismiss** the case under the doctrine unless the **plaintiff** has another **forum** open to him.

EXAMPLE: A truck lightly hits the rear end of a car, but, because of the vehicle's construction, the car bursts into flames and the driver is seriously injured. The driver, who is from another state, wants to have the case heard in his home state. The car company asks the court to invoke the *forum non conveniens* doctrine and have the case transferred to the state where the accident occurred. That request is granted because the witnesses to the accident, as well as the actual scene, are both in the other state, and it would be more inconvenient to have that information brought to the driver's home state than to have the driver go to the state where the accident occurred.

FOUNDER one who provides the first gift to establish a charitable institution, such as a college.

FOURTEENTH AMENDMENT one of the so-called "Civil War Amendments" to the Constitution in that it was ratified after the Civil War; protects all persons from state laws that attempt to deprive them of "life, liberty, or property, without due process of law,'' or that attempt to deny them **equal protection of the laws.** The amendment has been used to extend the protection of almost all of the provisions of the **Bill of Rights** to citizens of every state.

FRANCHISE 1. a special privilege that is conferred by the government upon individuals and that does not of common right belong to the citizens of the country. For example, a municipality may grant to a local bus company a franchise that will give it sole authority to operate buses in the municipality for a certain number of years. 2. the right given to a private person or **corporation** to market another's product within a certain area. 3. ELECTIVE FRANCHISE (sometimes called simply ''the franchise'') refers to the right of citizens to vote in public elections.

FRAUD intentional deception resulting in **injury** to another. Fraud usually consists of a misrepresentation, concealment or nondisclosure of a material fact, or at least misleading conduct, devices or contrivance.

CONSTRUCTIVE [OR LEGAL] FRAUD comprises all acts, omissions and concealments involving **breach** of **equitable** or **legal duty,** or trust and resulting in damage to another. It is thus fraud that is presumed from the circumstances, without the need for any actual proof of intent to defraud.

EXTRINSIC [OR COLLATERAL] FRAUD fraud that prevents a party from knowing about his rights or **defenses** or from having a fair opportunity to present or litigate them at a trial. It is a ground for **equitable** relief from a **judgment.**

EXAMPLE: Jane obtains a court order requiring a company to give her all relevant information concerning a certain product that she claims injured her. At trial, a judge finds her evidence insufficient and dismisses her claim. Afterwards, Jane finds other documents in the company's possession that she never received but that would have proved her case. The *extrinsic fraud* committed upon her gives rise to both a suit against the company for the fraud and a right for Jane to have a new trial with the new documents.

FRAUD IN FACT [POSITIVE FRAUD] actual fraud; deceit; concealing something or making a false representation with an evil intent [**scienter**] when it causes injury to another. It is used in contrast to CONSTRUCTIVE FRAUD, which does not require evil intent.

FRAUD IN LAW fraud that is presumed from circumstances, where the one who commits it need not have any evil intent to commit a fraud; it is a CONSTRUCTIVE FRAUD or legal fraud.

FRAUD IN THE FACTUM generally arises from a disparity between the **instrument** executed and the one intended to be **executed,** as for example when a blind or illiterate person executes a deed when it has been read falsely to him after he asked to have it read.

FRAUD IN THE INDUCEMENT intentional fraud that causes one to execute an instrument, or make an agreement, or render a **judgment.** The misrepresentation does not mislead one as to the paper he signs but rather misleads as to the facts of a situation, and the false impression it causes is a basis of a decision to sign or render a judgment.

INTRINSIC FRAUD fraudulent representation that is considered in rendering a judgment.

FRAUDULENT CONVEYANCE any conveyance made, or presumed to have been made, with the intention to delay or defraud **creditors,** where such intention is known to the party to whom the conveyance is made. It is generally characterized by a lack of fair and valuable **consideration** and is usually made by a debtor to place his **property** beyond the reach of creditors.

FREE ALONGSIDE [F.A.S.] a commercial delivery term that signifies that the seller must at his own risk and expense deliver the **goods** to the side of the transporting medium in the usual manner and obtain and **tender** a receipt for the goods in exchange for which the carrier must issue a **bill of lading.** Compare **free on board [f.o.b.].**

FREE AND CLEAR unencumbered. In property law, a **title** is free and clear if it is not encumbered by any **liens** or restrictions; one conveys land free and clear if he transfers a **good title** or **marketable title.**

FREEDOM OF CONTRACT the liberty or ability to enter into agreements with others, which is a fundamental right reserved to citizens by the United States Constitution.

FREEDOM OF INFORMATION ACT a federal law requiring that, with specified exceptions, documents and materials generated or held by federal agencies be made available to the public and establishing guidelines for their disclosure.

FREE EXERCISE CLAUSE a provision in the First Amendment to the United States Constitution providing that "Congress shall make no laws . . . prohibiting the free exercise" of religion. The "free exercise clause" guarantees against government compulsion in religious matters, while the **establishment clause** insures that the government will maintain neutrality towards religion.

FREEHOLD [ESTATE] an estate in **fee** or a **life estate;** an **estate** or **interest** in **real property** for life or of uncertain duration.

FREE ON BOARD [F.O.B.] a commercial term that signifies a contractual agreement between a buyer and a seller to have the subject of a sale delivered to a designated place, usually either the "place of shipment" or the "place of destination," without expense to the buyer. Thus a shipment "f.o.b. shipping point" requires the seller to bear the expense and the risk of putting the subject of the sale into the possession of the carrier, but the **duty** to pay the transportation charges from the f.o.b. point is on the buyer. Where the shipment is "f.o.b. destination point," the seller is required to bear the transportation charges and the risk of transport until the buyer point of destination. Compare **free alongside [f.a.s.].**

FRESH PURSUIT in criminal law, the **common law** right of a police officer to cross jurisdictional lines in order to arrest a **felon.** The term also refers to the power of a police officer to make an **arrest** without a **warrant** when he is in immediate pursuit of a criminal.

FRIENDLY SUIT an action authorized by law brought by agreement between the **parties,** to secure a **judgment** that will have a binding effect in circumstances where a mere agreement or settlement will not, as, for example where a claim in favor of an infant or another lacking legal capacity to enter into a binding contract can for that reason be settled only through the entry of a judgment. Suits that are **collusive,** on the other hand, will be **dismissed.** Compare **declaratory judgment.**

FRIEND OF THE COURT see **amicus curiae.**

FRISK quick, superficial search; patting outer clothing to detect, by the sense of touch, if a concealed weapon is being carried.

FRIVOLOUS clearly insufficient as a **matter of law;** presenting no debatable question. A **claim** is frivolous if it is insufficient because unsupported by the facts or because the law recognizes no **remedy** for the claim.

FRONT-END LOAD PLAN a contractual agreement to buy **mutual fund** shares through periodic payments, usually monthly, in which the sales commission and other expenses, called load, are taken out of the initial payments.

FRUIT OF THE POISONOUS TREE DOCTRINE a rule under which **evidence** that is the direct result of illegal conduct on the part of an official is inadmissible in a criminal trial against the victim of the conduct. The doctrine draws its name from the idea that once the tree is poisoned (the primary evidence is illegally obtained) then the fruit of the tree (any secondary evidence) is likewise **TAINTED** and may also not be used.

EXAMPLE: The police illegally break into Rob's house and obtain a confession from him as to his drug-dealing activities. He also tells the police where they can find more drugs that he intended to sell. The police attempt to use the confession and the drugs to convict Rob. Under the *fruit of the poisonous tree doctrine,* neither the confession nor the drugs can be used against him because they are the product of an illegal entry by the police.

FRUSTRATION OF PURPOSE a doctrine under which the occurrence of unexpected events may justify one of the parties to a contract in **rescinding** the contract. Such frustration (also called COMMERCIAL FRUSTRATION) typically occurs when an implied **condition** of an agreement (a circumstance without which the contract would never have been made) does not occur or ceases to exist without fault of either party, so that the absence of the implied condition "frustrates" one party's intentions in making the agreement.

EXAMPLE: Andy signs a contract with a real estate salesman to purchase a house, with the understanding that he will be able to get a zoning change and use part of the house for his office. Contrary to what either party expected, the zoning change is not approved. Andy may seek to renege on his contract to purchase the house because his purpose in purchasing the house has been *frustrated*.

See also **impossibility.**

FUGITIVE FROM JUSTICE one who commits a crime within a state, and then leaves that state without awaiting the consequences of the crime he committed there; also, one who conceals himself within the state in order to avoid its **process.**

FULL FAITH AND CREDIT the federal constitutional requirement that the public acts, records and judicial proceedings of one state be respected by each of the other states. Thus, if a **judgment** is conclusive in the state where it was pronounced, it is equally beyond dispute everywhere in the courts of the United States. The judgment is entitled to full faith and credit when the second court's inquiry discloses that the same questions were properly before the first court and were fully and fairly **litigated** and finally decided there.

EXAMPLE: Following a long trial, a company is found negligent in manufacturing a product that caused Lance substantial hair loss. The manufacturer's assets in that state are insufficient to cover the full amount of the judgment. Lance can take that judgment to another state where the manufacturer has assets, sue upon that judgment, and by applying the *full faith and credit* principle, obtain another judgment and collect whatever he is still owed.

FUNDED DEBT see **floating debt.**

FUNGIBLE a term applied to **goods** that are interchangeable or capable of substitution by nature or agreement. Oil, grain and coal are examples of naturally fungible goods. When storing fungible goods, warehousemen are exempt from the legal requirement of keeping stored goods from one depositor separate from the goods of another. **Securities** of the same issue are considered fungible; hence a person obligated to deliver securities may deliver any security of the specified issue.

FUTURE INTEREST an **interest** in presently existing **real property** or **personal property,** or in a **gift** or **trust,** that will commence in **use, possession** or enjoyment in the future. A **legatee** to receive an annual income upon reaching the age of twenty-one has a future interest that, when that age is reached, will ripen into a present interest. Future interests may constitute either **vested** or **contingent estates.**

EXAMPLE: A father conveys two hundred shares of stock to Beth, his daughter, but if Beth dies before the father, the stock goes to Marcy. Marcy has a *future interest* in the stock that is contingent on Beth's predeceasing the father. If Beth does predecease the father, Marcy's future interest then vests.

FUTURES agreements whereby one person agrees to sell a commodity at a certain time in the future for a certain price. The buyer agrees to pay that price, knowing that the person has nothing to deliver at the time, but with the understanding that when the time arrives for delivery the buyer is to pay him the difference between the market value of that commodity and the price agreed upon if the commodity's value declines; and if it advances, the seller is to pay to the buyer the difference between the agreed-upon price and the market price. Thus, if the price of the commodity rises, the buyer makes a profit, and if the price declines, the buyer suffers a loss.

G

GAG ORDER a court-imposed order to restrict information or comment about a case. The ostensible purpose of such an order is to protect the interests of all parties and preserve the right to a fair trial by curbing publicity likely to prejudice a jury. A gag order cannot be directly imposed on members of the press because this constitutes an impermissible prior restraint and violates the First Amendment.

GAINFUL EMPLOYMENT [OR OCCUPATION] employment suited to the ability of the one employed. For purposes of disability covered by insurance, it may mean the ordinary employment of the insured, or other employment approximating the same livelihood as the insured might be expected to follow in view of his circumstances and physical and mental capabilities.

GARAGEMAN'S LIEN see **lien** [MECHANIC'S LIEN].

GARNISH to bring a **garnishment** proceeding or to **attach** wages or other property pursuant to such a proceeding.

EXAMPLE: Charles owes money to a department store for several appliances that he purchased on credit. Once Charles stopped paying, the store brought a *garnishment* proceeding against him for the money owed. If the court agrees with the store, it will order that a part of Charles' wages go directly to the store and not to Charles.

GARNISHEE a person who receives notice to retain, until he receives further notice from the court, **custody** of **assets** in his control that are owed to or belong to another person. The garnishee merely holds the assets until legal **proceedings** determine who is entitled to the property. The term thus signifies one on whom process of **garnishment** is served. In a statutory garnishment proceeding, the garnishee (often an employer) may be directed to pay over to the **creditor** a portion of the **debtor's** property (such as an employee's wages) that is in the garnishee's possession.

GARNISHMENT process in which money or **goods** in the hands of a third person, which are due a **defendant,** are attached by the **plaintiff.** It is a statutory **remedy** that consists of notifying a third party to retain something he has that belongs to the defendant (debtor), to make disclosure to the court concerning it, and to dispose of it as the court shall direct.

GENERATION SKIPPING TRANSFER a generation skipping transfer is one more than a single generation removed from the transferor; e.g., a transfer by a grandfather to a grandchild. A **GENERATION SKIPPING TRUST** is created to make a generation skipping transfer. Certain generation skipping transfers made by a generation skipping trust or its equivalent are subject to a generation skipping transfer tax. If the transfer is not by a **trust** but directly by the donor, such transfer is subject to **tax [UNIFIED ESTATE AND GIFT TAX],** regardless of whether it skips a generation.

GERRYMANDER to create a civil division of an unusual shape within a particular locale for improper purpose; to redistrict a state, creating unnatural boundaries and isolating members of a particular political party, in the hope that a maximum number of the elected representatives will be of that political party.

EXAMPLE: A political party finally wins control of a state legislature. At the same time, the legislative districts must be restructured to account for population shifts. The party in power uses the opportunity to insure future control of the legislature by *gerrymandering* the districts. The end result is to create unnatural boundaries that will give the party the least opposition for future elections. The object of gerrymandering is to create districts in which the controlling party maintains a majority among registered voters.

GIFT a voluntary transfer of property made without **consideration,** that is, for which no value is received in return, which is accepted by the recipient. In federal tax law, a gift is excluded from the gross **income** of the recipient, but the transferor may be subject to the unified estate and gift tax. See **tax [UNIFIED ESTATE AND GIFT TAX].**

SPLIT GIFT a transfer in which the person receiving the property makes a payment that is less than the value of the property transferred.

GIFT IN CONTEMPLATION OF DEATH any gift made by a person within three years of death. Such transfers (except if less than $3,000) are subject to the unified estate and gift tax as if they had occurred at death.

GIFT OVER an estate that is to follow upon the expiration of a **preceding estate.**

GOOD CAUSE substantial or legally sufficient reason for doing something. For example, if a statute provides for granting a new **trial** upon a showing of good cause, such good cause might include the existence of **fraud,** lack of **notice** to the **parties** or newly discovered **evidence.**

EXAMPLE: Motions submitted before a judge, which in essence ask the judge to do something, must be supported by a showing of *good cause*. On a motion to exclude or suppress evidence for trial, good cause must be shown by example of illegal police conduct in the seizing of the evidence. For the motion to be granted, the judge must be convinced the conduct occurred and is enough to justify exclusion.

GOOD FAITH total absence of intention to seek unfair advantage or to defraud another party; an honest intention to fulfill one's obligations; observance of reasonable standards of fair dealing.

EXAMPLE: Don purchases securities for 60 percent of their face value from an associate. The associate had obtained the securities fraudulently, and the real owner then sued Don for their return. Don is protected from the owner's claims if he acted in *good faith* and is thus a **bona fide purchaser.** The owner states that Don could not have acted in good faith since he purchased them at such a low cost in comparison with their face value. But that fact alone does not preclude Don's good faith defense, since the low price can be justified by the associate's dire need for quick cash.

In property law, a good faith purchaser of land pays value for the land and has no knowledge or notice of any facts that would cause an ordinary, prudent person to make inquiry concerning the validity of the conveyance.

GOODS any species of **property** that is not **real estate,** **CHOSE IN ACTION** (see **chose**), investment **securities** or the like.

GOOD TITLE a **clear title** free from present **litigation,** obvious defects and grave doubts concerning its validity or **merchantability;** a title valid in fact that is **marketable** to a reasonable purchaser or **mortgaged** as security for a loan of money to a person of reasonable prudence. In a **contract** to **convey** good title, the term also signifies that there are no **encumbrances** on the land. See also **recording acts; warranty.**

GOODWILL an intangible but recognized business asset that is the result of such features of an ongoing enterprise as the production or sale of reputable brand-name products, a good relationship with customers and suppliers, and the standing of the business in its community. Goodwill can become a **balance sheet** asset when a going business is acquired at a price exceeding the net asset value (**assets** less **liabilities**).

GOVERNMENTAL IMMUNITY the **common law** doctrine that the government, be it federal, state or local, is not amenable to **suit** unless it consents to be sued. See **federal tort claims act; sovereign immunity.**

GRACE PERIOD in general, any period specified in a **contract** during which payment is permitted, without penalty, beyond the due date of the debt. In the insurance context, it is a span of time after an insurance policy premium was due to be paid, during which the insurance nevertheless remains in force.

GRADED OFFENSE one where an offender is subject to different penalties for various degrees of the offense, according to terms of a statute. Modern criminal codes rely upon degrees of an offense to vary **sanctions** according to the level of harm to others caused or risked by the actor.

GRAFT fraudulent obtaining of public money by the corruption of public officials; a dishonest advantage that one person by reason of his position, influence or trust acquires from another.

GRANDFATHER CLAUSE a provision permitting persons engaged in an activity before passage of a law affecting that activity to receive a license or prerogative without the necessity of fulfilling all that is legally required of persons subsequently undertaking the same activity.

EXAMPLE: Felix has been selling hot dogs on the street for fifteen years. The town council then decides to require licenses for all street vendors. Because the measure includes a *grandfather clause*, Felix can continue selling his food without a license.

GRAND JURY see **jury.**

GRAND LARCENY see **larceny.**

GRANT to give, allow or transfer something to another, with or without compensation; especially, a **gift** of land made by one having authority over it. The one giving the gift or making the transfer is the **grantor.** The recipient is the **grantee.**

GRANTOR-GRANTEE INDEX see **chain of title.**

GRATIS free; given or performed without reward or **consideration.**

GRATUITOUS BAILMENT see **bailment.**

GRATUITOUS PROMISE one by which a person promises to do, or refrain from doing, something without requiring **consideration** in return.

GRAVAMEN the essence of a **complaint, charge, cause of action,** etc.

EXAMPLE: A complaint is filed against Bruce alleging that he seriously hurt someone in a barroom brawl and then fled the scene. The *gravamen* of the complaint is that Bruce seriously hurt someone.

GREAT WRIT see **habeas corpus.**

GREEN CARD a common name for the alien registration card carried by permanent resident aliens in the United States. Permanent resident status is a first step towards becoming a **naturalized citizen.**

GRIEVANCE one's allegation that something imposes an illegal burden, or denies some equitable or legal right, or causes injustice. An employee may be entitled by a **collective bargaining** agreement to seek relief through a **GRIEVANCE PROCEDURE.**

GROUND RENT an **estate of inheritance** in the **rent** of lands, i.e., an inheritable interest in and right to the rent collected through the **leasing** of certain lands. It is a **freehold** estate, and as such is subject to **encumbrance** by **mortgage** or **judgment (lien, attachment,** etc.). The ground rent is an interest distinct from that held by the owner of the property, whose estate is in the land itself.

GROWTH STOCK the **stock** of a company that has achieved above-average earnings growth in the past and has good prospects for continued increases in the future.

GUARANTEE 1. to agree or promise to be responsible for the **debt, default** or miscarriage of another; 2. a promise or contract to answer for the debt, default or miscarriage of another; 3. one who receives a guaranty. Compare **save harmless.**

GUARANTEE CLAUSE Article IV, Section 4 of the United State Constitution, which states that "the United States shall **guarantee** to every state in this Union a republican form of government."

GUARANTEED SECURITY a **bond** or **stock** that is **guaranteed** as to principal or interest or both by someone other than the issuer.

GUARANTOR one who makes a **guaranty.**

GUARANTY 1. a promise to be responsible for the **debt, default** or miscarriage of another; 2. a **warranty** or promise to undertake an original obligation; 3. something given as security for the performance of an act or the continued quality of a thing. See **surety.**

GUARDIAN one who legally has care and management of the person or **estate,** or both, of an **incompetent;** an officer or agent of the court who is appointed to protect the interests of minors or incompetent persons and to provide for their welfare, education and support. See also **committee; next friend; ward.**

GUARDIAN AD LITEM a person appointed by the court to protect the interests of a ward in a legal proceeding. Compare **next friend.**

GUEST 1. a transient who rents a room at a hotel; 2. someone to whom hospitality is extended without charge.

An AUTOMOBILE GUEST is one who rides in an automobile for his own benefit without giving the driver compensation for the ride; designated by the law as such for purposes of determining **liability** of the owner or driver of the automobile. See **guest statute.**

For purposes of **tort** law, a SOCIAL GUEST is considered a **licensee** with respect to his entry upon the host's premises, so that no duty of affirmative care or inspection of the premises for defects is owed to him.

EXAMPLE: After a late night of drinking, the host invited Steve to spend the night at his house. As Steve was getting into bed, the wooden frame cracked and injured Steve's foot. Steve has no cause of action against the host since Steve was only a **guest** and not a paying customer.

GUEST STATUTE a law that provides that a lesser standard of care is owed by an automobile owner or driver toward his nonpaying passenger **[guest].** These statutes differ from state to state, but all require more than ordinary **negligence** on the part of an owner or driver for an automobile guest to recover **damages** in a **civil suit.**

GUILTY the condition of having been found by a **jury** to have committed the crime **charged,** or some **lesser-included offense.** The term may, though rarely does, refer to the commission of a **civil** wrong or **tort.** Compare **conviction.**

GUN CONTROL LAW a law restricting or regulating the sale, purchase or possession of firearms, or establishing a system of licensing, registration or identification of firearms or their owners or users.

HABEAS CORPUS *(hā'-bē-ŭs kôr'-pŭs)* Lat.: you have the body. The **writ** of habeas corpus, known as the **GREAT WRIT,** has varied use in criminal and civil contexts. It is a procedure for obtaining a judicial determination of the legality of an individual's custody. Technically, it is used in the criminal law context to bring the petitioner before the court to inquire into the legality of his confinement. The writ of federal habeas corpus is used to test the constitutionality of a state criminal conviction.

EXAMPLE: Sandy believes that his conviction in the trial court was obtained unconstitutionally in that he was not provided counsel until three days before his trial. He raised the issue on appeal in the state court system but was denied a new trial. Having exhausted all state remedies, Sandy files a writ of *habeas corpus* in the federal district court, alleging that his conviction and present confinement violate his Sixth Amendment right to counsel.

The writ is used in the civil context to challenge the validity of child **custody** and deportations.

HABENDUM that clause of the **deed** that names the **grantee** and defines the **estate** to be granted. It begins with the words "to have and to hold. . . ."

HABITUAL OFFENDER see **criminal.**

HARASSMENT 1. a **prosecution** brought without reasonable expectation of obtaining a valid conviction; 2. unnecessarily oppressive exercise of authority; 3. conduct motivated by a malicious or discriminatory purpose.

HARMLESS ERROR **error** that is not sufficiently prejudicial to the losing party in a lawsuit to warrant the **appellate court's**

modifying the lower court's decision. A conclusion that an error is harmless reflects the reviewing court's determination that the lower court's decision would have been the same with or without the purported error. Compare **plain error.**

EXAMPLE: The confessions of two codefendants are improperly introduced at Ray's trial. An appellate court may find that the violation was merely *harmless error* and does not require a new trial for Ray if the confessions had little or no effect upon the jury's determination of Ray's guilt.

HEADNOTE summary, placed at the beginning of a case report, of points discussed and issues decided in a case.

HEAD OF HOUSEHOLD an unmarried **taxpayer** who maintains as his home a household that is the principal residence of a designated **dependent.** A qualified head of household is subject to a lower **tax rate** than that applied to a person not a head of household.

HEARING a **proceeding** where **evidence** is taken to determine an issue of fact and to reach a decision on the basis of that evidence; describes whatever takes place before **magistrates** sitting without **jury.** Thus a hearing, such as an **ADMINISTRATIVE HEARING,** may take place outside the judicial process, before officials who have been granted judicial authority expressly for the purpose of conducting such hearings.

FINAL HEARING is sometimes used to describe that stage of proceedings relating to the determination of a **suit** upon its **merits,** as distinguished from those of preliminary questions. See also **fair hearing.**

HEARING DE NOVO see **de novo [DE NOVO HEARING].**

HEARSAY RULE a rule that declares not **admissible** as **evidence** any statement other than that by a **witness** while testifying at the **hearing** and offered into evidence to prove the truth of the matter stated. The hearsay statement may be oral or written and includes nonverbal conduct intended as a substitute for words. The reason for the hearsay rule is that the credibility of the witness is the key ingredient in weighing the truth of his statement; so when that statement is made out of court, without benefit of cross-examination and without the witness' demeanor being subject to assessment by the trier of fact (judge or jury), there is generally no adequate basis for determining whether the out-of-court statement is true.

EXAMPLE: At Doug's trial, a witness testifies that a bartender told him that Doug had admitted robbing a bank. If that testimony is used to prove that Doug did in fact tell the bartender of the crime, the testimony is not admissible under the *hearsay rule*.

HEIR APPARENT one who has the rights to **inheritance** provided that he lives longer than his donor ancestor. An **anti-lapse statute** may operate to save a **gift** to the estate of an heir apparent who predeceases the **testator.**

HEIRS strictly, those whom statutory law would appoint to inherit an **estate** should the ancestor die without a **will [intestate];** sometimes referred to as **HEIRS AT LAW, RIGHTFUL HEIRS, LEGAL HEIRS.** The term is often applied indiscriminately to those who inherit by will or **deed,** as well as by **operation of law.**

AND HIS HEIRS in **common law,** these words had to be included in order to convey a **fee simple.** The formal requirement has been abolished or modified by statute in most of the states, and now one may **convey** or **devise** an absolute interest in **real property** without using these technical words.

HEIRS OF THE BODY **issue** of the body, offspring engendered by the person named as parent. These words are used in instruments of conveyance, such as **deeds** and **wills,** to create a **conditional fee** or a **fee tail.**

HEREDITAMENTS anything that can be inherited, including **real property** or **personal property. CORPORAL HEREDITAMENTS** generally are tangible property. **INCORPOREAL HEREDITAMENTS** are less tangible rights connected to land, such as an **easement** or right to **rent.**

HEREDITARY SUCCESSION the passing of **title** according to the laws of descent; acquisition of title to an **estate** by a person by **operation of law** upon the death of an ancestor who has not left a valid **will** affecting the property inherited. See **descent and distribution.**

HIDDEN ASSET a property value that is understated on the **balance sheet** of a company because of accounting convention and/or deliberate action of management.

EXAMPLE: Glory Corporation is fearful of being taken over by a large international company and thereby losing its independence. To prevent the takeover, it undervalues the worth of its real estate holdings to make Glory look as though the corporation were not worth buying. The real estate holdings constitute *hidden assets*.

HIDDEN INFLATION a price increase implemented by offering a smaller quantity or poorer quality for the old price.

HIDDEN TAX an indirect tax paid unwittingly by the consumer, such as taxes levied on goods at some point in their production or transport prior to retail sale.

HIT-AND-RUN STATUTES statutes requiring that a motorist involved in an accident stop and identify himself and give certain information about himself to the other motorist and to the police. These laws have been upheld as not violative of the privilege against **self-incrimination** on the ground that they call for neutral acts, not intended to be probative of guilt, and pose only an insignificant hazard of self-incrimination.

HOARDING excess accumulation of commodities or currency in anticipation of scarcity and/or higher prices.

HOBBY LOSS a loss incurred by a **taxpayer** in an activity not pursued for profit. In general, hobby losses are deductible only to the extent of income generated by the hobby.

HOLDER a person in possession of a document of **title** or an **instrument** or an investment **security drawn,** issued or **indorsed** to him or to his **order** or to **bearer** or in blank.

HOLDER IN DUE COURSE a **good faith holder** who has taken a **negotiable instrument** for value, without **notice** that it was overdue or had been **dishonored** or that there was any **defense** against or **claim** to it. In property law, the innocent buyer or holder in due course is referred to as a **bona fide purchaser.**

EXAMPLE: People's Finance Company regularly buys promissory notes from stores that require the customers to sign these notes in return for merchandise. People's is a *holder in due course* of these notes since it has given value for them. That status protects People's from almost all claims against the notes.

HOLDING 1. in commercial and property law, **property** to which one has legal **title** and of which one is in **possession.** The term may be used to refer specifically to ownership of **stocks** or **shares** of **corporations.** 2. in **procedure,** any ruling of the court, including rulings upon the **admissibility** of **evidence** or other questions presented during trial. See **dictum.**

HOLDING COMPANY 1. a **corporation** organized to hold the **stock** of other corporations; 2. any company, incorporated or unincorporated, that is in a position to control or materially influence the management of one or more other companies by virtue, in part at least, of its ownership of **securities** in the other company or companies.

HOLDING PERIOD the period during which property must be held before its disposition will give rise to long-term **capital gain or loss.**

HOLDOVER TENANCY see **tenancy** (TENANCY AT SUFFERANCE).

HOLOGRAPHIC WILL a **will** entirely written, dated and signed by the **testator's** own hand. The word is sometimes written OLOGRAPHIC. In some states, such a will need not be witnessed and is valid, under a statute of **descent and distribution,** to pass **property.** In other states, such a will is invalid.

HOME RULE a means of apportioning power between state and local governments by granting power to the electorate of a local government unit to frame and adopt a charter of government. The effect of this grant is to enable local government to legislate without first obtaining permission from state legislatures.

EXAMPLE: Since the city was first chartered, it has been run by a mayor with virtually no check on his exercise of power. Exercising their rights under *home rule,* the residents vote to install a city council, which must approve any actions taken by the mayor.

See also **preemption.**

HOMESTEAD Any house, outbuildings and surrounding land owned and used as a dwelling by the head of the family. Under modern HOMESTEAD EXEMPTION LAWS, enacted in most states, any property designated as a homestead is exempt from **execution** and **sale** by **creditors.** This homestead exemption applies in some states to property taxes as well.

The exemption from claims of creditors may be extended by a **probate** court upon the death of the head of the family to ensure the surviving spouse and minor children uninterrupted **possession** and **enjoyment** of the family home. A home so protected is referred to as a PROBATE HOMESTEAD. See **life estate.**

HOMICIDE any killing of a human being by the act, agency, procurement or **culpable** omission of another. An unlawful homicide, or one resulting from an unlawful act, may constitute **murder** or **manslaughter.**

JUSTIFIABLE HOMICIDE the killing of a human being by commandment of the law, in the execution of public justice, in **self-defense,** in defense of habitation, property or person.

HORNBOOK LAW those principles of law known generally to all in the legal profession and free from doubt and ambiguity. They are therefore such as would probably be enunciated in a **HORNBOOK** (a primer of fundamentals).

HORS *(ôr)* Fr.: outside of, besides, other than. [Sometimes **DEHORS** *(dĕ-ôr')*.]

HOSTILE POSSESSION actual occupation or **possession** of real estate, coupled with a claim, express or implied, of ownership, without permission of the holder of **paramount title.** Hostile possession differs from **holding** in subordination to the true owner, as in possession under a **lease.** Hostile does not imply ill will but merely that the occupant claims ownership against all others, including the owner of **record.** The term is usually used as a condition for **adverse possession.** See also **notorious possession.**

EXAMPLE: For fifteen years, Ken has lived in a cabin he built in a wooded section of the state. He has cleared an area adjacent to the house where he grows whatever he uses to live, plus some extras to share with neighbors. Ken is not the owner of the land he lives on, but, because no one has come by in fifteen years to assert ownership of the land or even to ask him to get off, he claims it as his and is therefore in *hostile possession* of it.

HOSTILE WITNESS see **witness [ADVERSE** (or **HOSTILE) WITNESS].**

HUNG JURY one whose members [jurors] cannot reconcile their differences of opinion and that therefore cannot reach a **verdict** by the degree of agreement required (generally unanimity, but sometimes a substantial majority).

HYPOTHECATE to pledge something as security without turning over possession of it. Hypothecation creates a right in the **creditor** to have the pledge sold to satisfy the claim out of the sale proceeds.

EXAMPLE: Nathan needs a large amount of cash to put together a business deal. To acquire money from the bank, he *hypothecates* (pledges) his diamond ring as security. The bank allows Nathan to retain the ring because he is a good customer and they are not afraid he will disappear with the money and the ring. The loan agreement between Nathan and the bank is a hypothecation contract.

A **mortgage** on real property is a form of hypothecation **contract. Intangibles** and **securities** are most often the subject of hypothecation contracts. In the case of buying stock on **margin** the owner signs a hypothecation agreement with the broker who handles the transaction; the broker is then free to pledge the customer's securities as **collateral** for a bank loan or to lend the customer's securities in connection with **selling short.** Compare **replevin.**

I

IBID. *(ĭb′-ĭd)* Lat.: in the same place or manner, at the same time; abbreviation of ibidem. Used to mean "in the same book" or "on the same page"; functions in citations to avoid repetition of source data in the reference immediately preceding.

ID. *(ĭd)* Lat.: the same; abbreviation of idem. Used in citations to avoid repetition of author's name and title when a reference immediately follows another to the same item.

IGNORANTIA LEGIS NON EXCUSAT *(ĭg-nō-rän′-shē-à lā′-gĭs nŏn ĕks-kū′-zät)* Lat.: ignorance of the law is no excuse. The fact that a defendant did not think his act was against the law does not prevent the law from punishing him for the prohibited act.

ILLEGITIMATE illegal or improper. Applied to children, it means born out of wedlock, **bastards.**

ILLUSORY PROMISE a promise too indefinite to be enforced or, because of provisions in the promise itself, one whose fulfillment is optional. Since such a promise is not legally binding, it is not sufficient as **consideration** for a reciprocal promise and thus cannot create a valid **contract.**

EXAMPLE: Walter promises his neighbor that, if he remembers, he will water the neighbor's plants twice a week while the neighbor is on vacation. When the neighbor returns, all the plants, including three prize ferns, are dead from lack of water. The neighbor cannot sue Walter for the value of the ferns because, legally, Walter gave the neighbor only an *illusory promise* that is not enforceable nor is its failure actionable in court.

IMMATERIAL not material; **irrelevant,** nothing to do with the case; not significant.

EXAMPLE: At Doug's trial for robbery, the prosecution wants to introduce evidence that Doug and his wife argue frequently. That evidence is considered *immaterial* and is not allowed at the trial.

IMMORAL CONDUCT behavior opposed to accepted community standards of what is right.

IMMUNITY right of exemption from a duty or penalty; benefit granted in exception to the general rule. Immunity from prosecution may be granted a **witness** to compel answers he might otherwise withhold because of the constitutional privilege to avoid **self-incrimination.**

EXAMPLE: Ben asserts his privilege against self-incrimination when the grand jury asks probing questions about his activities. If the grand jury gives Ben *immunity* from criminal prosecution for anything to which he testifies before the grand jury, Ben can no longer use the privilege. The privilege is only available when Ben is subject to prosecution for what he says, a fear that the immunity eliminates.

OFFICIAL IMMUNITY the immunity of a public official from liability to anyone injured by actions in his exercise of official authority or duty.

See **sovereign immunity.**

IMPANELING 1. selection and swearing in of jurors; 2. listing of those selected for a particular jury.

IMPEACH 1. to charge a public official with wrongdoing while in office; 2. to question the truthfulness of the **testimony** of the **witness** by means of **evidence** that the witness is unworthy of belief.

IMPLEADER the procedure by which the **plantiff's** primary **claim** against the original **defendant,** as well as any alleged **liability** of a third party, may be settled in one **action** by joining the third party in the original action; a **procedural** device available to a defendant where a third party may be liable to him for any obligation that the defendant is found to have toward the plaintiff. The defendant is then a third-party plantiff with respect to the third party so joined. The device is also available to a plantiff against whom a **counterclaim** has been made.

IMPLICATION intention, meaning; though not expressly stated, a deduced state of mind or facts.

NECESSARY IMPLICATION a conclusion resulting from so strong a probability of intention that an opposite intention is incredible.

IMPLIED not explicitly written or stated; determined by deduction from known facts.

IMPLIED CONSENT consent that is found to exist solely because certain actions or signs would lead a **reasonable person** to believe that consent is present, whether or not that consent is even specifically expressed; in criminal law, generally used as a defense against rape, whereby the defendant claims that he acted under a reasonable and honest belief based on the fact that the woman consented to his advance.

IMPOST 1. a tax; 2. a charge or levy in the nature of a tax.

IMPOUND to place merchandise, funds or records in the **custody** of an officer of the law.

IMPOUNDING [IMPOUNDMENT] in **common law,** the second step in a **distress** action, in which the distrainer, having seized the **chattels,** must bring the goods to a public pound pending the outcome of the **action.**

IMPOSSIBILITY 1. a **defense** of nonperformance of a **contract** when **performance** is impossible because of destruction of the subject matter of the contract (as, for example, by fire) or death of a person necessary for performance. Performance is then excused and the contract duty terminated. See also **frustration of purpose.**

EXAMPLE: Grace contracts to purchase a boat at a nearby marina. Before the boat is ready for use, a storm destroys the marina and all the boats with it. Grace has an *impossibility* defense against performing the contract because the boat no longer exists.

2. in **civil law,** an excuse for nonperformance of a contract where the promised performance has become illegal. 3. in **criminal** law, applies to situations in which facts or circumstances render commission of the crime impossible. Thus, it is impossible to **murder** another if he is already dead.

EXAMPLE: A mugger brings his victim into an alley, robs him and in a fit of rage shoots him dead. Several hours later, a major drug deal is transacted in the same alley. One of the dealers sees the person lying there, believes the person is just drunk and shoots him because he wants no witnesses to the deal. The dealer has an *impossibility* defense to a murder charge because it is impossible to kill a person who is already dead. The dealer may, however, be subjected to prosecution for attempted murder.

IMPROVEMENT any permanent, fixed development of land or buildings through expenditure of money or labor that more than merely replaces, repairs or restores to original condition, and supposedly increases the value of the property.

IMPUTE to assign legal responsibility for the act of another, because of the relationship between those made liable and the actor, rather than because of participation in or knowledge of the act. See **vicarious liability.**

IN ABSENTIA *(ĭn ăb-sĕn'-shē-ȧ)* Lat.: in absence.

EXAMPLE: A defendant who leaves the courtroom without permission after a trial begins may be tried *in absentia*. Such proceedings otherwise require the actual presence of the defendant at all critical stages.

INALIENABLE RIGHTS fundamental rights, including the right to practice religion, freedom of speech, due process and equal protection of the laws, that cannot be transferred to another nor surrendered except by the person possessing them. See **Bill of Rights.**

IN CAMERA *(iň kă'-mĕ-rà)* Lat.: in chambers. A term designating a judicial act while court is not in session in the matter acted upon. Confidential or otherwise sensitive documents are often examined in camera to determine whether information should be revealed to the *jury* and so become public record.

INCAPACITY lack of legal, physical or intellectual power. See **incompetency; minority.** Compare **insanity.**

INCARCERATION confinement in prison.

INCENDIARY 1. arsonist; one who maliciously sets property on fire; 2. an object capable of starting and sustaining a fire, an incendiary device. See **arson.**

INCEST a criminal offense of sexual intercourse between members of a family, or those between whom marriage would be illegal because of blood relationship.

INCHOATE not yet completed. In inchoate offenses, something remains to be done before the crime can be accomplished as contemplated. See **attempt; conspiracy; solicitation.**

INCHOATE DOWER the **interest** that a wife has in her husband's lands before his death, and contingent upon his predeceasing her. The right of **dower** is considered inchoate until the husband's death, at which time the widow has a **vested** right to a **life estate.**

INCLOSURE see **enclosure.**

INCOME an economic benefit; money or value received.

ADJUSTED GROSS INCOME the gross income of the taxpayer reduced by specified **deductions,** generally business deductions.

CASH EQUIVALENT DOCTRINE the doctrine that property received by a taxpayer is includable in income if it can be converted into cash. The amount of income is the amount of such cash.

CONSTRUCTIVE RECEIPT OF INCOME a doctrine under which a taxpayer is required to include in gross income amounts that, though not actually received, are deemed received during the tax year. Thus there is constructive receipt when income is made available to a taxpayer without substantial restriction or condition on the taxpayer's right to exercise control over the income. Under this theory, interest credited on a savings account must be included in income even though the taxpayer does not withdraw it, since he had the right to withdraw it. The doctrine is to be distinguished from the cash equivalent doctrine.

GROSS INCOME the total of the taxpayer's income from any source, except items specifically excluded by the Internal Revenue Code and other items not subject to tax, such as **capital** income and FRINGE BENEFITS (see **benefit**).

IMPUTED INCOME economic benefit a taxpayer obtains through performance of his own services or through the use of his own property. In general, imputed income is not subject to INCOME TAXES (see **tax**). For example, if a taxpayer is a plumber and repairs his own toilet, such repair service is not subject to tax.

INCOME IN RESPECT OF A DECEDENT income earned by a taxpayer before his death but received by, and taxed to, the taxpayer's **heirs** or personal representatives.

ORDINARY INCOME income that is fully subject to ordinary income tax rates, as distinguished from income that is subject to the benefit of special deductions for **capital gains and losses.**

TAXABLE INCOME gross income reduced by deductions allowable in obtaining adjusted gross income and further reduced by deductions allowable in calculating itemized deductions.

INCOME AVERAGING a method of calculating tax liability to minimize adverse consequences to a **taxpayer** with substantial fluctuations in income from year to year; permits a taxpayer to compute his tax as if the higher amount of income had been earned equally over that year and the previous four years.

INCOME SPLITTING a device that allows married taxpayers to calculate their joint taxes as if one half of their joint taxable income were earned by each spouse. See **return, income tax [JOINT RETURN].**

INCOME STATEMENT a financial statement that gives operating results, such as net income and loss, depreciation, for a specific period; also referred to as earnings report, operating statement and profit-and-loss statement. See also **balance sheet.**

INCOME TAX see **tax; return, income tax.**

INCOMPETENCY inability, disqualification, **incapacity.** 1. lack of legal qualifications or fitness to discharge a required duty; 2. lack of physical, intellectual or moral fitness.

EXAMPLE: Herman is arrested for assault. Prior to his trial, a judge determines that he is *incompetent,* that he cannot aid in his defense nor can he endure the rigors of a criminal trial without suffering a mental breakdown. Herman may at some point be declared competent to stand trial, but at the present time his trial for assault is postponed.

When a person is adjudicated incompetent, a **guardian** is appointed to manage the incompetent's affairs, unless the incompetent recovers competency to the satisfaction of the court. An adjudicated incompetent lacks capacity to **contract** and his contracts are void. Compare **competent.**

INCOMPETENT EVIDENCE **evidence** that is not **admissible.** Compare **competent.**

INCONVENIENT FORUM see **forum non conveniens.**

INCORPORATE to organize and be granted status as a **corporation** by following prescribed legal procedures.

INCORPOREAL see **corporeal.**

INCORPOREAL HEREDITAMENT see **hereditament.**

INCORRIGIBLE uncorrectable; one whose behavior cannot be made to conform to standards dictated by law. See **criminal** [HABITUAL OFFENDER]; **recidivist.**

INCREMENT an amount of increase in number or value.

INCRIMINATE 1. to hold another, or oneself, responsible for criminal misconduct; 2. to involve someone, or oneself, in an accusation of a crime.

INCULPATORY tending to **incriminate** or bring about a criminal conviction. Compare **exculpatory.**

INCUMBRANCE see **encumbrance.**

INDEFEASIBLE incapable of being defeated or altered. An indefeasible **estate** is absolute and cannot be changed by any **condition.**

EXAMPLE: A sister conveys an *indefeasible* estate to her brother. The brother has perfect title to the land and can do with it as he pleases, since there is no circumstance that can operate to deprive him of title.

IN DELICTO *(ĭn dĕ-lĭk′-tō)* Lat.: at fault.

INDEMNIFY 1. to insure; to secure against loss or damage that may occur in the future; 2. to compensate for loss or damage already suffered; 3. to **save harmless.** See **damages; insurance.**

INDEMNITY 1. the obligation to make good any loss or damage another person has incurred or may incur; 2. the right that the person suffering loss or damage is entitled to claim.

EXAMPLE: John buys a piece of land from Pat. Unbeknown to John, the land was encumbered by a lien for several years of back taxes that Pat had not paid. John pays the taxes but has a right of *indemnity* against Pat for the tax liability.

Compare **contribution.**

INDENTURE 1. a **deed** between two parties conveying **real estate** by which both parties assume obligations. Indenture implies a **sealed instrument.** 2. a lengthy written agreement that sets forth terms under which **bonds** or **debentures** may be issued.

INDEPENDENT CONTRACTOR see **contractor.**

INDETERMINATE SENTENCE see **sentence.**

INDICIA *(ĭn-dĭ′-shē-ȧ)* Lat.: indications. Signs or circumstances that tend to support a belief in a proposition. Compare **circumstantial evidence.**

INDICTABLE OFFENSES crimes that can be prosecuted by the GRAND JURY (see **jury**) indicting the accused. In **common law,** these crimes were known as **felonies** and were defined by the punishment for them—either death, **forfeiture**

of all one's property or mutilation. The crimes included **murder, treason, robbery, assault, rape, arson, burglary** and **larceny.** These crimes could also be prosecuted by individuals bringing lawsuits against the **defendants.** Today felonies, as defined by modern **statutes,** are still prosecuted by **indictment.** Compare **misdemeanor.** See **crime; prosecution; suit.**

INDICTMENT a formal written **accusation,** drawn up and submitted under **oath** to a GRAND JURY (see **jury**) by the public prosecuting attorney, charging one or more persons with a **crime.** The grand jury must determine whether the accusation, if proved, would be sufficient for **conviction** of the accused, in which case the indictment is indorsed by the foreman as a TRUE BILL. Once an indictment is filed, the matter passes to the Court. Indictments also serve to inform an accused of the offense with which he is charged and must be clear enough to enable him to prepare his defense adequately. Compare **charge; complaint; information; presentment.**

INDIGENT 1. generally, a person who is poor, financially destitute; 2. in a legal context, a person found by a court to be unable to hire a lawyer or otherwise meet the expense of defending a criminal matter, at which point defense **counsel** is appointed by the court.

INDIGNITY affront to the personality of another; lack of reverence for the personality of one's spouse. Indignity is a ground for **divorce** in some states; may consist of vulgarity, unmerited reproach, malignant ridicule and any other plain expression of settled hate or estrangement. See **mental cruelty.**

INDISPENSABLE EVIDENCE **evidence** necessary to prove a submitted fact.

INDISPENSABLE PARTY a **party** who has such an interest in the **litigation** that a final **decree** cannot be issued without either affecting that interest or determining the controversy in a way inconsistent with **equity** and good conscience. Therefore, an **action** may not proceed without an indispensable party, who must be **joined** to the action, because his nonjoinder would result in prejudice to his rights and the rights of other parties to the action.

INDIVIDUAL RETIREMENT ACCOUNT [IRA] a retirement account for individuals not eligible to participate in a qualified pension or profit-sharing plan for an entire **taxable year.** Such individuals may pay into the account a specified sum (in general, no more than the lesser of $1,500 or 15 percent of compensation or personal service income). Such amounts are deductible to the employee and the income earned thereon is not recognized if the account provides that the employee may not make withdrawals, except if he dies or becomes disabled, prior to age 59½ and that withdrawal must commence no later than age 70½.

INDORSEMENT signature on the back of an **instrument,** with or without other words, the effect of which is to transfer the instrument and to create a new, independent **contract** by which the indorser becomes a party to the instrument and liable, on certan conditions, for its payment.

ACCOMMODATION INDORSEMENT one made without **consideration,** solely to extend **credit** to the holder by the indorser, generally to enable the holder to obtain credit or money from another on the basis of the indorsement.

BLANK INDORSEMENT one that specifies no particular party to whom the indorsed instrument is exclusively payable, and that therefore authorizes negotiation by the **bearer** upon **delivery** alone.

RESTRICTIVE INDORSEMENT one that limits transferability of the instrument.

SPECIAL INDORSEMENT one that specifies to whose **order** the instrument shall be payable. The instrument is then negotiable only by such person unless he makes a further indorsement.

IN EXTREMIS *(ĭn ĕks-trĕ'-mĭs)* Lat.: in extreme circumstances; especially, on the brink of death. Compare **causa [CAUSA MORTIS].**

INFAMOUS CRIME a crime that, in **common law,** rendered the convicted person **incompetent** as a **witness,** because of presumed untrustworthiness. See **crimen falsi; felony; treason.**

INFANCY the legal status preceding **majority; minority.**

IN FEE [IN FEE SIMPLE] absolute ownership of an **estate** in land.

INFERENCE a process of reasoning by which a proposition is derived as a logical consequence from given facts.

INFEUDATION the act of granting a **freehold estate;** same as **feoffment** or enfeoffment.

IN FORMA PAUPERIS *(in fôr'-mȧ paw-pĕr'-ĭs)* Lat.: in the manner of a pauper. In **pleadings,** in forma pauperis grants the right to sue without assuming the burden of **costs** or formalities of pleading. A criminal **defendant** granted permission to proceed in forma pauperis may be entitled to court-appointed counsel.

INFORMATION a written accusation of crime signed by the **prosecutor,** charging a person with the commission of a crime; an alternative to **indictment** as a means of starting a criminal prosecution. The purpose of an information is to inform the **defendant** of the charges against him and to inform the court of the factual basis of the charges.

INFORMATION AND BELIEF verification short of actual knowledge, but based on reasonable, **good faith** efforts to determine truth or falsity. The term is used with reference to documents requiring verification, such as requests for **search warrants,** responses to **interrogatories, complaints, pleadings,** etc.

INFORMED CONSENT consent given only after full disclosure of what is being consented to; constitutionally required in certain areas where one may consent to what otherwise would be an unconstitutional violation of a right.

EXAMPLE: Jan is arrested for burglary. She decides to handle her case by herself, without the assistance of an attorney. Since she has a constitutional right to an attorney and to have one appointed if she cannot afford one, a judge must insure that her decision is based on *informed consent*. Such consent would include an understanding of her right to an attorney and what her decision entails.

The phrase is also used in **tort** law, where a patient must be told the nature and risks of a medical procedure before the physician can validly claim exemption from **liability** for **battery** or from responsibility for medical complications.

Compare **Miranda rule; self-incrimination, privilege against.**

INFRA *(ĭn'-frȧ)* Lat.: below. In text the term refers to a discussion or a citation appearing subsequently; the opposite of **supra** (above).

INFRINGEMENT see **patent infringement.** See also **copyright; trademark; plagiarism.**

IN FUTURO *(ĭn fū-tū'-rō)* Lat.: in the future; at a later date.

IN GENERE *(ĭn gĕ'-nĕ-rā)* Lat.: in kind; of the same class or species.

INGRESS AND EGRESS 1. entrance and departure; 2. means of entering and leaving; 3. the right to do so.

INHERIT technically, to take as an **heir at law** solely by **descent,** rather than by **devise;** more commonly used to signify taking either by devise (i.e., by **will**) or by descent (i.e., from one's ancestor by **operation of law**).

INHERITANCE **real property** or **personal property** that is received by **heirs** according to the laws of **descent and distribution.** A nontechnical meaning of inheritance includes property passed by **will.**

IN HOC *(ĭn hŏk)* Lat.: in this; in reference to this.

INJUNCTION a judicial **remedy** awarded to restrain a particular activity; first used by **courts of equity** to prevent conduct contrary to **equity** and good conscience.

The injunction is a preventive measure to guard against future injuries, rather than one that affords a remedy for past injuries.

MANDATORY INJUNCTION one requiring positive action, rather than one forbidding a party to act.

EXAMPLE: A landlord refuses to supply his tenants with heat during the winter months. Regardless of the reasons for the landlord's action, a court might issue a *mandatory injunction* forcing the landlord to supply heat.

PERMANENT INJUNCTION one issued upon completion of a trial in which the injunction has been actively sought.

TEMPORARY [OR INTERLOCUTORY] INJUNCTION one that will expire at a particular time, and that is typically used to maintain the **status quo** or preserve the subject matter of the **litigation** during trial.

INJURIA ABSQUE DAMNO *(ĭn-jū'-rē-ȧ äb'-skwā däm'-nō)* Lat.: wrong without damage; insult without damage. Where a **cause of action** requires that damages be **pleaded,** this maxim expresses the rule that a wrong which causes no legally recognized damage cannot give rise to a cause of action. But see **damages [NOMINAL DAMAGES].**

INJURIA NON EXCUSAT INJURIAM *(ĭn-jū'-rē-ȧ nŏn ĕx-kū'-zät ĭn-jū'-rē-äm)* Lat.: one wrong does not justify another.

INJURY wrong or damage done to another, either in his person, rights, reputation or property. **LEGAL INJURY** is any damage that results from a violation of a legal right and that the law will recognize as deserving of redress. Compare **damnum absque injuria; depreciation; fault.** See also **relief; remedy.**

EXAMPLE: Federal law prohibits discrimination based on race. May, a black woman, is refused a job because of her race. Even if she gets another job and although no physical injury resulted to her, she has been *injured* in the eyes of the law and can pursue a monetary remedy or an award of the job she was refused.

IN KIND 1. of the same or similar type or quality; 2. in the same or similar manner.

IN LOCO PARENTIS *(ĭn lō'-kō pä-rĕn'-tĭs)* Lat.: in the place of a parent. Refers to a person or agency who has assumed the obligations of a parent. Commonly refers to the role of a residential institution such as a boarding school, in relation to the **minors** in its care.

INNS OF COURT four private societies in England that prepare students for the practice of law and that alone may admit them to the bar; that is, confer the rank of **barrister.** The four inns of court are Inner Temple, Middle Temple, Lincoln's Inn, Gray's Inn.

INNUENDO that part of a **pleading** in an **action** for **libel** that explains, improperly, the spoken or written words that are the basis of the action, thereby attaching to those words more than their plain meaning. The **plaintiff** in a libel action cannot enlarge or change original language by innuendo, since the purpose of innuendo is to explain the application of words used, and words that are not libelous in themselves cannot be made so by innuendo.

IN OMNIBUS *(ĭn ŏm'-nĭ-bŭs)* Lat.: in all things; in all the world; in all nature; in all respects.

IN PAIS *(ĭn pĕ'-ĭs)* Fr.: in the country, neighborhood. Applies to a transaction handled outside the court or without a legal **proceeding.**

IN PARI DELICTO *(ĭn pä'-rē dĕ-lĭk'-tō)* Lat.: in equal fault. Refers to an exception to the general rule that illegal transactions or **contracts** are not legally enforceable; thus, where the parties to an illegal agreement are not in pari delicto, the agreement may nevertheless be enforceable at **equity** by the innocent or less guilty party. See also **clean hands; duress; fraud.**

IN PARI MATERIA *(ĭn pä'-rē mä-tĕr'-ē-ȧ)* Lat.: on like subject matter. **Statutes** or document provisions that relate to the same person or subject. In the **construction** or interpretation of a statute or instrument, the various provisions of the statute or instrument and all other acts or instruments on the same subject or having the same purpose are to be read together as one law or agreement, giving equal importance to each.

IN PERPETUITY existing forever.

IN PERSONAM *(ĭn pĕr-sō'-näm)* Lat.: into or against the person. In **pleading,** an **action** against a person or persons, founded on personal **liability** and requiring **jurisdiction** by the court over the person sought to be held liable, i.e., the **defendant.**

EXAMPLE: David causes an accident while driving recklessly. He is sued *in personam* in the state where the accident occurred, but he claims that as an out-of-state driver the courts of that state do not have jurisdiction over him and cannot force him to answer the suit. Although that might be true without applicable statutes, every state has laws automatically establishing jurisdiction over persons using their highways. If the victim of the accident wins this suit, based on the merits, he can use the judgment against David in any other state.

In such an action, the **plantiff** seeks either to subject defendant's general **assets** to **execution** in order to satisfy a money **judgment,** or to obtain a judgment directing defendant to do an act or refrain from doing an act.

Compare **in rem.**

IN PRAESENTI *(ĭn prā-zĕn'-tē)* Lat.: in the present. Often signifies a presently effective act or interest, distinguished from one effective **in futuro.**

IN QUANTUM MERUIT see **quantum meruit.**

INQUEST 1. a judicial inquiry; 2. an inquiry made by a **coroner** to determine cause of death of one who has been killed, has died suddenly, or under suspicious circumstances or in prison.

IN RE *(ĭn rā)* Lat.: in the matter of. Usually signifies a legal proceeding with no opponent, but rather judicial **disposition** of a thing, or **res,** such as the **estate** of a decedent.

IN REM *(ĭn rĕm)* Lat.: into or against the thing. Signifies actions against the **res,** or thing, rather than against the person. The goal of a proceeding in rem is the **disposition** of property without reference to the **title** of individual **claimants.** Compare **in personam.**

ACTIONS IN REM those that seek not to impose personal **liability** but rather to affect the **interests** of persons in a specific thing (or **res**). A few such actions purport to affect the interests of all persons ("all the world") in the same thing as, for example, in actions to protect the environment; most of them seek to affect the interests of only particular persons in the thing. Typical modern examples are actions for **partition** of, or for **foreclosure** of a **lien** upon, or to **quiet title** to, real estate. The concept of in rem actions has been extended to those that seek to affect the condition of a thing as well as the thing itself.

ACTIONS QUASI IN REM actions based on a claim for money damages begun by **attachment** or **garnishment** or other seizure of property where the court has no **jurisdiction** over the person of the defendant but has jurisdiction over a thing belonging to the defendant or over a person who is indebted or under a duty to the defendant.

INSANITY mental illness. The term may be used to signify lack of criminal responsibility, need for commitment to a mental institution, inability to transact business, inability to stand trial (i.e., to assist in one's own defense). Compare **incompetency; non compos mentis; non sui juris.** See **Durham rule; M'Naghten rule.**

INSANITY, PLEA OF see **plea.**

IN SE *(ĭn sā)* Lat.: in and of itself.

INSIDER a person whose opportunity to profit from his position of power in a business is limited by law to safeguard the public good. Both federal securities acts and state **blue sky laws** regulate stock transactions of individuals with access to inside information about a corporation, since the prospect of **insider trading** may inhibit investment by the general public due to their concern that the price of securities has been artificially inflated or deflated by such trading.

INSIDER TRADING buying or selling of corporation stock by a corporate officer who profits by his access to information not available to the public. Corporate **insiders** who trade on the basis of nonpublic corporate information may be exposed to **liability** under state or federal law, because of a policy that everybody should have equal access to information and that insiders should not profit personally from something that belongs to the corporation.

INSOLVENCY 1. inability to meet financial obligations as they mature in the ordinary course of business; 2. excess of liabilities over assets at any given time. In the absence of definition by statute, the first definition is more widely recognized; however, statutory definition is common today. See also **bankruptcy.**

EXAMPLE: Baden Company borrows money from a bank to pay overdue debts in the hope that business will improve. That hope is not realized, and payments to the bank as well as other debts begin to develop again. Baden is finally declared *insolvent*. If any assets remain in the company, Baden's creditors and/or a court will divide them in some fair fashion.

IN SPECIE *(ĭn spē'-shē)* Lat.: in like form. To repay a loan in specie is to return the same kind of goods as were borrowed.

INSPECTON OF DOCUMENTS right of parties in a **civil action** to view and copy documents in the possession of the court and essential to the **adverse party's cause of action.** This is done as part of the **discovery** process before trial; but apart from the production for pretrial inspection, a party may by the use of a **subpoena duces tecum** require the production of documents at the time of trial for the purpose of introducing them into **evidence.**

INSTALLMENT CONTRACT a contract in which the obligation of one or more of the parties—such as an obligation to pay money, deliver goods or render services—is divided into a series of successive performances.

EXAMPLE: Flavor Bread Company wants to insure supplies of wheat over the next five years. It writes an *installment contract* with a farmer's cooperative to deliver monthly shipments of wheat to its plant over the five-year period, with Flavor's obligation to pay likewise apportioned over the five-year period. Since the contract is long-term, prices are arrived at by a formula that can vary each month.

IN STATU QUO *(ĭn stä'-tū kwō)* Lat.: in the existing situation or condition. In the same position a party is in currently or was in at some relevant prior time.

INSTRUCTION the judge's directions to the **jury** before their deliberation, informing them of the law applicable to the **case,** to guide them in reaching a verdict according to law and the **evidence.** An instruction to the jury is a **charge** to the jury, more a command than a request.

INSTRUMENT in commercial law, a written formal document that records an act or agreement and provides the **evidence** of that act or agreement.

INSUFFICIENT EVIDENCE a term usually referred to in a decision by a judge that a prosecutor or other party charged with proving a crime has failed to provide the minimum of **evidence** necessary to even ask a jury to decide a **question of fact;** results in a **directed verdict** in favor of a defendant. If an **appellate court** decides that the evidence at a defendant's trial is insufficient, it will reverse the conviction and dismiss the charges that the State failed to prove at the trial.

INSURABLE INTEREST a relationship with a person or thing that supports issuance of an **insurance** policy. A person having an insurable interest can derive financial advantage from preservation of the subject matter insured or suffer loss from its destruction.

An insurable interest in the life of another requires that the continued life of the insured be of real interest to the insuring party. The connection may be financial (as when a **creditor** insures the life of his **debtor**) or it may consist of familial or other ties of affection.

EXAMPLE: A basketball team drafts Astor, the best player in college. His contract will pay him over a million dollars a year for ten years. The team has an *insurable interest* in Astor and will undoubtedly take out an insurance policy to protect their investment.

INSURANCE the benefit from an agreement by one party (insurer) to provide the other (insured), for a **consideration,** money or some other benefit in the event of the loss of, or injury to, a specified person or thing in which the other has an interest.

ENDOWMENT INSURANCE insurance for a specified amount payable to the insured at the expiration of a certain period or to a designated **beneficiary** immediately upon the death of the insured.

TERM INSURANCE insurance for the period for which a premium has been paid. With life insurance it is a **contract** in which the insured pays the actual cost of insurance for each assessment period, without defraying a future deficit from the cost of insuring older persons. Economical premium eliminates cash surrender value and loan value.

WHOLE LIFE INSURANCE insurance upon the life of the insured for a fixed death benefit at a definite annual premium; synonymous with ordinary life insurance or straight life insurance.

INSURED the person whose interests are protected by an **insurance** policy; the person who **contracts** for a policy of insurance that **indemnifies** him against loss of **property,** life or health.

INTANGIBLE PROPERTY possessions that only represent real value, such as **stock certificates, bonds, promissory notes, franchises.**

INTEGRATION 1. the process by which the parties to an agreement adopt a writing or writings as the full and final expression of their agreement; 2. the writing or writings so adopted.

INTENT a state of mind wherein the person knows and desires the consequences of his act. For criminal and certain types of civil **liability,** intent must exist at the time the offense is committed. See **animo; mens rea; scienter.**

INTER ALIA *(ĭn'-tèr ä'-lē-à)* Lat.: among other things.

INTEREST 1. in commercial law, **consideration** or **compensation** for the use of money loaned or forbearance in demanding it when due. 2. in legal practice, a term connoting bias or concern for the advantage or disadvantage of a party to the **action** or of the subject matter of the action. Interest affects the credibility of **witnesses.** Interest is required for the **intervention** of third parties in a lawsuit and is also a ground for disqualifying a judge or juror. 3. in real property, the broadest term applicable to claims on **real estate,** including any right, **title** or **estate** in or **lien** on real property. Interest thus refers to the legal concern of a person in the property, or in the right to some of the benefits from which the property is inseparable.

EXECUTED INTEREST an interest in property presently enjoyed and possessed by a party.

EXECUTORY INTEREST interest in property that may become actual in the future or upon some event.

COMPOUND INTEREST interest that is paid not only upon the principal sum, but also upon the interest previously paid on that sum. Thus, interest already paid or accrued becomes part of the principal, for purposes of subsequent interest calculations.

SHIFTING INTEREST a future interest arising in derogation of or out of a preceding interest.

SPRINGING INTEREST a future interest arising from an **estate** in the grantor. Compare **chain of title.**

VESTED INTEREST one in which there is a present fixed right of present or future enjoyment.

INTERIM ORDER a temporary order, made until another or FINAL ORDER (see **order**) takes its place or a specific event occurs.

INTERLOCUTORY provisional; temporary. An **order** or **judgment** that does not determine the **issues** but directs further **proceeding** preliminary to a final order or **decree.** Until final decree, an interlocutory judgment is subject to change by the court to meet the needs of the case and is often not appealable except by leave of court.

EXAMPLE: Fran wins a suppression motion to exclude certain evidence against her in an upcoming trial. Before the trial begins, the prosecutor seeks leave from the judge to file an *interlocutory* appeal from the suppression order, rather than wait until the trial is concluded before appealing the judge's ruling on Fran's motion. If the prosecutor's request is granted, Fran's trial will not proceed until an appellate court rules on the motion.

INTERNAL REVENUE CODE the massive **statute** providing the foundation for all federal tax law. This statute is located in Title 26, United States Code. Its various subtitles include **tax** provisions relating to the INCOME TAX, GIFT TAX and ESTATE TAX (now UNIFIED ESTATE AND GIFT TAX), as well as other less important and less well-known taxes. As with all federal statutes, it is enacted and amended by Congress, and is implemented through the **Internal Revenue Service** by the Commissioner of Internal Revenue, appointed by the President.

INTERNAL REVENUE SERVICE [IRS] the federal agency primarily concerned with the administration of the federal tax laws.

INTERNATIONAL COURT OF JUSTICE the principal tribunal of the United Nations, consisting of 15 members elected by the General Assembly and the Security Council for a definite, limited term. The only **appeal** from a **judgment** of this Court is to the U.N. Security Council. The seat of the Court is at the Hague, though it may meet elsewhere at its discretion.

INTERNATIONAL LAW the law governing relations of nations with one another, which arises principally from international agreements or from customs that nations adopt.

In a broader sense, international law includes both public law and private law. The public law regulates political relations between nations. The private law is the **comity** nations grant to each other's laws in enforcing rights arising under foreign law.

INTER PARES *(ĭn'-tėr pär'-ās)* Lat.: among peers; among those of equal rank.

INTER PARTES *(ĭn'-ter pär'-tās)* Lat.: between the parties.

INTERPLEADER an equitable **action** in which a **debtor,** not knowing to whom among his **creditors** a certain debt is owed, and having no **claim** on the property in dispute, will petition a court to require the creditors to litigate the claim among themselves. The person interpleading is called the **stakeholder.** Interpleader is used to avoid multiple **liability** on the part of the debtor and is used often by insurance carriers, who deposit the proceeds of a policy in court where several persons with conflicting rights have made claims.

EXAMPLE: An insurance company immediately realizes that an airline it insures is responsible for a crash that has killed twenty people. The company, by way of *interpleader,* is able to deposit with the court the maximum liability for which the airline is insured for these twenty people and thereby lets the families of each person and the court determine how the money will be allocated.

Compare **cross-claim; joinder.**

INTERROGATION the process by which suspects are rigorously questioned by police. See **Miranda rule.**

INTERROGATORIES in **civil actions,** a pretrial **discovery** tool in which one party's written questions are served on the **adversary,** who must serve written replies under oath. Interrogatories can only be served on **parties** to the **action,** and while not as flexible as **depositions,** which include opportunity of **cross-examination,** they are regarded as a good and inexpensive means of establishing important facts held by the adversary.

IN TERROREM *(ĭn tĕ-rô'-rĕm)* Lat.: in fear. A CONDITION SUBSEQUENT (see **condition**) placed in a **will** or **contract** that, although unenforceable, has the purpose of intimidating the beneficiary and thereby perhaps securing his compliance.

INTER SE [INTER SESE] *(ĭn'-tėr sā; ĭn'-tėr sĕ'-sā)* Lat.: among or between themselves; commonly applied to **trust**

instruments to signify that only the rights of **shareholders** and **trustees** are involved.

INTERSTATE COMMERCE business activity among inhabitants of different states, including transportation of persons and property and navigation of public waters for that purpose, as well as purchase, sale and exchange of commodities.

INTERVAL OWNERSHIP see **time-sharing.**

INTERVENING CAUSE see **cause.**

INTERVENTION a **proceeding** permitting a person to enter a law**suit** already in progress; in **civil law,** admission of a person not an original **party** to the suit, to protect a right or **interest** allegedly affected by the proceedings. The **INTERVENOR** may wish to join the **plaintiff** or the **defendant** or demand something adverse to both. A person generally can become an intervenor only by proving he has an interest in the subject matter of the original **litigation.** The purpose of intervention is to prevent delay and unnecessary duplication of lawsuits; it may be denied, however, if it interferes excessively with the rights of original parties to conduct the suit on their own terms.

EXAMPLE: A family sues Durable Paperboard Company for using chemicals that contain carcinogens in phone repair products. Two other companies use the same chemicals and fear that a decision adverse to Durable will result in many lawsuits against them based on the same claim. The companies therefore seek to *intervene* in the suit between the family and Durable.

INTER VIVOS *(ĭn'-tėr vē'-vōs)* Lat.: between the living. Transactions inter vivos are made while the parties are living, and not upon death (as in **inheritance**) or upon contemplation of death **(causa mortis).** A **deed,** therefore, is an **instrument** that **conveys** inter vivos a present **interest** in land. **Gifts** are either inter vivos, causa mortis or by **will.**

INTESTATE [INTESTACY] the condition of having died without leaving a valid **will.** An intestate **estate** is property that a **testator** has failed to dispose of (**devise**) by will.

INTESTATE SUCCESSION the disposition of property to **heirs** according to the laws of **descent and distribution** upon the death of a person who has left no **will** or who has left a portion of his **estate** unaccounted for in his will. See **inheritance.**

IN TOTO *(ĭn tō'-tō)* Lat.: in total.

INTOXICATION state of drunkenness, or a similar condition caused by use of drugs other than alcohol.

INTRINSIC FRAUD see **fraud.**

INURE to take effect; to serve to the benefit of someone; in property, to **vest.**

INVASION OF PRIVACY the wrongful intrusion into a person's private activities by other individuals or by the government. See also **due process of law.**

INVESTMENT the purchase of property with the expectation of obtaining **income** or **capital gain** in the future.

INVEST to transfer **capital** to an enterprise in order to secure income or profit for the investor.

INVESTMENT BANKER a **broker** of **stocks** who acts as an **underwriter** of **securities.** The investment banker can act as **principal** by buying the entire issue from the selling **corporation** or from selling **shareholders,** or as **agent** by selling the offering on a "best-efforts" basis. In either event the investment banker sells the issue to other dealers who together with the lead banker have formed an underwriting **syndicate.** Members of the syndicate in turn sell the **shares** to the investing public and to institutional investors such as pension funds (see **retirement plan**) or **mutual funds.** Investment banking is not banking as generally defined, and investment banking activities are illegal for commercial banks.

INVESTMENT COMPANY [OR TRUST] a company or trust formed to pool the money resources of many individual investors in a large fund offering potential for investment diversification and professional management. Such a corporation typically invests in real estate or stocks and bonds, distributing the profit therefrom to its shareholders in the form of **dividends.**

INVITEE one who comes upon private land by the owner's invitation, whether express or implied. In **tort** law, the owner is not an insurer of the safety of invitees, but he owes a duty to them to exercise reasonable care for their protection against **latent defects** in the premises that might cause them injury.

EXAMPLE: John has a vacation home in a wooded area where he lays traps to catch animals. He invites neighbors to take a walk with him in some of the back parts of the property to enjoy the scenic view. One of these *invitees* steps on a trap that was buried below the ground and injures his foot. John is responsible for the invitee's damages.

INVOLUNTARY unwilling; forced; opposed; in criminal law, can act as a defense to a charge of committing a crime. See **duress.**

EXAMPLE: Bernice is forced at gunpoint to accompany several men into a bank to aid them in a robbery. Since her actions are *involuntary* and performed under duress, she cannot be charged with criminal responsibility in the crime.

IPSE DIXIT *(ĭp'-sā dĭks'-ĭt)* Lat.: he himself said it. Refers to an assertion the sole authority for which is that the speaker has said it.

IPSO FACTO *(ĭp'-sō făk'-toō)* Lat.: by the fact itself; in and of itself.

IPSO JURE *(ĭp'-sō jū'-rā)* Lat.: by the law itself; merely by the law.

IRA see **Individual Retirement Account.**

IRRELEVANT **immaterial;** not relevant; generally used in the context of a rule of evidence, whereby one party objects to the introduction at trial of evidence that is not connected to the issue being decided.

IRREPARABLE INJURY [OR DAMAGE OR HARM] a type of **injury** for which no **remedy at law (damages)** suffices, and that thus requires a **court of equity** to intervene, often by issuing an **injunction** to prevent the conduct or conditions that are causing or threatening the injury. In fact, showing of imminent irreparable injury is ordinarily prerequisite to a request for an injunction.

ISSUE 1. as a verb, to put into circulation, as to a buyer. 2. In **corporation** law, a STOCK ISSUE is the process by which a corporation authorizes, executes and delivers shares of stock for sale to the public. The term also describes the shares offered by the corporation at a particular time. 3. in the law of **real property,** the noun issue means descendants.

EXAMPLE: Paula's will declared that any part of her estate not specifically distributed to someone else be divided among her *issue*. Her children tried to claim the full amount of this residual property, but, as the children were reminded by the court in a lawsuit against them, "issue" refers to all descendants, including children, grandchildren and other more remote descendants.

4. in legal practice, a point of fact or law disputed between **parties** to the **litigation,** generally an assertion by one side and a denial by the other.

J

JEOPARDY the danger of conviction and punishment in which a person is placed when he is put on trial for a criminal offense. See **double jeopardy.**

JOBBER a middleman in the **sale** of **goods**; one who buys from a **wholesaler** and sells to a retailer. A jobber, who actually purchases goods himself and then resells them, is distinguished from a **broker** or **agent,** who sells goods on another's behalf.

JOHN/JANE DOE fictional names used to identify persons in a hypothetical situation in order to explain an issue; name used when a person refuses to identify himself or when a person cannot be identified.

JOINDER uniting of several **causes of action** or **parties** in a single **suit.** In federal practice, a party may join as many claims as he has against the opposing party. Compare **class action; impleader; misjoinder.**

COMPULSORY JOINDER mandatory joining of a person needed in an action for a just adjudication of the **controversy.** All related claims against another must be joined, or the claimant faces the possibility of being barred from **litigating** claims separately on the grounds that such action constitutes **multiplicity of suits.** A defendant must raise related claims as compulsory **counterclaims.**

PERMISSIVE JOINDER the joining of persons, so that in a single lawsuit a plaintiff may raise all his unrelated claims against another party with the court **severing** claims that ought not be tried together. A defendant may **plead** in his **answer** any PERMISSIVE COUNTERCLAIMS against the plaintiff.

JOINDER OF ISSUE the act by which an **issue** is formally structured for its determination by a court.

JOINT a common as opposed to individual interest or liability.

JOINT ACCOUNT a bank account belonging to two or more persons, with funds in **JOINT TENANCY.** (see **tenancy**).

JOINT AND SEVERAL refers to the sharing of rights and **liabilities** among a group of persons collectively and also individually. Thus, if **defendants** in a **negligence** suit are jointly and severally liable, all may be sued together or any one may be sued for **satisfaction** to the injured party.

EXAMPLE: Sue is injured when a bottle of soda she purchased at a store explodes. She sues both the owner of the store and the manufacturer of the soda. If they are both found liable, their liability will probably be *joint and several.* Sue may choose to collect her entire damage award from one of the parties or may apportion the total owed to her between the two defendants in any manner she chooses.

See **contribution; indemnity.** Compare **severally.**

JOINT CUSTODY see **custody of children.**

JOINT ENTERPRISE undertaking founded on mutual agreement of parties; essential elements are agreement, common purpose, community of interest and equal right of control. Those who engage in a joint enterprise that is unlawful or causes injury may be **liable** as **joint tortfeasors, accessories** or **conspirators.**

JOINT LIABILITY shared **liability** that allows a sued person the right to insist that others be sued jointly with him.

JOINT STOCK COMPANY see **company.**

JOINT TENANCY see **tenancy.**

JOINT TORTFEASORS two or more persons who owe to another person the same **duty** and whose **negligence** results in injury to such other person, thereby rendering the tortfeasors both **jointly and severally** [individually] **liable** for the injury. To be liable as joint tortfeasors, the parties either must act in concert or must by independent acts cause a single injury.

EXAMPLE: Two friends practice their hunting skills on a reservation that does not permit hunting. A hiker is injured by a stray bullet from one of the friend's guns. Since it cannot be determined which friend shot the bullet that injured the hiker, both friends are liable for the injury as **joint tortfeasors.**

Compare **conspiracy.**

JOINTURE an **estate** or **property** secured to a prospective wife as a marriage settlement, to be **enjoyed** by her after her husband's decease. The estate existed under the **common law** as a means of protecting the wife's future, upon the death of her husband, in place of **dower.**

JOINT VENTURE a business undertaking by two or more parties in which profits, losses and control are shared. Though the term is often synonymous with **partnership,** a joint venture may indicate an enterprise of more limited scope and duration, though there is the same mutual **liability** of the participants for debts and **torts** of the venture.

EXAMPLE: Several business associates develop a new method of marketing pet food. A *joint venture* is established, limiting business activity to the marketing scheme and obliging each associate to contribute enough money for the new company to last one year. If the company is not successful by that time, any remaining money will be distributed to the associates and the venture will be dissolved.

JUDGE-MADE LAW law made in the **common law** tradition; law arrived at by judicial **precedent** rather than by statute.

JUDGMENT the determination of a court of competent **jurisdiction** upon matters submitted to it.

ESTOPPEL BY JUDGMENT **estoppel** brought about by the judgment of a court because a similar question or fact in dispute has been determined by a court of competent jurisdiction between the same parties or their **privies.**

FINAL JUDGMENT a conclusive determination of the rights of the parties, disposing of the entire **controversy** before the court, or of some separable portion of the dispute, so that immediately after the judgment or an appeal, therefore, the only judicial business that remains is enforcement of that judgment. The term also refers to the **sentence** imposed in a criminal case. See **final decision.**

JUDGMENT BY DEFAULT see **default; default judgment.**

JUDGMENT IN REM one pronounced upon the status of a particular subject matter, property or thing, as opposed to one pronounced upon persons.

JUDGMENT N.O.V. see **n.o.v.**

JUDGMENT OF CONVICTION the **sentence** in a criminal case formally entered in the clerk's records.

JUDGMENT ON THE MERITS a binding judgment determined by analysis and adjudication of the factual issues presented, rather than by the existence of a technical or **procedural** defect that requires one party to prevail.

EXAMPLE: Alice files a lawsuit but inadvertently names the wrong parties as defendants. When her case comes to trial, it may be dismissed as against the people she wanted to sue because they were not named. That dismissal would not be a *judgment on the merits,* since the court's action in doing so is necessitated by a procedural error committed by Alice.

JUDGMENT CREDITOR a **creditor** who has obtained against a **debtor** a **judgment** through which the creditor can obtain the sum due him. The effect of becoming a judgment creditor is to create against other creditors a certain priority right to have the debt satisfied out of the debtor's assets, and to extend the life of the claim under the **statute of limitations** so that the judgment debt may be sued upon for a longer period than would be possible for a debt without a judgment.

JUDGMENT DEBTOR a person against whom there is a legal **judgment** for repayment of a **debt.** The effect of becoming a judgment debtor is that the debtor's property may be subject to **creditor's** claims. See **creditor's bill; garnishment; judgment creditor; lien; sheriff's sale; writ of execution.** Compare **bankruptcy.**

JUDICIAL DISCRETION see **discretion.**

JUDICIAL NOTICE the court's recognition of facts that can be confirmed by consulting sources of unquestioned accuracy, thus removing the burden of producing **evidence** to prove these facts. A court can admit facts that are common knowledge to an average, well-informed citizen.

EXAMPLE: Doug claims that on the day of the accident the roads were very slick as a result of a torrential downpour. However, the victim of the accident brings in several weather maps and reports showing that for seven days prior to and including the day of the accident, there was not a single raindrop. A court can take *judicial notice* of the maps and reports.

JUDICIAL SALE see **sale [FORCED SALE].**

JUMP BAIL colloquial expression meaning to leave the **jurisdiction** or to avoid **appearance** as a **defendant** in a **criminal** trial after **bail** has been posted, thus causing a **forfeiture** of bail; to **abscond** after the posting of bail. See also **flight.**

JURAT *(jūr'-ät)* Lat.: has been sworn; The clause at the end of an **affidavit** with the date, location and person before whom the statement was sworn.

JURISDICTION 1. power to hear and determine a case; may be established and described with reference to a particular subject or to parties in a particular category. In addition to power to adjudicate, a valid exercise of jurisdiction requires fair **notice** and opportunity for affected parties to be heard. 2. the geographic or political entity governed by a particular legal system or body of laws.

APPELLATE JURISDICTION the power vested in a superior **tribunal** to correct legal errors of inferior tribunals and to revise their **judgments** accordingly.

CONCURRENT JURISDICTION equal jurisdiction; jurisdiction exercisable by different courts at the same time, over the same subject matter and within the same territory, so that litigants may, in the first instance, resort to either court.

DIVERSITY JURISDICTION jurisdiction that federal courts have when the opposing parties are from different states.

IN PERSONAM JURISDICTION jurisdiction over the person of the **defendant;** necessary where the action is **in personam.**

SUBJECT MATTER JURISDICTION the **competency** of the court to hear and determine a particular category of cases.

See also **ancillary jurisdiction; federal question jurisdiction; limited jurisdiction; original jurisdiction; pendent jurisdiction.**

JURISDICTIONAL AMOUNT the minimum value a lawsuit must have for certain courts to have **jurisdiction** to hear the case. The method of determining the jurisdictional amount may vary with the nature of the case; it may be the amount of **damages** claimed, money demanded, the value of **property** in disputed ownership, or the value of a claimed right. In some classes of federal cases, for example, a minimum amount of $10,000 must be in controversy to confer jurisdiction on the federal courts.

JURISPRUDENCE 1. the science of law; the study of the structure of legal systems, such as equity, and of the principles underlying that system; 2. a collective term denoting the course of judicial decision, i.e., case law, as opposed to legislation; 3. sometimes a synonym for law.

JURIST 1. a legal scholar; one versed in law, particularly the **civil law** or the law of nations; 2. a judge.

JUROR 1. person sworn as member of a **jury;** 2. person selected for jury duty, but not yet chosen for a particular case.

JURY a group, composed of the peers of the **parties** or a cross section of the community, summoned and sworn to decide on the facts in issue at a **trial.**

BLUE RIBBON JURY a jury that was chosen from prominent members of the community, such as well-educated persons or persons in positions of high responsibility, thought to be particularly well qualified to serve as jurors. These juries were used for certain highly publicized cases where ordinary juries were thought to be too influenced to judge impartially. Such special juries raised serious constitutional questions of the right to trial by a jury of one's peers and so are no longer used.

EXAMPLE: The murder of a beautiful actress made headlines and television reports across the nation. When someone was finally arrested for the crime, a *blue ribbon jury* was chosen from among bankers, doctors and leaders of the business community. These people were selected for their perceived ability to separate the news stories from the facts they would hear at trial.

GRAND JURY a jury to determine whether the facts and accusations presented by the **prosecutor** warrant an **indictment** and eventual trial of the **accused;** called grand because of the relatively large number of jurors **impaneled** (traditionally twenty-three) as compared with a petit jury.

PETIT (PETTY) JURY. ordinary trial jury, whose function is to determine issues of fact in **civil** and **criminal** cases and to reach a **verdict** in conjunction with those **findings.** While the number of jurors has historically been twelve, many states now permit six-member juries in civil cases, and some states permit six-member juries to hear criminal cases as well.

JURY OF THE VICINAGE literally, a jury from the neighborhood where a crime was committed; a jury of peers. See **vicinage.**

See also **evidence; hung jury.**

JUST COMPENSATION full **indemnity** for the loss or damage sustained by the owner of property taken or injured under the power of **eminent domain.** The measure generally used is the fair **market value** of the property at the time of taking.

JUS TERTII *(yūs tĕr′-shē-ī)* Lat.: the right of a third; the legal right of a third. The term often appears in the context of **actions** involving claims of **title** to **real property,** where it is said that because a possessor's title is good against all the world except those with a better title, one seeking to oust a possessor must do so on the strength of his own title, and may not rely on a jus tertii, or the better title held by a third party.

JUSTICE OF THE PEACE a judicial officer of inferior rank, who presides in a court of statutorily limited **civil jurisdiction** and who is also a conservator of the peace with limited jurisdiction in criminal **proceedings, prosecutions,** and commitment of offenders, as fixed by **statute.**

JUSTICIABLE 1. capable of being tried in a court of law or **equity;** 2. feasible for a court to carry out and enforce its decision, as opposed to having **jurisdiction** — the authority to hear a case. A court can have jurisdiction, but at the same time have a nonjusticiable **issue** before it.

EXAMPLE: A governor is required by law to extradite a person sought by another state when that state institutes proper legal proceedings. Still, the governor may decide not to extradite if, for example, he sees an obvious life-threatening situation should the person be returned to the state seeking him. In such instances, a court will usually deem the failure to extradite as a *nonjusticiable* controversy and will take no action to force the governor to extradite.

JUSTICIABLE CONTROVERSY a real **controversy** appropriate for judicial determination, as distinguished from a hypothetical dispute; a dispute that involves legal relations of **parties** who have real adverse **interests,** and upon whom **judgment** may effectively operate through a conclusive **decree.**

JUSTIFIABLE HOMICIDE see **homicide.**

JUSTIFICATION 1. just and lawful cause or excuse; 2. showing in court sufficient reason the **defendant** did what he is called upon to **answer** to, so as to excuse liability.

JUVENILE COURTS tribunals designed to treat **youthful offenders** separately from adults. The purpose of this has been to place the state, through the presiding judge, in the position of **parens patriae,** to replace the adversary nature of normal proceedings with paternal concern for the child's wellbeing.

JUVENILE DELINQUENT a **minor** who has committed an offense ordinarily punishable by criminal processes, but who is under the age, set by **statute,** for criminal responsibility. When a juvenile commits an offense it is considered an act of JUVENILE DELINQUENCY. See **juvenile courts.**

K

KANGAROO COURT a court that has no legal authority and that disregards all the rights normally afforded to persons; its conclusions are not legally binding. This is a slang term referring to a court that is biased against a party and thus renders an unfair **verdict** or **judgment.**

KIDNAPPING unlawful carrying away of a person against his will; **false imprisonment** coupled with removal of the victim to another place. Kidnapping was only a **misdemeanor** in **common law,** but is a serious **felony** in the United States. Compare **abduction.** See **ransom.**

KING'S BENCH [QUEEN'S BENCH] Court of King's Bench or Court of Queen's Bench (depending on the reigning monarch); the highest English **common law** court, both civil and criminal, so called because the king or queen formerly presided; now known as the King's Bench or Queen's Bench Division of the High Court of Justice, embracing the **jurisdiction** of the former Courts of Exchequer and Courts of Common Pleas.

KNOWINGLY see **mens rea.**

L

LABOR UNION an association of workers for the purpose, in whole or in part, of bargaining on behalf of workers with employers about the terms and conditions of employment.

LACHES a doctrine providing a party an **EQUITABLE DEFENSE** (see **defense**) where long-neglected rights are sought to be enforced against him. Laches signifies an undue lapse of time in enforcing a right of **action,** and **negligence** in failing to act more promptly. It recognizes that on account of the delay the defendant's ability to defend may be unfairly impaired because **witnesses** or **evidence** may have become unavailable or been lost. The doctrine also recognizes that if the delay has led the adverse party to change his position as to the **property** or right in question, it is inequitable to allow the negligent delaying party to be preferred in his legal right. The consequent barring of the negligent party's action is a kind of equitable **estopel** known as **ESTOPPEL BY LACHES.**

EXAMPLE: Believing that he had good title to property, Jason constructs an office building and fully rents it out. George watches Jason construct the building and waits an additional ten years before asserting an ownership interest in the property. A court might apply the doctrine of *laches* and bar George's claim for two reasons. George was aware of the construction and took no action until the building was completed, a point at which Jason had invested a considerable amount of money. Also, George took an inordinate amount of time to raise his claim.

LAND 1. **real estate** or **real property,** or any tract that may be **conveyed** by **deed.** 2. an **estate** or **interest** in real property; often refers not only to the earth itself but also to things of a permanent nature found or affixed there.

LANDLORD one who leases **real property.** See **lease.**

LAPSE to expire. Generally refers to termination of a right or **privilege** that can no longer be exercised because of a particular contingency or the passage of time.

EXAMPLE: Fred signs a thirty-day option to purchase a home. That option gives him the exclusive right to purchase the home within thirty days. If thirty days expire and Fred does not purchase the house, the option *lapses*.

LARCENY the **felonious** taking and carrying away of the **personal property** of another, without his consent, by a person not entitled to **possession,** with intent to deprive the owner of the property and to convert it to the use of the taker or another person other than the owner.

Larceny is sometimes classified as either **GRAND LARCENY** or **PETIT (PETTY) LARCENY,** according to the value of the property taken or the method employed. Compare **embezzlement.**

LAST ANTECEDENT DOCTRINE in statutory **construction,** the doctrine under which relative or modifying phrases are to be applied only to words immediately preceding them, and are not to be construed as extending to more remote phrases unless this is clearly required by the context of the statute or the reading of it as a whole.

LAST CLEAR CHANCE the doctrine that a **defendant** may still be **liable** for the injuries he caused, even though the **plaintiff** was guilty of **CONTRIBUTORY NEGLIGENCE** (see **negligence**), if the defendant could have avoided injury to the plaintiff by exercising ordinary care at the last moment and after the plaintiff's negligence had ceased.

EXAMPLE: A passerby without a hard hat walks on a construction site that is clearly marked ''Hard Hats Required.'' A worker is throwing garbage out of a window so that it will fall into a garbage dump below. One of the pieces of garbage hits the passerby. Although the passerby is at fault for not wearing a hard hat, the worker may be held liable since he had the *last clear chance* to avoid the injury either by being more careful with the garbage or by carrying it to the dump site.

LAST-IN, FIRST-OUT [LIFO] see **first-in, first-out.**

LAST WILL AND TESTAMENT see **will.**

LATENT DEFECT a defect that is hidden from knowledge as well as from sight and one that would not be discovered even by the exercise of ordinary and reasonable care.

EXAMPLE: A part of a new car engine was prone to wearing down after a few hundred miles, causing the engine to stop immediately. The part was inside the engine and could not be detected by even a very thorough examination unless the engine was dismantled. The faulty part was a *latent defect* of the engine.

Compare **patent defect.** See also **warranty [WARRANTY OF HABITABILITY].**

LAW 1. the legislative pronouncement of rules to guide one's actions in society; 2. the total of those rules of conduct put in force by legislative authority or court decisions, or established by local custom.

AT LAW see **at law.**

LAW MERCHANT a body of **commercial law** governing merchants in England, particularly noted for contributions to the law of **negotiable instruments.** The law merchant was the **common law's** recognition of usages and procedures that had developed over a long period among merchants in England and other European countries. As part of the common law of England, it was incorporated into American law and has been largely supplemented by common law evolution and statutory enactment.

LAW OF ADMIRALTY see **maritime law.**

LAW OF THE CASE doctrine whereby courts will refuse to consider matters of law that have been already **adjudicated**

by **motion** or **appeal** in the same cause; reflects the courts' unwillingness to reopen **issues** already finally determined in a suit.

EXAMPLE: A judge schedules a pre-trial hearing to decide what evidence will be allowed at trial. Each party is given an opportunity to make arguments, and the judge decides not to allow a statement by one of the plaintiff's witnesses. At trial, the plaintiff attempts to argue for the introduction of the statement. Because of the pre-trial decision, the judge applies the *law of the case* doctrine and refuses to allow the introduction of the statement.

Compare **collateral** [COLLATERAL ESTOPPEL]; **double jeopardy.**

LAW OF THE LAND 1. phrase first used in **Magna Carta** to refer to the then established law of the kingdom as distinguished from Roman or **civil law;** 2. today, basic principles of justice in agreement with **due process of law;** those rights that the legislature cannot abolish or significantly limit, because they are fundamental to our system of liberty and justice. 3. the law as developed by the courts or in **statutes** in pursuance of those basic principles or rights. The United States Constitution (Article 6, Section 2) establishes itself, and laws made under its authority, and treaties of the United States, as the "supreme law of the land."

LAWSUIT see **suit.**

LEADING QUESTION a question posed by a trial lawyer that is sometimes improper because it suggests to the **witness** the answer he is to deliver, or in effect prompts answers in disregard of actual memory.

EXAMPLE: In direct examination during the trial, the witness is asked, "Isn't it true that you saw Rich standing outside the store waiting for a friend when the robbery occurred?" That question will be objected to as a *leading question* since it suggests to the witness how he should explain or recall the event, instead of simply inquiring how the event actually took place. However, leading questions are proper as part of cross-examination since the object of such examination is to test the credibility of the statement made during direct examination.

LEASE 1. an agreement by the **lessor** temporarily to give up **possession** of **property** while retaining legal ownership (**title**); 2. an agreement by the owner **landlord** to turn over, for all purposes not prohibited by terms of the lease, specifically described **premises** to the exclusive possession of the **lessee** for a definite period and for a **consideration** called **rent.**

PROPRIETARY LEASE the kind of lease that the resident/stockholder in a cooperative apartment maintains, with the cooperative as owner of the building. See **condominium.**

LEASEHOLD the **estate** in **real property** of a **lessee,** created by a **lease;** generally an estate of fixed duration, but may also describe **tenancy at will,** a month-to-month tenancy, PERIODIC *tenancy*, etc. (see **tenancy**).

LEGACY a disposition by **will** of **personal property;** synonymous with **bequest,** but properly distinguished from **devise,** which is a disposition of **real property.**

LEGATEE recipient of personal property by virtue of a will—i.e., the recipient of a legacy.

LEGAL AID SOCIETY state-funded and state-administered offices established throughout the country to deliver legal services to financially needy **litigants,** that is, those unable to afford to retain private **counsel.**

LEGAL DUTY that which the law requires be done or forborne. **Breach** of a legal duty owed another is an element of **negligence** and is the essence of most actions in **tort.** Legal duties not otherwise imposed may be created by a **contract** or by one's entering into some other such relationship (**landlord-tenant,** host-**invitee,** etc.).

EXAMPLE: In an apartment house, a landlord usually has the *legal duty* to keep the common areas, such as a hallway, clean and in good repair. If a tenant injures himself because a light bulb in a hallway has gone out and the landlord has been made aware that the bulb is not working, the landlord's breach of the legal duty makes him liable.

LEGAL FICTION a fact presumed in law, regardless of its truth, for the purpose of justice or convenience. For example, the **domicile** of the owner is presumed to be the situs of **personal property** for taxing purposes regardless of where it is actually located. The term legal fiction commonly occurs in cases where adherence to the fiction is perceived as working an injustice. Thus, when the personal property has never been in the state where the owner is domiciled and it would clearly be unfair to tax the property, the court will dispense with the situs presumption as a mere legal fiction.

LEGAL IMPOSSIBILITY see **impossibility.**

LEGAL SEPARATION see **divorce** [SEPARATION]; **separation agreement.**

LEGAL TENDER the kind of money lawfully acceptable for payment of a **debt** where the medium of payment is not specified by **statute** or agreement. All legal tender is money, but not all money is legal tender. Congress has the power to determine what is legal tender. All coins and paper money of the United States, as well as **Federal Reserve** notes and circulating notes of Federal Reserve banks and national banking associations, are legal tender.

LEGATEE one who takes a **legacy.**

LESSEE one who holds an **estate** by virtue of a **lease;** the **tenant** of a **landlord.**

LESSER-INCLUDED OFFENSE 1. a violation of law that is necessarily established by proof of a greater **offense** and that is properly submitted to the **jury,** should the **prosecution's** proof fail to establish **guilt** of the greater offense charged, without necessity of multiple **indictment;** 2. that necessarily committed lesser offense accompanying the conduct leading to a greater offense.

EXAMPLE: Jenny is charged with robbery, which is the taking of property by threat or fear of violence. If Jenny cannot be convicted of robbery because there is insufficient proof of a threat or fear, she could still be convicted of larceny, which is simply the taking of another's property. Larceny is a *lesser-included offense* in relation to robbery.

See also **graded offense; plea bargaining.**

LESSOR one who grants a **lease** to another, therby transferring to him exclusive temporary right of **possession** of certain **property,** subject only to rights expressly retained by the owner.

LET to **lease;** 1. to grant the use of **realty** for a compensation. 2. The term does not always connote the act of leasing, but the granting of a **license.**

LETTER OF CREDIT in commercial law, a promise by a bank or other issuer that it will honor on behalf of one of its customer's demands for payment upon compliance with specified conditions; intended to facilitate long-distance sales by allowing a buyer to establish a credit line against which a seller can draw. Letters of credit guard against risk **insolvency** and uncertainty in delivery and settlement due to market fluctuations.

LETTERS ROGATORY see **rogatory letters.**

LETTER STOCK a category of stock that derives its name from an inscription on the face of the **stock certificate,** indicating that the shares have not been registered with the **Securities and Exchange Commission** and, therefore, cannot be sold to the general public.

LEVERAGE the use of **debt** to finance **capital investment,** for the purpose of increasing the investor's rate of return on his **equity.** As long as the return income and appreciation on the total investment exceed the interest paid on the borrowed money, the investor benefits.

LEVY 1. to raise or collect; 2. to seize; 3. to assess, as to levy a tax; 4. a seizure or levying, as of land or other **property** or rights, through lawful **process** or by force. When one places a levy upon some property, right or a CHOSE IN ACTION (see **chose**), it is seized and may be sold to satisfy a **judgment.** See **writ of execution.**

LEX LOCI DELICTI *(lŏks lō'-kē dĕ-lĭk'-tē)* Lat.: law of the place of the wrong. See **conflict of laws.**

LEX LOCI CONTRACTUS *(lĕks lō'-kē kŏn-trăk'-tūs)* Lat.: law of the place of making a contract. See **conflict of laws.**

LIABILITY 1. an **obligation** to do or refrain from doing something; 2. a **duty** that eventually must be performed; 3. an obligation to pay money; 4. money owed, as opposed to an **asset;** 5. responsibility for one's conduct, such as **contractual** liability, **tort** liability, **criminal** liability, etc. See **limited liability; strict liability; vicarious liability.**

EXAMPLE: Lauren runs a red light and hits another car, injuring both the driver and the passenger. Lauren has incurred *tort liability* for her action.

CURRENT LIABILITIES in accounting, **debts** due within one year, including salary payable to employees, purchase costs payable to suppliers, taxes and annual portion due on long-term debt.

LONG-TERM LIABILITIES in accounting, debts due after one year, including term bank loans, **mortgages** payable, **bonds** outstanding and liabilities under long-term **lease** and rental agreements.

LIABILITY WITHOUT FAULT see **strict liability.**

LIABLE responsible for; obligated in law.

LIBEL a **tort** consisting of a false, **malicious,** unprivileged publication aiming to defame a living person or to mar the memory of one dead. Printed or written material, signs or pictures that tend to expose a person to public scorn, hatred, contempt or ridicule may be considered libelous.

EXAMPLE: A candidate for public office reads in the paper of an earlier conviction against him for bribery. After some investigation, the candidate finds out that Vic, who is in contact with his opponent, had planted the story, which is unquestionably false, in order to ruin the candidate's standing in the election. The candidate can sue Vic or the newspaper for *libel.*

See **slander.** Compare **privileged communications.**

LIBERTY freedom; the ability to enjoy all the rights granted by the United States and a particular state's constitution, as well as other rights such as the right to earn a living, the right to acquire knowledge, the right to marry, etc.; refers to the fullest scope of freedoms one has but at the same time limits those freedoms so as not to interfere with another person's exercise of them.

LICENSE a grant of permission needed to legalize doing a particular thing, exercising a certain privilege or pursuing a particular business or occupation. Licenses may be granted by private persons or by governmental authority.

In the law of **property,** a license is a personal privilege or permission with respect to some use of **land,** and is revocable at the will of the landowner. The privilege attaches only to the party holding it and not to the land itself, since, unlike an **easement,** a license does not represent an **estate** or **interest** in the land.

EXAMPLE: When Linda opens a new shop in a small shopping center, a neighboring businessman gives her *license* to use some of his storage space. The businessman can deny Linda the use of that space at any time, and, most importantly, if Linda ever sells her store, she could not guarantee that storage space to the purchaser.

Compare **franchise; lease; monopoly.**

LICENSEE one to whom a **license** has been granted; in **property,** one whose presence on the **premises** is not invited, but tolerated. Thus, a licensee is neither a customer, nor a servant, nor a **trespasser,** and does not stand in any contractual relation with the owner of the premises, but is permitted expressly or impliedly to go upon the property of another merely for his own interest, convenience, or gratification. Compare **invitee.**

LICENSER one who grants a **license.**

LIE DETECTOR TEST see **polygraph.**

LIEN a charge, hold or claim upon the **property** of another as **security** for some **debt** or charge. The term connotes the right the law gives to have a debt satisfied out of the property to which it attaches, if necessary by the sale of the property.

EQUITABLE LIEN a right in **equity,** but not **at law,** to have specific property applied in satisfaction of a debt. Whenever parties enter into an agreement indicating an intention to post some particular property as security for an obligation, an equitable lien is created on such property. An equitable lien may also be created by implication and is based on the doctrine of **unjust enrichment.**

FACTOR'S LIEN a lien that the **factor** has on goods **consigned** to him while in his possession for any advances made by him and for his **commissions.** In **common law,** it was purely a possessory lien and was lost by surrender of **possession,** but today, under the Uniform Commercial Code, a written security agreement is a sufficient substitute for possession.

FEDERAL TAX LIEN a lien of the United States on all property and rights to property of a taxpayer who fails to pay a tax for which he is liable to the federal government.

FLOATING LIEN in commercial law, one that covers not only inventory and accounts possessed by the debtor at the time of the original loan, but also his **after-acquired property** of inventory or accounts. The floating lien allows a buyer's operations to be completely financed with periodic advances and repayments secured by changing **collateral** of raw materials, work in progress, finished goods, proceeds, etc. This financing may be accomplished in a single security agreement, with only one filing required.

LANDLORD'S LIEN in common law, the **landlord's** right to **levy (distress)** upon the **goods** of a **tenant** in satisfaction of unpaid **rents** or property damage; now generally a statutory lien giving the **lessor** status of a preferred **creditor** with regard to the **lessee's** property.

MECHANIC'S LIEN one created to secure **priority** of payment for value of work performed and materials furnished in erecting or repairing a structure; attaches to the land as well as its buildings and improvements. **Statutes** according priority to the satisfaction of the debt represented by a mechanic's lien are found in most **jurisdictions** and extend to automobiles and other goods as well as to structures. As applied to automobiles, the claim is sometimes called **GARAGEMAN'S LIEN.**

EXAMPLE: Standard Heating and Air Conditioning Company has installed all the ventilation in an office complex. The owner of the complex falls into bankruptcy and cannot pay Standard. By operation of the law of the state in which the work was done, Standard has a *mechanic's lien* equalling the value of the work it performed. That lien attaches to the office complex, so that Standard has a priority of payment for any money that is paid to the complex.

LIEN JURISDICTION **jurisdiction** in which **title** to the **mortgaged premises** remains with the **mortgagor** pending payment of the mortgage price. See **title jurisdiction.**

LIFE ESTATE an **estate** whose duration is limited by the life of the person holding it or by that of some other person **[per autre vie].** It is a **freehold** interest in land.

EXAMPLE: A grandfather conveys his summer home to his daughter for life and then to his three grandchildren. Since the daughter's interest in the house exists only so long as she is alive, her interest is considered a *life estate*.

LIFO last-in, first-out. See **first-in, first-out.**

LIMITATIONS PERIOD see **statute of limitations.**

LIMITATIONS, STATUTE OF see **statute of limitations.**

LIMITED JURISDICTION refers to courts that are only authorized to hear and decide certain or special types of cases; also known as SPECIAL JURISDICTION. See **jurisdiction.**

EXAMPLE: The **Court of Claims** has *limited jurisdiction* to only hear claims against the United States based on certain types of violations.

A small claims court is limited to a specified dollar amount that it can litigate.

LIMITED LIABILITY the limitation placed on the amount an investor of a corporation can lose resulting from a lawsuit against the corporation or other loss suffered by the corporation; the **liability** for losses that is limited to the amount an investor or shareholder invests in the corporation. The corporation itself also enjoys limited liability inasmuch as the corporation's obligations are always limited to its **assets** unless, with regard to particular transactions, personal responsibility is assumed by an officer or shareholder of the corporation.

EXAMPLE: Phil purchases ten shares of a corporation's stock for $5 a share. If the corporation becomes bankrupt with many creditors who are unpaid, Phil's *liability* is *limited* to the $50 he invested. He can never be charged for a greater amount.

LIMITED PARTNERSHIP see **partnership.**

LINEAL refers to **descent** by a direct line of **succession** in ancestry.

LINEUP the police procedure in which a person suspected of a crime is placed in a line with several other persons and a witness to the crime attempts to identify the suspect as the person who committed the crime. The procedure must not be "unduly suggestive," or the identification will not be admissible in a criminal trial.

LIQUIDATE to settle; to determine the amount due, and to whom due, and then to extinguish the indebtedness. Although the term more properly signifies the adjustment or settlement of **debts,** to liquidate often means to pay.

LIQUIDATE A BUSINESS to assemble and mobilize the **assets** of the business, settle with **creditors** and **debtors,** and apportion remaining assets, if any, among the **shareholders** or owners.

LIQUIDATE A CLAIM to determine by agreement or **litigation** the precise amount of the claim, and to settle it on the basis of that determination.

LIQUIDATED DAMAGES a stipulated **contractual** amount that the **parties** agree is a reasonable estimation of the **damages** owing to one in the event of a **breach** by the other.

EXAMPLE: Safety Corporation and Fire Prevention, Inc., enter into a long-term contract whereby Fire Prevention supplies Safety with all the sprinkler systems safety needs. Instead of leaving a damage figure to a court decision if either party should breach the agreement, the parties include a *liquidated damages* clause in the contract. That clause provides both a dollar figure and a formula for calculating damages, with the higher of the two figures constituting the maximum damages either party could charge.

LIQUIDATION DIVIDEND see **dividend.**

LIS PENDENS *(lēs pĕn'-dĕns)* Lat.: a pending lawsuit. Refers to the maxim that pending the **suit** nothing should be changed; thus, for example, one who acquired an interest in **property** from a party to **litigation** respecting such property takes that interest subject to the **decree** or **judgment** in such litigation and is bound by it.

NOTICE OF LIS PENDENS in in some **jurisdictions,** a publicly recorded notice required to warn persons (such as prospective purchasers) that **title** to the property is in litigation and that they will be bound by a possibly adverse judgment.

LISTED STOCK a company's stock that is traded on an organized **stock exchange.** To be listed, the company must meet requirements of the selected exchange and file application for listing with both the exchange and the **Securities and Exchange Commission.**

LITE PENDENTE see **pendente lite.**

LITIGANTS the parties actively involved in a lawsuit; **plaintiffs** or **defendants** involved in **litigation.**

LITIGATION a judicial contest aiming to determine and enforce legal rights.

LIVING TRUST see **trust.**

LOBBYIST one engaged in the business of persuading legislators to pass laws that are favorable, and to defeat those that are unfavorable, to the interests of the lobbyist or of his clients.

LOCO PARENTIS see **in loco parentis.**

LOCUS *(lō'-kŭs)* Lat.: the place.

LOCUS CONTRACTUS *(kŏn-trăk'-tūs)* Lat.: the place where the contract was made.

LOCUS DELICTI *(dĕ-lĭk'-tē)* Lat.: the place where the wrong occurred.

LOCUS IN QUO *(ĭn kwō)* Lat.: the place where or in which. Refers to a locale where an offense was committed or a **cause of action** arose.

LOCUS POENITENTIAE *(pō-ĕ-nĭ-tĕn'-shē-ī)* Lat.: a place for repentance. The opportunity for one to change his mind.

LOCUS SIGILLI *(sĭ-jĭl'-lē)* Lat.: the place of the **seal;** usually abbreviated L.S. Commonly used within brackets on copies of documents to indicate the position of the seal in the original; also used to call attention of the signer to the place for his seal.

LOGROLLING refers to schemes by legislators to force passage of desired bills without convincing their colleagues of the merits of their proposals. One type of logrolling is the inclusion under one bill of secondary bills, each of which probably would not be approved if voted on singly.

EXAMPLE: Conservative legislators are finding it very difficult to get their bills passed on the strength of the bills' own merits. In an attempt to sidestep this problem, the legislators tack their proposals onto a tax bill that has to be passed or government employees cannot be paid. This attempt is called *logrolling*.

Another practice is for legislators to agree to vote for each other's bills, even if neither has any interest in the other's bill.

LOITER to linger for no evident reason, particularly in a public place, near a school or a transportation facility. There are criminal prohibitions of such behavior as loitering for purposes of begging, gambling, soliciting another to engage in sexual intercourse, or for the purpose of selling or using drugs; being masked or disguised in an unusual manner; or simply not being able to give a satisfactory explanation of one's behavior. Compare **probable cause; void for vagueness.**

LONG-ARM STATUTES laws that allow a local **forum** to obtain **jurisdiction** over nonresident **defendants** when the **cause of action** is generated locally and affects local **plaintiffs.** Such expanded jurisdiction is authorized where the contacts of the nonresident defendant with the forum are regarded as sufficiently substantial.

EXAMPLE: Federated Television Company sells many televisions in a particular state, but the company does not maintain any sales offices, have any corporate headquarters or employ any sales agents in the state. When one of its televisions explodes and burns down Bob's house, Bob can use the state's *long-arm statute* to bring Federated into the state court. Without the statute, there may be a procedural difficulty in forcing Federated to come in to Bob's state and defend against the action or pay for the damages caused.

Long-arm statutes are commonly employed to allow a local court to exercise jurisdiction over nonresident motorists who cause automobile accidents within the state.

LONG-TERM CAPITAL GAIN see **capital; capital gains or losses.**

LOST PROPERTY **property** involuntarily lost to the owner through neglect, carelessness or oversight. Compare **abandonment; mislaid property.**

M

MAGISTRATE 1. a public **civil** officer, invested with some part of the legislative, executive or judicial power. 2. In a narrower sense, the term includes only inferior judicial officers, such as **justices of the peace.**

MAGNA CARTA [MAGNA CHARTA] the "great charter" to which King John gave his assent in 1215, and which is considered the fundamental guarantee of rights and privileges under English law.

MAIL BOX RULE a rule that an **acceptance** made in response to an **offer** is valid and forms a binding **contract** at the time of dispatch of the acceptance, as when it is placed in the mailbox, if that method of accepting is a reasonable response to the offer.

MAINTENANCE see **criminal maintenance.**

MAJORITY, AGE OF the age when a person is considered legally responsible for all his activities and becomes entitled to the legal rights held by citizens generally.

MAKER in commercial law, he who **executes** a **note,** or **indorses** it before its delivery to the **payee,** and who thereby assumes an absolute obligation to make payment on the note.

EXAMPLE: Before a supplier ships any goods to Creative Bottle Company, the supplier requires the company to sign a promissory note explaining payment terms and dates and also obliging Creative Bottle to meet those terms. Creative Bottle is the *maker* of the note since it is the one who has to make the payments.

MALFEASANCE 1. the doing of a wrongful and unlawful act; 2. any wrongful conduct that interrupts or interferes with the performance of official duty.

MALICE the state of mind that accompanies the intentional doing of a wrongful act without **justification** and in **wanton** or **willful** disregard of the plain likelihood that harm will result.

With respect to **slander** and **libel,** malice is the mental state that accompanies a false statement when the maker knows it to be false or when the maker recklessly disregards the truth or falsity of it. **Tort liability** may also attend the malicious disclosure of true but private facts.

In **malicious prosecution,** there is intent to institute a **prosecution** for a purpose other than bringing an offender to justice.

MALICE AFORETHOUGHT the distinguishing state of mind that may render **homicide murder** in common law; characterized by a life-endangering mental disposition for which there is no justification. Compare **manslaughter; premeditation.**

MALICIOUS ARREST the arresting of a person on a criminal **charge** without **probable cause,** with knowledge that the person did not commit the offense charged. See **malicious prosecution.** Compare **false arrest.**

MALICIOUS PROSECUTION an action for recovery of **damages** that have resulted to person, **property** or reputation from previous unsuccessful **civil** or criminal **proceedings** that were prosecuted without **probable cause** and with **malice.**

EXAMPLE: Martha wants to persuade her estranged husband Peter to pay her generous alimony and child support. She contrives a story, which she tells the local prosecutor, connecting Peter with child abuse. Her misuse of the criminal process is an example of *malicious prosecution,* for which Peter may be able to sue her.

MALPRACTICE a professional's improper or immoral conduct in the performance of his duties, done either intentionally or through carelessness or ignorance; commonly applied to physicians, surgeons, dentists, lawyers and public officers to denote negligent or unskillful performance of duties where professional skills are obligatory on account of the **fiduciary** relationship with patients or clients.

MALUM IN SE *(mă'-lŭm ĭn sā)* Lat.: evil in itself. Evil, as adjudged by a civilized community; refers to an act or case involving conduct punishable because of the nature of the conduct, not only because the law has declared it punishable.

MALUM PROHIBITUM *(mă'-lŭm prō-hĭ'-bĭ-tŭm)* Lat.: wrong because it is prohibited. Made unlawful by **statute** for the public welfare, but not inherently evil and not involving **moral turpitude.** Compare **malum in se.**

MANDAMUS Lat.: we command. An extraordinary **writ,** issued from a court to an official, compelling performance of an act that the law recognizes as an absolute duty, as distinct from acts that may be at the official's discretion.

EXAMPLE: A state legislature passes a law which provides that, upon request, a person has the right to see any information the government has on file for that person. Kathy files such a request with the State's Attorney General and is refused access to her information. Unless the refusing party can show some compelling need for secrecy, a court will issue a writ of *mandamus* to the holder of the records, directing him to release the information.

See **ministerial act.**

MANDATE a judicial command; 1. an official mode of communicating the **judgment** of the **appellate court** to the lower court; 2. a **bailment** of something for the performance of some **gratuitous** service with respect to it by the **bailee.**

MANDATORY INJUNCTION see **injunction.**

MANN ACT a federal statute prohibiting the transportation of a woman or girl in interstate or foreign commerce for the purpose of **prostitution,** debauchery or any other immoral purpose; also known as the WHITE SLAVE TRAFFIC ACT.

MANSLAUGHTER unlawful killing of another person without **malice** aforethought; distinguished from **murder** with possible attendant death penalty; an explainable, less extreme **homicide.** Most **jurisdictions** distinguish between voluntary and involuntary manslaughter. VOLUNTARY MANSLAUGHTER is intentional killing committed under circumstances that, although they do not justify the homicide, reduce its evil intent. A charge of manslaughter is appropriate where the **defendant** killed the victim in rage, terror or desperation. INVOLUNTARY MANSLAUGHTER consists of a homicide resulting from criminal negligence or recklessness.

MARGIN the payment, a percentage of purchase cost, that a buyer of regulated **securities** must make when buying on **credit** from a stock**broker.**

MARITAL DEDUCTION an ESTATE TAX (see **tax**) deduction permitting a spouse to take, tax free, up to one half the value of the decedent spouse's total **estate.** The marital deduction thus permits **property** to pass to the surviving spouse without being depleted by the federal estate tax; enacted for all to have tax treatment similar to that enjoyed by surviving spouses in the several **community property** states, where one half of the decedent's gross estate was presumed by law to already belong to the surviving spouse and hence was not subject to an estate tax.

MARITIME LAW the traditional body of rules and practices related to business transacted at sea or to navigation, ships, seamen, harbors and general maritime affairs. It is, and always has been a body of law separate from every other jurisprudence. See **admiralty and maritime jurisdiction; admiralty courts.**

MARKETABLE TITLE one that a reasonably well-informed purchaser would, in the exercise of ordinary business prudence, be willing to accept. A **title,** to be marketable, need not be free from every technical criticism, but it must be demonstrated to be reasonably free of **encumbrances.**

MARKET VALUE the price that **property** would bring in a market of willing buyers and willing sellers, in the ordinary course of trade. Market value is generally established, if possible, on the basis of sales of similar property in the same locality. Market value is generally regarded as synonymous with **ACTUAL VALUE, CASH VALUE** and **FAIR MARKET VALUE.** See **book value.**

MARRIED WOMEN'S ACTS see **tenancy** [**TENANCY BY THE ENTIRETY**].

MARSHAL 1. an officer of the peace, appointed by authority of a city or borough, to answer calls within the general duties of a constable or sheriff; 2. an officer in each federal district who performs the same duties as sheriffs do for states.

MARSHALING arranging or ranking in order.

MARSHALING ASSETS a rule of ranking assets of a debtor that seeks equitable distribution of those assets among as many claims as possible according to the equities of the parties. Courts of equity sometimes invoke the rule to compel a **creditor,** who has the right to satisfy his **debt** out of either of two funds, to resort to the fund that will not interfere with the rights of another creditor who has recourse to only one of these funds.

EXAMPLE: When Triad Corporation goes bankrupt, it owes money to both secured and unsecured creditors. The secured creditors have priority claims over specific property, while the unsecured creditors get paid only after all secured creditors are paid. One of the secured creditors has a claim on Triad's computers. If that creditor now wants to satisfy its debt with something other than the computers and that action will adversely affect the unsecured creditors, a court might apply the rule of *marshaling assets* to force that creditor to take the computers. Under that rule, both types of creditors have a better chance of having their claims satisfied.

Probate courts marshall assets to meet the stated wishes of a **testator** (testatrix) in a **will** when appointed property (property disposed of in the will by **power of appointment**) would, because of technical impediments, pass into an inappropriate **residuary clause** rather than be distributed as intended by the testator. Marshaling of assets in probate courts to achieve this objective is also called **SELECTIVE ALLOCATION.**

MARTIAL LAW law of military necessity, where the military exercises great control over civilian affairs, generally because of war or civil insurrection. When instituted, martial law represents the unchecked will of the commander, controlled only by consideration of strategy and policy. In America, the President, as Commander-in-Chief of the Armed Forces, would assume unreviewable discretion were martial law declared. Compare **separation of powers.** See also **court-marshal.**

MASSACHUSETTS TRUST a business **trust** that confers limited liability on the holders of trust certificates; also called a common law trust; a voluntary association of investors who transfer contributed cash or other property to trustees with legal authority to manage the business. Ownership **interest** is represented by transferable certificates of beneficial interest, also called trust certificates, and, less properly, **shares.** The business trust is a common form of organization among **real estate investment trusts (REITs).**

MASTER [MASTER IN CHANCERY; SPECIAL MASTER] 1. a judicial officer, often expert in the field with which the litigation is concerned, appointed by **courts of equity** to hear **testimony** and make reports that, when approved by the presiding judge, become the decision of the courts; 2. the employer in an employment relationship. See **master and servant.**

MASTER AND SERVANT the relation that develops from an **express** or **implied** employment **contract** between a master, or employer, and a servant, or employee. See **agent; respondeat superior; servant.**

MATERIAL necessary, meaningful, pertinent to a given matter. In contract law, a material **breach** excuses further performance by the **aggrieved party** and can give rise to an **action** for breach of contract.

EXAMPLE: a contract between Plastics, Inc., and a cassette recording company called for twelve separate shipments of plastic cassettes. The first three shipments were defective and were returned to Plastics. The recording company was falling behind in its production schedule when the fourth shipment arrived and that shipment was also defective. The four defective shipments constitute a *material* breach of the contract and permit the company to cancel the contract and perhaps to institute a lawsuit against Plastics as well.

MATERIAL WITNESS see **witness.**

MATTER OF FACT see **question of fact.**

MATTER OF LAW see **question of law.**

MATURITY the date at which legal rights in something ripen. In the context of **commercial paper [negotiable instruments],** it is the time when the paper becomes **due** and demandable, that is, the date when an **action** can enforce payment.

MAXIMS statements espousing general principles of law; not usually used to justify a court decision based on law, but frequently used to determine the equities of a situation.

EXAMPLE: "Equity treats as done what ought to be done": The court will order the party to do what he or she should in good conscience already have done:

"First in time is first in right": If the claim of two parties is equal, the first in time is the party who will normally prevail.

MAYHEM the common law **felony** of **malciously** maiming, dismembering or in any other way depriving another of the use of part of his body so as to render the victim less able to fight in the king's army. Many states today treat mayhem as AGGRAVATED ASSAULT (see **assault**).

MC NABB-MALLORY RULE a judicial policy, based on federal law, that renders **incriminating** statements not **admis-**

sible in federal court if obtained from a suspect held in violation of the speedy **arraignment** provisions of federal law, i.e., if there is unreasonable delay in arraignment.

MECHANIC'S LIEN see **lien.**

MEDIATE DATA facts from which **ultimate facts** may be inferred for purposes of COLLATERAL ESTOPPEL (see **estoppel**).

MEDIATELY indirectly; having been deduced from proven facts.

MEDIATION a method of settling disputes outside of a court setting; the imposition of a neutral THIRD PARTY (see **party**) to act as a link between the parties; similar to **arbitration** and conciliation. Compare **negotiation.**

EXAMPLE: Jane and Ed desire to obtain a divorce. Hoping to avoid undue litigation and emotional trauma, they secure the help of a professional divorce mediator, who attempts a *mediation* of their affairs.

MEETING OF MINDS mutual assent to terms by parties to a **contract.** A traditional rule of contract law is that the agreement, to be legally enforceable, must be accurately expressed within the terms of the contract the parties create for therein lies the required meeting of the minds; a hidden intent of either party will not change the agreement as expressed.

MEMBER BANK a member of the **Federal Reserve System.**

MEMBER CORPORATION a **securities brokerage** firm, organized as a **corporation,** with at least one member of the **New York Stock Exchange** who is a director and a holder of voting **stock** in the corporation. See **member firm.**

MEMBER FIRM a **securities brokerage** firm organized as a **partnership** and having at least one general partner who is a member of the **New York Stock Exchange.** See **member corporation.**

MEMORANDUM 1. an informal record; 2. a brief note, in writing, of some transaction; 3. an outline of an intended instrument; 4. an instrument written in concise summary.

MEMORANDUM OF LAW an argument by an **advocate** in support of his position; like a **brief** but less formal.

OFFICE MEMORANDUM informal discussion of the merits of a matter pending in a lawyer's office; usually written by a law clerk or junior associate for a senior associate or partner.

MEMORANDUM CHECK see **check.**

MENS REA *(mĕns rā'-à)* Lat.: a guilty state of mind. The mental state accompanying a forbidden act. Criminal offenses are usually defined with reference to one of four recognized criminal states of mind: (1) **intent;** (2) knowledge; (3) recklessness; (4) gross (criminal) **negligence.** See **assault; larceny.** Compare **insanity.**

MENTAL ANGUISH compensable **injury** embracing all forms of mental pain, distinguished from physical pain, including deep grief, distress, anxiety and fright. See **pain and suffering.**

MENTAL CRUELTY a ground for **divorce,** consisting of behavior by one spouse toward the other that so imperils the mental and physical health of the other that continuation of the marriage is unbearable.

MERCANTILE LAW the branch of law (often called **commercial law**) that deals with rules and institutions of commercial transactions; derived from the **law merchant.**

MERCHANTABLE 1. salable; 2. reasonably fit for the purpose for which an article is manufactured and sold; 3. having at least average quality, compared to similar products.

MERCHANTABLE TITLE see **marketable title.**

WARRANTY OF MERCHANTABILITY see **warranty.**

MERGER 1. in criminal law, the process by which, when a single criminal act constitutes two offenses, the **lesser-included offense** merges with the more serious offense for purposes of **conviction** and **sentence.**

2. In the law of **corporations,** a merger is effected when one corporation ceases to exist by becoming part of another continuing corporation. The company that continues to exist retains its name and identity and acquires the **assets, liabilities, franchises** and powers of the corporation that ceases to exist. CONSOLIDATION, by contrast, occurs when two or more corporations unite to form a new corporation and all the original corporations cease to exist.

3. Procedurally, merger describes the effect of a **judgment** in a **plaintiff's** favor. Such a judgment extinguishes the entire **claim** or **cause of action** that was the subject of a former action, so that it becomes merged in the judgment. Plaintiff is then precluded from making any further claim that was or could have been part of the action that has been ended.

4. In the conveyancing of **real property,** once the **deed** is accepted, representations and agreements made before delivery of the executed deed are said to merge with the deed, which is the final expression of the mutual rights and obligations of the parties, replacing the contract of sale and other prior understandings.

5. In **property** law, merger is the absorption of a lesser **estate** into a higher estate when the two estates meet in the same person at the same time, without any intermediate estate separating them. Thus, when a TENANT FOR YEARS purchases or **inherits** the **reversion** in **fee simple,** the **tenancy terminates** in ownership.

EXAMPLE: Irwin has the right to possess and use a farm until his death, at which time the land passes to his sister. The sister has no desire to farm or own a country house, so she sells her interest to Irwin. Irwin's right of possession until his death *merges* with the interest he purchases from his sister to give him full ownership of the land forever. The result is that Irwin can now dispose of the property in whatever manner he desires.

Similarly, when the owner of an easement becomes the owner of the land, the easement is terminated by merging into the **possessory interest.**

6. The term also applies to the process by which, since the **Statute of Uses, equitable** ownership becomes legal ownership and conveyance of the former effectively conveys the latter.

MERGER CLAUSE see **parol evidence** [PAROLE EVIDENCE RULE].

MERITS the various elements that qualify **plaintiff's** right to the **relief** sought, or **defendant's** right to prevail in his defense.

MESNE intermediate; between two extremes.

MESNE PROFITS profits obtained from the land by one without legal right to the land and who thus curtails the rights of the owner.

METES AND BOUNDS the territorial limits of property expressed by measuring distances and angles from designated landmarks and in relation to adjoining properties.

MINISTERIAL ACT an act performed according to explicit directions (often embodied in a **statute**) by a subordinate official, allowing no judgment or **discretion** on the part of that official. See **mandamus.**

MINORITY condition of being under legal age.

MINUTES a transcription or other written record of judicial proceedings. While the minutes kept by the **judge** are neither a memorial of the **judgment** nor a legally required **record,** they are legal **evidence** of the **judgment,** and as such they may serve as the foundation for the correction of **errors.**

MIRANDA RULE the requirement to inform a person of his privilege against **self-incrimination** (right to remain silent) and his right to the presence and advice of a retained or appointed attorney before any custodial **interrogation** by law enforcement authorities. Prior to any questioning, the person must also be warned that any statement he does make may be used as **evidence** against him.

Statements and evidence obtained in violation of this rule, unless these rights have been knowingly **waived** (and the evidence voluntarily provided), are not **admissible** in the defendant's criminal **trial** and are grounds for federal constitutional challenge to any **conviction** obtained thereby.

MISADVENTURE an accidental and unintentional homicide, distinguished from involuntary **manslaughter** in that the homicide by misadventure must be the result of a lawful act unaccompanied by criminal carelessness or recklessness.

MISAPPLICATION [MISAPPROPRIATION] OF PROPERTY the conscious illegal use of funds or property for a wrongful purpose; particularly applies to the acts of a **fiduciary** [one in a position of trust], public servants as well as private **trustees.** The terms can include misapplication of funds intended for another purpose, e.g., the misapplication of public money, or the **conversion** of another's funds for one's own benefit. Compare **embezzlement; larceny.**

MISCARRIAGE OF JUSTICE damage to the rights of one **party** to an **action** that results from errors made by the court during trial and that is sufficiently substantial to require **reversal.** Where the **appellate court** is seriously doubtful that without committed errors the result in the case would have been the same, the errors may require a reversal on the grounds of a miscarriage of justice. See **plain error.**

MISCEGENATION in America and England, a marriage between a Caucasian and a member of any of the other races; the mixture of races in a marriage or cohabitation in a state of **adultery** or **fornication** by a white and a black person.

MISDEMEANOR a class of criminal offenses less serious than **felonies** and sanctioned by less severe penalties. In a **jurisdiction** where there are no felonies, the more serious misdemeanors are called **HIGH MISDEMEANORS.**

MISFEASANCE the wrongful or injurious performance of an act that might have been lawfully done.

MISJOINDER 1. the improper joining together in one trial of distinct unrelated **counts** in a single **indictment** or **complaint;** 2. the improper joining of **parties** or criminal **defendants** in a single action. See **joinder.**

MISLAID PROPERTY **property** that the owner has intentionally placed where he can resort to it, but which place is then forgotten. Compare **abandonment; lost property.**

EXAMPLE: Ken inadvertently leaves his briefcase at the train station. Later that evening, Ken realizes he no longer has the briefcase and cannot remember where it is. The briefcase is *mislaid property,* and Ken still has an ownership interest in it. He did not leave the property where he had no intention of recovering it. In that case the property would have been abandoned.

MISNOMER a mistake in a person's name. The **MISNOMER RULE,** which affords relief from the **statute of limitations,** applies when the **plaintiff** has sued and **served** the party he intends to sue but has mistakenly used the wrong name of the **defendant.**

MISPRISION OF FELONY in common law, the **misdemeanor** of observing the committing of a felony and failing to prevent it, or of knowing about a felony and failing to disclose its occurrence, or of concealing the felony without any previous agreement with or subsequent assistance to the **felon** as would make the concealer an **accessory** before- or after-the-fact. Today, to be guilty of the federal crime of misprision of felony, in addition to knowing about a felony and failing to disclose information about it, one must take an affirmative step to conceal it.

EXAMPLE: Mark observes a bank robbery taking place at a federally insured bank. As a believer in the axiom of stealing from the rich to give to the poor, Mark not only does not call the police but picks up a pair of gloves the thieves left behind. Those gloves, which might help solve the crime, are destroyed by Mark. That destruction makes Mark guilty of the federal crime of *misprision of felony*.

MISREPRESENTATION See **false pretense.**

MISTAKE an act or omission arising from ignorance or misconception, which may, depending upon its character or the circumstances surrounding it, justify **rescission** of a **contract,** or exoneration of a **defendant** from **tort** or criminal **liability.**

MISTAKE OF FACT mistaken notion as to circumstances, events or facts.

MISTAKE OF LAW ignorance of the legal consequences of one's conduct, though he may be cognizant of the facts and substance of that conduct. Compare **ignorantia legis non excusat.**

MUTUAL [or BILATERAL] MISTAKE in **commercial law,** an error on the part of both parties regarding the same matter—for example, where both parties understood that the real agreement was what one party alleges it to be, but had unintentionally executed a contract that did not express the true agreement.

EXAMPLE: Steve buys his mother a raincoat for her birthday. The sales person tells him that one size fits all and believes that to be the case. In fact, the particular coat is tailored for a very large person and is manufactured in several different sizes. The mutual *mistake* will allow the sale to be cancelled by Steve even though it was a final sale with no returns.

UNILATERAL MISTAKE a mistake on the part of only one of the parties.

MISTRIAL a **trial** that has been terminated and declared void prior to the **jury's** returning a **verdict** (or the judge's declaring his verdict in a nonjury trial) because of some extraordinary circumstance (such as death or illness of a necessary **juror** or of an attorney), or because of some fundamental error prejudicial to the **defendant** that cannot be cured by appropriate instructions to the jury (such as the inclusion of highly improper remarks in the prosecutor's summation), or most commonly because of the jury's inability to reach a verdict because it is hopelessly deadlocked in its deliberations (**hung jury**). Mistrial does not result in a **judgment** for any party, but merely indicates a failure of **trial.** Compare *double jeopardy*.

MITIGATION OF DAMAGES 1. a requirement that one injured by another's **breach** of an agreement or **tort** employ reasonable diligence and care to avoid aggravating the injury or increasing the **damages;** 2. a defendant's request to the court for a reduction in damages owed to the plaintiff, a request that the defendant justifies by evidence demonstrating that the plaintiff is not entitled to the full amount that might otherwise be awarded.

DUTY TO MITIGATE DAMAGES the rule that in some circumstances one who is wronged must act reasonably to avoid or limit losses, because he cannot recover damages that could have been avoided.

EXAMPLE: Rusty signs a three-year lease with a landlord but has to move out of the apartment after one year. For two years, the landlord lets the apartment stay vacant, even though several people are interested in renting that specific apartment. When the landlord sues Rusty for rent due over the two-year period, Rusty will claim that the landlord's right to collect should be limited because of the landlord's failure to *mitigate his damages*. In this instance, the landlord may have easily rented the apartment to another person so that the landlord's losses, and therefore his damage claims, would have been greatly reduced. The offset for rents that could have been collected will be allowed.

MITIGATING CIRCUMSTANCES a set of conditions that, while not exonerating the accused, might reduce the **sentence** or the **damages** arising from the offense. Compare **defense.**

M'NAGHTEN RULE the **common law** test of criminal responsibility under which a person was not responsible for criminal acts and was thus entitled to an **acquittal** by reason of **insanity** if as a result of a mental disease or defect he did not understand what he did or that it was wrong, or if he was under a delusion (but not otherwise insane) that, if true, would have provided a good **defense** (as where the defendant thought he was acting in **self-defense** or carrying out the will of God). This is called the RIGHT AND WRONG TEST because it is often said that one was not insane under the M'Naghten rule if he could distinguish right from wrong. The test has been criticized as too restrictive and has been changed in many **jurisdictions.** See **Durham rule.**

M.O. see **modus operandi.**

MODUS OPERANDI *(mō'-dŭs ŏp-er-än'-dē)* Lat.: the manner of operation. The means of accomplishing an act; especially, the characteristic method employed by **defendant** in repeated criminal acts.

MOIETY the half part.

MOLLITER MANUS IMPOSUIT *(mō'-lĭ-tėr mä'-nŭs ĭmpō'-zū-ĭt)* Lat.: the gentle laying upon of hands. In a **tort** action, the term refers to an assertion by one of the **parties** that he used only the force necessary to protect himself or his property from injury by the other party. Compare **self-defense.**

MONOPOLY 1. a market condition where all or so nearly all of an article of commerce within a district is brought within the control of one person or company, that competition or free traffic in that article is excluded. See **antitrust laws.**

2. a privilege or **license** granting a group or company sole authority to deal in certain products, or provide a product or service in a specified area.

EXAMPLE: Public Utilities Gas Company is granted the exclusive right to supply gas to the northern part of a state. The right is granted out of convenience and necessity, since it would be impractical to have several gas company lines running underground. Moreover, it is desirable to have the state control pricing of a necessary item for any household. As a grant by the state, the *monopoly* in favor of Public Utilities is a lawful monopoly.

MOOT CASE a case that seeks to determine an abstract question that does not rest upon existing facts or rights, or that seeks a **judgment** in a pretended controversy, or one that seeks a decision about a right before it has actually been asserted or contested, or a judgment upon some matter that, when rendered for any cause, cannot have any practical effect upon the existing controversy. See **advisory opinion.**

EXAMPLE: Tina files a lawsuit against Private University, claiming that the university has denied her admission because of her race. Before the case reaches the trial court, Private admits Tina as a student. Because of the school's actions, the case between Tina and Private is rendered *moot.* Tina can no longer claim that race was a factor in denying her admission, since she has been admitted.

MOOT COURT a fictitious court established to argue a **moot case.** Law schools form moot courts as an instrument of learning.

MORAL CERTAINTY certainty beyond a **reasonable doubt;** a conviction based on persuasive reasons and excluding doubts that a contrary conclusion can exist. A juror is said to be morally certain of a fact when he would act in reliance upon its truth in matters of greatest importance to himself.

MORAL TURPITUDE vileness or dishonesty of a high degree. A crime of moral turpitude demonstrates depravity in the private and social duties a person owes to others, contrary to what is accepted and customary.

MORTGAGE in **common law,** a conveyance of, or granting of a **lien** upon, **real property** of a **debtor** to his **creditor,** intended as a security for the repayment of a loan, usually the purchase price (or a part thereof) of the **property** so conveyed or **encumbered.** The transfer was rendered **void** upon repayment of the loan; i.e., the property reverted to the debtor upon the discharge of the mortgage by timely payment of the sum loaned.

TITLE THEORY refers to the modern version of the common law mortgage under which the creditor has the legal right to possession (though in fact the debtor remains in possession of his property). Under the **HYBRID THEORY** the creditor's right to possession arises only upon **default** by the debtor. Under the **LIEN THEORY,** the mortgagee (creditor) takes a lien on the property, and is not entitled to possession until he has pursued his remedy in **foreclosure** and the mortgaged **premises** have been sold; i.e., the right to possession arises only when the mortgagor's (debtor's) **equity of redemption** has been foreclosed. In the mortgage relationship, the debtor is called the mortgagor and the creditor is called the *mortgagee*.

ASSUMPTION OF MORTGAGE taking upon oneself the obligations of a mortgagor towards a mortgagee, generally as part of the purchase price of a parcel of real estate. By assuming the mortgage rather than taking subject to the mortgage, the purchaser becomes personally **liable** on the debt.

EXAMPLE: Ed wants to buy Frank's home for $80,000. He can afford a $16,000 down payment and is willing to assume Frank's $64,000 mortgage. If the bank agrees to the assumption of its mortgage, Ed will be personally responsible for the mortgage payments. If Ed should default, the bank can still hold Frank liable, since he was the original mortgagor, unless he is released by the bank as part of the assumption.

SUBJECT TO MORTGAGE a condition of sale whereby the purchaser takes land encumbered by a preexisting mortgage. The purchaser's obligation to the mortgagee is limited to the value of the property subject to the mortgage, unless the purchaser becomes personally liable on the debt by assuming the mortgage.

CHATTEL MORTGAGE conveyance of a present **interest** in **personal property,** generally as security for payment of money, such as the purchase price of property, or for the performance of some other act. Like a mortgage of **real property,** it operates in some states to pass **title** to the mortgagee, but in other states merely to create a **lien;** but in either case the mortgagor retains possession. It is thus distinguished from a **pledge,** which establishes a **bailment** and which therefore establishes the pledgee as bailee and grants him possession of the **personalty.**

EQUITABLE MORTGAGE security transaction that fails to satisfy the legal requirements of a mortgage but that nevertheless is treated in **equity** as a mortgage. It includes cases in which **interest** in the property in the hands of the creditor is full legal ownership, and the aid of equity is necessary to reduce it to a security interest and to establish the rights of the debtor as a mortgagor. Also included are cases where the transaction is technically insufficient to create a mortgage **at law,** but where equity intervenes to protect the mortgagee.

MORTGAGEE the party lending the money to a **mortgagor,** who takes a security interest in property owned by the mortgagor.

MORTGAGOR the party borrowing money from a bank or other lending agency, who secures the loan with property the party owns in whole or in part.

MORTIS CAUSA see **causa [CAUSA MORTIS].**

MORTMAIN literally, dead hand; applies to all **property** that, from the nature of the purposes to which it is devoted, or the character of the **ownership** to which it is subjected, is for every practical purpose not freely **alienable.**

MOTION an application to the court requesting an **order** in favor of the applicant. Motions are generally made in reference to a pending **action** and may be addressed to a matter within the discretion of the judge, or may concern a point of law. Motions may be made orally or, more formally, in writing.

MOVANT the moving party; applicant for an **order** by way of **motion** before a court.

MOVE to make a **motion;** in practice, to make application to a court or other tribunal for a ruling, **order** or particular **relief.**

MULTIFARIOUS refers to a suit where independent matters are improperly **joined** and thereby confused; also refers to **misjoinder** of **causes of action** and misjoinder of **parties** in a suit.

MULTIPARTITE consisting of two or more parts or **parties,** as where several nations join in a treaty.

MULTIPLICITY OF SUITS the existence of several separate **actions at law** brought against the same defendant to **litigate** the same right. In the exercise of its **equity** powers, a court can **enjoin** the proceedings at law and hear all of the claims at a single proceeding.

MUNICIPAL BOND a **bond** issued by a state or local government body such as a county, city or town.

MUNICIPAL CORPORATIONS usually **incorporated** cities, towns and villages having subordinate and local powers of legislation. The term is sometimes used in a broader sense to include every **corporation** formed for governmental purposes, so as to embrace counties, townships, school districts and other governmental subdivisions of the state.

MUNICIPAL COURT city court that administers the law within the city. These courts generally have exclusive **jurisdiction** over violations of city **ordinances** and may also have jurisdiction over minor criminal cases arising within the city and over certain **civil** cases.

MURDER unlawful killing of another human being with premeditated intent or **malice** aforethought.

FIRST DEGREE MURDER unlawful killing that is deliberate and premeditated.

SECOND DEGREE MURDER unlawful killing of another with malice aforethought but without deliberation and premeditation. Such malice may be in the form of express malice as the actual intention to kill, or of implied malice where there is no intent, but where death is caused by an act which discloses such a reckless state of mind as to be equivalent to an actual intent to kill.

EXAMPLE: Tom becomes very angry at his business partner, Andy, and throws a brick at him. Since Tom intended to hurt Andy, if death results the act will be second degree murder. If the provocation was sufficient, the crime might be reduced by the jury to manslaughter. If Tom planned the attack on Andy and intended to inflict grievous injury, it might be first degree murder.

See also **homicide; manslaughter.**

MUTUAL FUND an investment company that sells its own shares to investors and then invests the proceeds from that sale in other securities, thus affording its investors a diversified **portfolio.** OPEN-END MUTUAL FUNDS do not have a fixed **capitalization** and may issue new shares on a customer-demand basis. CLOSED-END MUTUAL FUNDS do have a fixed capitalization and may sell only as many shares as were authorized in the first instance.

MUTUALITY OF OBLIGATION responsibilities imposed on each of the parties to a **contract,** which must be mutual and by which each must be bound. Unless each **party** is bound to perform in some way, the agreement will lack **consideration.**

MUTUALITY OF REMEDY a doctrine that one party should not obtain from **equity** that which the other party could not obtain. Accordingly, whenever a **contract** is incapable of being specifically enforced against one **party** because of the personal nature of the contract, that party cannot specifically enforce it against the other. However, the general requirement of mutuality does not compel each party to have precisely the same remedies available against each other, since the means of enforcement may differ without necessarily affecting their reciprocal obligation. See **mutuality of obligation.**

MUTUAL MISTAKE see **mistake.**

N

NATIONAL LABOR RELATIONS BOARD [NLRB] an independent agency created by Congress that oversees relationships between unions and employees. The Board has the power to adjudicate claims before it and to enforce its judgments in the federal courts.

NATURALIZED CITIZEN one who, having been born in another country or otherwise reared as a foreigner, has been granted U.S. citizenship and the rights and privileges of that status. The process by which such a person attains citizenship is called **NATURALIZATION.**

NATURAL LAW law that so necessarily agrees with the nature of human beings, that without observing its maxims, the peace and happiness of society cannot be preserved; that law, knowledge of which may be attained merely by the light of reason, and from the facts of its essential connection with human nature. Natural law exists regardless of whether it is enacted as **positive law.** See also **positivism.**

NATURAL LAW THEORY in jurisprudence, the view that the nature and value of any legal order is best understood by studying how the positive law of that legal order agrees or contrasts with natural law.

NATURAL PERSON a human being, as opposed to an artificial or fictitious person such as a **corporation.**

N.B. see **nota bene.**

NECESSARY INFERENCE deduced fact that is unavoidable from the standpoint of reason, so that no other inference may be reasonably drawn from the facts as stated.

EXAMPLE: Mark is in a maximum security prison when a robbery occurs in a local jewelry store. Several witnesses to the robbery are shown pictures of criminals at police headquarters, and one of those witnesses identifies Mark as the robber. Mark cannot be charged because there is a *necessary inference* that he could not have committed the robbery in town while an inmate at a maximum security prison.

Compare **presumption.**

NECESSARY PARTY see **party.**

NECESSITY, DEFENSE OF see **justification.**

NEGATIVE PREGNANT in pleading, a **denial** that implies an affirmation of a substantial fact and hence is beneficial to the opponent. Thus, when only a qualification or modification is denied while the fact itself remains undenied, the denial is pregnant with an affirmation of that fact.

NEGLIGENCE failure to exercise a degree of care that a person of ordinary prudence (a **reasonable man**) would exercise under the same circumstances. The term refers to conduct that falls below the standard established by law for the protection of others against unreasonable risk of harm.

COMPARATIVE NEGLIGENCE the proportionate sharing between **plaintiff** and **defendant** of responsibility for injury to the plaintiff based on the relative negligence of the two. It results in a reduction of the **damages** recoverable by the negligent plaintiff in proportion to his fault.

EXAMPLE: John runs across a busy street at a point between two trucks, so that both his vision and the vision of other vehicles is impaired. A car travels down the street over the speed limit, but not excessively fast, and hits John. A jury finds John 30 percent responsible for the accident and the driver 70 percent. Under a *comparative negligence* theory, if John would have normally recovered $10,000 in damages, he now only recovers $7,000.

CONCURRENT NEGLIGENCE the wrongful acts or omissions of two or more persons acting independently but causing the same injury. The independent actions do not have to occur at the same time, but must produce the same result. The actors are all responsible for paying the damages and can usually be sued together in one lawsuit or individually in separate lawsuits.

CONTRIBUTORY NEGLIGENCE conduct on the part of the plaintiff that falls below the standard to which he should conform for his own protection, and that is a legally contributing cause cooperating with the negligence of the defendant in bringing about the plaintiff's harm. In **common law,** the plaintiff's contributory negligence precludes his right to recover from the defendant.

EXAMPLE: On the same facts as in the example under comparative negligence, if the jurisdiction John sues in follows a theory of *contributory negligence,* John's fault will prevent any recovery against the other driver since John's negligence contributed to his injury.

CRIMINAL [or CULPABLE] NEGLIGENCE such negligence as is necessary to incur criminal liability. In most jurisdictions, culpable negligence is more than the ordinary negligence necessary to support a **civil action** for damages. Thus, culpable negligence is a reckless disregard of consequences or a heedless indifference to the personal safety of others.

GROSS NEGLIGENCE an intentional or willful failure to perform a clear duty, recklessly disregarding the consequences of injury to person or property that attend such failure.

NEGLIGENCE PER SE negligence as a matter of law; an act or omission recognized as negligent either because it is contrary to the requirements of law or because it is so opposed to the dictates of common prudence that one could say without doubt that no careful person would have committed the act or omission. While negligence ordinarily must be found by the trier of fact (see **fact finder**) from the facts and circumstances disclosed by the **evidence,** negligence per se arises from a violation of a specific requirement of law or ordinance, the only fact for determination by the trier of fact being the omission or commission of the specific act prohibited or required.

NEGOTIABLE INSTRUMENT a writing signed by the **maker** or **drawer,** containing an unconditional promise or order to pay a specific sum, payable on demand or at a definite time, and payable to **order** or to **bearer.** A **draft, check, certificate of deposit** and **note** may or may not be negotiable instruments, depending upon whether the elements of negotiability are satisfied.

EXAMPLE: Mickey takes a loan from a bank and signs a promissory note to repay the bank in twelve months. That note is a *negotiable instrument* and can be transferred by that bank to any other party. Because it is freely transferable, Mickey does not repay the note unless he knows who possesses it, and demands that, upon payment, the note be returned to him so that it is not transferred to another party.

An ordinary check issued by an employer to an employee or by a customer to a store is also a negotiable instrument.

NEGOTIATION a method of dispute resolution where either the parties themselves or the representatives of each party attempt to settle conflicts without resort to the courts; an impartial third party is not involved. Compare **arbitration; mediation.**

NEMO EST SUPRA LEGIS *(nā'-mō ĕst sū'-prȧ lā-gĭs)* Lat.: nobody is above the law.

NET ASSET VALUE an accounting term similar in meaning to **book value** and net worth; most often used in reference to value of **mutual fund** shares and similar investment companies. Investment companies compute their net asset value at the end of each market day by taking the total market value of securities, cash, etc., owned, less any **liabilities.** See **balance sheet.**

NET ESTATE **estate** that under federal and state statutes is subject to an **estate tax;** generally that estate remaining after all debts of decedent, funeral and administrative expenses, and other deductions prescribed by law have been subtracted from the GROSS ESTATE (total valuation of the estate's assets at decedent's death). The term thus refers generally to that estate left to be distributed after all deductions have been made.

NET INCOME the gross [total] income less the deductions and exemptions allowed by law.

NET OPERATING LOSS the excess of allowable **deductions** over GROSS INCOME (see **income**) with certain specific adjustments set forth in the **Internal Revenue Code,** which are generally designed to limit the net operating loss deductions of individual **taxpayers** to business losses. A net operating loss reduces the TAXABLE INCOME (see **income**) of the taxpayer for the **taxable year** by the amount of such net operating loss.

NET WORTH one of several methods used by the **Internal Revenue Service** to reconstruct a **taxpayer's income** when it is determined that either the taxpayer has failed to file a **return** or the tax liability shown is not correct. Under this method the taxpayer's net worth for the start of the period in question is determined, and his net worth at the end of the period is also calculated, with the difference, less any nontaxable amounts received, deemed to be the taxpayer's income for the period. This approach is often used in cases involving suspected **evasion** by the taxpayer, but it is also used in normal civil or civil fraud contexts.

NEW MATTER matters raised by **defendent** that go beyond mere denials of **plaintiff's** allegations. New matter consists of new issues, with new facts to be proved, and purports to show that the alleged **cause of action** never did exist and that material allegations are not true.

NEW YORK STOCK EXCHANGE [NYSE] the oldest organized stock exchange in the United States, which has been active, since its organization, in establishing listing requirements for companies whose stocks are traded on the Exchange and in encouraging accurate and timely disclosure of listed company **income statement** and **balance sheet** results.

NEXT FRIEND a **competent** person who, although not an appointed **guardian,** acts in behalf of a party who is unable to look after his own interests or manage his own **suit;** one who represents an infant, married woman or other party, who by reason of some disability, is not **sui juris.** A next friend is not considered a party to the suit, but is regarded as an **agent** or **officer** of the court to protect the rights of the disabled person.

NIHIL *(nĭ'-hĭl)* Lat.: nothing; not at all, in no respect; NIL is an often-used form of the noun. Most commonly used to describe a sheriff's **return** after an unsuccessful attempt to **serve** a **summons** or otherwise gain **jurisdiction** over an individual.

NIL see **nihil.**

NISI *(Nē'-Sē)* Lat.: unless. Used in law after **decree, order,** rule to indicate that the adjudication shall take permanent effect at a specified time unless cause is shown why it should not or unless it is changed by further proceedings. More particularly, a decree nisi is a conditional **divorce,** which becomes absolute upon the expiration of a stipulated period unless cause to the contrary is shown within the time period.

NISI PRIUS *(nē'-sē prē'-ŭs)* Lat.: unless the first. In American law, sometimes used to describe any court where a case is first heard by a **judge** and **jury,** distinguishing such courts from the **appellate courts.** See **original jurisdiction.**

NO FAULT a system of **insurance** whereby all persons who are injured in an automobile accident may be compensated for any injuries resulting therefrom, without regard to who was at fault.

EXAMPLE: At one o'clock in the morning, two automobile drivers get into an accident. Each claims that the other ran a red light. Under a *no-fault* insurance plan, the argument as to who ran the light is irrelevant. The plan provides each driver with compensation for his injuries from his own insurance company. If the injuries are substantial, fault may be relevant, as suit is generally permitted based on fault, even in no-fault jurisdictions, for injury that exceeds some specified dollar amount. Under a no-fault system, most cases, however, can be settled without litigation.

NO-FAULT DIVORCE see **divorce.**

NOLO CONTENDERE *(nō'-lō kŏn-tĕn'-dĕ-rā)* Lat.: I do not wish to contend, fight or maintain (a **defense**). A statement that the **defendant** will not contest a **charge** made by the government. Like a **demurrer** to an **indictment,** it admits all facts stated in the indictment for the purposes of a particular **case,** but it cannot be used as an **admission** elsewhere, or in any other proceeding, such as a **civil** suit arising from the same facts.

EXAMPLE: Dan is charged with careless driving. He pleads "nolo contendere" and is fined by the court. Since he did not admit guilt, his plea cannot be used against him if he is sued by an injured party.

NOMINAL DAMAGES see **damages.**

NOMINAL PARTY see **party.**

NON ASSUMPSIT *(nŏn ȧ-sŭmp'-sĭt)* Lat.: he did not promise; he did not undertake. A form of **pleading** in which the defendent claims that he did not undertake or promise any obligation in the manner or form that is set forth in the **plaintiff's complaint.** See **assumpsit.**

NON COMPOS MENTIS *(nŏn kŏm'-pōs mĕn'-tĭs)* Lat.: not having control over the mind or intellect; not of sound mind; insane. In certain circumstances its effect is lessened to mean only not legally **competent.**

NONCONFORMING USE a **use** of land that lawfully existed before enactment of a **zoning** ordinance and that may be maintained after the effective date of the ordinance although it no longer complies with use restrictions newly applicable to the area. Continuation of the existing use includes preservation of both the functional use of the land and the physical structures thereon, and neither of these aspects of use may be extended once the zoning restriction has taken effect.

EXAMPLE: Prior to any zoning restrictions, Russ opens a doctor's office adjacent to his home. Subsequently, the town passes an ordinance prohibiting any business in Russ's section of town. Russ is permitted to continue operating his office as a *nonconforming use,* but he cannot expand his office without express permission from the zoning officials.

See also **grandfather clause.** Compare **variance.**

NONCONTESTABILITY CLAUSE a provision in an **insurance** policy that precludes the insurer from disputing the validity of the policy on the basis of **fraud** or **mistake** after a specified period. If the insurer wishes to contest the policy on any grounds that would justify **rescission,** it must do so within the prescribed period, either by suing to cancel the policy or by asserting fraud or **misrepresentation** as a **defense** in an action instituted by the policyholder or **beneficiary.** The purpose of the clause is to require the insurer to investigate with reasonable promptness the accuracy of information provided by the policyholder. It prevents the insurer from lulling the policyholder into a sense of security during the time when facts could best be ascertained, only to **litigate** them belatedly.

NONCUSTODIAL SENTENCE see **sentence.**

NONDISCRETIONARY TRUST [FIXED INVESTMENT TRUST] an **investment trust** that may buy only those **securities** on a list set forth when the trust is organized. The percentage of total assets that may be invested in a specific security or type of securities is usually predetermined. See **unit investment trust.**

NONFEASANCE in the law of agency, the total omission or failure of an **agent** to perform a distinct duty that he has agreed with his **principal** to do; also, the neglect or refusal, without sufficient excuse, to do what is an officer's legal duty to do. Nonfeasance differs from **misfeasance,** which is the improper doing of an act that one might lawfully do, and from **malfeasance,** which is the doing of an act that is wholly wrongful and unlawful.

NONMEMBER BANK a bank that is not a member of the **Federal Reserve System** and is regulated only by the banking laws in the state in which it is chartered.

NONNEGOTIABLE INSTRUMENTS see **negotiable instruments.**

NON OBSTANTE VEREDICTO see **n.o.v.**

NONPROFIT CORPORATION [NOT-FOR-PROFIT CORPORATION] an incorporated organization chartered for other than profit-making activities and exempt from corporation income tax. Most such organizations are engaged in charitable, educational or other civic or humanitarian activities, although nonprofit corporations are not restricted to such activities.

NONREBUTTABLE PRESUMPTION see **presumption [CONCLUSIVE (NONREBUTTABLE) PRESUMPTION].**

NON SEQUITUR *(nŏn sĕ'-kwĭ-tūr)* Lat.: it does not follow; it does not come after (in time); abbreviated non seq. A non sequitur action or decree is unrelated to the preceding events. A non sequitur has no logical, temporal, or spatial purpose for its place in the progression of events.

NONSTOCK CORPORATION a corporation owned by its members under the membership charter or agreement, rather than through the issue of shares.

NON SUI JURIS *(nŏn swē jū'-rĭs)* Lat.: not by his own authority or legal right. Refers to those who are not legally **competent** to manage their own affairs as regards **contracts**

and other causes in which this **incompetency** restricts exercise of sound judgment. Compare **non compos mentis.**

NONSUIT a **judgment** rendered against a **plaintiff** who fails to proceed to trial or is unable to prove his case. Since the adjudication is made when the plaintiff has failed to provide **evidence** sufficient to establish a case, it does not decide the **merits** of his **cause of action,** and thus does not preclude his bringing it again. The term is sometimes broadly applied to various terminations of an action that do not amount to a judgment **on the merits.**

EXAMPLE: Rose sues a local appliance store for selling her a defective washing machine. At the beginning of the trial, she cannot produce any evidence to show that she bought the machine at that particular store. The judge declares a *nonsuit* against Rose and dismisses her claim.

Compare **acquit.**

NON VULT *(nŏn vŭlt)* Lat.: abbreviation of non vult contendere (''He will not contest''). Refers to a plea by one charged with a crime which does not expressly admit guilt, but acknowledges that the defendant will not contest the charge and therefore agrees to be treated as though he had been found guilty. See also **nolo contendere.**

NO-PAR STOCK stock issued with no value stated on the stock certificate.

NOTA BENE *(nō'-tȧ bā-nā)* Lat.: note well. Written on the original note **N.B.** to indicate an important portion of the text to be studied.

NOTARY PUBLIC a public officer authorized to administer oaths, to attest to and certify certain types of documents, to take **depositions,** and to perform certain acts in commercial matters. The seal of a notary public authenticates a document. In some **jurisdictions** an attorney admitted to practice within the jurisdiction can act as a notary public. In many jurisdictions private persons can apply for and receive authority to act as notaries to witness documents.

NOTE a written paper that acknowledges a **debt** and promises payment to a specified party of a specific sum, and that describes a time of **maturity** that is either definite or will become definite. See **commercial paper.**

NOT GUILTY a **plea** by the **accused** in a criminal **action** that denies every essential **element** of the offense charged. A **plea** of not guilty on **arraignment** obliges the government to prove the defendant's guilt beyond a reasonable doubt and preserves the right of the accused to defend against the charge. A jury **verdict** of not guilty does not mean the jury found the accused innocent, but simply that the state failed to prove its case beyond a reasonable doubt.

NOT GUILTY BY REASON OF INSANITY a special form of verdict or finding that is usually followed by commitment of the defendant to a mental institution. The insanity defense differs from other defenses in that, if successful, it is not an **acquittal** and does not result in the outright release of the accused.

NOTICE information concerning a fact actually communicated to a person by an authorized person, or actually derived by him from a proper source. Notice to a **defendant** of a lawsuit that has been instituted against him or of an **action** in which he may have an interest to defend is accomplished by **service of process** on him.

AVERMENT OF NOTICE a statement in the **pleadings** declaring that a **party** to an action has received proper notice thereof.

CONSTRUCTIVE NOTICE notice presumed by law to have been acquired; often accomplished by posting of notices or by mailing of notification to the defendant if he cannot be personally **served** with **process.**

EXAMPLE: Neil sues Jim for a debt incurred when Neil painted his house. One requirement of filing the suit is that Neil personally notify Jim of the court action. After several unsuccessful attempts to meet Jim and physically hand him a copy of the complaint, Neil satisfies the notice requirement by sending a copy to Jim's business and home addresses and by tacking a copy on Jim's door. Jim is considered to have received *constructive notice* of the action whether or not he actually learned of it.

INQUIRY NOTICE with respect to one who claims to have been a **bona fide purchaser** without notice of adverse claims to the purchased property, information from whatever source derived that would create in an ordinary mind apprehension about the actual state of ownership of the property and that would prompt a person of average prudence to make inquiry.

JUDICIAL NOTICE see **judicial notice.**

NOTICE BY PUBLICATION method of bringing a lawsuit to the attention of parties who may have an interest therein by publishing notification of it in a newspaper of general circulation; permissible only where specifically allowed by **statute** and generally limited to actions involving **land, estates** or status.

NOTORIOUS POSSESSION **possession** of **real property** that is open, undisguised, generally known or recognized. The term is one of the elements in defining or determining existence of **adverse possession,** which involves a claim of right to property not by **title** but by possession for a prescribed period.

N.O.V. [NON OBSTANTE VEREDICTO] *(nŏn ŏb-stăn'-tā vĕr-ĕ-dĭk'-tō)* Lat.: notwithstanding the verdict. A JUDGMENT N.O.V. is one by the trial court that reverses the determination of the **jury,** granted when it is obvious that the jury **verdict** had no reasonable support in fact or was contrary to law. The motion for a judgment n.o.v. provides a second chance for the trial court to render what is, in effect, a **directed verdict** for the **moving** party.

NOVATION substitution of another **party** for one of the original parties to a **contract,** with the consent of the remaining party. The old contract is then extinguished, and a new contract, with the same content but with at least one different party, is created. A novation often involves a transaction whereby the original **debtor** is discharged from liability to his **creditor** by substitution of a second debtor.

NOW ACCOUNT [NEGOTIABLE ORDER OF WITHDRAWAL ACCOUNT] an interest-bearing savings account against which depositors are permitted to write checks. See **bank.**

NSF CHECK nonsufficient funds **check.** If the **drawee** (bank) discovers that the **drawer** lacks funds to cover the presented check, the drawee can **dishonor** the check, and the presenter is powerless to make the drawee pay.

NUDUM PACTUM *(nū'-dŭm păk'-tŭm)* Lat.: a bare **contract.** A **promise** naked of obligation on one side; not enforceable, since contracts must generally be supported by a **consideration** on each side. See **mutuality of obligation.**

NUGATORY void; invalid; for example, judicial **proceedings** in courts that lack **jurisdiction.** See **voidable.**

NUISANCE 1. anything that disturbs the free use of one's property, or that renders its ordinary use uncomfortable; 2. in **tort** law, a wrong arising from unreasonable or unlawful use of property to the annoyance or damage of another or of the public.

EXAMPLE: Gail rents an apartment in a residential apartment building. In the adjacent apartment, a politically active group meets very frequently at late hours to discuss strategy and to type press releases. The apartment is at no time used for sleep. Even if the group's activities are legal, Gail has a *nuisance* action against the group. Their late hours disturb her, and the apartment is not used for its normal and intended purpose.

ABATABLE NUISANCE a nuisance that can be suppressed, extinguished or rendered harmless, and whose continued existence is not authorized under law.

ABATEMENT OF A NUISANCE the removal or termination of a nuisance by **self-help.**

ATTRACTIVE NUISANCE see **attractive nuisance.**

PRIVATE NUISANCE an **actionable** interference with a person's interest in the private **use** and enjoyment of his land.

PUBLIC [or COMMON] NUISANCE an unreasonable interference with a right common to the general public; behavior that unreasonably interferes with the health, safety, peace, comfort or convenience of the community.

NULLITY in law, a **void** act; a defective proceeding or one expressly declared by **statute** to be a nullity.

NUNC PRO TUNC *(nŭnk prō tŭnk)* Lat.: now for then.

NUNC PRO TUNC ORDER an **order** used by the courts to correct the **record** usually after a proceeding has been concluded. It supplements a prior **judgment** or order in any matter over which the court originally had **jurisdiction.**

O

OATH an affirmation of the truth of a statement. See **affidavit.** Compare **perjury.**

OBITER DICTA *(ō'-bĭ-tėr dĭk'-tȧ)* Lat.: passing or incidental statements. Statements made or decisions reached in a court opinion that were not necessary to disposition of the case; plural of obiter dictum. See **dictum.**

OBJECT a procedure whereby a party asserts that a particular witness, line of questioning, piece of evidence or other matter is improper and should not be continued, and asks the court to rule on its impropriety or illegality.

EXAMPLE: Michael is on trial for theft. The prosecution asks a witness whether Michael ever owned a gun. Michael's attorney will *object* and seek to exclude the question and answer on the grounds that the question will introduce improperly "other crimes" (i.e., possession of a gun) into the case.

OBLIGATION OF A CONTRACT the term refers not to any duty that rises out of the contract itself, but to the legal requirements that bind the contracting parties to the performance of their undertaking.

IMPAIR THE OBLIGATION OF A CONTRACT to weaken the contract in any respect. Any law that changes the intention and legal effect of the original parties, giving to one a greater and to the other a lesser **interest** in the contract, that hastens or postpones the prescribed time of performance, or imposes conditions not included in the contract, or dispenses with the performance of those that are included, impairs the obligation of a contract. Impairment also exists where the right to enforce a contract is eliminated or substantially lessened. State statutes that impair contract obligations are prohibited by Article I, Section 10 of the United States Constitution.

OBSCENE MATERIAL material that, taken as a whole, appeals to the prurient interest of the average person, depicts sexual conduct in a patently offensive manner, and lacks serious literary, artistic, political or scientific value. Matter so classified is not protected by the free speech guarantee of the First Amendment.

OBSOLESCENCE the process by which property becomes useless, not because of physical deterioration, but because of scientific or technological advances.

OBSTRUCTION OF JUSTICE the impeding of those who seek justice in a court, or of those who have duties or powers of administering justice therein; includes attempting to influence, intimidate or impede any **juror, witness** or officer in any court regarding the discharge of his duty.

EXAMPLE: Ned possesses telephone recordings of a contractor offering a bribe to secure a construction grant. When Bill, another contractor, sues to have the grant overturned because of the possibility of a bribe, he requests that Ned give him the recordings. If Ned destroys or otherwise loses the recordings after they are requested, he will be charged with *obstruction of justice*.

Statutes addressing this subject may reach beyond interference with the judicial process and also proscribe interference with police officers and other such administrative officials. See **embracery.**

OCCUPANT one who has the actual use or possession of property. See **tenant.** Compare **landlord; title.**

OCCUPATIONAL DISEASE a disease that is the natural result of a particular employment, where that employment involves a risk of contracting the disease greater than the risk in employment and living conditions in general, and that usually develops gradually from the effects of long-continued work at the employment.

OCCUPATIONAL HAZARD a risk distinctively associated with a particular type of employment or workplace.

OCCUPYING THE FIELD see **preemption.**

ODD LOT in the **securities** trade, **stocks** or **bonds** in a block of fewer than 100 **shares.** In buying or selling an odd lot, a **premium** or **discount** to the round lot price is charged; this charge is referred to as the **ODD LOT DIFFERENTIAL.**

OF COUNSEL refers to an attorney who aids in the preparation of a case, but who is not the principal attorney of record for the case. He usually assists the attorney who has been hired for the case.

OFFENSE any violation of law for which a penalty is prescribed, including both **felonies** and **misdemeanors.**

OFFER 1. a manifestation of willingness to enter into a bargain, so made as to justify another person in understanding that his assent to that bargain is invited and will establish a **contract.**

EXAMPLE: A representative of Clay Brick Company sends a letter to a large outlet store informing them of an overstock in several types of bricks the company is hoping to eliminate. The store responds that it will buy the full overstock for the price stated in Clay's letter, and includes a check with their response. The store views Clay's letter as an *offer*. By sending a positive response and a check to Clay, the store believes that a bargain has been struck and a valid contract established.

2. a promise, a commitment to do or refrain from doing some specified thing in the future. 3. In the **securities** trade, an offer indicates price and volume available from open market sellers of **stocks** and **bonds.** 4. an **underwriting** in which a **broker** offers a large quantity of a specific **issue** at a fixed price, called an offering.

OFFICER 1. a person invested with the authority of a particular position or office; may be public or private in that the occupied office may or may not be invested with a **public trust.** 2. corporate personnel appointed by the directors and charged with the duty of managing the day-to-day affairs of the **corporation.**

OFFICIAL IMMUNITY see **immunity.**

OFFICIOUS INTERMEDDLER one who performs an act that confers a **benefit** upon another, although he had neither a contractual duty nor a legally recognized interest in performing the act, and who nevertheless seeks **restitution** for the benefit conferred.

OFFSET see **setoff.**

OLIGOPOLY 1. an industry in which a few large sellers of substantially identical products, such as automobiles, dominate the market; 2. the condition of a specific products market so dominated. An oligopolistic industry is more concentrated than a competitive one but less concentrated than a **monopoly.**

OMISSION a failure to do something; something left undone; the neglect to perform what the law requires. Omission will not give rise to **liability** unless there is a **duty** to act.

EXAMPLE: A motorist sees an accident on the highway late at night but fails to call anyone, although a telephone is just a few hundred yards away. As a result of that *omission,* one of the victims of the accident dies. Although common standards may view the motorist as somewhat responsible for the death, the motorist cannot be found liable in a court of law since he has no legal duty to report the accident. If he had been involved in the accident, he would have had a legal duty to summon help. His *omission* in that instance would be the subject of civil and possibly criminal action.

Compare **actus reus.**

OMNIBUS CLAUSE a clause in an automobile liability insurance policy that gives categories of persons, in addition to the person named as **assured** (see **insured**), the benefit of the policy, within specified limitations. The clause extends protection to one permitted to use the car, although the assured may not be liable for an accident under the doctrine **respondeat superior.** The object is to cover the liability of the operator of the car as unnamed assured, and to protect any injured person by giving him a **cause of action** against the insurer for injuries deemed by law to have been caused by the operation of the car. **Statutes** have been passed in some **jurisdictions** requiring the inclusion of omnibus clauses for the protection of automobile accident victims.

ON ALL FOURS describes a case similar to or identical with the case at hand and therefore possibly useful as **precedent;** derived from the Latin maxim, ''Nullum simile est idem nisi quattuor pedibus currit'': Nothing similar is identical unless it runs on all four feet.

ON DEMAND when asked for. For example, a note payable on demand is payable when the sum is requested; called a **demand note** if no due date is included.

ON THE MERITS refers to a **judgment** based upon the essential facts of the case rather than upon a technical rule of practice, such as failure of proper **service** or other **jurisdictional** defect. A decision on the merits is rendered after a full presentation of the **evidence** and determines finally the rights of the parties, barring **appeal** or subsequent relitigation.

EXAMPLE: After several weeks of preparation, the attorneys for both sides presented their arguments to the judge. By carefully considering all the evidence and relevant legal theory, the judge was able to base his decision *on the merits.* Had the judge dismissed the case because one of the attorneys failed to comply on time with a rule of court, the case would have been dismissed because of a procedural flaw and not on the merits.

OPEN COURT a court that is formally opened and engaged in the transaction of judicial affairs, to which all persons who conduct themselves in an orderly manner are admitted. Most legal proceedings take place in open court except where confidentiality is a recognized interest (e.g., matrimonial, adoption or juvenile delinquency proceedings).

OPEN POSSESSION see **notorious possession.**

OPEN PUBLIC MEETINGS LAWS see **Sunshine laws.**

OPEN SHOP an enterprise that employs workers without regard to whether they are members of a labor union.

OPERATION OF LAW the determination of rights and obligations through the automatic effects of the law and not by any private agreement or direct act of the party affected.

EXAMPLE: A husband and wife own a home as tenants by the entirety. Under that principle of property, when either dies, the surviving spouse has sole ownership of the home. Since this event occurs automatically, it is said to occur by *operation of law*.

OPINION the reason given for a court's **judgment, finding** or conclusion, as opposed to the decision, which is the judgment itself. When the court is composed of more than one judge or justice, and more than one opinion has been written in a given case, the opinion that expresses the view of the majority of the judges presiding, and thus announces the decision of the court, is referred to as the **MAJORITY OPINION.**

CONCURRING OPINION a view basically in accord with the majority opinion, but written to express a somewhat different perception of the issues, to illuminate a particular judge's reasoning or to expound a principle which he holds in high esteem. An opinion that concurs "in the result only" is one that rejects the reasoning and conclusions concerning the law or the facts on the basis of which the majority reached its decision, and that expresses a different view that has coincidentally led the judge or justice to recommend the same **disposition** as was agreed upon by the majority.

DISSENTING OPINION a view that disagrees with the disposition made of the case by the court, with the facts or law on the basis of which the court arrived at its decision, or the principles of law announced by the court in deciding the case. Opinions may also be written that express a dissent "in part."

PER CURIAM OPINION an opinion "by the court," which expresses its decision in the case without identifying the author.

Opinion also refers to the conclusions reached by a **witness** that are drawn from his observations of the facts. See **expert witness.**

OPTION a **contract** that gives the holder a right or option to buy or sell specified property, such as **stock** or **real estate,** at a fixed price for a limited period.

ORAL CONTRACT see **contract.**

ORDER 1. a direction of the court on a matter incident to the main proceeding that adjudicates a preliminary point or directs some step in the proceeding. If an order closes the matter and precludes future **hearing** and investigation, it is a FINAL ORDER; but an order that does not completely dispose of the subject matter of the controversy and settle the rights of the **parties** is not final. A final order is an **appealable** order. See **interlocutory.**

2. In the **securities** trade, an instruction to buy or sell a specified security under specified conditions.

ORDER PAPER see **order paper.**

ORDERED LIBERTY a concept in constitutional law that the **due process** requirements applicable to the states through the Fourteenth Amendment to the United States Constitution do not incorporate all the provisions of the first ten amendments (the **Bill of Rights**), but only those measures essential for the preservation of a scheme of ordered liberty.

This restrictive view of due process has been largely replaced by a broader view of incorporating nearly all of the Bill of Rights as representing a national standard of fundamental fairness.

ORDER PAPER in commercial law, a **negotiable instrument** that by its terms is payable to a specified person or his **assignee,** rather than, for instance, to cash or to bearer. The **payee** must be named or otherwise indicated with reasonable certainty. Compare **bearer paper.**

ORDINANCE a local law that applies to persons and things subject to the local **jurisdiction.** Usually it is an act of a city council or similar body that has the same force as a **statute** when it is duly enacted. See **home rule.**

ORDINARY COURSE OF BUSINESS the common practices of commercial transactions; refers to a necessary activity that is normal and incidental to the business.

ORIGINAL JURISDICTION authority to consider and decide cases in the first instance, as distinguished from APPELLATE JURISDICTION (see **jurisdiction**), which is the authority to review a decision or **judgment** of an inferior tribunal.

EXAMPLE: The Constitution of the United States provides that the Supreme Court has *original jurisdiction* in all cases affecting ambassadors. Notwithstanding any issue of diplomatic immunity, if an ambassador from France were sued, the Supreme Court, rather than some lower court, would hear the case.

OSTENSIBLE AUTHORITY see **apparent authority.**

OUSTER the wrongful **dispossession** or exclusion of a person, usually associated with the acts of a co-owner that exclude other co-owners from their legal right to share **possession.**

OUTPUT CONTRACT see **contract.**

OVERBREADTH the overbroad aspect of a **statute** forbidding or inhibiting conduct that is constitutionally protected. Compare **chill** [CHILLING EFFECT].

OVERREACHING in commercial law, the taking of unfair advantage through cunning, cheating, fraud or abuse of superior bargaining power. **Contracts** that are the product of overreaching may be unenforceable under modern concepts of fraud or the **unconscionability** doctrine.

OVERRULE 1. to overturn or make **void** the **holding** (decision) of a prior case; generally accomplished in a different and subsequent case, when a court renders a decision that is substantially opposite the decision made in the prior case. A decision can be overruled only by the same court or a higher court within the same **jurisdiction.** The overruling of a decision generally destroys its value as **precedent.** Compare *reversal*.

2. to deny a **motion,** objection or other point raised to the court.

OVERT ACT open act; especially, an outward act done in furtherance of a crime and as a manifestation of **intent** to accomplish the crime. See also **attempt; conspiracy; treason.**

EXAMPLE: Sal and Ed agree to rob a bank. In preparation, Sal steals a car and Ed buys a ski mask. Both the theft of the car and the purchase of the ski mask as well as any other acts innocent or criminal may be *overt acts* if they are done in furtherance of a criminal conspiracy.

OVER-THE-COUNTER MARKET [OTC] a **securities** dealers market that handles trading in securities that are not **listed stocks** on an organized exchange. OTC trading differs from exchange trading in two significant ways: (1) transactions are carried out through telephone contact and negotiation with a number of dealers, called market makers, as compared to the single specialist, single location auction market mechanism used for listed securities trading, and (2) the market maker acts as principal in the transaction that involves the dealer as buyer and seller from his own inventory. The bulk of **bond** trading is carried out in the OTC market.

OWNERSHIP exclusive right of possessing, **enjoying,** and disposing of a thing; often said to include the concept of **possession** and that of **title,** thus to be broader than either.

ALLODIAL OWNERSHIP free ownership, not subject to the restrictions or obligations associated with feudal tenures.

TENURIAL OWNERSHIP the holding of land subject to specific **services** or obligations owed to another. See **fee simple.**

OYER AND TERMINER in English law, special tribunals empowered to hear and determine cases within their criminal **jurisdiction,** commissioned by the king when the delay involved in ordinary prosecution could not be tolerated, as in the case of sudden insurrection. The term has been sometimes used in American law to identify high courts of criminal jurisdiction in some states.

P

PACTUM *(päk'-tŭm)* Lat.: pact, **contract,** agreement. See also **nudum pactum.**

PAIN AND SUFFERING a species of **damages** that one may recover for physical or mental pain that results from a wrong done. See also **survival statute.**

PALIMONY an award of support like **alimony** but made to a partner in a dissolved nonmarital relationship. Where the partners had an **express contract,** founded on consideration other than sexual services, some courts have held the contract enforceable; where no such formal agreement exists, the court may determine whether the conduct of the parties warrants a finding of **implied** contract or other understanding to support an award.

PANDER to pimp, to cater to the lust of another. A PANDERER is a pimp, procurer, male bawd. PANDERING is 1. the crime of inducing a female to become a prostitute; 2. the promotion of obscene literature or movies by appeals to prurient interests. See **aid and abet; solicitation.**

PAR equal to the established value; denotes the face amount or stated value of a **negotiable instrument, stock** or **bond,** and not the actual value it would receive on the open market. Bills of exchange, stocks and the like are AT PAR when they sell for their stated value.

PAR VALUE is the stated or **face value** of a stock or bond. It has little significance for common stock; current practice is to issue **no-par stock** or stock with an arbitrary low value to avoid taxes. In the case of **preferred stock,** par takes on added importance since it specifies the dollar value upon which dividends are paid, and preferreds are usually offered for sale or exchange at par value. The par value on bonds specifies both the maturity payment and interest base.

PARALEGAL one not a member of the bar who is employed, usually by a law office, to perform a variety of tasks associated with a law practice, any of which may be performed properly and conveniently by one not trained or authorized to practice law.

PARAMOUNT TITLE a **title** that will prevail over another asserted against it; signifies immediate right of **possession,** and is generally referred to as the basis for **eviction** of a **tenant** by one with a right of possession superior to that of the tenant.

PARAMOUR one's lover; one in the place of a husband or wife, but ordinarily without the legal rights attached to the marital relationship. See **palimony.**

PARCENER in **common law,** one who, jointly with others, as **coparcener,** holds an **estate** by virtue of **descent** (i.e., **inheritance**). The holding of a parcener is generally known as an estate in coparcenary and usually refers to the estate held by each inheritor before the inheritance has been divided (i.e., **partitioned**). The term is no longer widely used, since it is now said to be indistinguishable from a TENANCY IN COMMON (see **tenancy**).

PARDON an exercise of the **sovereign** prerogative to relieve a person from further punishment and from legal disabilities resulting from a crime of which he has been **convicted.** Its effect is that of relaxing the punishment and blotting out guilt, so that in the eyes of the law the offender is as innocent as if he had never committed the offense.

EXAMPLE: Joyce is convicted of destroying government property in a protest march. As a result of that conviction, Joyce can no longer keep her job as a state employee. A few years later, serious questions are raised as to some of the witnesses' truthfulness, especially in light of the excellent reputation Joyce enjoyed before her conviction. After being presented with the issues, the governor grants Joyce a *pardon*. That pardon enables Joyce to work once more for the state.

CONDITIONAL PARDON any pardon imposing some condition, precedent or subsequent, before it will become effective.

See **amnesty; commutation; executive clemency.**

PARENS PATRIAE *(pă'-reňz pă'-trē-ī)* Lat.: parent of his country. The role of the state as sovereign and guardian of persons under legal disability. By exercising this authority the state emphasizes that a child is not the absolute property of a parent but is a **trust** reposed in a parent by the state as parens patriae.

PARENT CORPORATION see **subsidiary.**

PARI DELICTO see **in pari delicto.**

PAROLE in criminal law, a conditional release from imprisonment that entitles the person receiving it to serve the remainder of his term outside prison if he complies with all the conditions connected with his release. Compare **probation.**

PAROL EVIDENCE oral rather than written **evidence.**

PAROL EVIDENCE RULE [MERGER CLAUSE] a rule that declares that when terms of a **contract** have been embodied in a writing (called the **integration** of the agreement) to which both parties have assented, *parol* (oral) evidence of contemporaneous or prior oral agreements is not **admissible** for the purpose of varying or contradicting the written contract.

EXAMPLE: Mike signs a contract with a home improvement builder to construct a pool at certain specifications. When the project is completed, Mike claims that the builder orally agreed to change the specifications at Mike's request. Because the specifications were never changed, Mike refuses to pay, and the builder sues him. Unless the circumstances allow Mike to introduce as *parol* [oral] *evidence* the builder's statement agreeing to the changes, the builder will probably prevail on the basis of his written contract with Mike.

PARTIAL BREACH a **breach** that gives rise to a claim for **damages** but that is so slight that it does not substantially impair the value of the **contract** to the injured party and thus does not give the injured party cause to abandon the whole contract.

PARTICULARS, BILL OF see **bill of particulars.**

PARTITION a judicial separation of the respective interests in land of joint owners or TENANTS IN COMMON (see **tenancy**), so that each may take **possession** of, **enjoy** and control his separate **estate.** Partition is thus the dissolution of the **unity** of possession existing between common owners, with the result that the parties hold their estates in **severalty.** Partition is available whenever desired by any **co-tenant** in a tenancy in common.

A JOINT TENANCY (see **tenancy**) can be destroyed by either the **sale** or the **mortgaging** of a joint owner's interest in the estate, and the resultant tenancy in common is then subject to partition, thus defeating the **survivorship** rights of other joint tenants in the sold or mortgaged property.

EXAMPLE: Pat and his friend own a large piece of undeveloped land as tenants in common. Pat uses his ownership interest to obtain a loan from the bank. When he defaults on the loan, the bank can seek a *partition* of the land. With a partition, the bank owns one-half of the land and Pat's friend owns one-half. Subsequent to a partition, the parties own particular portions of the land. If the land cannot be divided equitably, the land would be sold and the proceeds divided.

PARTNERSHIP 1. a **contract** of two or more persons to place their money, effects, labor and skill, or some or all of them, in lawful business, and to divide the profit and bear the loss in certain proportions; 2. an association of two or more persons to carry on as co-owners a business for profit. Partners are individually liable for the **debts** of the partnership, and assets individually owned will be subject to **execution** to satisfy any such debt when partnership assets are insufficient. A partnership is not subject to tax; rather the income is divided and taxed as personal income to the individual partners, unlike profits in corporations. The decision whether to form a partnership or to incorporate is generally controlled by the tax consequences.

LIMITED PARTNERSHIP an entity in which one or more persons, with unlimited liability (called **GENERAL PARTNERS**), manage the partnership, while one or more other persons contribute only **capital.** This latter group of partners (called **LIMITED PARTNERS**) have no right to participate in the management and operation of the business and assume no liability beyond the capital contributed. Compare **corporation.**

PARTY 1. in a judicial **proceeding,** a **litigant (plaintiff** or **defendant);** a person directly interested in the subject matter of a case; one who would assert a **claim,** make a **defense,** control proceedings, examine **witnesses** or **appeal** from the **judgment.** 2. a person or entity that enters into a **contract, lease, deed,** etc.

INDISPENSABLE PARTY one whose involvement in the subject matter of a **controversy** is such that his **interests** will be affected, or one whose **joinder** in the **action** is required to enable a complete **adjudication** of the issues as well as the fashioning of an effective **remedy.** A **suit** cannot in **equity** and good conscience proceed without one who is regarded as an indispensable party.

EXAMPLE: Ball Corporation is the largest maker of a chemically based ceiling tile, although other smaller companies also produce the product. The tiles were installed in school buildings, and the chemical in them has had an adverse effect on the children. It could not be determined which company's tiles had been used, but only the smaller companies are named in a suit by the children. Ball is never mentioned. The other companies want Ball named as an *indispensable party* because, by numbers alone, it is most likely that Ball's tiles were used in schools. Ball also wants to be named because it fears that a judgment against the other companies will be used against it, even though it did not have an opportunity to participate in the litigation, and because otherwise a favorable outcome for the other companies would not prevent Ball from being sued later for the same thing.

NECESSARY PARTY one whose interests will be affected by the suit or without whom complete relief cannot be granted, but who will not be joined if doing so would deprive the court of **jurisdiction** in the case.

NOMINAL PARTY party appearing on the **record** not because he has any real interest in the case, but because technical rules of **pleading** require his presence in the record.

PROPER PARTY one who has an interest in the subject matter of the **litigation,** but without whom a substantial **decree** may nevertheless issue, though such decree will not settle all questions in the controversy with respect to such party.

REAL PARTY IN INTEREST see **real party in interest.**

THIRD PARTY someone other than the parties directly involved in the action or transaction; an outsider with no legal interest in the matter.

PARTY WALL a dividing wall between adjoining landowners that exists for the common benefit of both properties that it separates, and of which any use may be made by either party, so long as such use is not detrimental to the other. The two landowners own the wall as TENANTS IN COMMON, (see **tenancy**), where the wall stands upon ground which is itself held in common, or where it stands partly upon each of the two adjoining properties. A party wall may be constructed wholly upon property belonging to one of the parties, or it may be owned entirely by only one of them; in either case the wall is subject to an **easement** to have it maintained. A party wall is often one that provides support for one or more separately owned structures.

PATENT evident; obvious.

PATENT OF INVENTION (often called simply a patent) a grant of right to exclude others from the making or selling of an invention during a specified time. It gives to its owner a legitimate **monopoly.** See **patent infringement.**

PATENT PENDING (often abbreviated PAT. PEND.) a notice that the product on which it is inscribed has been the subject of an application for patent protection and that if a patent does issue, those with notice will be subject to the applicant's prior rights.

PATENT OF LAND an instrument by which the government conveys a **fee simple** interest in land to another.

PATENT DEFECT a defect that could be recognized upon reasonably careful inspection or through ordinary diligence.

EXAMPLE: Alex examines a warehouse space prior to renting it for himself. Normal examination would reveal that water leaked into the warehouse in several spots. Some of Alex's property in the warehouse is subsequently damaged by water. Since the leakage is a *patent defect,* which he should have discovered, Alex cannot sue for the damage.

Compare **latent defect.**

PATENT INFRINGEMENT the act of trespassing upon the rights secured by a **patent.** The test of infringement is whether the device in question does substantially the same work in substantially the same way and accomplishes the same result as the device that has been patented.

Copyrights and **trademarks** can also be the subject of an infringement action.

PATERNITY SUIT [BASTARDY PROCEEDINGS] a suit initiated to determine the paternity of a child born out of wedlock and to provide for the support of that child once paternity is proved.

PAT. PEND. see **patent** [PATENT PENDING].

PATRICIDE the killing of one's own father.

PAWN to deposit personal property with another as security for the payment of a **debt.**

PAYABLES see **liabilities.**

PAYABLE TO BEARER see **bearer paper.**

PAYABLE TO ORDER see **order paper.**

PAYEE any **person** to whom a **debt** should be paid; one to whose order a **bill of exchange, note** or check is made payable.

PAYMENT IN DUE COURSE payment of a **negotiable instrument** at or after its date of maturity, made to its **holder** in good faith and without notice of any defect in his **title.**

EXAMPLE: Mark fraudulently obtains a negotiable promissory note made out by Paul and payable to a third party. When the note becomes due, Mark presents it to Paul and Paul *pays it in due course*. The third party cannot force Paul also to pay him, because Paul had no knowledge of the earlier fraud and, therefore, had no reason to suspect that the third party did not legitimately negotiate the note to Mark.

PEACEABLE POSSESSION possession that is not interrupted by adverse **suits** or other hostile action intended to **oust** the possessor from the land. The existence of adverse claims is not precluded, so long as no actual attempt to **dispossess** is made. See **quiet title.**

PEACEFUL ENJOYMENT see **quiet enjoyment.**

PECULATION the fraudulent **misappropriation** to one's own use of money or goods entrusted to his care. See also **embezzlement; larceny.**

PECUNIARY consisting of money or that which can be valued in money. A **PECUNIARY LOSS** is a loss of money or one that can be translated into economic loss.

PENAL INSTITUTION any place of confinement for **convicted** criminals.

PENAL LAW a law to preserve public order that defines an offense against the public and inflicts a penalty for its violation. **Statutes** that grant a private **(civil) action** against a wrongdoer are not considered penal, but **remedial,** in nature.

PENDENTE LITE [LITE PENDENTE] *(pĕn'-dĕn'-tā lē'-tā)* Lat.: suspended by the lawsuit; pending the lawsuit. Contingent upon the determination of a pending lawsuit.

EXAMPLE: Tenants in an apartment building sue their landlord for not providing heat. The tenants do not want to pay full rent since they are not getting heat, but state law requires full rent each month or else the landlord can evict. To protect themselves, the tenants commence a lawsuit and set up a bank account *pendente lite* where they deposit their rent each month while the suit is in court. At the end of the suit, the money in the account is applied to past-due rents less whatever amount the court says the tenants are entitled to for lack of heat.

A wife will seek alimony and child support payments *pendente lite* in most cases after she sues for divorce.

See also **lis pendens.**

PENDENT JURISDICTION federal court doctrine where-by a plaintiff, notwithstanding the limitations of **federal question jurisdiction,** may rely upon both federal and nonfederal grounds for the **relief** sought in a **complaint.** Thus, where the plaintiff joins a federal claim with a state law claim based on closely related or identical conduct of the defendant, the federal courts have jurisdiction to hear and determine the state law claims as well as those arising under federal law. See **abstention; ancillary jurisdiction.**

PENSION FUND see **retirement plan.**

PER ANNUM *(pĕr ăn'-nŭm)* Lat.: by the year; annually.

PER [PUR] AUTRE VIE *(pĕr [pūr] ô'-tr vē)* Fr.: for or during the life of another. A **life estate** measured by the life of a third person rather than the life of the **grantee.**

PER CAPITA *(pĕr kăp'-ĭ-tȧ)* Lat.: by the heads. Anything figured per capita is calculated by the number of individuals, (heads) involved and is divided equally among all.

PER CURIAM *(pĕr kū'-rē-äm)* Lat.: by the court. See **opinion [PER CURIAM OPINION].**

PER DIEM *(pĕr dē'-ĕm)* Lat.: by the day. 1. pay for a day's services. 2. Government and private business travel allowances are often allocated on a per diem basis.

PEREMPTORY absolute, final, not admitting of question or appeal. A peremptory trial date may be established by the court on its own **motion** or at the request of a **party** to insure timely disposition of the case. In selection of a **jury** each side has a right to a fixed number of PEREMPTORY CHALLENGES to the seating of potential **jurors,** which means that **counsel** may reject a certain number of potential jurors for any reason, or for no reason. See **peremptory writ.**

PEREMPTORY CHALLENGE see **challenge.**

PEREMPTORY PLEA see **plea.**

PEREMPTORY WRIT a peremptory **writ** is a form of **mandamus** that requires the act commanded be done absolutely. In comparison, a usual writ of mandamus permits the public official the choice of either doing the act commanded or showing legal cause why it need not be done. Before a peremptory writ can issue, the official must be given notice of the legal action and an opportunity to defend.

In **common law,** peremptory writs were a species of original writs by which lawsuits were begun. The peremptory original writ commanded the sheriff to cause the **defendant** to appear in court and to defend the suit. It was used when general damages to be assessed by the jury were requested. A suit was otherwise begun by the use of an optional writ, which commanded the defendant to do the acts requested or to show cause why they should not be done. This writ was used when the plaintiff requested a specific remedy, such as the return of a parcel of land or the payment of a specific sum.

PERFECTED completed, executed, enforceable, merchantable; refers especially to the status ascribed to **security interests** after certain events have occurred or certain prescribed steps have been taken, such as filing evidence of the interest, taking possession of the collateral, etc. A perfected security interest has **priority** over an unperfected interest. The date of perfection is also the time from which courts judge priority contests among other holding perfected interest.

In practice, after the accomplishment of all steps necessary to entitle a litigant to proceed in an **appellate court,** the appeal is said to be perfected.

PERFORMANCE the fulfillment of an obligation or a promise; especially, completion of one's duty under a **contract.** Compare **obligation of a contract.**

PERIODIC TENANCY see **tenancy.**

PERJURY criminal offense of making false statements under **oath.** In **common law,** only a willful and corrupt sworn statement made without sincere belief in its truth, and made in a judicial **proceeding** regarding a material matter, was perjury. Today, **statutes** have broadened the offense so that in some **jurisdictions** any **false swearing** in a legal instrument or legal setting is perjury.

EXAMPLE: Sheila is charged with robbery. At her trial, Tom, Sheila's boyfriend, admits to the crime, which results in a "not guilty" verdict for Sheila. Because of a procedural technicality, Tom cannot be tried for the robbery. But if the prosecution can prove that Tom lied about committing the crime, he could then be prosecuted for *perjury*.

PERMANENT INJUNCTION see **injunction.**

PERMISSIVE COUNTERCLAIM see **counterclaim; joinder [PERMISSIVE JOINDER].**

PERMISSIVE JOINDER see **joinder.**

PERMISSIVE WASTE see **waste.**

PER MY ET PER TOUT *(pĕr mē ā pĕr tū)* Law Fr.: by half and by whole. In joint **tenancy,** each tenant's share is the whole, for purposes of **tenure** and **survivorship** [tout], and each share is an **aliquot** portion for purposes of **alienation** [my].

PERPETUITIES, RULE AGAINST see **rule against perpetuities.**

PERPETUITY see **in perpetuity.**

PER QUOD *(pĕr kwŏd)* Lat.: through which; by which; whereby. Requiring extrinsic circumstances (context); acquiring meaning only by reference to external facts.

PER SE *(pĕr sā)* Lat.: through itself, by means of itself. Not requiring extraneous evidence or support to establish its existence.

PERSON in law, an individual or **incorporated** group having certain legal rights and responsibilities.

PERSONAL JUDGMENT **judgment** imposed on defendant requiring sums to be advanced from whatever assets he has within the jurisdiction of the issuing court, as opposed to a judgment directed against particular property (called an **in rem** judgment) or a judgment against a **corporate** entity. See **jurisdiction** [IN PERSONAM JURISDICTION].

PERSONAL JURISDICTION see **jurisdiction** [IN PERSONAM JURISDICTION].

PERSONAL PROPERTY [PERSONALTY] things movable, as distinguished from **real property** or things attached to the **realty.**

EXAMPLE: An agreement between a buyer and seller of a house provides that the sale covers only the land and home and not the seller's *personal property*. This agreement means that the seller can remove items such as furniture and rugs, but not the heating system.

PERSONAL SERVICE see **service.**

PERSONALTY see **personal property.**

PER STIRPES *(pĕr stûr'-pāz)* Lat.: through or by roots; by family stock representation. The essential characteristic of a distribution of an **intestate's estate** per stirpes is that each beneficiary receives a share in the property, representing the accurate fraction of the fraction to which the person through whom he claims from the ancestor would have been entitled. It is distinguished from a distribution **per capita.**

EXAMPLE: Frank dies without a will. His wife has predeceased him, and he is survived by two children. A third child has also predeceased him but has left two children. Under a *per stirpes* distribution, Frank's two children each receive one-third of his estate. The remaining one-third is distributed to the children of the third child who had predeceased Frank.

PER TOUT ET NON PER MY *(pĕr tū ā nōn pĕr mē)* Law Fr.: by the whole and not by the half. Describes the type of **seisin** that exists in a JOINT TENANCY or TENANCY BY THE ENTIRETY (see **tenancy**). Thus, the joint tenants or man and wife who own property by the entirety own an **undivided interest** in the whole of the property but not an individual interest in only a part of the property. See **partition; tenancy** [TENANCY IN COMMON].

PETITION in **equity** procedure, the functional equivalent of a **complaint at law.** It is a written application addressed to a court or judge, stating facts and circumstances relied upon as a cause for judicial action, and containing a **prayer** (formal request) for relief.

PETITIONER one who presents a petition to a court or other body either to institute an **equity** proceeding or to take an **appeal** from a **judgment.** The adverse party is called the **respondent.**

PETIT JURY [PETTY JURY] see **jury.**

PETIT LARCENY [PETTY LARCENY] see **larceny.**

PHYSICAL WASTE see **waste.**

PHYSICIAN-PATIENT PRIVILEGE see **privileged communication.**

PICKETING the practice, used in labor disputes, of patrolling, usually with placards, to publicize a dispute or to secure support for a cause; a constitutionally protected exercise of free expression when done peaceably.

PIERCING THE CORPORATE VEIL the process of imposing liability for corporate activity, in disregard of the corporate entity, on a person or entity other than the offending **corporation** itself.

Generally, the corporate form isolates both individuals and PARENT CORPORATIONS (see **subsidiary** [SUBSIDIARY CORPORATION] from liability for corporate misdeeds. However, there are times (such as when incorporation itself was accomplished to perpetrate a **fraud**) when the court will ignore the corporate entity and strip the organizers and managers of the corporation of the limited liability that they usually enjoy. In doing so, the court is said to pierce the corporate veil.

PLAGIARISM appropriation of the literary composition of another and passing off as one's own the product of the mind and language of another. The offense of plagiarism, known in the law as INFRINGEMENT OF COPYRIGHT, comes into being only when the work allegedly copied is protected by **copyright.**

PLAIN ERROR rule applicable to **appellate courts** that requires the **reversal** of a conviction and the award of a new trial where an obvious error in the trial **proceedings** affecting the fundamental right of the accused to a fair trial was not objected to at the time it occurred and went uncorrected by the trial court.

EXAMPLE: The prosecutor introduces very prejudicial evidence at Roy's trial. The judge fails to instruct the jury to limit their consideration of that evidence, despite the obvious need for such an instruction. Roy is convicted and the case is appealed. Even though Roy's attorney did not object to the introduction at the time it occurred—a procedure that would normally be required before a new trial could be granted—the appellate court may apply the *plain error* rule and grant Roy a new trial.

Compare **harmless error; miscarriage of justice.**

PLAINTIFF the one who initially brings the **suit;** he who, in a personal **action,** seeks a **remedy** in a court of justice for an injury to, or a withholding of, his rights.

PLAINTIFF IN ERROR one who appeals from a judgment against him in a lower court, whether he was plaintiff or defendant in that court.

THIRD PARTY PLAINTIFF refers to a **defendant** who files a **complaint** against a third party not named as a defendant by the plaintiff, and so not otherwise a party to the **proceeding.**

PLAIN VIEW a doctrine that may legitimize a search or **seizure** without a **search warrant,** which otherwise is generally required.

EXAMPLE: While walking on the sidewalk, a policeman sees a marijuana plant growing in someone's house. Under the *plain view* doctrine, the policeman can enter the house without a search warrant, even though a house represents a highly protected privacy area that in almost every other instance requires a search warrant prior to a policeman's entrance.

PLEA 1. in **equity,** a special answer relying upon one or more things as a reason for the **suit** to be dismissed, delayed or barred; 2. **at law,** broadly, any one of the common law **pleadings;** 3. technically, the **defendant's** or **respondent's** answer by matter of fact to the **plaintiff's** petition or **complaint,** as distinguished from a **demurrer,** which is an answer by a matter of law. 4. In criminal procedure, the defendant will enter a plea, at his **arraignment,** of not guilty, guilty or, in some jurisdictions, **nolo contendere** or **non vult** (meaning no contest). Pleas are either dilatory or peremptory.

DILATORY PLEA one that tends to defeat the actions to which it refers by contesting grounds other than the **merits** of plaintiff's case. Hence, the plea raises issues such as improper **jurisdiction,** wrong defendant, or other procedural defects.

INSANITY PLEA one by which the defendant claims innocence because of a mental disorder or inability to reason that prevented him from having a culpable mental state, i.e., from having the sense of purposefulness (intent, willfulness, recklessness) that is a necessary element of the crime charged.

PEREMPTORY PLEA one that answers the plaintiff's material contention, responding to the **merits** of plaintiff's case.

PLEA IN ABATEMENT one that does not deny the truth of plaintiff's contention, but introduces **new matter** to avoid what would otherwise be the effect of the pleader's failure to deny plaintiff's allegations.

PLEA BARGAINING the process whereby the accused and the prosecutor negotiate a mutually satisfactory disposition of the case. The defendant may plead guilty to a lesser offense or to only one or some of the courts in a multicount **indictment.** In return, the defendant seeks concessions on the type and length of his **sentence** or a reduction of counts against him.

EXAMPLE: Fred is charged with robbery while armed with a deadly weapon. All witnesses say that Fred was seen with a gun. However, the only gun found at the scene of the crime is on Fred's partner. In Fred's state, robbery with a deadly weapon carries a much greater sentence than robbery. Fred *plea bargains* with the prosecutor, offering to plead guilty to robbery if the prosecutor will dismiss the charge relating to the weapon and thus insure a shorter sentence. The State is spared the expense and uncertainty attendant to a trial, and defendant minimizes his overall exposure.

PLEAD 1. to make any **pleading;** 2. to answer **plaintiff's common law declaration;** 3. in criminal law, to answer to the **charge,** either admitting or denying guilt.

PLEADING BURDEN see **burden of proof.**

PLEADINGS statements, in logical and legal form, of the facts that constitute plaintiff's **cause of action** and defendant's ground of **defense.** Pleadings are either **allegations** by the parties affirming or denying certain matters of fact, or other statements in support or derogation of certain principles of law, which are intended to describe to the court or jury the real matter in dispute.

PLEADING THE FIFTH AMENDMENT see **Fifth Amendment; self-incrimination, privilege against.**

PLEA IN ABATEMENT see **dilatory plea.**

PLEDGE a deposit of **personal property** as security for a **debt;** delivery of goods by a **debtor** to a **creditor** until the debt is repaid; generally defined as a **lien** or a **contract** that calls for the transfer of personal property only as **security.** See **bailment; collateral.**

PLENARY full or unqualified. In judicial proceedings, denotes a complete, formally **pleaded** suit wherein a **petition** or **complaint** is filed by one or more persons against one or more other persons who file an **answer** or a response. A PLENARY ACTION is one in which a full trial or PLENARY HEARING is had on the merits of a complaint following full **discovery,** as distinguished from a **summary proceeding.**

POLICE COURT an inferior **municipal court** with limited **jurisdiction** in criminal cases. Minor cases can be disposed of by such courts, but otherwise they generally have power only to **arraign** the **accused** and set **bail.**

POLICE POWER inherent power of state governments, often delegated in part to local governments, to impose upon private rights those restrictions that are reasonably related to promotion and maintenance of the health, safety, morals and general welfare of the public. Restrictions upon the use of one's property, such as **zoning** laws, or upon the conduct of one's business, such as environmental regulations, are imposed by state and local governments pursuant to the police power.

EXAMPLE: A federal law sets out certain requirements for processing milk. One state has conclusively found that, because of conditions peculiar to the state, the requirements are insufficient to protect its citizens' health. Under the state's *police power,* the state legislature may enact greater precautions that all milk must meet to be sold in that state.

POLITICAL ASYLUM see **asylum.**

POLITICAL CORPORATION see **corporation, [PUBLIC CORPORATIONS].**

POLITICAL QUESTION a question that a court determines not to be properly subject to judicial determination (not to be **justiciable**), because resolution is committed exclusively to the jurisdiction of another branch of government (legislative or executive), or because adequate standards for judicial review are lacking, or because there is no way to insure enforcement of the court's judgment.

EXAMPLE: The Constitution provides that the Senate shall have advise and consent power for all treaties entered into by the President with other nations. After the Senate consents to a certain treaty, a suit is brought challenging the extent to which the Senate deliberated over the treaty. A court will rule that the issue is a *political question* that cannot be decided by the judiciary.

POLL TAX a direct tax of a fixed amount upon all persons, or upon all persons of a certain class, resident within a specified territory, without regard to their property or their occupation.

POLYGAMY in criminal law, the offense of having more than one husband or wife at one time.

POLYGRAPH a lie detector; an electromechanical instrument that measures and records certain physiologic changes that it is believed are involuntarily caused by the subject's conscious attempts to deceive the questioner. Once the machine has recorded the subject's responses to the questions propounded by the operator, the operator interprets the record and determines whether the subject is lying.

PORTFOLIO a group of **securities** held by an individual or institutional investor, which may contain a variety of common and preferred **stocks,** corporate and municipal **bonds, certificates of deposit** and **treasury bills**—that is, appropriate selections from the **equity, capital** and money markets.

POSITIVE FRAUD see **fraud [FRAUD IN FACT].**

POSITIVE LAW standards of conduct dictated by validly enacted laws, rather than by principles of **natural law.**

POSITIVISM in **jurisprudence,** the view that any legal system is best studied by concentrating on the **positive law** of that system. Compare **natural law.**

POSSE COMITATUS *(pŏ'-sā kŏm-ĭ-tä'-tus)* Lat.: able to be an attendant. Refers to those called to attend the sheriff to assist him in making an **arrest** for a **felony.** A person so summoned is neither an officer nor a mere private person, but occupies the legal position of a posse comitatus, and, while acting under the sheriff's orders, is as much clothed with the protection of the law as the sheriff himself. See **immunity.**

POSSESSION the having, holding or detention of **property** in one's control. When distinguished from mere **custody,** possession involves custody plus the assertion of a right to exercise dominion.

ACTUAL POSSESSION immediate and direct physical control over property. In **real property,** it involves actual occupation of the property or direct appropriation of the benefits it yields.

CONSTRUCTIVE POSSESSION the condition of having the conscious power and intention to exercise control over property, but without direct control or actual presence upon it.

EXAMPLE: Ken is arrested for unlawful possession of handguns found in the trunk of his car. Ken argues that he did not have *actual possession* of the guns, since the trunk was locked and he was driving the car. Although that fact may be true, he is still liable for prosecution if he had *constructive possession,* which in this case is shown by the fact that he is the only person with keys to the trunk.

CRIMINAL POSSESSION possession for which criminal sanctions are provided, because the thing (or property) either may not lawfully be possessed, may not be possessed by a particular category of persons or may not be possessed under certain circumstances.

POSSESSORY ACTION a lawsuit brought for the purpose of obtaining or maintaining possession of real property. See **tenancy** [TENANCY AT SUFFERANCE].

POSSESSORY INTEREST a right to exert exclusive control over certain land, coupled with intent to exercise that right. Compare **remainderman.**

POSSIBILITY OF A REVERTER the possibility of the return of an **estate** to the **grantor,** should a specified event occur or a particular act be performed in the future. It is thus a **reversionary** interest subject to a CONDITION PRECEDENT (see **condition**). The possibility does not itself constitute an estate, present or future. It describes the interest remaining in the grantor who conveys a **conditional** or **determinable fee.**

EXAMPLE: A father conveys a piece of real estate to his daughter as long as she remains unmarried. The possibility of the land returning to the father or his estate if the daughter marries creates a *possibility of a reverter* in the father.

Compare **reentry.**

POSTCONVICTION RELIEF PROCEEDINGS [PCR ACTIONS] a statutory or court rule procedure whereby a criminal **defendant** may challenge collaterally a **judgment** of **conviction** which has otherwise become final in the normal **appellate** review process. See **collateral** [COLLATERAL ATTACK]. Compare **habeas corpus.**

A **writ of coram nobis** is available in some states as a form of PCR. In other states an out-of-time motion for a new trial to correct a miscarriage of justice can afford this relief.

POST FACTO see **ex post facto.**

POSTING to affix physically in order to display. 1. In civil procedure, posting of certain required information is a substitute form of **service of process.** 2. In commercial law, posting is the procedure that a bank follows in deciding to finally pay a **negotiable instrument** and in recording its payment. It includes verifying any signature, ascertaining that sufficient funds are available, marking the item paid, charging the customer's account and correcting or reversing an entry or erroneous action with regard to the item. 3. Posting also refers to the exhibition of notices on real property, warning potential trespassers that trespass for fishing or hunting is not permitted by the property owner.

POST MORTEM *(pōst môr'-tĕm)* Lat.: after death. Examination of the body of a deceased to detemrine cause of death; may comprehend only examination by a **coroner** and may consequently not produce a true medical determination of cause of death, which involves **autopsy** and dissection. See **inquest.**

POUROVER 1. a provision in a will, or a whole will, that distributes money or other valuables to a previously established **trust;** 2. in rare instances, a provision in a trust placing the trust assets in a will.

POWER OF ACCEPTANCE the abiity of an offeree to create a binding **contract** by consenting to the terms of an **offer.**

An offer can be accepted only by the individual invited by the offeror to furnish the **consideration.**

The power of acceptance is always terminated by rejection or counteroffer by the offeree, **revocation** by the offeror, lapse of time specified in the offer, or death or incapacity of the offeror or offeree.

POWER OF APPOINTMENT authority given to a person to dispose of **property** of another, or of an **interest** therein. The authority must be to do an act that the grantor of the authority might lawfully do. **Title** to the property or interest passes directly from the **donor** of the power; the party having the power of appointment acts merely as a conduit through which title passes.

A power of appointment does not itself constitute an **estate** or interest, but the **donee** of the power may also be granted, in the same **instrument,** a present or **future interest** in the subject or property over which the power is to be exercised. The donee is then said to have a **POWER COUPLED WITH AN INTEREST**.

Powers of appointment are exercisable **inter vivos** (by **deed** or similar instrument) or by **testamentary disposition (will.)** A **GENERAL POWER** may be exercised by the donee in favor of any person(s) he chooses, including himself or his estate. The donee of a **SPECIAL POWER** is limited in the choice of **beneficiaries** by the donor of the power, and so must appoint in favor of member(s) of the class specified in the instrument creating the power.

EXAMPLE: A trust instrument created by a grandmother gives her son a special *power of appointment* to distribute the income generated by the trust principal to all of the grandmother's living grandchildren. The son has no power to touch the principal, but he has discretion to determine which grandchildren get how much of the interest.

POWER OF ATTORNEY an **instrument** in writing by which one person, as **principal,** appoints another as his **agent** and confers upon him the authority to perform certain specified acts or kinds of acts on behalf of the principal. The primary purpose of a power of attorney is to evidence the authority of the agent to third parties with whom the agent deals.

PRACTICE refers to the rules governing all aspects of a court proceeding.

PRAYER [FOR RELIEF] request contained in a **complaint** or **petition** that asks for relief to which plaintiff thinks himself entitled.

PREAMBLE an introductory clause in a **constitution, statute** or other legal instrument that states the intent or underlying reason for the instrument.

PRECATORY advisory or in the form of a recommendation or request rather than a command; applied to language, usually in a **trust** or a **will,** by which the **settlor** or **testator** expresses a wish to benefit another but does not impose an enforceable **obligation** upon any party to carry out this wish. Depending upon how equivocal the language is, the trust or disposition may or may not be enforceable by the person whose benefit the testator seeks.

EXAMPLE: The mother's will leaves her home to her son. Other language in the will provides that if her home is ever sold by the son, she hopes that it will be sold to some other member of the family. That *precatory* language creates a doubt as to whether the son has an obligation to sell the house to another family member and as to what will happen should the son sell to someone else.

PRECEDENT previously decided case recognized as authority for the disposition of future cases. In **common law,** precedents were regarded as the major source of law. A precedent may involve a novel question of common law or it may involve an interpretation of a **statute.** To the extent that future cases rely upon the precedent or distinguish it from themselves without disapproving of it, the case will serve as a precedent for future cases under the doctrine of **stare decisis.**

PRECEDENT CONDITION see **condition.**

PRECEDING ESTATE a prior estate upon which a **future interest** is limited. Thus, a **remainder** is said to **vest** upon the termination of a preceding estate, such as a **life estate.**

PREEMPTION a doctrine based on the **supremacy clause** of the federal constitution, under which a state may be deprived of **jurisdiction** over matters embraced by an Act of Congress, regardless of whether the state law coincides with, is complementary to or opposes the federal legislation. When Congress legislates in an area of federal concern, it may specifically preempt all state legislation (thus OCCUPYING THE FIELD) or may bar only inconsistent legislation; where Congress does not directly indicate its intention in this regard, the court will determine that intention based on the nature and legislative history of the enactment.

EXAMPLE: A state owns a railroad that operates in interstate commerce and uses guidelines to insure safety. Congress then passes legislation establishing greater safety requirements for railroads nationwide. Since Congress has the power to regulate interstate commerce, its guidelines *preempt* the state guidelines and the state must follow the national requirements.

State legislatures may preempt local governments in the same manner.

In international law, the term expresses the right of a nation to detain goods of a stranger in transit so as to afford its citizens a chance to purchase those goods.

PREEMPTIVE RIGHTS the right specified in the **charter** of a **corporation,** granting to existing **shareholders** the first opportunity to buy a new issue of **stock.** Corporations implement such a charter provision by distributing, in advance of a new issue, subscription rights or **warrants** to existing shareholders in proportion to their current holdings. Shareholders have the choice of exercising the rights by purchasing shares of the new issue or of selling the rights in the open market. Rights usually have market value due to pricing of the new issue slightly below the prevailing market.

PREFERENCE the paying or securing by an **insolvent debtor,** to one or more of his **creditors,** the whole or a part of their claims, to the exclusion or detriment of other creditors. Under the Bankruptcy Act, a **bankrupt** is deemed to have given a preference if within four months preceding the filing of his petition for bankruptcy he procures or suffers a judgment against himself or makes a transfer of any of his assets; the effect of this is to give a creditor a greater percentage of his debt than any other creditor of the same class.

PREFERRED DIVIDEND see **dividend.**

PREFERRED STOCK part of the CAPITAL STOCK (see **capital**) of a **corporation** that enjoys **priority** over the remaining stock, or **common stock,** in the distribution of profits and, in the event of dissolution of the corporation, in the distribution of assets as well.

PREJUDICE see **dismissal** [**DISMISSAL WITH PREJUDICE; DISMISSAL WITHOUT PREJUDICE**].

PREJUDICIAL ERROR see **reversible error.**

PRELIMINARY HEARING in criminal law, 1. a **hearing,** before **indictment,** to determine whether **probable cause** for the arrest of a person existed; 2. a hearing to determine whether there is sufficient **evidence** to warrant the **defendant's** continued detention and whether submission of such evidence to the GRAND JURY (see **jury**) is warranted. Compare **arraignment.** See also **fair hearing.**

PREMEDITATION forethought. As one of the **elements** of first-degree murder, the term is often equated with **intent** and deliberateness.

PREMISES land and its **appurtenances;** land or a portion thereof and the structures thereon. For purposes of insurance on a building, or in defining the crime of **burglary,** or with respect to the scope of a **search warrant,** the range of the term may vary.

EXAMPLE: A search warrant lists 118 South Street as the *premises* to be searched. If there is a garage at 118 South Street that is not attached to the house, the warrant would not extend to the garage. It is not considered part of the premises, because a search warrant must list with particularity the places to be searched. To cover the garage, the warrant would have to list 118 South Street and the adjacent garage.

With respect to **Workers' Compensation Acts,** premises may include any place where the employee may go in the course of his employment.

PREMIUM 1. the sum paid to the insurer as **consideration** for a policy of **insurance;** 2. money paid by a buyer for an **option** to buy or sell corporate **stock;** 3. a reward for an act done.

PREPONDERANCE OF THE EVIDENCE general standard of **proof** in civil cases. The phrase refers to the degree of proof that will lead the **TRIER OF FACT** (see **fact finder**) to find that the existence of the fact in issue is more probable than not. See **clear and convincing.**

PREROGATIVE WRIT a written order issued by a court in furtherance of its **discretionary** powers. The prerogative writs are the writs of **procedendo, mandamus, prohibition, quo warranto, habeas corpus** and **certiorari.**

EXAMPLE: A corporation files a suit in federal district court challenging a part of a federal securities statute. It loses in the district court and also in the Court of Appeals. It asks the Supreme Court to issue a writ of certiorari to the Court of Appeals so that the Supreme Court can rule on the question. The Supreme Court has the discretion to issue the writ, making the writ a *prerogative writ*.

PRESCRIPTION a means of acquiring an **easement** on the land of another by continued regular use over a specified period of time. Compare **adverse possession.**

PRESCRIPTIVE EASEMENT see **easement.**

PRESENTMENT 1. a written accusation of crime by the **GRAND JURY** (see **jury**) upon its own initiative, without consent or participation of a prosecutor, in the exercise of the jury's lawful inquisitorial powers; 2. the presenting of a **bill of exchange** or **promissory note** to the party on whom it is **drawn,** for his acceptance, or to the person bound to pay, for payment.

PRESUMPTION an assumption of fact resulting from a rule of law that requires such fact to be assumed from another fact or set of facts. The term indicates that the law accords to a given evidentiary fact heavy enough weight to require the production of contrary **evidence** to overcome the assumption thereby established. This rule of evidence thus has the effect of shifting either the **burden of proof** or the burden of producing evidence.

EXAMPLE: Bill writes a check to a car repair establishment that the bank refuses to cash. The law in Bill's state establishes a *presumption* that he knowingly intended to write a bad check if (1) there is no account in Bill's name at the bank named on the check or (2) the shop was refused payment for lack of funds within thirty days of the date on the check and Bill did not pay the amount owed within ten days of being informed of the bank's refusal to honor the check.

Compare **inference.**

CONCLUSIVE [OR NONREBUTTABLE] PRESUMPTION one that no evidence, however strong, no argument, or consideration will be permitted to overcome. Since a presumption always properly refers to a rebuttable assumption of fact, when the term presumption is used in this conclusive sense, it is not a true presumption but is a statement by the court of a rule of law.

REBUTTABLE PRESUMPTION an ordinary presumption that, as a matter of law, must be made once certain facts have been proved, thus establishing a certain conclusion **prima facie;** but it may be rebutted. If it is not overcome through contrary evidence, it becomes conclusive. The prevailing doctrine is that competing facts are weighed on their own merits, without further reference to the presumption.

PRESUMPTION OF INNOCENCE prevailing assumption that the **accused** is innocent until proven **guilty.** Because of this **presumption,** the government bears the **burden of proof** that the **defendant** is guilty beyond a **reasonable doubt.**

PRESUMPTIVE EVIDENCE evidence that is indirect or **circumstantial; prima facie** evidence or evidence that is not conclusive and admits of explanation or contradiction; evidence that must be treated as sufficient unless rebutted by other evidence, such as evidence that a **statute** deems to be presumptive of another fact unless rebutted.

PRETRIAL DISCOVERY see **discovery.**

PRETRIAL INTERVENTION [PTI] a remedial program by which first-time or petty criminal offenders are not subjected to the regular judicial process, but rather are immediately placed under probationary supervision for a period usually no longer than one year. The program allows persons accused of crime to avoid the stigma of conviction and a permanent criminal record by correcting their criminal behavior during the period of probation. Pre-conviction probationary programs divert persons from the ordinary criminal process without an admission of guilt or a conviction, and, for this reason, are called **DIVERSIONARY PROGRAMS**.

PRICE FIXING under federal **antitrust laws,** a combination or **conspiracy** for the purpose and with the effect of raising, lowering or stabilizing the price of a commodity in interstate commerce.

HORIZONTAL PRICE FIXING price fixing engaged in by competitors at the same commercial level.

VERTICAL PRICE FIXING price fixing engaged in by members of different levels of production, such as manufacturer and retailer.

PRIMA FACIE *(prī'-mà fā'-shà)* Lat.: at first view, on its face. Not requiring further support to establish existence, validity, credibility.

EXAMPLE: Sid is caught with untaxed cigarettes. In the state where he is caught, untaxed cigarettes are designated *prima facie* contraband and are immediately subject to forfeiture to the state.

PRIMA FACIE CASE 1. a case sufficient on its face, supported by at least the requisite minimum of **evidence,** and free from obvious defects; 2. state of facts that entitles a party to have his case go to the **jury;** 3. a case that will usually prevail in the absence of contradictory evidence; 4. a case in which the evidence is sufficient to support, but not to compel, a certain conclusion and does no more than furnish evidence to be weighed, but not necessarily to be accepted, by the **TRIER OF FACT** (see **fact finder**).

PRIMOGENITURE *(prē-mō-jĕn'-ĭ-tūr)* ancient **common law** doctrine governing **descent,** under which the eldest son takes all property of decedent father. The opposite of primogeniture, **BOROUGH ENGLISH**, existed under local custom in at least one **jurisdiction** even while primogeniture prevailed elsewhere in England; the youngest son inherited on the death of the father. Under the local custom of gavelkind all sons took equally. In the event all **issue** of the decedent were daughters, they took equal shares in **coparceny.**

PRINCIPAL most important. 1. in criminal law, one who commits an offense, or an **accomplice** actually or constructively present during commission of the offense. 2. in commercial law, the amount received in loan, or the amount upon which interest is charged; 3. in the law of **agency,** one who has permitted or engaged another to act for his benefit, in accordance with his direction and subject to his control.

DISCLOSED PRINCIPAL one whose identity is known to the party dealing with the agent.

PARTIALLY DISCLOSED PRINCIPAL one whose identity is not known, but whose existence is known, to the party with whom the agent deals.

UNDISCLOSED PRINCIPAL one of whose existence the party

dealing with the agent is not aware—i.e., the third party does not know he is dealing with an agent.

EXAMPLE: Henry buys property for Sphinx Mall Company. Sphinx desires to be an *undisclosed principal* because it believes that land prices would skyrocket if sellers knew who the real purchaser is.

PRIORITY preference; the condition of coming before, or of coming first, in a **bankruptcy** proceeding; the right to be paid before other **creditors** out of the assets of the bankrupt party. The term may also be used to signify such a right in connection with a **prior lien,** prior **mortgage,** etc.

PRIOR LIEN a first or superior **lien,** entitled to satisfaction before others.

PRIVATE CORPORATION see **corporation.**

PRIVATE NUISANCE see **nuisance.**

PRIVATE RULING see **revenue ruling** [PRIVATE RULING].

PRIVILEGE 1. a particular benefit enjoyed by a person, company or class beyond the advantages of other citizens; 2. an exceptional exemption, or an immunity held beyond the course of the law; 3. an exemption from some burden or attendance, with which certain persons are indulged, from a supposition of the law that the public offices or duties require so much time and care that, without this indulgence, their duties could not be performed to the advantage that the public good demands. See **privileged communication.**

EXAMPLE: All citizens of a county are required to be available for jury duty. Doctors are *privileged* to avoid this requirement, because of their constant need to attend to their patients.

PRIVILEGE AGAINST SELF-INCRIMINATION see **self-incrimination, privilege against.**

PRIVILEGED COMMUNICATION communication that occurs in a setting of legal or other recognized professional confidentiality. Designating a communication as privileged allows the speakers to resist legal process to disclose its contents. When communications are termed privileged, a **breach** by one party of the concurrent confidentiality can result in a **civil suit** in **tort** by the othe party to the communication. Communications that are privileged may include: (1) communications in the sanctity of the marital relationship; (2) communications between a physician and his patient; (3) communications of psychological counselors and their clients; (4) priest-and-penitent communications; (5) communications between attorney and client; and (6) in some **jurisdictions,** communications between a journalist and his sources.

ATTORNEY-CLIENT PRIVILEGE an evidentiary **privilege** protecting the confidential communications between a client and his or her attorney from disclosure to any other party; can be waived by the client but not by the attorney.

EXAMPLE: John discusses with his attorney a past wrong he is alleged to have committed. If the attorney is asked to discuss this without John's permission, he will not be permitted to do so since the communication was privileged.

PRIVITY a relationship between parties out of which arises mutuality of interest.

PRIVITY OF CONTRACT the relationship between two or more contracting parties. To maintain an **action** on any contract, there must be a privity between the plaintiff and defendant in respect to the matter sued on.

PRIVITY OF ESTATE mutual or successive relation to the same right in the same property. A privy in **estate** derives from another person's **title** to property, by contract (**grant, will** or other voluntary transfer of possession) or law (**descent, judgment,** etc.).

HORIZONTAL PRIVITY privity of estate between the covenantor and covenantee. Horizontal privity is satisfied any time an estate is **conveyed** from one party to another, provided that the **covenant** is made at the time of the transfer.

EXAMPLE: Julie sells some of her land to a neighbor, who by the sale acquires ownership of a lake. Three months later the neighbor conveys to Julie the right to use the lake. Julie then sells her portion of the land to another party. That party does not have the right to use the lake. The requirements of *horizontal privity* are not met because the covenant is made after the transfer of the land between Julie and the neighbor.

VERTICAL PRIVITY the privity of estate between the covenantor and his successor in interest who acquires the property subject to the *covenant*.

See **easement** [RECIPROCAL NEGATIVE EASEMENTS]; **run with the land.**

PRIVY a person connected with another or having mutual interest with him in the same **action** or thing, by **contract** or otherwise.

PROBABLE CAUSE a requisite element of a valid **arrest** or **search and seizure;** consists of knowledge of facts and circumstances sufficient in themselves to warrant belief that a crime has been committed (in the context of an arrest) or that property subject to seizure is at a designated location (in the context of a search and seizure). Compare **stop and frisk.**

EXAMPLE: A policeman, patrolling a high crime area where narcotics offenses are particularly troublesome, observes two men exchange money on a street and then go to a nearby car to retrieve a package from the trunk. One of the men sticks his finger in the bag, puts his finger in his mouth to taste something, stuffs the bag in his pocket and walks away. This routine occurs several times. The owner of the vehicle is known to the officer as a drug dealer. The policeman has *probable cause* to obtain a warrant to search the vehicle and any person who receives a package from the trunk.

PROBATE 1. act of proving that an **instrument** purporting to be a **will** was signed and otherwise executed in accordance with the legal requirements for a will, and of determining its validity; 2. combined result of all procedures necessary to establish the validity of a will. In some **jurisdictions** a PRO-

PROBATE COURT is a special court having jurisdiction of proceedings incident to the settlement of a decedent's **estate.**

PROBATION procedure whereby a **defendant** found guilty of a crime, upon a **verdict** or **plea** of guilty, is released by the court without imprisonment, subject to conditions imposed by the court, under the supervision of a PROBATION OFFICER. Compare **parole.**

PROBATIVE tending to prove a particular proposition or to persuade one of the truth of an allegation.

PROBATIVE FACTS 1. matters of **evidence** required to prove **ultimate facts;** 2. facts from which the ultimate and decisive facts may be properly inferred.

PROBATIVE VALUE the relative weight properly accorded particular evidence.

EXAMPLE: The prosecutor wants to introduce an accused's past criminal record as evidence of the accused's guilt of the offense with which he is presently charged. In the past the accused has committed similar offenses. The accused replies that if his record is introduced, the jury might convict him exclusively because of his prior record as opposed to the evidence before it. The judge refuses to allow the introduction of the evidence, finding that the *probative value* of the prior record is far outweighed by the prejudicial effect it will have on the jury's consideration of the evidence. Although the prior record is relevant, that relevance is not sufficient to overcome the right of the accused to be judged on the basis of the evidence of the present offense and not upon demonstration of a criminal disposition. If the defendant decides to testify, the record may be used to impugn his credibility. In that event, the court will instruct the jury that it may only consider the prior record for that limited purpose. Such instructions are rarely effective.

PRO BONO PUBLICO *(prō bō'-nō pūb'-ly-kō)* Lat.: for the public good or welfare. When an attorney takes a case without compensation to advance a social cause, or to fill a perceived social need to offer legal representation to the poor, the attorney represents the party pro bono publico. The phrase pro bono is sometimes used.

PROCEDENDO *(prō-sā-dĕn'-dō)* Lat.: duty to have proceeded. Refers to a **writ** issued by a superior court when a cause has been improperly removed to it, as by **certiorari,** commanding the inferior court from which it was removed to assume **jurisdiction** and proceed to judgment on the cause. It is more frequently called a **remand.**

PROCEDURAL DUE PROCESS see **due process of law.**

PROCEDURE legal method; the machinery for carrying on the **suit,** including **pleading, process, evidence** and **practice.** The term thus refers to the mechanics of the legal process—the body of rules and practice by which justice is meted out by the legal system—rather than the substance and content of the law itself. See **adjective law.** Compare **substantive law.**

EXAMPLE: The Federal Rules of Civil Procedure guide the federal courts in conducting all aspects of cases before them, from the filing of a suit to the trial itself. The rules also instruct attorneys how they must proceed with these cases. Although these rules govern only *procedure,* not the actual merits of the case, a failure to abide by the rules could easily result in a valid claim being dismissed by the court. Each state court also has rules of procedure.

PROCEEDING 1. the succession of events in the process of judicial action; 2. the form in which actions are to be brought and defended, the manner of intervening in suits, of conducting them; the mode of deciding them, of opposing and of executing **judgments.**

PROCESS 1. a formal writing **(writ)** issued by authority of law; 2. any means used by the court to acquire or to exercise its **jurisdiction** over a person or over specified property; 3. usually refers to the method used to compel attendance of a **defendant** in court in a **civil** suit. See **service of process.**

PROCTOR 1. one who manages another's affairs, acting as that person's **agent;** 2. an attorney who is admitted to practice in a **probate, admiralty** or ecclesiastical court. Compare **administrator.**

PRODUCTION BURDEN see **burden of proof.**

PRODUCTS LIABILITY a concept in the law of **torts** holding a manufacturer **strictly liable** in tort when an article he places on the market, knowing it is to be used without inspection for defects, proves to have a defect that causes injury to a human being. One who sells any defective product unreasonably dangerous to the consumer or to his property may be liable for physical harm thereby caused to the consumer or to his property, even though there is no contractual or other relationship between seller and user, and even though the seller has not been **negligent.** See **warranty.**

EXAMPLE: A manufacturer sells a food processor to a department store, which in turn sells it to Ann. The rotary mechanism in the machine has a tendency to engage when the top of the processor is off. Ann's finger is cut when this problem occurs. She can sue the manufacturer under a *products liability* theory.

PROFFER to offer **evidence** at **trial.** The **admissibility** of evidence so offered is governed by the appropriate **jurisdiction's** rules of evidence.

PRO FORMA *(prō fôr'-mȧ)* Lat.: for the sake of form; as a matter of form. 1. In practice, the term usually means that an **appealable decree** or **judgment** was entered by the court, not because of an intellectual conviction that the decision rendered was right, but merely to facilitate further proceedings. 2. In accounting, the term is used in reference to the presentation of financial statements that represent proposed events in the form in which they would appear if or when the event actually occurred. Examples include presentation of consolidated statements in connection with a proposed corporate **merger** and presentation of **balance sheet** data showing the effect of a proposed financing.

PRO HAC VICE *(prō häk vē'-chā)* Lat.: for this turn; for this one particular occasion. The allowance of that which under ordinary circumstances is not permitted. Usually the term is used to describe the permission granted an out-of-state lawyer to appear in a particular case with the same standing as a local attorney admitted to practice in the **jurisdiction.**

PROHIBITION see **writ of prohibition.**

PROMISE a declaration of one's intention to do or to refrain from doing something.

BREACH OF PROMISE see **breach** [BREACH OF PROMISE].

ILLUSORY PROMISE see **illusory promise.**

PROMISSORY ESTOPPEL an **equitable** doctrine that declares that if injustice can be avoided only by enforcement of a promise, the pledge is binding, though there is no **consideration** for the promise and it cannot therefore be enforced as a contract. The promisor, having induced in the promisee **reliance** on the promise for certain action or forbearance, is said to be **estopped** to deny the existence of a contract, though in fact one has not been made. Compare **assumpsit.**

PROMISSORY NOTE a kind of **negotiable instrument** wherein the **maker** agrees to pay a specific sum at a definite time.

PROOF the quantity or quality of **evidence** that tends to establish the existence of a fact in issue. See also **burden of proof; inference; moral certainty; preponderance of the evidence; presumption; reasonable doubt.**

PROOF BEYOND A REASONABLE DOUBT see **reasonable doubt.**

PROPER PARTY see **party.**

PROPERTY every species of valuable right or **interest** that is subject to **ownership,** has an exchangeable value or adds to one's wealth or **estate.** Property describes one's exclusive right to possess, use and dispose of a thing, as well as the object, benefit or prerogative that constitutes the subject matter of that right.

COMMON PROPERTY 1. that which belongs to the citizenry as a whole; 2. property owned by **TENANTS IN COMMON** (see **tenancy**), or in some **jurisdictions** where designated by **statute,** that owned by husband and wife. Compare **community property.**

PERSONAL PROPERTY see **personal property.**

REAL PROPERTY see **real property.**

PROPORTIONAL REPRESENTATION a system of election designed to insure that different groups will have their interests represented, something that may not necessarily occur in a majority rule scheme.

EXAMPLE: A university faculty is comprised of 65 percent full-time and 35 percent part-time members. Under a *proportional representation* system for election of an appointments committee, each class will be able to have a voice on the committee.

PROPRIETARY INTEREST any right in relation to a **chattel** that enables a person to retain its **possession** indefinitely or for a period of time.

PRO RATA *(prō rā'-tȧ)* Lat.: according to the rate, i.e., in proportion. According to a measure that fixes proportions. Thus, a lease terminated by agreement before the expiration of the full term may call for the payment of rent on a pro rata basis for the expired term of the lease.

PRO SE *(prō sā)* Lat.: for himself; in one's own behalf. One appears pro se in a legal **action** when he represents himself without aid of counsel.

PROSECUTION 1. the act of pursuing a lawsuit or criminal **trial;** 2. the party initiating a criminal **suit,** i.e., the state. Where the civil **litigant,** or the state in a criminal trial, fails to move the case towards final resolution or trial as required by the court schedule, the matter may be dismissed for **WANT OF PROSECUTION** or for **FAILURE TO PROSECUTE.**

PROSECUTOR public official who prepares and conducts the **prosecution** of persons accused of **crime.** In certain cases, the legislature may appoint a **SPECIAL PROSECUTOR** to conduct a limited investigation and prosecution. The state prosecutors are usually called district attorneys or county prosecutors. The federal prosecutor is known as the United States Attorney for a certain federal district. The prosecutor is charged with the duty to see that the laws of his **jurisdiction** are faithfully executed and enforced.

PROSECUTORIAL DISCRETION see **discretion.**

PROSTITUTION the giving or receiving of the body for sexual intercourse for hire. A person who sells his or her body for sexual intercourse is a **PROSTITUTE.** See **pander; solicitation.**

PRO TANTO *(prō tän'-tō)* Lat.: for so much; to the extent, but only to the extent.

PRO TEMPORE [PRO TEM] *(prō tĕm'-pō-rā)* Lat.: for the time being.

PROTEST 1. a demand for payment of a **note,** its nonpayment, and consequent **dishonor;** 2. a formal certification by a consul, **notary** or the like that an **instrument** has been dishonored. A protest must identify the instrument and certify that due **presentment** has been made, or show why it has been excused, and that the instrument has been dishonored by nonacceptance or nonpayment.

EXAMPLE: Frank deposits one of his customer's checks in the bank, but the check is returned for lack of sufficient funds in the customer's account. Frank files a *protest* with the customer and demands that the debt now be paid in cash.

PROVISIONAL REMEDY see **remedy.**

PROVISO a condition or stipulation. Its general function is to except something from the basic provision, to qualify or restrain its general scope, or to prevent misinterpretation.

PROXIMATE CAUSE see **cause** [PROXIMATE CAUSE].

PROXY 1. recipient of a grant of authority to act or speak for another; 2. one permitted to vote in place of a **stockholder** of a **corporation,** who is thereby presumably voicing the will of his **principal.** 3. the instrument used to grant this authority.

PRUDENT-MAN RULE a flexible legal investment standard that allows a **fiduciary** to purchase **securities** that a person of discretion and intelligence would choose to earn a reasonable income and to preserve the **principal.** See also **trustee.**

EXAMPLE: A father sets up a trust for his two sons, naming a bank as trustee. The trust instrument provides no definition of how the trust principal should be invested. The trustee is bound by the *prudent-man rule* and must purchase securities that may not offer the highest return possible but are very safe investments.

PUBLIC CORPORATION see **corporation.**

PUBLIC DOMAIN 1. all lands and waters in the possession of the United States, and all lands owned by the several states, as distinguished from lands possessed by private individuals or corporations; 2. information, the source of which is available to anyone and is not subject to **copyright.**

PUBLIC EASEMENT any **easement** enjoyed by the public in general, such as the right of passage over the surface of streets and highways. Also called a DEDICATION, meaning that use of the land has been devoted for such purposes by the owner of the **fee.**

EXAMPLE: A developer wants to construct a tall office building but needs part of the sidewalk adjacent to the area. The city is willing to allow this infringement of a *public easement* if the builder will provide other access to the public, such as an open passageway through the building or an alternate facility for public usage.

PUBLIC NUISANCE see **nuisance [PUBLIC or COMMON NUISANCE].**

PUBLIC PROPERTY that which is dedicated to the use of the public, or that over which the state has dominion; describes the use to which the property is put, or the character of its ownership. Compare **public domain; public easement.**

PUBLIC SALE see **sale.**

PUBLIC SECURITIES see **securities.**

PUBLIC TRUST 1. CHARITABLE TRUST (see **trust**); 2. the public's confidence reposed in their elected officials and expectation that these elected officials will faithfully perform the duties of public office.

PUBLIC TRUST DOCTRINE A doctrine under which the state is said to own lands lying under navigable waters and to hold such lands in trust for the benefit of the people of the state. According to this doctrine, these submerged lands may not be sold or otherwise alienated by the state except in a manner that promotes the public interest.

PUBLIC USE the public's right to use or to benefit from the use of **property** condemned by the government through the exercise of its power of **eminent domain.** One of the limitations upon the use of this power is that property so taken must be for a public use.

PUFFING a statement of belief not meant as fact; a seller's extravagant statements, made to enhance his wares and induce others to enter into a bargain. Salesmanship talk, characterized as puffing, cannot be the basis of a charge of **fraud** or **express warranty,** since the buyer is said to have no right to rely on sales talk.

EXAMPLE: Tim *puffs* his cooking utensils by stating that they are the best quality utensils money can buy or the easiest to clean or the least expensive compared to other brands. A purchaser of these utensils then finds a nearly identical set that costs a few dollars less. Tim's comments cannot be taken as facts and do not give rise to a cause of action against Tim by the customer for misleading advertising or the like.

PUNITIVE DAMAGES see **damages** [EXEMPLARY DAMAGES].

PUR AUTRE VIE see **per autre vie.**

PURCHASE-MONEY SECURITY INTEREST see **security interest.**

PURLOIN to steal; to commit **larceny.**

PURVIEW the enacting part of a statute distinguished from other parts, such as the **preamble.** Conduct is WITHIN THE PURVIEW of a statute when such conduct properly comes within the statute's purpose, operation or effect.

EXAMPLE: The legislature passes a statute prohibiting the possession of burglar's tools. Workmen such as locksmiths or window repairmen commonly have these tools as part of their trade. Their possession of the tools would not come *within the purview* of the statute.

PUTATIVE alleged; supposed. Thus, a putative marriage is one that is actually void, but that has been contracted in good faith by the two parties, or by one of the parties. The putative father in a **paternity suit** is the person alleged to have fathered the child whose parentage is at issue in the suit.

PUT OPTION see **stock option** [PUT OPTION].

PYRAMIDING the use of paper profits from an investment to finance purchases of additional investments. Compare **margin.**

Q

QUAERE *(kwē'-rē)* Lat.: a **query.**

QUANTUM MERUIT *(kwän'-tūm mĕ'-rū-ĭt)* Lat.: as much as he deserved. 1. Historically, it was a common **count** in the action of **assumpsit,** allowing recovery for services performed for another on the basis of a **contract** implied in law or an implied promise to pay the performer for what the services were reasonably worth.

2. It refers today to a theory under which a **plaintiff** may recover for reasonable value of services or materials furnished to another who has enjoyed those materials or services under circumstances that reasonably notified him that the plaintiff expected to be paid. The doctrine imposes **liability** for a contract implied by law, which arises not from the consent of the parties but from the law of natural justice and **equity,** and which is based on the doctrine of **unjust enrichment.** See **quasi** [QUASI CONTRACT].

EXAMPLE: A physician renders emergency services to an unconscious accident victim. Consent to those services by the injured party is implied in law, so that the physician may bring an action in *quantum meruit* to recover the reasonable value of the services.

QUARE CLAUSUM FREGIT *(kwä'-rā klaü'-zūm frā'-gĭt)* Lat.: wherefore he broke the close. An early form of **trespass** designed to obtain **damages** for an unlawful entry upon another's **land.** The **form of action** was called trespass quare clausum fregit, or trespass qu. cl. fr. **BREAKING A CLOSE** was the technical **common law** expression for unlawful entry upon land. Even without an actual fence the complainant would **plead** that the "defendant with force and arms broke and entered the close of the **plaintiff,**" since in the eyes of the common law every unauthorized entry upon the soil of another was a trespass.

QUASH to annul, overthrow or vacate by judicial decision.

QUASI *(kwā'-zi; kwä'-zē)* Lat.: as it were, so to speak; about, almost, like.

QUASI CONTRACT one that, unlike a true **contract,** is not based on the apparent intention of the **parties** to undertake the **performances** in question, but is an obligation created by law for reasons of justice and fairness. The doctrine of quasi-contract is based upon the principle that a party must pay for a benefit he desired and received under circumstances that render it inequitable for him to retain it without making compensation. See **quantum meruit; unjust enrichment.**

EXAMPLE: A car owner brings his car in for brake repairs. The mechanic fixes the brakes and in doing so he also fixes a separate part of the axle that has a direct relationship to the car's ability to brake correctly. Although the axle repair was not specifically contracted for, a *quasi contract* is implied for which the owner must pay the mechanic.

QUASI CORPORATION see **corporation.**

QUASI-CRIMINAL describes a **proceeding** that, though not actually a criminal **prosecution,** is sufficiently similar in terms of the substantial **sanction** (civil fine, loss of employment, loss of license, suspension from school, etc.) or the stigma attached to warrant some of the special **procedural** safeguards of a criminal proceeding. See also **due process.**

QUASI IN REM describes proceedings that are not purely **in rem** but that are brought against the **defendant** personally, although the real object is to deal with particular property; refers to **actions** for money **damages** begun by **attachment, garnishment** or other seizure of property, where the court has no **jurisdiction** over the defendant but has jurisdiction over a thing belonging to the defendant or over a person who is indebted or under a duty to the defendant.

QUEEN'S BENCH see **King's Bench.**

QUERY question; indicates that the proposition or rule it introduces is unsettled or open to some question.

QUESTION OF FACT disputed factual contention that is traditionally left for the **jury** to decide, unless the judge is serving as TRIER OF FACT (see **fact finder**) in the case.

EXAMPLE: The jury is asked to decide if Fred developed a product while he was employed by his company or after he was fired. That issue is a *question of fact,* and the legal significance of the answer (who is entitled to what) is for the judge to determine.

Compare **question of law.**

QUESTION OF LAW disputed legal contentions that are traditionally left for the judge to decide. The occurrence or nonoccurrence of an event is a **question of fact;** its legal significance is a question of law.

EXAMPLE: Two parties stipulate [agree] on the facts of the situation in which they are involved. The judge is then asked to only rule on the *question of law* that those facts present.

QUID PRO QUO *(kwĭd prō kwō)* Lat.: something for something. In some legal contexts, synonymous with **consideration;** sometimes referred to as the quid and always indicating that which a party receives or is promised in return for something he promises, gives or does.

QUIET ENJOYMENT the right to unimpaired use and enjoyment of **property.** For **leased** premises, a guarantee of quiet enjoyment is usually expressed by a COVENANT OF QUIET ENJOYMENT in a written lease, but such a **covenant** may be implied today from the landlord-tenant relationship, even where it is not so expressed. This covenant is violated if the tenant's enjoyment of the premises is substantially disturbed either by wrongful acts or omissions of the landlord or by persons claiming a superior **title** against the landlord.

EXAMPLE: A company agrees to lease a warehouse owned by a landlord. When the company's lease is to begin, the tenants who were in the warehouse are still there. Their presence violates the company's right to *quiet enjoyment.* A few states may place the burden of removing the tenants on the company, but most states place the burden on the landlord.

In that majority of states, if those tenants do not leave after a certain amount of time, the company can rescind the lease without penalty.

The covenant may be and often is included in a **deed** conveying title to property. If it is present in a deed, the **grantor** is obligated to protect the estate of his **grantee** against lawful claims of ownership by others.

QUIET TITLE a **suit** in **equity** brought to obtain a final determination as to the **title** of a specific piece of property. A quiet title action is distinguished from an action to REMOVE CLOUD ON TITLE, which is brought to determine and resolve problems of **instruments** conveying a particular piece of land, rather than to resolve the actual claims to that land.

EXAMPLE: Evan believes he is the rightful owner of a parcel of land, but there is a question concerning the transfer of the land twenty-five years ago. In order to satisfy any doubts so that he may sell the property, Evan brings a *quiet title* action to confirm his ownership by judicial decree.

QUITCLAIM DEED a **deed** that conveys only that right, **title** or **interest** that the **grantor** has, or may have, and that does not warrant that the grantor actually has any particular title or interest in the property. The grantor under a quitclaim deed represents merely that whatever interest he may have he conveys to the grantee.

QUORUM the number of members of any body who must necessarily be present in order to transact the business of that body.

QUOTATION 1. in commercial usage, a statement of the price of an item; 2. the price stated in response to an inquiry.

QUOTIENT VERDICT see **verdict.**

QUO WARRANTO *(kwō wär'-rän-tō)* Lat.: by what right or authority. An ancient **common law writ** that was issued out of **chancery** on behalf of the king against one who claimed or usurped any office, **franchise** or liberty, to inquire by what authority he asserted such a right, in order that the legitimacy of the assertion might be determined. Formerly a criminal method of **prosecution,** it has long since lost its criminal character and is now a **civil** proceeding, expressly recognized by **statute,** and usually employed for **trying the title** to a corporate franchise or to a corporation or public office.

Quo warranto proceedings may be brought against **corporations** where the company has abused or failed for a long time to exercise its franchise. In the case of an official, it may be brought to cause him to forfeit an office for misconduct. If in these cases a quo warranto proceeding determines that a company no longer properly holds a franchise or that an officer no longer properly holds his office, it will oust the wrongdoer from enjoying the franchise or office. The purpose of the writ is not to prevent an improper exercise of power lawfully possessed; its purpose is to prevent an official, corporation or persons acting as such from usurping a power that they do not have.

R

RACE see **recording acts.**

RANSOM 1. money or other consideration paid for the release of a kidnapped or otherwise captured person or thing; 2. to redeem from captivity by payment.

RAPE act of unlawful sexual intercourse accomplished through force or threat of force by one party and implying lack of consent and resistance by the other party.

CARNAL KNOWLEDGE was the original term for the act itself and is retained in many **statutes** that proscribe "carnal knowledge of a child," regardless of purported consent. This offense is often called STATUTORY RAPE.

RATABLE proportional, capable of estimation; taxable. Thus, a ratable **estate** is a taxable estate. In **bankruptcy,** a ratable distribution is a **pro rata** share of the bankrupt's **assets.** Ratable does not mean equal, but rather pro rata according to some measure fixing proportions.

RATIO DECEDENDI *(rä'-shē-ō dā-sā-dĕn'-dē)* Lat.: the reason for the decision; the principle that the case establishes.

RATIO LEGIS *(rä'-shē-ō lā'-gĭs)* Lat.: legal reasoning or grounds; the underying principle; theory, doctrine or science of the law.

EXAMPLE: A loitering statute permits law enforcement officers to disperse crowds of people rather than arrest each person and go through a series of formalities not actually necessary in the circumstances. The *ratio legis* of the statute is to allow the officers more latitude in attempting to prevent crime rather than to rely solely on apprehension and sentencing as a deterrent.

RAVISH generally, synonymous with **rape.** Literally, to ravish is to seize or snatch by force. Traditionally, a valid **indictment** for rape required the use of the term ravished, which implied force or violence; it would thus constitute an essential word in all indictments for rape, importing not only violence on the part of one party but resistance on the part of the other.

REAL ESTATE every possible **interest** in land, except for a mere **chattel** interest.

REAL ESTATE INVESTMENT TRUST [REIT] a specialized investment organization that functions as a financial intermediary in the real estate debt market and that qualifies under Internal Revenue Code requirements to act as a conduit with respect to income distributions. The **Massachusetts Trust** is a popular legal form for REITs. **Trusts** fall into two basic categories: **equity** trusts, which invest in income properties under terms that provide equity ownership and/or participation in income, and **mortgage** trusts that lend funds on a short-term basis for development and construction and on a long-term basis for first and second mortgages.

REALIZATION 1. the conversion of an asset into money; 2. in tax law, the occurrence of a transaction deemed to be a sufficiently substantial economic change for the **taxpayer** to warrant imposition of INCOME TAX (see **tax**). If the tax is imposed, the event gives rise to **recognition.**

GAIN OR LOSS REALIZED the difference between the amount realized on a **sale or exchange** of an asset and the taxpayer's **basis** in such asset.

EXAMPLE: A taxpayer buys stock for $5 a share. Ten years later, he sells the stock for $15. The taxpayer has a *realization* of $10 on each share and must pay tax on the total gain. If the stock is sold at $1, he has a loss of $4 a share, and his income is reduced by that amount before his tax liability is calculated.

REAL PARTY IN INTEREST the person who will be entitled to the benefits of the legal **action** if it is successful; one who is actually and substantially interested in the subject matter, as opposed to one who has only a nominal, formal or technical interest in it. For example, if an insurance company pays its insured for damage done his automobile under a collision insurance provision of his policy and if the insurance company attempts to collect its loss from the responsible party, the suit may be brought in the name of the insured, but the real party in interest will be the insurance company.

REAL PROPERTY 1. land and whatever is erected or growing on it, or affixed to it; 2. rights issuing out of, annexed to, and exercisable within or about, the land. Compare **chattel.**

REALTY an interest in land; another word for **real property.**

REAPPORTIONMENT changing of a legislative district or of the number of seats a state is entitled to in the Congress to more clearly reflect the population of that district or state; an attempt to meet the right of every person to vote on a one-person, one-vote basis. Compare **gerrymander.**

EXAMPLE: Each legislative district elects one person to represent them in Congress, but one district has only 10,000 people whereas another district covers 20,000 people. *Reapportionment* will attempt to make each district equal in size.

REASONABLE DOUBT refers to the degree of certainty required of a **juror** before he can make a legally valid determination of the guilt of a criminal **defendant.** These words are used in **instructions** to the **jury** in a criminal trial to indicate that innocence is to be presumed unless the jury can see no reasonable doubt of the guilt of the person charged. The term does not require that proof be so clear that no possibility of error exists; it means that the evidence must be so conclusive that all reasonable doubts are removed from the mind of the ordinary person. See also **moral certainty.**

EXAMPLE: Jay is charged with first degree murder, which requires that he intentionally planned the death. At his trial, he attempts to show that the killing occurred on the spur of the moment in a fit of rage. He is trying to create in the jurors a *reasonable doubt* that he planned the murder. If he is successful in that effort, he may lower the degree of his guilt to **manslaughter.**

REASONABLE MAN [OR PERSON] a phrase used to denote a hypothetical person who exercises qualities of attention, knowledge, intelligence and judgment that society requires of its members for the protection of their own interest and the interests of others. Thus, the test of **negligence** is based on either a failure to do something that a reasonable person, guided by considerations that ordinarily regulate conduct, would do, or on the doing of something that a reasonable and prudent person would not do.

REBUTTABLE PRESUMPTION see **presumption.**

REBUTTAL EVIDENCE any **evidence** that refutes, counteracts or explains away evidence given by a **witness** or an adverse party. Rebuttal evidence is offered to contradict other evidence or to rebut a **presumption** of fact.

REBUTTER a form of common law **pleading** that was a defendant's answer of fact to the plaintiff's response to the defendant's **rejoinder.**

RECAPITALIZATION a recasting of the **capital** structure of a **corporation.** A typical **capitalization** will contain **bonds** (called funded debt), **preferred stock** and **common stock.** Voluntary recapitalization could involve exchanging an existing bond issue or exchanging a preferred stock issue for bonds.

EXAMPLE: A corporation finds that the amount of its outstanding loans to banks is greater than the corporation wants. The directors *recapitalize* the corporation by exchanging shares of the corporation's stock for money to repay the loans. The corporation thus receives additional equity investors in return for reduction of its debt.

Recapitalizations are common when public companies emerge from **bankruptcy.**

See **refinancing.**

RECAPTURE a term generally applied when an event or transaction requires a **taxpayer** to repay earlier tax savings by payment of additional tax in the present **taxable year.** Thus, upon a **sale** or **exchange** of property that constitutes a **CAPITAL ASSET** (see **capital**), the gain realized on such sale or exchange constitutes **capital gain.** However, under certain circumstances, if the taxpayer has taken excess **depreciation** (**ACCELERATION DEPRECIATION** over **STRAIGHT LINE DEPRECIATION**) with respect to real property or any depreciation with respect to personal property, to the extent of such depreciation the gain realized on the sale or exchange of that property is taxed as **ORDINARY INCOME** (see **income**) and not as capital gains. This taxation of the proceeds of the sale or exchange or the capital asset as ordinary income is recapture.

RECEIVABLES see **accounts receivable; balance sheet.**

RECEIVER 1. a neutral person appointed by the court to receive and preserve the property that is the subject of **litigation** during the period of litigation, or to manage and dispose of the property as the court or officer may direct. The court takes possession of the property in controversy through its **agent,** the receiver, during the litigation or after the **decree** or **judgment,** for the benefit of the people entitled to the property, when the court does not deem it proper that either party have control of it during that time. Although the assets involved in the litigation are in **custody** of the receiver, **title** to the assets remains in the owners who are parties to the litigation, and the receiver manages the property for the benefit of the parties.

A receiver is frequently appointed in **insolvency** proceedings to manage the property of the insolvent for the benefit of his **creditor.**

2. In criminal law, one who obtains possession of property that he knows or believes to have been stolen is a receiver of stolen property and commits an offense thereby.

RECEIVERSHIP 1. an **equitable** remedy whereby property is by order of the court placed under the control of a **receiver** so that it may be preserved for the benefit of affected parties. A failing company may be placed in receivership in an **action**

brought by its **creditors.** The business is often continued but is subject to the receiver's control. A receivership is ancillary to or in aid of the main **relief** sought in an action; it is sometimes used to carry out an **order** or **decree** but is generally used for the purpose of preserving property during **litigation** involving rights in the property. 2. the status of property affected by this remedy; property is said to be in receivership.

EXAMPLE: The Antique Furniture Company is heavily indebted to several creditors and is only showing average sales. In a court-approved agreement between the owners of the company and the creditors, Antique is placed in *receivership*. The court appoints a receiver to oversee Antique's expenditures and orders. At the same time, the creditors settle for a partial payment of the debt and dismiss the rest of the debts against Antique.

Compare **bankruptcy.**

RECESS 1. temporary adjournment of a trial or hearing after commencement of the trial or hearing. The recess may be short, for lunch, overnight or for a few days. If it amounts to a substantial delay in the proceedings, it is called a **continuance.** 2. the intermission between sittings of the same legislative body at its regular or adjourned session, but not the interval between the final adjournment of one body and the convening of another at the next regular session. Compare **sine die.**

RECIDIVIST a second offender or habitual criminal, who is often subject to extended terms of imprisonment under habitual offender statutes. See **criminal.**

RECIPROCITY generally, a relationship between persons, corporations, states, or countries whereby privileges granted by one are returned by the other. Compare **comity.**

RECKLESS careless, inattentive to duty; foolishly heedless of danger; rashly adventurous; indifferent to consequences; mindless; very negligent.

In criminal law, the term connotes conscious disregard of

a substantial and unjustifiable risk, a gross deviation from the standard of care that a **reasonable person** would observe in the actor's situation, a wanton indifference to the consequences of one's acts.

RECKLESS DISREGARD refers to conduct without concern for consequences or danger. Compare **negligence.**

EXAMPLE: Fully aware that his conduct creates a risk of harm, Richard lights a pack of firecrackers and throws them into a crowd. Regardless of whether anyone is hurt, Richard has acted with *reckless disregard.*

RECOGNITION imposition of tax under the federal income tax system. Income or loss that the **taxpayer** has **realized** is recognized when it is subject to **tax.**

RECOGNIZANCE, ONE'S OWN see **release on recognizance [R.O.R.].**

RECORD 1. to preserve in a writing, printing, on film, tape, etc.; 2. a precise history of a **suit** from beginning to end, including the conclusions of law thereon, drawn by the proper officer to perpetuate the exact facts.

EXAMPLE: A court rule provides that a judge must inform a person convicted of a crime of his right to an attorney to pursue his appeal if he so desires. Since all comments by the judge are transcribed, a *record* is produced that will eliminate any question whether the person was informed of his rights.

The RECORD ON APPEAL consists of those items introduced in **evidence** in the lower court, as well as a compilation of **pleadings, motions, briefs** and other papers filed in the proceeding in the inferior court. 3. in real property law, to enter in writing in a repository maintained as a public record any mortgage, sale of land or other interest affecting real property located within the jurisdiction of the government entity maintaining the public record.

RECORDING ACTS in real property law, statutes that afford a means of giving CONSTRUCTIVE NOTICE (see **notice** to others of ownership respecting **estates** or **interests** in land, by providing for recording the existence of that estate or interest. These statutes generally provide for recording **deeds, mortgages,** EXECUTORY CONTRACTS (see **executory**) of sale and **leases** of specified duration. When one's interest or ownership in land is recorded, the recording prevents a subsequent purchaser or **mortgagee** of the land from qualifying as a **bona fide purchaser** for value without notice, because the instrument recorded would provide at least constructive notice of another's prior ownership or interest in the land.

Under a RACE type of recording act, the first person who records takes in preference to other persons who receive an interest from the same source, even if the first recorder had notice of a prior unrecorded conveyance. A RACE-NOTICE type of act operates like the race statute, but only if the first recorder had no notice of the prior unrecorded conveyance. NOTICE type recording acts provide that a bona fide purchaser is favored even though a prior purchaser is the first to record, so long as the second purchaser had no knowledge of the prior conveyance at the time he made his purchase.

Where there is a GRACE PERIOD provided by a recording act, a prior conveyee is protected against a subsequent conveyee even if he doesn't record first, as long as he records within the period of grace defined by the recording act. See also **chain of title.**

RECOUPMENT 1. the right of **defendant** to have **plaintiff's** award of **damages** against defendant reduced; 2. a right of deduction from the amount of the plaintiff's claim by reason of either a payment thereon or some loss sustained by the defendant because of the plaintiff's wrongful or defective **performance** of the **contract** out of which his claim arose; 3. a withholding, for an equitable reason, of something that is due. The word is nearly synonymous with discount, deduction or reduction. Compare **counterclaim; cross-claim.**

RECOVERY 1. the establishment of a right by the **judgment** of a court, though recovery does not necessarily imply a return to whole or normal; 2. the amount of the judgment; 3. the amount actually collected pursuant to the judgment.

RECUSAL disqualification of a judge, jury or administrative officer for prejudice or interest in the subject matter. A judge may be recused as a result of objection by either party, or he may voluntarily disqualify himself if he fears he may not act impartially, or that some circumstance will lead to a suspicion of bias.

EXAMPLE: Jerry has been before a judge several times on criminal charges and has been acquitted each time. After each trial, the judge makes certain disparaging comments indicating to the press that he believes Jerry is guilty. When Jerry comes before the judge again, Jerry seeks a *recusal* based on the earlier comments. Jerry contends that the comments indicate prejudice on the judge's part and will prevent his getting a fair trial.

In most states, a judge may also be disqualified because he is related within certain degrees to a party litigant.

REDEEMABLE BOND a bond that is callable for payment by the issuer.

REDEMPTION a regaining of possession by payment of a stipulated price; especially, the process of annulling a **defeasible title,** such as is created by a **mortgage** or tax sale, by paying the **debt** or fulfilling other obligations.

For tax purposes, a redemption is any purchase by a **corporation** of its own stock.

RIGHT OF REDEMPTION statutory right in some jurisdictions to redeem property that has been **forfeited** because the **mortgagor** had **defaulted** on the mortgage payments. It can be exercised only after the **foreclosure** and sale of the property, by paying the amount due on the mortgage, plus interest. It is a personal privilege and not an interest or **estate** in land, and it can be exercised only by the persons and on the condition named in the statute that grants the right. This right arises only after the **equity of redemption** period ends. It frequently applies to foreclosure under tax foreclosure statutes.

REDUCTIO AD ABSURDUM *(rā-dŭk'-tē-ō äd äb-sûr'-dŭm)*

Lat.: to reduce to the absurd. To disprove a legal argument by showing that it ultimately leads to an absurd position.

REENTRY the resumption of **possession** pursuant to a right reserved when the former possession was surrendered. It was a remedy given by the feudal law for nonpayment of rent, and also refers to a right reserved in the conveyance of a **fee** that is subject to a CONDITION SUBSEQUENT (see **condition**). See **conditional fee.** Compare **ejectment; quiet title.**

REFEREE a quasi-judicial officer appointed by a court for a specific purpose, to whom the court refers power and duty to take **testimony,** determine issues of fact and report the findings for the court to use as a basis for judgment.

REFERENDUM referring of legislative acts to the voters for final approval or rejection.

REFINANCING **refunding** existing elements of the **capital** structure; usually implies selling a new **bond** issue to provide funds for **redemption** of a maturing issue. See **recapitalization.**

REFORMATION an **equitable** remedy consisting of a revision of a **contract** by the court, in cases where the written terms of the contract do not express what was actually agreed upon. Thus, reformation is generally only decreed upon a **clear and convincing** showing of MUTUAL MISTAKE (see **mistake**); if only one party was mistaken, reformation is not appropriate unless the mistake of one party resulted from the other party's **fraud.**

EXAMPLE: Two parties negotiate a contract that inadvertently calls for a delivery date that predates the signing of the contract. Neither party realizes this mistake at the time, but, subsequently, one of the parties tries to use this fault as a reason for cancelling the contract. Since a delivery date can never come before a contract is completed, the court *reforms* the contract and does not permit the one party to cancel.

REFUNDING the process of selling a new **issue** of **securities** to obtain funds needed to retire existing securities. Debt refunding is done to extend maturity and/or to reduce debt service cost. See **refinancing.**

REGIONAL STOCK EXCHANGE a domestic exchange located outside New York City. See **stock exchange.**

REGISTER to record formally and exactly; to enroll; to enter precisely in a list or the like. For **corporations,** to record the names of **stock** and **bond** holders on the books of the company. The **REGISTRAR** may be an **agent,** such as a bank, or it may be the corporation. The registrar is responsible for preventing unauthorized issuance of stock by a company.

REGISTERED BOND see **bond.**

REGISTERED COUPON BOND see **bond.**

REGISTERED REPRESENTATIVE a commission sales person who is qualified to take orders for **securities** from the general public. A securities sales trainee must be trained in the securities trade for at least six months and must pass tests prepared by the **National Association of Securities Dealers** [NASD] and the **New York Stock Exchange;** when training and testing are successfully completed, the trainee is registered with the **Securities and Exchange Commission,** the NASD, the American and New York Stock Exchanges and regional exchanges, and is registered in the various states in which the sales person intends to do business.

REGISTRAR see **register.**

REGISTRATION STATEMENT a document that must be approved by the **Securities and Exchange Commission [SEC]** before a company makes a public offering of new securities through the mails or in interstate commerce. The registration statement must describe the securities and must disclose in detail information on the nature of the business, including accounting statements, the identity of the management and key stockholders, the purpose of the offering, and the use to be made of the proceeds.

REGISTRY [OF DEEDS] an officially maintained book that provides a place and mechanism for registering evidences of **conveyances** of interests in **real property,** so that notice may be available to all third parties that there has been a change in the ownership of property effected by a conveyance of that property.

REGULATION T a regulation of the **Securities and Exchange Commission** that governs the maximum amount of credit that **securities** brokers and dealers may extend to customers for the initial purchase of regulated securities.

REGULATION U a rule of the **Securities and Exchange Commission** that governs the maximum amount of credit that banks may extend for the purchase of regulated **securities.**

REGULATION Z the body of regulations promulgated by the Federal Reserve Board pursuant to the federal **Truth in Lending Act** that entrusts that administrative agency with supervision of compliance by all banks in the Federal Reserve System with the cost of credit disclosure requirements established under the Act.

REGULATORY AGENCY a government body responsible for control and supervision of a particular activity or area of public interest. For example, the Federal Communications Commission (FCC), in addition to its other duties, administers the laws regulating access to communication facilities such as television and radio airwaves. Regulatory agencies are also called ADMINISTRATIVE AGENCIES.

EXAMPLE: The Environmental Protection Agency was created by Congress to protect the quality of the nation's air, water and land. Pursuant to that goal, the agency monitors air pollution in cities, sewage treatment plants, chemical landfills, etc. The Federal Trade Commission regulates commercial practices and takes action against deceptive advertising and monopolistic activity. There are many federal and state *regu-*

latory agencies that enforce federal and state policies in particular areas of governmental regulation.

REGULATORY OFFENSE a deed that is not inherently evil but is a crime only because prohibited by legislation, i.e., **malum prohibitum.** Regulatory offenses are also called STATUTORY OFFENSES and may impose **strict liability** upon defendants for their violation.

REHEARING a **retrial,** a new hearing and a new consideration of the case by the court (or other body) in which the suit was originally heard, and upon the **pleadings** and **depositions** already in the case.

REHEARING EN BANC see **en banc.**

REJOINDER in **pleadings,** in **common law,** an answer to **plaintiff's** replication by some matter of fact, in an **action at law.**

RELATION BACK the principle that an act done at a later time is deemed by law to have occurred at a prior time, often for purposes of the **statute of limitations** or rules of procedure permitting amendment of **pleadings.**

RELEASE a written document or the act of writing by which some **claim,** right or interest is given up to the person against whom the claim, right or interest could have been enforced.

In the law of property, the holder of a **fee simple** may **convey** to another a term of years and then subsequently release his **reversionary** interest (LEASE AND RELEASE) to the possessor of the term of years.

RELEASE ON RECOGNIZANCE [R.O.R.] a method by which an individual is released in lieu of providing **bail,** upon his promise to appear and answer a criminal charge. The R.O.R. procedure permits release on nonmonetary conditions, generally involving only the promise to appear, but sometimes involving special conditions (e.g., remaining in the **custody** of another, abiding by travel restrictions).

RELEVANT MARKET a term used by the courts in determining whether a violation of an **antitrust** statute has occurred. Identification of the relevant market of a product takes into account not only the product but also its geographic area of distribution. Compare **monopoly.**

RELIANCE dependence, confidence, repose of mind upon what is deemed sufficient authority.

DETRIMENTAL RELIANCE reliance by one party on the acts, representations, or promises of another, which causes the first party to allow or to effect a worsening change in his position.

RELICTION gradual and imperceptible withdrawal of water from land that it covers, by lowering of the water's level from any cause. If the retreat of the waters is permanent, not merely seasonal, the owner of the contiguous property acquires ownership of the dry land thus created. Compare **avulsion; dereliction.**

RELIEF the redress or assistance awarded to a **complainant,** by the court, especially a **court of equity,** including such **remedies** as **specific performance, injunction, rescission** of a contract, etc.

EXAMPLE: Carl ordered two hundred items at a set price from a company that happens to be the only manufacturer of the item. Although his order has been produced, the company refuses to deliver unless Carl pays a price increase. Carl seeks *relief* from a court, which in this instance should be to order delivery since the item cannot be purchased elsewhere.

The term generally does not comprehend an award of money **damages.** Thus the term AFFIRMATIVE RELIEF is often used to indicate that the gist of relief is protection from future harm rather than compensation for past injury.

RELIEF TO LITIGANTS see **contempt of court.**

RELINQUISHMENT see **abandonment.**

REMAINDER that part of an **estate** in land that is left upon the termination of the immediately preceding estate (often a life estate or estate for a term of years) and that does not amount to a **reversion** to the original grantor or his heirs. The remainder must be created by the same **conveyance** and at the same time, as the preceding estate; the remainder must **vest** in right during the continuance of the preceding estate; and no remainder can be created in connection with a **fee simple.**

CONTINGENT [EXECUTORY] REMAINDER any remainder subject to a CONDITION PRECEDENT (see **condition**), created in favor of an unborn person, or in favor of an existing but unascertained person. Such an interest was not, according to the older **common law** definition, an estate, but the possibility of an estate. A contingent remainder becomes a **vested** remainder only if any condition precedent is fulfilled and the **remainderman** is identified prior to the termination of the preceding estate.

EXECUTED REMAINDER a remainder interest that is vested as of the present time, though the enjoyment of it may be withheld until a future date.

VESTED REMAINDER a remainder created in favor of an existing and ascertained person who has the right to immediate possession at the termination of the preceding estate, or estates, subject only to another person's prior right to possession.

EXAMPLE: A grandfather conveys a house to his son for life, then to his oldest grandson. The grandson has a *vested remainder* in the house since he is entitled to it at the son's death. If the grandson predeceases the son, the house is distributed according to the provisions of the grandson's will.

REMAINDERMAN one who has an interest in the **estate** that becomes possessory **in futuro,** after the termination, by whatever reason, of a present possessory interest. Remainderman usually refers to one who holds an interest in a **remainder** whether **vested** or **contingent.**

REMAND to send back, as for further deliberation; to send back to the tribunal (or body) from which the matter was appealed or moved. When a judgment is **reversed,** the **appellate court** usually remands the matter for a new trial to be carried out consistent with the principles announced by the appellate court in its opinion ordering the remand.

REMEDY the means employed to enforce or redress an injury. The most common remedy **at law** consists of money **damages.**

EXTRAORDINARY REMEDY a **remedy** not usually available in an action at law or in **equity,** and ordinarily not employed unless the **evidence** clearly indicates that such a remedy is necessary to preserve the rights of the party. Examples include the appointment of a **receiver,** a decree of **specific performance,** the issuing of a writ of **mandamus** or **writ of prohibition** or of an **injunction.**

PROVISIONAL REMEDY one provided pursuant to a proceeding incidental to and in connection with a regular **action,** invoked while the primary action is pending, to assure that the claimant's rights will be preserved or that he will not suffer irreparable injury. Its connection to the primary action is termed **collateral.** Examples include **attachment,** temporary **restraining orders,** preliminary **injunctions,** appointment of **receivers.**

REMITTER the act by which a person, who has a good **title** to land, and enters upon the land with less than his original title, is restored to his original good title; the doctrine whereby the law will relate back from a defective title to an earlier valid title.

REMITTITUR *(rē-mĭ'-tĭ-tūr)* Lat.: reduction. The procedural process by which the **verdict** of a **jury** is diminished; describes any reduction made by the court, without the consent of the jury, to decrease an excessive verdict.

EXAMPLE: A jury awards several million dollars to a small electronics corporation as compensation for anticompetitive practices by a multinational company. The judge is unsure whether the evidence supports a finding against the large company but is not willing to overturn the jury's decision on that issue. Still, he feels that the award is much too great and by *remittitur* reduces the award to one million dollars. If the reduction is not accepted by the plaintiff, the judge will set the entire verdict aside and order a new trial.

REMOVAL 1. a change in place or position, as the removal of a **proceeding** to another court, especially from state to federal court; 2. the process by which a public official is stripped of his office for cause.

REMOVE CLOUD ON TITLE see **quiet title.**

RENT a profit in money, goods, or labor issuing periodically out of land and **tenements,** constituting a return for the privilege of use.

RENUNCIATION in criminal law, the voluntary and complete abandonment of criminal purpose prior to the commission of a crime, or an act otherwise preventing its commission. In some jurisdictions it is an **affirmative defense** (see **defense**) to inchoate, or incipient, offenses such as **attempts, conspiracy, solicitation** or offenses dependent upon the conduct of another (i.e., **accessorial** crimes).

EXAMPLE: Eric devises an intricate plan to rob a bank, but, on the evening on which he plans to carry it out, he finds that workmen are redecorating the bank's interior. He postpones the robbery until he can formulate a new plan. He has not *renunciated* the crime since he plans to rob the bank at another opportunity, even if that opportunity never arises or the new plan is not carried out. If he has a genuine change of heart and voluntarily destroys the blueprint of the bank, this might satisfy the requirements of *renunciation*.

Compare **withdrawal.**

REORGANIZATION the transaction by which the **stock** of property of one **corporation** is exchanged for the stock or property of another corporation. The **shareholders** of the old corporation generally hold the same proportion of stock in the new corporation. The term is most often used to mean reorganization under Chapter X of the Federal Bankruptcy Act. See **bankruptcy.**

REPEAL abrogation or annulling of a previous law by the enactment of a subsequent statute, which either expressly declares that the former law shall be revoked, or contains provisions so irreconcilable with those of the earlier law as to abrogate the earlier law by necessary **implication.**

REPLEVIN a legal form of **action** ordinarily employed only to recover **possession** of specific **personal property** unlawfully withheld from the plaintiff, plus **damages** for its detention. In this primarily possessory action, the issues ordinarily are limited to the plaintiff's **title** to the goods.

EXAMPLE: Arthur leaves a shipment of goods in a warehouse and prepays storage costs for three months. At the end of that time, he goes to pick up the goods, but the warehouse refuses to release them until he pays for the storage. Arthur sues for *replevin* to obtain the goods.

REPLEVY to secure, especially by an **action** in **replevin,** redelivery of goods that have been kept from the rightful owner.

REPLY a defensive **pleading** by one who has made a complaint; the sole purpose of reply is to interpose a **defense** to **new matter** pleaded in the **answer.** In modern practice a reply is an extraordinary pleading and is not permitted except to respond to a **counterclaim** or by leave of court to an answer or third-party answer.

EXAMPLE: A store owner sues Ed for failure to pay a debt. Ed files a counterclaim against the store owner claiming that the washer and dryer Ed purchased, which gave rise to the debt, have never worked properly. The store owner can *reply* to the counterclaim that he is not responsible for the problem or that Ed has not operated the machines correctly.

REPOSSESSION **seizure** or **foreclosure.** Either by judicial action or **self-help,** the secured **creditor,** to satisfy the **debtor's** obligation, takes **possession** of the **property** after the debtor **defaults** on his payments.

REPRIEVE in criminal law, the postponement of a **sentence** for an interval in which the **execution** is suspended. Compare **commutation; pardon.**

REPUDIATION refusal by one party to perform a contractual obligation to another party. See **anticipatory breach.**

REQUIREMENTS CONTRACT see **contract.**

RES *(rās)* Lat.: a thing. The subject matter of **actions** that are primarily **in rem,** i.e., actions that establish rights in relation to an object, as opposed to a person (**in personam**). For example, in an action that resolves a conflict over **title** to **real property,** the land in question is the res. Tangible **personal property** can also be a res, as in the **corpus** of a **trust.**

EXAMPLE: A mother creates a trust for her children, providing that the rentals from an office building be distributed to each child every month. The office building is the trust *res* since it generates the income that is distributed to the children.

In a QUASI IN REM (see **quasi**) **proceeding,** land or **chattels** that are seized and **attached** at the beginning of the action, in order that they may later be used to satisfy a personal **claim,** are the res of such suits. The term refers as well to the status of individuals. Thus, in a divorce suit, the marital status is the res. The purpose of a res is to establish a court's **jurisdiction:** if the property lies within the state where the action is brought, or an individual in a divorce action is a **domiciliary** of the state, then jurisdiction is established.

RES AJUDICATA see **res judicata.**

RESCIND to abrogate a **contract,** release the parties from further obligations to each other and restore the parties to the

STATUS QUO ante, (see **status quo**) or the positions they would have occupied if the contract had never been made.

RESCISSION cancellation of a **contract** and the return of the parties to the positions they would have occupied if the contract had not been made (see **status quo** [STATUS QUO ANTE]). Grounds for rescission may include original invalidity of the agreement, **fraud,** failure of **consideration,** or **material breach** or **default.** Rescission may be brought about by the mutual consent of the parties, by the conduct of the parties or by a decree by a **court of equity.**

RESCUE DOCTRINE tort rule that holds a **tortfeasor** liable to his victim's rescuer, should the latter injure himself during a reasonable rescue attempt. The premise is that the wrong is not only to the imperiled victim, but also to his rescuer.

RESERVATION 1. a clause in any **instrument** of **conveyance,** such as a **deed,** that creates a lesser **estate,** or some right, interest or profit in the estate granted, to be retained by the **grantor.** 2. a tract of land, usually substantial, set aside for specific purposes such as military grounds, parks, Indian lands. Compare **reversion.**

RES GESTAE *(rās gĕs'-tī)* Lat.: the thing done. The undersigned, necessary incidents of the **litigated** act are **admissible** as **evidence** when illustrative of such act and if they are part of the immediate preparations for or emanations of such act, and are not produced by the calculated policy of the actors. Declarations that are subject to the **hearsay rule** may be admissible if they qualify as res gestae; i.e., if they constitute a part of the thing done under a recognized exception to the hearsay rule.

RESIDENCE broadly, any place of abode that is more than temporary. Compare **domicile.**

RESIDENT ALIEN see **alien.**

RESIDUARY BEQUEST see **bequest; residuary legacy.**

RESIDUARY CLAUSE clause in a **will** that conveys to the beneficiary of a **residuary legacy** (residuary **legatee**) everything in a **testator's estate** not **devised** to a specific legatee; a testamentary clause that includes in its gift any property or interest in the will that, for any reason, eventually falls into the general residue, because specific legacies were **void,** the disposition was illegal, or because for any other reason it was impossible that the legacy should take effect; and it includes such legacies as may lapse by events subsequent to the making of the will. It operates to transfer to the residuary legatee such portion of his property as the testator has not perfectly disposed of.

EXAMPLE: In his will Manny leaves his antique car to a cousin who predeceases him. He also provides a *residuary clause* that leaves any of his property not already disposed of in the will to his oldest son. In addition to receiving all of Manny's property not left to others, the son, as the residuary legatee, also receives the antique car.

RESIDUARY ESTATE that part of a **testator's estate** that remains undisposed of after all of the estate has been discharged through the satisfaction of all claims and specific legacies with the exception of the dispositions authorized by the **residuary clause.**

RESIDUARY LEGACY a general **legacy** into which all the assets of the estate fall after satisfaction of other legacies, payment of all debts of the estate and all costs of administration.

RES IPSA LOQUITUR *(rās ĭp'-sȧ lō'-kwĭ-tûr)* Lat.: the thing speaks for itself. Refers to a rule of **evidence** whereby **negligence** of the alleged wrongdoer may be inferred from the mere fact that the accident happened, provided (1) that in the absence of negligence the accident would not have occurred and (2) the thing that caused the injury is shown to have been under the exclusive control of the alleged wrongdoer. The procedural effect of successful invocation of the doctrine is to shift the **burden** of going forward with the evidence, normally borne by the plaintiff, to the defendant, who is thereby charged with introducing evidence to refute the **presumption** of negligence that has been created.

EXAMPLE: An accident occurs when the brakes of a new car fail on its first trip from the dealer. The victim claims negligence on the part of the car manufacturer and points to the failed brakes as evidence. Under the doctrine of *res ipsa loquitur,* the manufacturer must now provide evidence to show that some cause other than its negligence is responsible for the accident.

RESISTING ARREST common-law offense involving physical efforts to oppose a lawful arrest.

RES JUDICATA *(rās jū-dĭ-kä'-tȧ)* Lat.: a thing decided; a matter adjudged. The phrase reflects a rule by which a final **judgment** by a court of competent **jurisdiction** is conclusive upon the **parties** in any subsequent **litigation** involving the same **cause of action.**

EXAMPLE: Two parties litigate an issue in one federal district court, and the defendant loses. Under the principle of *res judicata,* the defendant could not then go to another federal district court and litigate the same issue a second time.

Compare **collateral [COLLATERAL ESTOPPEL].**

RESPITE 1. a delay, postponement or **forbearance** of a **sentence,** not comprehending a permanent suspension of **execution** of the **judgment;** 2. a delay in repayment, granted to a debtor by his creditor. See **reprieve.**

RESPONDEAT SUPERIOR *(rā-spôn'-dā-ät sū-pĕr'-ē-ôr)* Lat.: let the superior reply. This doctrine is invoked when there is a master-**servant** relationship between two parties. The premise is that when an employer (master) is acting through the facility of an employee or **agent** (servant), and tort **liability** is incurred during the course of this **agency** because of some fault of the agent, then the employer or master must accept the responsibility. Implicit is the **common law** notion that everyone must conduct his affairs without injuring another, whether or not he employs agents or servants.

EXAMPLE: A truck driver employed by a manufacturing company causes an accident while delivering a shipment to a buyer. The doctrine of *respondeat superior* allows the victims to sue the company for any injuries caused by the driver. Under normal principles of tort responsibility, the driver can also be sued. Since it is unlikely that he has the money to pay a damage award, the doctrine acts to assure that the victims will be paid the full amount of the award because the company by law will be required to carry adequate insurance or have sufficient assets for such contingencies. Absent this doctrine, companies would be able to hire judgment-proof drivers and in that fashion avoid all liability for injuries caused by such drivers.

RESPONDENT 1. in **equity,** the party who answers a **pleading.** 2. the party against whom an **appeal** is prosecuted.

RESPONSIVE PLEADING see **answer.**

RESTATEMENT an attempt by the American Law Institute to present an orderly statement of the general **common law** of the United States, including not only the law developed by judicial decision, but also the law that has evolved from the application of statutes by the courts. Restatements are compiled according to subject matter: **contracts, torts, property, trusts, agency, conflict of laws, judgments, restitution, security** and foreign relations.

RESTITUTION act of making good or of giving the equivalent for loss, damage or injury. As a remedy, restitution is available to prevent **unjust enrichment,** to correct an erroneous payment and to permit an **aggrieved party** to recover deposits advanced on a contract. As a contract remedy, restitution is limited to the value of a performance rendered by the injured party, and ordinarily requires that both parties to a transaction be returned to the STATUS QUO (see **status quo**).
In criminal law, restitution is sometimes ordered as a condition of a **probationary sentence.** Compare **indemnity.**

RESTRAINING ORDER an **order** granted without notice or hearing, demanding the preservation of the **status quo** until a hearing to determine the propriety of **injunctive** relief, temporary or permanent. A restraining order is always temporary, since it is granted pending a hearing; thus it is often called a **T.R.O.** [**temporary restraining order**].

EXAMPLE: A federal agency grants a lumber company permission to cut wood on federal lands. An environmental group immediately goes to court and seeks a *restraining order* prohibiting the cutting of any trees until the validity of the grant is determined. The order probably will be issued since irreparable damage will be caused by cutting the trees, provided the group can produce a minimum of evidence that their position as to the illegality of the grant is correct.

RESTRAINT OF TRADE in common law and as used in the antitrust laws, illegal restraints interfering with free competition in commercial transactions, which tend to restrict production, affect prices or otherwise control the market to the detriment of consumers of goods and services.

RESTRAINT ON ALIENATION restriction on the ability to **convey** real property interests, any attempt at which is in **derogation** of the **common law** policy in favor of free alienability. Such restrictions often are void or voidable as unlawful restraints on **alienation.**

RESTRICTIVE COVENANT a promise as part of an agreement, restricting the use of **real property** or the kind of buildings that may be erected. The promise is usually expressed by the creation of a **covenant, reservation** or exception in a **deed.** In order for a grantor to enforce the covenant against remote grantees [subsequent owners who take **title** from the first grantee], the covenant must **run with the land.**

EXAMPLE: When Marshall sells a plot of land next to his house, he includes a *restrictive covenant* with the deed that no structure over two and one-half stories will be constructed on the land. Since the covenant is included with the deed, it is valid against any and all other purchasers of the land.

RESTRICTIVE INDORSEMENT see **indorsement.**

RESULTING TRUST see **trust.**

RESULTING USE see **use.**

RETAINER compensation paid in advance to an attorney for services to be performed in a specific case. A retainer may be the whole sum to be charged (plus expenses) but more often is a deposit, with the attorney furnishing a periodic or final statement of how much the client owes for services rendered.

RETIRE 1. in reference to **bills of exchange,** to recover or redeem by payment of a sum of money; to withdraw from circulation or from the market.

2. A **jury** is retired when the judge has submitted the case for its consideration and **verdict.**

RETIREMENT PLAN a plan provided by an employer or a self-employed individual for an employee's or self-employed individual's retirement. Because of the tax advantages, most retirement plans are designed to insure a present **deduction** to the employer while the employee is permitted to avoid **recognizing** the **income** until he has actually or **constructively** received it.

DEFERRED COMPENSATION a plan under whose terms an employee defers payment of a portion of his salary in return for the employer's promise to pay the employee the salary at some time in the future. Generally, if such plan is not financed by irrevocably setting the fund aside for the employee or guaranteed by insurance, the employee will not recognize income from such plan until he is actually paid, and the employer does not obtain a deduction under such plan until the employee recognizes the income.

INDIVIDUAL RETIREMENT ACCOUNT [IRA] an account to which the employee pays a specified tax-exempt sum, whose earned income is also tax-exempt when specified limitations upon withdrawal are adhered to.

KEOGH PLAN a pension or profit-sharing plan set up by a self-employed individual.

NONQUALIFIED PENSION OR PROFIT-SHARING PLAN a plan created by an employer for an employee that does not qualify for a present deduction to the employer and deferral of income recognition to the employee. In such cases the employer is generally not permitted to take a deduction for the amount set aside until the employee recognizes such amount as income.

QUALIFIED PENSION OR PROFIT-SHARING PLAN a plan set up by an employer for an employee or a group of employees that allows the employer to pay into a **trust** a certain sum or percentage of compensation for the employees. The employer obtains a present deduction for the contributions but the employee does not recognize the income until it is actually paid to him.

ROLLOVER a method whereby an employee converts from one qualified plan to another without the recognition as income of the sum rolled over.

RETRACTION the withdrawing of a **plea,** declaration, **accusation,** promise, etc.

RETRIAL a new trial in which an issue or issues already litigated, and as to which a verdict or decision by the court has been rendered, are reexamined by the same court for some sufficient reason, such as a recognition that the initial trial was improper or unfair as a result of procedural errors. Compare **mistrial.**

RETROACTIVE refers to a rule of law, whether legislative or judicial, that relates to things decided in the past. ''Retroactive'' includes both retrospective and **ex post facto,** the former technically applying only to **civil** laws, the latter to criminal or penal laws. A RETROSPECTIVE LAW is one that relates back to a previous transaction and gives it some different legal effect from that which it had under the law when it occurred. A retrospective law is constitutionally objectionable if it impairs **vested** rights acquired under existing laws, or creates a new obligation or attaches a new disability with respect to past transactions. Similarly, an ex post facto law retroactively imposes criminal liability on behavior that took place prior to enactment of the criminal statute. State constitutions may prohibit their legislatures from enacting retrospective laws; ex post facto laws are prohibited by the Constitution of the United States.

Judicially created law (common law) is often retroactive in its effect, since the court's decision is made on the basis of old facts as to which the litigants could not possibly have predicted at the time of their actions the court's eventual interpretation of the law; nevertheless they are bound by it.

In constitutional law, decisions announcing new or different rights favoring criminal defendants are often given full retroactive effect so as to permit a **COLLATERAL ATTACK** (see *collateral*) on previously finalized judgments.

EXAMPLE: The state supreme court rules that any person affected by the use of a particular police procedure can exclude evidence so obtained. The court also rules that this right is only available after the date of this decision. The latter ruling means that the law is prospective only and has no *retroactive* effect and that any person already tried cannot take advantage of the new rule. If the decision had retroactive effect, every person who has been convicted or whose trial is in progress and who has not been permitted to challenge the legality of the evidence used against him could now raise the issue.

Compare **statute of limitations.**

RETROSPECTIVE see **retroactive.**

RETURN 1. a report from an official, such as a sheriff, stating what he has done in respect to a command from the court, or why he has failed to do what was requested. See **false return.**

2. a report from an individual or **corporation** as to its earnings, etc., for tax or other governmental purposes.

RETURN, INCOME TAX a document by which a **taxpayer** or his representative provides information to the **Internal**

Revenue Service relevant to the determination of the taxpayer's tax liability for a specified period.

AMENDED RETURN a return by which a taxpayer or his representative corrects information contained in an earlier return. An amended return may require an additional payment of tax (possibly with interest and/or penalties) or be accompanied by a **claim for refund.**

DECLARATION OF ESTIMATED TAX a return required of those taxpayers who do not regularly withhold income, as in the case of self-employed taxpayers, who expect that the total amount of their withholdings will not cover their tax liability for the tax year, and whose filing is accompanied by payments of estimated tax.

INFORMATION RETURN any of a number of returns that only communicate information to the Service relevant to tax liability but that do not compute the actual liability of any taxpayer or accompany the actual payment of tax.

JOINT RETURN a return filed by a husband and wife, setting forth tax information concerning each of them, and computing a joint tax liability.

REVENUE RULING a published decision by the **Internal Revenue Service** in the Internal Revenue Bulletin applying the federal tax laws to a particular set of facts. Revenue Rulings (as opposed to PRIVATE RULINGS) may be relied upon by **taxpayers** in determining the **tax** impact upon them of a similar set of facts.

PRIVATE RULING a determination by the Internal Revenue Service issued to a taxpayer who has asked for a determination as to the tax impact upon such taxpayer of a particular transaction. The determination is binding with respect to that taxpayer only and may not be relied upon by other taxpayers. These private rulings are published with the identifying characteristics of the taxpayer and the transaction deleted.

REVERSAL as used in **opinions, judgments** and **mandates,** the **vacating** or changing to the contrary the decision of a lower court or other body. Compare **overrule; remand.**

REVERSIBLE ERROR error substantially affecting **appellant's** legal rights and obligations that, if uncorrected, would result in a miscarriage of justice and that justifies **reversing** a **judgment** in the inferior court; synonymous with PREJUDICIAL ERROR. See **plain error; harmless error.**

EXAMPLE: In his summation to the jury, a prosecutor makes disparaging remarks concerning the defendant Jim's failure to take the stand, thus violating the defendant's constitutional right to remain silent. The defendant objects and the judge tells the jury to disregard the remarks. The jury finds Jim guilty. On appeal, the appellate court finds the prosecutor's remarks so blatant that no amount of instructions by the judge could eliminate the prejudice that was caused. The remarks constitute *reversible error,* and Jim is granted a new trial.

REVERSION an **interest** created by operation of law by a **conveyance** of less than an absolute interest in property that thus leaves in the **grantor** some right or interest in the property to arise in the future; a FUTURE ESTATE (see **estate**) created by operation of law to take effect in possession in favor of a **lessor** or a grantor of his **heirs,** or the heirs of a **testator,** after the natural termination of a prior particular estate **leased,** granted or **devised.** Compare **remainder.**

REVERTER see **possibility of a reverter.**

REVIEW judicial reexamination of the proceedings of a court or other body; a reconsideration by the same court or body of its former decision; also, an **appellate court's** examination of the **record** of a lower court or agency's determination that is on **appeal** to the appellate court.

REVISED STATUTES statutes that have been altered, reorganized or reenacted. Their enactment is generally regarded as repealing and replacing the former laws.

REVOCATION 1. recall of authority conferred; 2. cancellation of an **instrument** previously made; 3. cancellation of an **offer** by the offeror, which, if effective, terminates the offeree's power of **acceptance.**

EXAMPLE: Steel Pipe Company offers to buy used pipe from a supplier at fifteen cents a foot. Before the supplier responds, Steel realizes it has offered to buy the wrong type of pipe and *revokes* its offer. Since the supplier has not acted, the revocation is effective.

REVOKE 1. to recall a power previously conferred; 2. to **vacate** an **instrument** previously made; 3. to annul, **repeal, rescind** or cancel privileges, e.g., **parole, probation,** driver's license.

REVOLVING CREDIT renewable **credit** line over a set period of time. The term refers generally to credit extended by a banker or merchant for a certain amount that can be paid off periodically.

RIDER 1. an amendment or addition attached to a document usually found as an attachment to an insurance policy identifying changes or increases in coverage; 2. in the legislative process, a provision in a bill that is not germane to the main purpose of the law.

EXAMPLE: The President wants to increase the federal excise tax on gasoline five cents to raise revenues needed to repair the nation's roads and bridges. Knowing that the President is anxious to approve the bill, a senator attaches to it as a rider an unrelated measure he was having difficulty getting support for by itself, a senator attaches a *rider* to it.

RIGHT OF ACTION see **cause of action.**

RIGHT OF FIRST PUBLICATION see **copyright.**

RIGHT OF REDEMPTION see **redemption.**

RIGHT OF REENTRY see **reentry.**

RIGHT OF WAY 1. in property law, an **easement** to use another's land for passage; 2. in the context of vehicular traffic, the right of a vehicle or pedestrian to proceed on the road, while others yield.

RIGHT OR WRONG TEST see **M'Naghten Rule.**

RIGHTS 1. individual liberties in a constitutional sense; 2. **proprietary,** contractual or legal rights. 3. in the context of securities trading, a negotiable privilege to buy a new **issue** of stock at a subscription price lower than the market price of outstanding stock. Compare **stock option.** See also **constitutional rights; vested [VESTED RIGHTS].**

RIGHT TO REMAIN SILENT see **Miranda rule.**

RIGOR MORTIS *(rĭ'-gôr môr'-tĭs)* Lat.: stiffness of death. Medical terminology depicting the rigidity of the muscles after death.

RIPARIAN RIGHTS rights that accrue to owners of land on the banks of bodies of water, such as the use of such water, and ownership of soil under the water. The lands to which these natural rights are attached are called in law **RIPARIAN LANDS.**

RIPENESS doctrine in constitutional law under which courts will not decide cases in advance of the necessity of deciding them, i.e., in advance of their being ripe for decision. Compare **justiciable; moot case.**

RISK OF LOSS 1. a phrase used to signify who bears the financial risk of damage or destruction when property is being transferred from a buyer to a seller.

EXAMPLE: In a contract between Dynamic Boat Company and a buyer, the buyer agrees to assume *risk of loss* only when the boat is in his possession. Therefore, if anything should happen to the boat after its completion but while it is being transported to the buyer, from the buyer's point of view Dynamic must take responsibility for the damage.

2. In insurance law, the term refers to the contingencies or unknown events that are contemplated by the insured and that are covered by the insurance.

ROBBERY forcible stealing; the **felonious** taking of property from the person of another by violence or by putting him in fear.

ARMED ROBBERY robbery aggravated by the fact that it is committed by a defendant armed with a dangerous weapon, whether or not the weapon is used in the course of committing the crime. Compare **burglary.**

ROGATORY LETTERS a formal communication from a court in which an **action** is pending, to a foreign court, requesting that the **testimony** of a **witness** residing in such foreign **jurisdiction** be taken under the direction of the court, addressed and transmitted to the court making the request.

ROLLOVER see **retirement plan.**

ROYALTY a share of the product or of the proceeds therefrom, reserved by an owner for permitting another to exploit and use his **property;** the rental paid to the original owner of property, based on a percentage of profit or production. The term is employed with respect to mining **leases, conveyances,** literary works, inventions and other intellectual productions. Compare **commission.**

RULE AGAINST PERPETUITIES the rule that no contingent **interest** is good unless it must **vest,** if at all, not later than twenty-one years after some life in being at the creation of the interest. The rule against perpetuities is directed against the remoteness of vesting of **estates** or interests in property, and against unreasonable restraints of the power of **alienation.**

RULE IN WILD'S CASE a rule of **construction** by which a **devise** to "B and his children," where B has no children at the time the gift **vests** in B, was read to mean a gift to B in **fee tail,** the words "and his children" thus being construed as **words of limitation** and not **words of purchase.** The popularity of the fee tail has declined, and most American jurisdictions have repudiated the Rule in Wild's Case, so that such conveyances are construed to be a gift of a **life estate** to B, with a **remainder** to his children.

RULE NISI procedure by which one party by an **ex parte** application or an order to **show cause** calls upon another to show cause why the rule set forth in his proposed order should not be made final by the court. If no cause is shown, the court orders the rule absolute (final), thereby requiring whatever was sought to be accomplished.

RULE OF LAW see **question of law.**

RUN WITH THE LAND a phrase used with respect to **covenants** in the law of real property to mean that the burdens and/or the benefits of the covenant pass to the persons who succeed to the interests of the original contracting parties. Covenants so characterized bind the owners of the property to which they attach (with which they ''run''), no matter who those owners are; such covenants therefore represent an essentially permanent limitation upon the **estate** held by the owner of the ''burdened'' property, and an enhancement of the estate held by the owner of the ''benefitted'' property.

EXAMPLE: Chris divides a large building so that he can sell one-half to another businessman. There is only one alley through which deliveries can be made, but the alley is on Chris's side of the property. In the deed of sale, Chris includes a covenant that allows the other businessman to use the alley. That covenant *runs with the land* so that anyone who buys the store from the other businessman can enforce the covenant against any owner of the other half of the building.

Compare **chain of title.**

S

SALE a **contract** by which property, real or personal, is transferred from the seller (**vendor**) to the buyer (**vendee**) for a fixed price in money, paid or agreed to be paid by the buyer. This is in contrast to BARTER, which is an exchange of goods or services for another's goods or services. See also **arm's length.**

ABSOLUTE SALE a sale whereby the property passes to the buyer upon completion of the agreement between the parties.

AUCTION SALE a public sale of goods or **real property** to the highest bidder, by public outcry and competitive bidding.

CONDITIONAL SALE 1. a sale in which the vendee receives **possession** and right of use of the **goods** sold, but transfer of title to the vendee is dependent upon **performance** of some condition, usually full payment of purchase price. The conditional sale becomes absolute on fulfillment of the condition. 2. a purchase accompanied by an agreement to resell upon particular terms. See also SALE ON APPROVAL.

EXECUTED SALE in contrast to an EXECUTORY SALE, one wherein nothing remains to be done by either party to effect **delivery** and complete transfer of title.

EXECUTION SALE see **sheriff's sale.**

EXECUTORY SALE in contrast to an EXECUTED SALE, an agreement to sell wherein something remains to be done by either party before delivery and passing of title.

FORCED SALE a sale that the seller must make immediately, without opportunity to find a buyer who will pay a sum approaching the reasonable worth of the item (often land). The phrase is synonymous with JUDICIAL SALE (see **sheriff's sale**), whereby the court forces the sale of property as a result of a prior **adjudication.**

EXAMPLE: Bob owes money to several creditors as a result of work they performed on a building he owns. He avoids the creditors, and they obtain a judicial order demanding payment. His continued refusal to pay results in a *forced sale* of the building. The excess of the sale price over the money owed is returned to Bob.

PUBLIC SALE a sale upon notice to the public and in which members of the public may bid.

SALE IN GROSS sale of land by the tract or as a whole, without **warranty** of quantity (acres); sometimes referred to as a **CONTRACT OF HAZARD.**

PUBLIC SALE a sale upon notice to the public and in which members of the public may bid.

SALE IN GROSS sale of land by the tract or as a whole, without **warranty** of quantity (acres); sometimes referred to as a **CONTRACT OF HAZARD.**

SALE BY SAMPLE a sale of **goods** in existence in bulk, but not present for examination, where it is mutually understood that the goods not exhibited will conform to the sample. Such a sale carries with it an **implied** warranty that the goods purchased conform to the sample.

SALE ON APPROVAL a transaction in which goods delivered primarily for use may be returned if the buyer is unsatisfied with them, even though they may conform to the contract. If the goods are delivered primarily for resale, rather than for use, the transaction is termed a **SALE OR RETURN,** or the arrangement is termed a **CONSIGNMENT.**

SALE OR EXCHANGE see **sale or exchange.**

SALE WITH RIGHT OF REDEMPTION sale where seller reserves the right to take back **title** to property he has sold upon repayment of the purchase price.

SHERIFF'S SALE see **sheriff's sale.**

TAX SALE a sale of land for the nonpayment of taxes.

SALE OR EXCHANGE disposition of property in a value-for-value exchange, as opposed to a disposition by **gift,** contribution or the like. For **income tax** purposes, the **realization** of **gain or loss** on the disposition of property is based on the sale or exchange of that property.

SANCTION 1. to approve; 2. to reward or punish; 3. a consequence of punishment for violation of accepted norms of social conduct, which may be of two kinds: those that redress **civil** injuries (civil sanctions) and those that punish crimes (penal sanctions).

SATISFACTION [OF A DEBT] a release and discharge of the obligation in reference to which performance is executed. See also **accord and satisfaction.**

SAVE HARMLESS protect from loss or liability; **indemnify;** guarantee.

In **contract** law, signifies a commitment by one party to **repay** another party to an agreement in the event of a specified loss.

EXAMPLE: A lease provides that the tenant shall *save harmless* the landlord against claims for injuries to persons on the premises. As a result of this clause, the tenant is required to reimburse the landlord in the event such a claim is successfully prosecuted and damages are recovered against the landlord.

SAVING CLAUSE a clause in a **statute** restricting the scope of the **repeal** of prior statutes; language inserted in a statute to maintain existing rights provided in the repealed law. See also **grandfather clause.**

SCIENTER *(sī'-ĕn-tûr)* Lat.: knowledge. Previous knowledge of operative facts; frequently signifies guilty knowledge. As used in **pleadings,** the term signifies that the alleged **crime** or **tort** was done designedly or with guilty knowledge. The term is usually employed in relation to **fraud,** and means a person's knowledge that he was making false representations, with **intent** to deceive.

EXAMPLE: A corporation files a registration statement, containing false representations, with the Securities and Exchange Commission so that the corporation may sell stock to the public. Applicable law holds a party liable if with *scienter* he signs a statement that contains false representations. The requirement of scienter means that the party must know of the false representations and know that the statement will be used to deceive others into purchasing stock.

See also **mens rea.**

SCOPE OF EMPLOYMENT those acts done while performing one's job duties. The phrase was adopted by the courts for the purpose of determining employer's **liability** for the acts of his employees. The master (usually, the employer) is said to be **vicariously liable** only for those torts of the servant (employee) that are committed within the range of his job activities. See **respondeat superior; employee's liability acts.**

EXAMPLE: A professional driver employed by Escort Service, Inc., decides to stop home and see his wife while he is driving from one job to another. As he drives to his home, he hits a child playing in the street. Escort will not be responsible for the injury to the child if the driver was not in the *scope of his employment*.

SCRIP DIVIDEND see **dividend.**

SCRIVENER 1. an old English term referring to a writer or scribe, particularly one who draws legal documents; 2. one who acts as **agent** for another, investing and managing that other's property for a fee.

SEAL in **common law,** an impression on wax or other substance capable of being impressed. The purpose of a seal is to attest to the execution of an **instrument.** The word seal or the letters **L.S.** (**LOCUS SIGILLI,** place of the seal) have the same significance and are commonly used for the same purpose today.

A seal of a corporation is sometimes called a **COMMON SEAL.**

SEALED INSTRUMENT one that is signed and has the **seal** of the signer attached. To render a **contract** a sealed instrument, it must be so recited in the body of the instrument and a seal must be placed after the signature. In **common law,** a sealed contract was a **FORMAL CONTRACT** (as opposed to a contract without a seal, called a **SIMPLE CONTRACT**) and is often called a **CONTRACT UNDER SEAL;** such a contract or a **deed** under seal did not require **consideration.** Today any symbol, even the printed word seal or the letters L.S. will, if so intended, constitute the necessary seal. In most states, **statutes** have eliminated most of the special effects of sealed instruments in common law.

SEALING OF RECORDS the sealing of criminal records, permitted in some states with respect to **youthful offenders,** so that such records may be examined only by court order.

SEARCH AND SEIZURE a police practice whereby a person or place is searched and **evidence** useful in the investigation and **prosecution** of crime is seized. The search and seizure is constitutionally limited by the Fourth Amendment and Fourteenth Amendment to the United States Constitution and by provisions in the several state constitutions, statutes and rules of court. See also **probable cause; search warrant.**

SEARCH WARRANT an order issued by a judge or **magistrate** authorizing certain law enforcement officers to conduct a search of specified premises for specified things or persons. In those cases where **warrants** are required, only a judge or magistrate who has not previously considered the facts giving rise to the application can issue a search warrant, and only upon a showing of **probable cause** that the described item is located in the designated place and that it was involved in the planning or commission of a crime.

SEASONABLE timely; in due season or time; the time in which action is appropriate and can be effective.

SECONDARY DISTRIBUTION an organized **offering** of **stock** that is already issued and outstanding, usually distributed by a **syndicate.** Typical sources of large blocks of stock for redistribution are **founders, insiders** and major investors.

SECONDARY PARTY a person obligated to pay a debt if the person incurring the debt fails to pay the **creditor.** The parties to whom the creditor may then go for repayment are secondarily **liable.**

EXAMPLE: Abe receives a check for a debt owed to him. He signs the check and turns it over to a friend to whom he owes money. Abe is *secondarily liable* on the check, so that if the check is dishonored, the friend can look to Abe for payment.

SECUNDUM *(sĕ-kūn'-dŭm)* Lat.: immediately after; next to.

SECURED TRANSACTIONS see **security interest.**

SECURITIES **stock certificates, bonds** or other **evidence** of a secured indebtedness or of a right created in the holder to participate in the profits or **assets** distribution of a profit-making enterprise; more generally, written assurances for the return or payment of money; **instruments** giving to their legal holders right to money or other property.

PUBLIC SECURITIES those certificates and other **negotiable instruments** evidencing the debt of a governmental body.

SECURITIES ACTS popular name of the two primary federal statutes regulating the issuing of and market trading in corporate **securities.** The Securities Act of 1933 deals primarily with initial distribution of securities by the issuer: its objective is to provide full disclosure of **material** facts about securities for sale so that investors may be able to make informed investment decisions. The Securities Exchange Act of 1934 is designed to regulate postdistribution trading in securities and provides for the registration and regulation of securities exchanges, as well as for the prohibition of fraud and manipulation in sale or purchase of securities.

SECURITIES AND EXCHANGE COMMISSION [SEC] the federal agency empowered to regulate and supervise the selling of **securities,** to prevent unfair practices on security exchanges and **over-the-counter markets,** and to maintain a fair and orderly market for the investor. See also **Administrative Procedure Act; proxy.**

SECURITIES INVESTOR PROTECTION CORPORATION [SIPC] a nonprofit corporation supported by its membership of **securities brokers** and dealers, developed to protect their customers and to promote confidence in the securities markets. In principle, SIPC provides certain amounts of insurance on cash and securities left on deposit in a brokerage account.

SECURITY DEPOSIT money that a **tenant** deposits with the **landlord** to assure that the tenant will abide by the **lease** agreements; a fund from which the landlord may obtain payment for **damages** caused by the tenant during his occupancy.

SECURITY INTEREST an **interest** in **real property** or **personal property** that secures the payment of an obligation. In common law, security interests are either consensual (by agreement) or arise by **operation of law,** as in the case of judgment **liens** and statutory liens.

EXAMPLE: In order to obtain a loan from a bank, Oscar uses a very valuable painting as collateral. The bank has a *security interest* in the painting and can acquire ownership of it if the loan is not repaid.

PURCHASE-MONEY SECURITY INTEREST one taken or retained by the seller of the **collateral** to secure all or part of its price.

SEDITION illegal action that tends to cause the disruption and overthrow of the government.

EXAMPLE: Cathy sabotages a Federal Bureau of Investigation computer that lists the names of all of the most wanted criminals, thus committing a *seditious* act. Liability for such an act extends beyond a mere charge of destroying government property.

See **treason.** Compare **clear and present danger.**

SEDITIOUS LIBEL in English law, a **misdemeanor** involving the publishing of any words or document, with **intent** to develop **contempt** or excite disaffection against the government or to promote feelings of ill will between the classes.

SEDUCTION inducing a chaste, unmarried woman, by means of temptation, deception, acts, flattery or a promise of marriage, to engage in sexual intercourse. Compare **rape.**

SEISED the condition of legally **owning realty.** The phrase imports legal **title** as opposed to **beneficial ownership.**

EXAMPLE: A father owning apartment houses that are fully rented conveys the houses to his son. The son is thus *seised* of the buildings. He has legal title to them, but, because the tenants have leases that allow them to remain in their apartments, he cannot do with the buildings as he pleases until all the leases expire.

SEISIN in early English property law, the term to describe the **interest** in land of one who held a **freehold estate.** The term **ownership** was not used, since the **sovereign** (king) was technically owner of all lands in England; a landholder was instead said to be **seised** of his estate. A voluntary transfer of the holder's interest was accomplished by **livery of seisin.** Today, seisin is generally considered synonymous with ownership.

SEIZURE 1. the act of forcibly dispossessing an owner of property, under actual or apparent authority of law; 2. the taking of property into the **custody** of the court in **satisfaction** of a **judgment,** or in consequence of a violation of law. See also **search and seizure.**

SELECTIVE ALLOCATION see **marshaling** [**MARSHALING ASSETS**].

SELF-DEALING type of securities trading in which a party acts upon secret information obtained by his or another's special position in the corporation. It may involve sale or purchase of stock by the director, officers and majority **shareholders** of a **corporation.** See also **fiduciary; insider.**

SELF-DEFENSE the self-protection of one's person, or preservation of members of one's family, and, to a lesser extent, one's property, from harm by an aggressor, in a way and under circumstances that the law recognizes as justifying the protective measures. It is a valid **defense** to a criminal **charge** or to **tort** liability.

EXAMPLE: Ken is assaulted and in an act of *self-defense* hits the mugger. Even if that blow was strong enough to knock the mugger unconscious, Ken still has a valid defense for his assault against the mugger. If the mugger is unconscious and Ken then hits him with a brick and kills him, Ken would not be able to assert he was acting in self-defense since the mugger was no longer in a position to harm him. Ken would be liable in that circumstance to prosecution for murder.

SELF-HELP the right or fact of redressing or preventing wrongs by one's own action, without resort to legal proceedings, but without **BREACH OF THE PEACE.** (see **breach**).

EXAMPLE: Tim's car is stolen. Two weeks later he sees the car in a downtown auto repair shop. Tim can employ *self-help* and drive the car away without calling the police to aid him if he so desires. Likewise, if Tim had been behind in his car payments, the creditor could come and take the car to satisfy the debt without legal process so long as there is no breach of the peace.

SELF-INCRIMINATION, PRIVILEGE AGAINST the constitutional right of a person to refuse to answer questions or otherwise give **testimony** against himself that will create substantial likelihood of criminal incrimination.

The privilege can be displaced by a grant of **USE IMMUNITY,** which guarantees that neither the compelled testimony nor any fruits will be used against the witness. Given such immunity, the witness is no longer exposed to the hazard of self-incrimination and thus must respond to questions or provide evidence. Some states still give such witnesses a broader form of immunity known as TRANSACTIONAL IMMUNITY, which protects the witness not merely from use of his testimony but from any prosecution relating to transactions about which relevant testimony was elicited. It should be emphasized that the privilege against self-incrimination, like all constitutional rights, may be **waived. Miranda** warnings are generally necessary before such a waiver will be found to qualify a **confession** as admissible evidence in a criminal trial.

See Fifth Amendment. Compare **contempt of court; immunity.**

SELLING SHORT the selling of **securities, commodities** or foreign currency that are not actually owned by the seller. In making the short sell, the seller hopes to cover—that is, buy back—sold items at a higher price and thus earn a profit.

COMMODITY SHORT SALES short sales accomplished in the **futures** market. A speculator wishing to take advantage of an expected decline in a commodity can sell a large quantity of the commodity for future delivery. Compare **margin.**

SENILE DEMENTIA insanity that occurs as the result of old age, progressive in character, and resulting in collapse of mental faculties that, in its final state, deprives one of **testamentary** capacity because of loss of power to reason or act sanely.

EXAMPLE: Warren had a valid will, but as he neared death, he changed certain provisions. When the will was read subsequent to Warren's death, there was a challenge as to Warren's capacity to change it. After hearing evidence that Warren claimed he spoke to dead people and was king of a nonexistent country, the court found that he had suffered from *senile dementia,* and therefore disallowed the changes.

See **competent; incompetency.**

SENTENCE punishment ordered by a court for a person convicted of a crime, usually either a NONCUSTODIAL SENTENCE such as **probation** or a fine, or a **CUSTODIAL SENTENCE** such as a term of imprisonment.

CONCURRENT SENTENCE a sentence that overlaps with another as opposed to a consecutive [cumulative] sentence, which runs by itself, beginning after or ending before the running of another sentence.

CONDITIONAL DISCHARGE SENTENCE see **SUSPENDED SENTENCE.**

CONSECUTIVE [or CUMULATIVE] SENTENCE a sentence that runs separately from one or more other sentences to be served by the same individual. The sentence is cumulative to the extent that it begins after an existing sentence has terminated either by expiration of the maximum term of the existing sentence, or by release from the present sentence through **parole.** If the consecutive sentence is a custodial one, the parole will be "to the cell" (called **CELL PAROLE**), so that the consecutive sentence may be served during the period of the parole.

INDETERMINATE SENTENCE a sentence for the maximum period prescribed by law for the particular offense committed, subject to the provision of the statute that the custodial portion may be terminated sooner by the board of parole any time after the expiration of the minimum period required for parole eligibility.

EXAMPLE: Jim, a youth, is given an *indeterminate sentence* for burglary. Since the maximum sentence for any youth in Jim's state is three years, his punishment will not exceed that length. But, as an indeterminate sentence, the time he actually serves will be determined by the prison authorities based on his adjustment at the prison. He is thereby encouraged to make a positive adjustment.

INTERLOCUTORY SENTENCE 1. a temporary or provisional sentence, pending the imposition of a final sentence; 2. a sentence on a supplementary question derived from the main cause of action.

SPLIT SENTENCE a sentence part of which is served in jail and the remainder of which is served on probation.

SUSPENDED SENTENCE one whose imposition or execution

has been withheld by the court on certain terms and conditions. An **implied** condition is always that the defendant not commit further violation of the law during a fixed period. Where no such period is fixed by the court, the practical effect of the suspended sentence is similar to an UNCONDITIONAL DISCHARGE sentence, i.e., the matter is terminated without conditions. A CONDITIONAL DISCHARGE is a suspended sentence on particular conditions for a period that is expressly fixed by the court or by statute. See also **pretrial intervention.**

SEPARATION AGREEMENT a written agreement by a husband and wife who are separated or about to separate or divorce; provides for the distribution of marital property and, when applicable, support by one spouse for the other. See **divorce** [SEPARATION].

SEQUESTER to separate from; to hold aside.

SEQUESTRATION 1. in **equity,** the act of **seizing** property belonging to another and holding it until profits have paid the demand for which the property was taken.

2. In **common law, juries** (at least in capital cases) were always sequestered, i.e., kept together throughout the trial and jury deliberations, and guarded from improper contact until they were discharged. This common law right to demand jury sequestration has been replaced in most **jurisdictions** with **discretion** in the trial court to grant sequestration in the interests of justice.

3. Sequestration of **witnesses** is frequently ordered by the court at the request of one of the parties to insure that in-court testimony of each witness not be colored by what another witness said.

EXAMPLE: The prosecutor was aware that defense witnesses might alter their versions of the facts if they were permitted to hear the State's witnesses testify. To avoid that problem, he asked for the *sequestration* of all witnesses. The judge agreed and excluded all potential witnesses from the courtroom until they were called to testify.

SERIAL BOND see **bond.**

SERIATIM *(sĕr'-ē-ä'-tĭm)* Lat.: in due order; in succession; one by one.

SERVANT one who works for, and is subject to, the control of his **master;** a person employed to perform services for another and who in the performance of the services is subject to the other's control or right to control.

In determining whether one acting for another is a servant or an independent contractor, the following matters of fact, among others, are considered: (1) the extent of control which, by the agreement, the master may exercise over the details of the work; (2) whether or not the one employed is engaged in a distinct occupation or business; (3) the kind of occupation, with reference to whether, in the locality, the work is usually done under the direction of the employer or by a specialist without supervision; (4) the skill required in the particular occupation; (5) whether the employer or the workman supplies the instrumentalities, tools and the place of work for the person doing the work; (6) the length of time for which the person is employed; (7) the method of payment, whether by the time or by the job; (8) whether or not the work is a part of the regular business of the employer; (9) whether or not the parties believe they are creating the relation of master and servant; and (10) whether the principal is or is not in business. A master is in many instances liable, under the theory of **respondeat superior,** for the torts of his servant, but not for those of an independent contractor. Compare **agent; contractor [INDEPENDENT CONTRACTOR].**

SERVICE [OF PROCESS] **delivery** of a **pleading,** notice or other paper in a **suit,** to the opposite party, to charge him with receipt of it and subject him to its legal effect; communication of the substance of the **process** to the defendant, either by actual delivery or by other methods, whereby defendant is furnished with reasonable notice of the proceedings against him to afford him opportunity to appear and be heard.

EXAMPLE: Al files a lawsuit against a company, but the company never responds. Before entering a default judgment against the company, the judge demands proof that the company was *served* with notice of the suit. Without such proof, the judge cannot be sure that the company knows there is a suit against it.

PERSONAL SERVICE actual delivery to the party to be served.

SERVICE BY PUBLICATION **constructive** service accomplished by publishing the **notice** in a newspaper designated by the court, and in some **jurisdictions,** by mailing that newspaper to the last-known address of the party.

SUBSTITUTED SERVICE constructive service accomplished by service to a recognized representative or **agent** of the party to be served.

SERVIENT ESTATE in relation to an **easement,** an **estate** that is **burdened** by the **SERVITUDE,** i.e., an estate that is subject to some use by the owner of the **dominant estate;** also called **SERVIENT TENEMENT.**

SESSION LAWS laws bound in volumes in the order of their enactment by a state legislature, before possible codification.

SET ASIDE to **annul** or make **void.** See also **reversal.**

SETOFF 1. a **counterclaim** by **defendant** against **plaintiff** that grows from an independent **cause of action** and diminishes the plaintiff's potential **recovery;** a counter-demand arising out of a transaction different from that on which the plaintiff's cause of action is based. It does not deny the justice of the plaintiff's claim but seeks to balance it in whole or in part by a counterobligation alleged to be due by the plaintiff to the defendant in another transaction.

2. In tax law, setoff allows the amount of refund that a **taxpayer** could claim to be offset against the amount of deficiency that could be properly assessed; conversely, the amount of deficiency the government could assess can be offset by the amount the taxpayer could properly claim as a refund for the same **taxable year.**

SETTLEMENT conclusive resolving of a matter; especially, a compromise achieved by **adverse parties** in a **civil suit** before final **judgment,** whereby they agree between themselves upon their respective rights and obligations, thus eliminating the necessity of judicial resolution of the controversy.

EXAMPLE: A company is accused of discriminatory hiring practices by the Equal Employment Opportunity Commission (EEOC). The Commission will usually file with the company a notice of its accusations and will attempt to reach a *settlement* before looking to the courts. That method generally gives each party more flexibility. In certain instances, a judge may have to approve the settlement.

Compare **plea bargaining.**

SETTLOR [DONOR; TRUSTOR] one who creates a **trust** by giving **real** or **personal property** in trust to another (the **trustee**) for the benefit of a third person (the **beneficiary**). One who gives such property is said to settle it on, or bring **title** to rest with, the trustee.

SEVERABLE CONTRACT one that, in the event of a **breach** by one of the parties, may be justly considered as several independent agreements expressed in a single **instrument.** Where a **contract** is deemed severable, a breach thereof may constitute a **default** of only part of the contract, saving the defaulting party from the necessity of responding in **damages** for breach of the entire agreement.

A severable contract may in fact be a series of DIVISIBLE CONTRACTS so that each part may be supported by a separate **consideration** and involve separate suits for breach of contract.

SEVERABLE STATUTE one the remainder of which is still valid when a portion has been declared invalid, because the parts of the **statute** are not wholly interdependent. If the remaining part of the statute is capable of separate enforcement, the statute is said to be severable. The legislature may express its intent in a SEVERABILITY CLAUSE at the end of the act.

EXAMPLE: Congress passes a comprehensive piece of legislation attacking racial discrimination in all areas. If the Supreme Court finds a part of the legislation unconstitutional, the Court will eliminate it. Since the legislation is *severable,* the rest of the provisions remain in force.

SEVERAL separate. 1. In a **note,** each who severally promises to pay is responsible separately for the entire amount. 2. In a **judgment** against more than one defendant, arising out of one **action,** each may be **liable** for the entire amount of the judgment, thereby permitting the successful plaintiff to recover the entire amount of the judgment from any defendant against whom he chooses to institute a suit. See **contribution; joint and several; joint tortfeasors.**

SEVERALTY refers to the sole holding of property. A tenant in severalty holds land exclusively for the duration of his or her **estate** without any other person holding **joint** rights.

SEVERANCE act of separating; state of being disjoined. 1. a process for selecting a particular **charge** against the **defendant,** so that only one charge or only properly joined charges are before the **jury** in one trial. 2. the disjoinder, for separate trials, of two or more **defendants** named in the same **indictment** or **information;** a useful device where prejudice might arise to one or more of the defendants if they were tried together.

EXAMPLE: Ned is on trial with two other well-known criminals. He feels that the association between him and the others will sway a jury to convict him regardless of the evidence. Ned asks the trial judge for a *severance* so that he will have a better opportunity for a fair trial.

3. Severance of **claims** is also available in **civil** trials to prevent prejudice or for the convenience of the parties. A court may sever the issue of **liability** from the issue of **damages** and direct that the question of liability be determined first. Once liability is established the parties may agree upon the damages, avoiding a lengthy trial on that issue.

SHAM PLEADING one so clearly false that it presents no **issue** of fact to be determined by a **trial.** A **complaint** or **answer** will be stricken as sham only when it is undisputed that the alleged claim or **defense** is wholly unsupported by facts.

SHARE a portion of something; an **interest** in a **corporation.** See **stock; stock certificate.**

SHAREHOLDER proprietor of one or more shares of the **stock** of a **corporation.** A stockholder possesses the evidence, usually **stock certificates,** of real ownership of a portion of the property in actual or potential existence held by the company in its name for the common benefit of all the owners of the entire **capital** stock of the company.

EXAMPLE: Grace feels that a small company named Venta has a great future profit potential. She has some money that she can afford to risk so she becomes a *shareholder* in Venta. By purchasing shares, she becomes a part owner of the company and is entitled to share in dividends and to vote on certain company affairs.

SHAREHOLDERS' DERIVATIVE ACTION see **stockholders' derivative action.**

SHAREHOLDER'S EQUITY see **equity.**

SHERIFF'S SALE [JUDICIAL SALE] a **sale** of **property** by the sheriff under authority of a court's **judgment** and **writ of execution** in order to satisfy an unpaid judgment, **mortgage, lien** or other **debt** of the owner **(judgment debtor).** See **sale.**

SHIELD LAWS in the case of news persons, laws designed to protect a journalist's confidential sources of information and to protect other information, notes and materials from disclosure. In the case of rape victims, laws that limit the questions a defendant may ask about the life-style of the victim unless those questions can be shown to be essential for a fair trial. See **privileged communication.**

SHIFTING INTEREST see **interest.**

SHIFTING THE BURDEN OF PROOF transferring to the other party in a litigation the burden that one party has in producing evidence to support his or her claim; requires that the person who originally had the burden make out a **prima facie** case or defense by some minimum of evidence. See **burden of proof.**

SHIFTING USE see **use.** See also **interest** [EXECUTORY INTEREST].

SHORT SELLING see **selling short.**

SHORT-TERM CAPITAL GAIN see **capital gains or losses.**

SHOW CAUSE ORDER an **order,** made upon the **motion** of one party, requiring a party to appear and show cause (demonstrate) why a certain thing should be permitted or not permitted. It requires that party to meet the **prima facie case** made by the applicant's verified **complaint** or **affidavit.** An order to show cause is an accelerated method of beginning a **litigation** by compelling the adverse party to respond in a much shorter period of time than he would normally have to respond to a complaint.

EXAMPLE: A group of prisoners petitions a court to allow them greater visitation rights than their present one-visit-a-month allotment. The judge is inclined to agree with them and orders prison officials to *show cause* why greater visitation privileges should not be granted immediately. The officials must then provide at least some rationale for the limit, or the court will order a change, pending a trial on the petition.

Compare **restraining order; summons.**

SIMPLE CONTRACT see **sealed instrument.**

SIMULTANEOUS DEATH ACT a uniform state law passed in most states providing for the distribution of property when distribution depends upon the time of death of more than one person and it cannot be determined that the persons died other than simultaneously. In cases governed by the Act, the law presumes each person died before the other, with the effect that one half of the property of each passes to the estate of the other.

SINE DIE *(sē'-nā dē'-ā)* Lat.: without day, without time. A legislative body adjourns sine die when it does not set the next date of assembly.

SINE QUA NON *(sē'-nā kwä nŏn)* Lat.: without which not. That without which the thing cannot be, i.e., the essence of something. Compare **cause.**

EXAMPLE: Betty purchases a new refrigerator. She puts the old one on the street to be carted away but does not remove the door or lock it shut. A child is severely injured when he is trapped inside the refrigerator. The *sine qua non* is Betty's failure to do something about the door, which made the refrigerator an attractive nuisance.

SINKING FUND an accumulation, by a corporation or government body, of money invested to repay a **debt.**

EXAMPLE: A university borrows money from a bank to build a library. In its appeal to alumni, the school stresses that it wants to develop a *sinking fund* to pay off the loan. It is hoped that the fund will generate enough interest income so that the principal is never touched.

In government bodies, a sinking fund, whose sources are taxes, **imposts** or duties, is appropriated toward payment of interest on a public loan and for eventual payment of the **principal.**

SLANDER to engage in **defamation** orally; spoken words that tend to damage another's reputation. If defamatory meaning is apparent on the face of the statement, it is said to be SLANDEROUS PER SE. If the defamatory meaning is not self-evident, but arises only from extrinsic facts, the statement is SLANDEROUS PER QUOD. Compare **libel.**

SODOMY **crime against nature,** including **bestiality,** buggery (copulation per anus) and, in many **jurisdictions,** other acts of unnatural sexual intercourse as defined and proscribed by statute. Sodomy was a common law **felony** in the United States.

SOLE PROPRIETORSHIP a business or financial venture that is carried on by a single person and that is not a **trust** or **corporation.**

SOLICITATION an **offense** developed by later common law courts to reach conduct whereby one incited another to commit a **felony** or certain **misdemeanors** injurious to public welfare. If the actor agrees to join the other in an offense, **conspiracy** can be established. Compare **aid and abet; pander.**

SOLICITOR see **barrister.**

SOLVENCY 1. ability to pay all **debts** and just claims as they come due; 2. term to signify that **property** is adequate to satisfy one's obligations when sold under **execution.** 3. In certain contexts, solvency is an excess of **assets** over **liabilities.**

SOUNDS IN has a connection with. Thus, though a party to a lawsuit has **pleaded damages** in **tort,** it may be said that the **action** nevertheless sounds in **contract** if the elements of the offense charged appear to constitute a contract, rather than a tort, action.

SOVEREIGN that which is preeminent among all others; the King; the State.

EXAMPLE: A state wants to build a highway that requires the use of private property. Negotiations with the property owners fail to persuade them to sell to the state. The state can then use its *sovereign* power of eminent domain over all property within the state to take private property and put it to public use upon payment of just compensation.

SOVEREIGN IMMUNITY **immunity** precluding **suit** against the **sovereign** (government) without the sovereign's consent when the sovereign is engaged in a government function. Compare **Federal Tort Claims Act.**

SPECIAL DAMAGES see **damages** [CONSEQUENTIAL DAMAGES].

SPECIAL JURISDICTION see **limited jurisdiction.**

SPECIAL LEGISLATION acts of the legislature for the benefit of a certain individual or group, as opposed to general legislation enacted for the general population. Special laws may be constitutional if there is a rational basis for limiting application of the statute to the special group, such as small municipalities.

EXAMPLE: A state legislature passes a law requiring all municipalities to provide sewage systems. Because of the peculiarities of the soil in one municipality, *special legislation* is passed postponing the requirements until appropriate technology can be developed.

SPECIE money with intrinsic value, e.g., gold and silver coins.

SPECIFIC PERFORMANCE an **equitable remedy** available to an aggrieved party when remedy **at law** is inadequate. A decree of specific performance requires the party guilty of BREACH OF CONTRACT (see **breach**) to complete performance of his obligations under the contract on pain of punishment for contempt. Money **damages,** in contrast, are enforceable only by a **judgment** against property. Specific performance is available only where the **subject matter** of the contract is unique such as a particular parcel of real property or a rare painting, or in other unusual circumstances.

SPECIFIC RELIEF see **specific performance.**

SPECULATION purchase of property with the expectation of obtaining a quick profit as a result of price change.

SPENDTHRIFT TRUST a **trust** to provide a fund for maintenance of a **beneficiary** that is so restricted that it is secure against the beneficiary's improvidence, and beyond the reach of his **creditors.**

EXAMPLE: Nathan is well-known for his ability to spend large sums of money quickly and foolishly. Fearful that his habits may one day leave him without enough to live on, his mother creates a *spendthrift trust* with Nathan as beneficiary. The trust is restricted so that he receives only income and cannot invade the principal except with special permission.

SPLITTING A CAUSE OF ACTION impermissible practice of bringing an **action** for only part of the **cause of action** in one **suit,** and initiating another suit for another part. Under the policy against splitting of causes of action, the law **mandates** that all **damages** accruing to one as a result of a single wrongful act be claimed in one action or not at all.

EXAMPLE: Matt develops a new product and obtains a patent for it. Two months later, one of Matt's assistants goes to work for a company that introduces the exact same product. Matt sues the company but *splits his cause of action* by filing one suit for copyright infringement and another for profits derived from the sale of his product. The court does not permit this and forces Matt to combine both suits at the same time in one action.

Compare **multiplicity of suits; joinder; misjoinder.**

SPRINGING INTEREST see **interest.**

SPRINGING USE see **use.** See also **interest** [EXECUTORY INTEREST].

STAKEHOLDER a third party chosen by two or more persons to keep in deposit **property** whose **title** is in dispute, and to deliver the property to the one who establishes his right to it.

STANDING the legal right to challenge in a judicial forum the conduct of another. In the federal system, **litigants** must satisfy constitutional standing requirements in order to create a legitimate **case or controversy** within the meaning of Article III of the Constitution. In construing this language, courts have held that the gist of the question of standing is whether the party seeking **relief** has alleged a personal stake in the outcome of the controversy so as to insure that real, rather than remote or possible, adverseness exists to sharpen the presentation of issues.

EXAMPLE: Payne, a resident of one state, files a suit claiming that another state prevents its own citizens from voting. Since Payne is not affected by the fact that citizens of another state may not be getting the opportunity to vote, he has no *standing* to bring this challenge. There are procedures whereby a court has the discretionary power to allow Payne to participate in a suit if someone files it who does have standing. Payne might also have standing in the suit first referred to if the challenged state action adversely impacts on a national election that affects Payne.

STANDING MUTE in a criminal trial, refusing to **plead;** today equivalent to a **plea** of **not guilty.** Compare **self-incrimination, privilege against.**

STARE DECISIS *(stä'-rā dĕ-sī'-sĭs)* Lat.: to stand by that which was decided. Rule by which **common law** courts are reluctant to interfere with principles announced in former decisions and therefore rely upon judicial **precedent** as a compelling guide to decision of cases raising issues, similar to those in previous cases.

EXAMPLE: A state supreme court rules that a person's privacy interests demand court protection of telephone toll records from police investigations. Several years later, the issue is brought back to the court. The prosecutor claims that other states allow the records to be used without interference in privacy and that other privacy protections can be employed if necessary. Even if some new members of the court agree with the prosecutor, the court most likely will apply *stare decisis* and abide by the previous decision.

STATU QUO see **in statu quo.**

STATUS QUO *(stă'-tŭs kwō)* Lat.: the positions or conditions that exist.

STATUS QUO ANTE the situation that existed at the inception of a **contract.**

See **injunction; rescission; restraining order.**

STATUTE an act of the legislature, adopted under its constitutional authority, by prescribed means and in certain form, so that it becomes the law governing conduct within its scope. Statutes are enacted to prescribe conduct, define crimes, create inferior government bodies, appropriate public monies, and in general to promote the public welfare. Compare **common law; judge-made law; ordinance; police power.**

STATUTE OF FRAUDS statutory requirement that certain kinds of **contracts** be in writing to be enforceable. Contracts to answer to a **creditor** for the **debt** of another, contracts made in **consideration** of marriage, contracts for the sale of land or affecting any **interest** in land and contracts not to be performed within one year from their making normally must be evidenced by a written memorandum and be signed by the **party** sought to be bound by the contract.

STATUTE OF LIMITATIONS any law that fixes the time within which **parties** must take judicial action to enforce rights or else be thereafter barred from enforcing them.

Equity proceedings are governed by an independent doctrine called **laches.** The enactment of such laws derives from the belief that there is a point beyond which a prospective defendant should no longer worry about a future possibility of an action against him, that the law disfavors "stale evidence," and that no one should be able to "sit on his rights" for an unreasonable time without forfeiting claims.

STATUTE OF USES an English statute, enacted in 1536, to prevent separation of legal and EQUITABLE ESTATES (see **estate**) in land, a separation that arose whenever a **use** was created at **common law.** The purpose was to unite all legal and equitable estates in the **beneficiary** (the holder of the equitable estate) and to strip the **trustee** (the holder of the legal **title**) of all interest.

STATUTE OF WILLS an early English statute prescribing conditions necessary for valid disposition through a **will.** Today the term is used broadly to refer to the statutory provisions of a particular **jurisdiction** relating to requirements for valid testamentary dispositions.

STATUTORY OFFENSE see **regulatory offense.**

STATUTORY RAPE see **rape.**

STAY a halt in a judicial **proceeding** where, by its **order,** the court will not take further action until the occurrence of some event.

STAY OF EXECUTION process whereby a **judgment** is precluded from being executed for a specific period.

EXAMPLE: An apartment dweller is found in default under his lease. He seeks a *stay of execution* of the eviction order until he can make new living arrangements. A stay may be granted, but not for an excessively long time.

STIPULATION an agreement or concession made by parties in a judicial proceeding or by their attorneys, relating to a matter before the court.

EXAMPLE: Two parties in a contractual dispute agree as to most of the facts except those occurring immediately prior to the breach of contract. To avoid unnecessary delays in proving facts that the parties agree on, they enter a *stipulation* with the court as to those facts. If one of those facts is actually a legal conclusion based on the facts, the court will not accept that part of the stipulation.

STIRPES see **per stirpes.**

STOCK 1. a merchant's inventory; 2. the **capital** of a corporation, consisting of proceeds from the sale of shares and evidenced by the total number of shares issued; 3. the number of shares owned by an individual shareholder and the proportionate **equity** interest in the corporation represented thereby.

BONUS STOCK see **bonus stock.**

COMMON STOCK see **common stock.**

PREFERRED STOCK see **preferred stock.**

NO-PAR STOCK see **par.**

STOCKBROKER see **broker** or **registered representative.**

STOCK CERTIFICATE written **instrument** evidencing a **share** in the ownership of a **corporation.**

STOCK DIVIDEND see **dividend.**

STOCK EXCHANGE a place where the business of buying and selling **securities** is transacted.

STOCKHOLDER see **shareholder.**

STOCKHOLDERS' DERIVATIVE ACTION a **suit** by the **corporation** in which the grievance to be redressed has been suffered primarily by the corporation, conducted by the **shareholders** as the corporation's representative. The shareholder is only a nominal **plaintiff,** and the corporation is the **real party in interest.** Where the corporation itself fails or refuses to act after a demand that it do so by the shareholders, their ultimate interest in the corporation is sufficient to warrant the prosecution of an action on behalf of the corporation that will ultimately recover for the corporation the rights or property of which it has been deprived by the wrongdoer.

Such suits are the only civil remedy a stockholder has for breach of a **fiduciary** duty by those entrusted with the management of their corporation.

EXAMPLE: The shareholders of a corporation believe that the corporation is not pressing a debt owed to it by another company. The shareholders bring a *stockholders' derivative action* to force the officers to take steps against the other company to secure payment of the debt.

STOCK MARKET an organized market, such as a **stock exchange** or an **over-the-counter market,** where **stocks** and **bonds** are actively traded.

STOCK OPTION the granting to an individual of the right to purchase a corporate stock at some future date at a price specified at the time the option is given rather than at the time the stock is obtained. The option may be purchased or sold, as in a **CALL OPTION,** or may be granted to an individual by the company as is an **EMPLOYEE STOCK OPTION.** The option will always involve a specified number of shares, state a time period within which it may be exercised and state a price to be paid upon exercise. A **PUT OPTION** is the reverse of a call option in that the holder has a right to compel the seller of the option to purchase his shares at a fixed price during a set time period for a pre-determined price per share.

EXAMPLE: Art acquires the right to buy *x* number of shares of corporate stock in two months at $20 a share. The price of the *stock option* depends on the price of the stock at the time the option is purchased. Art hopes that the stock will be worth over $20 in two months. If it is worth $25 at that time, he may decide to exercise his option to purchase at $20 and then choose to sell the stock immediately at a profit for its market value of $25. If it is worth less than $20 in two months, however, Art will probably not exercise his option and will only lose whatever he paid for the option. At any time before expiration, Art can sell the option for its then market value.

STOP AND FRISK in reference to police conduct on the street, a limited search for weapons confined to outer clothing.

EXAMPLE: A policeman observes two men walk in front of a jewelry store several times and discuss what they see after each trip. The policeman is permitted to *stop* the men and question them until the purpose of their activity is sufficiently explained. He can *frisk* them if he sees a bulge that appears to be a weapon or if he otherwise has a reasonable belief that one of them possesses a weapon. To do anything beyond this "stop and frisk" requires a more concrete belief that the pair will commit or have committed a crime.

Compare **search and seizure.**

STRAIGHT-LINE METHOD see **depreciation.**

STRAW MAN 1. a colloquial expression designating arguments in **briefs** or **opinions** created solely for the purpose of refuting them. Such arguments are like straw men because they are, by nature, insubstantial.

2. In commercial and property contexts, the term may be used when a transfer is made to a third party, the straw man, simply to retransfer to the transferror or to transfer to another in order to accomplish some purpose not otherwise permitted.

STREET NAME refers to **securities** held in the name of a **broker** or the broker's nominee instead of the name of the owner. This is required when securities are purchased on **margin.** Many cash buyers leave their securities with their broker, who normally holds them in street name, although arrangements can be made to hold the securities as custodian in the customer's name.

STRICT CONSTRUCTION 1. adherence to the literal meaning of the words in **statutes** or **contracts;** 2. an interpretation that confines a statute or **instrument** to subjects or applications obviously within its terms or purposes.

STRICT LIABILITY in **tort** and criminal law, liability without a showing of fault, or the need to show fault. See **ultrahazardous activity.**

EXAMPLE: Adrienne harbors wild animals on her estate. A child accidentally enters the estate and is harmed by one of these animals. Adrienne will usually be held *strictly liable* for the injury regardless of the fact that the child did not belong there or that the child scared the animal. Society imposes that cost on Adrienne merely for keeping the animals.

STRIKE SUIT a suit brought primarily for its nuisance value by a small **shareholder** whose interest in the corporation is insignificant. Knowing that the cost of defending such a suit is high, the shareholder sues hoping for a private settlement. These suits are also called BLACKMAIL SUITS and HOLDUP SUITS. Compare **stockholders' derivative action.**

SUA SPONTE *(sū'-à spŏn'-tā)* Lat.: of itself or of one's self. Without being prompted; refers especially to a court's acting of its own volition (on its own motion), without a **motion** being made by either of the **adverse parties.**

EXAMPLE: A party files a lawsuit and the opponent replies, so that both parties are prepared to litigate the issue. If the judge realizes for some reason that he has no jurisdiction over the case, he will on his own initiative dismiss the case. His action is taken *sua sponte*.

SUBCHAPTER S CORPORATION see **corporation** [SUBCHAPTER S].

SUBCONTRACTOR one to whom a principal (general) contractor or other subcontractor sublets part or all of a contract.

SUBJECT MATTER the thing in dispute; the nature of the **cause of action;** the real **issue** of fact or law presented for **trial;** also, the object of a **contract.**

SUBJECT MATTER JURISDICTION see **jurisdiction.**

SUB JUDICE *(sŭb jū'-dĭ-sā)* Lat.: under a court. Before a court or judge for consideration.

EXAMPLE: Two attorneys are arguing their respective positions before a judge. One attempts to prove his point by using related examples. The other, seeking to weaken his opponent's tactic, reminds the judge that the facts of the case *sub judice* are sufficiently different from the examples to warrant a different outcome.

SUBLEASE a transaction whereby a **tenant** (one who has **leased** premises from the owner, or **landlord**) grants to another an **interest** less than his own in the leased premises. Compare **assignment** [ASSIGNMENT OF A LEASE].

EXAMPLE: Marcy has two years remaining on her rental agreement when she marries her boyfriend and moves into his apartment. Except in rare circumstances, Mary will be able to *sublease* her apartment to someone else. But unless the landlord makes a different arrangement, Mary is still responsible for seeing that rent is paid each month.

SUBLET to make a **sublease.**

SUB MODO *(sŭb mō'-dō)* Lat.: under a qualification. Subject to a **condition.**

SUB NOMINE *(sŭb nō'-mē-nā)* Lat.: under the name; often abbreviated sub nom. Indicates that the title of a case has been altered after the beginning of the proceedings.

SUBORDINATION establishment of priority of one **claim** or **debt** over another. A SUBORDINATION AGREEMENT is one in which a **creditor** agrees in a **contract** that claims of other creditors must be fully paid before there is any payment to the subordinated creditor.

EXAMPLE: A company wants to borrow money from a lender, but it runs into difficulty because of two outstanding debts, both of which are owed to company directors. In order to obtain the money, the directors sign a *subordination agreement,* which provides that the lender will be fully repaid before the directors receive any money toward their loans.

In real estate law, subordination refers to the establishment of priority between different existing interests, claims, **liens** and **encumbrances** on the same parcel of land.

SUBORNATION OF PERJURY a crime consisting of encouraging and persuading another to make a false oath. See also **false swearing.**

SUBPOENA *(sŭ-pē'-nȧ)* Lat.: under penalty. A **writ** issued under authority of a court to compel the **appearance** of a **witness** at a judicial proceeding; disobedience may be punishable as **contempt of court.**

SUBPOENA AD TESTIFICANDUM *(ăd tĕs-tĭ-fĭ-kăn'-dūm),* subpoena to testify. Technical name for the ordinary subpoena.

SUBPOENA DUCES TECUM *(dū'-chĕs tā'-kūm)* under penalty you shall bring it with you. Type of subpoena issued by a court at the request of one of the parties to a **suit.** A witness having under his control documents relevant to the controversy is **enjoined** to bring such items to court during the trial or at the **deposition.**

EXAMPLE: Several years ago, Martin was a marketing consultant to a large firm. The firm is being sued by a company that claims the firm gave it false information. Martin is not personally being sued, but he is issued a *subpoena duces tecum* to testify at the trial and bring with him any papers relevant to the firm's relationship with the company.

SUBROGATION the substitution of another person, the **subrogee,** in the place of the **creditor,** to whose rights to the **debt** the other person succeeds; one's payment or assumption of an obligation for which another is primarily liable.

Subrogation typically arises when an insurance company pays its insured under the provisions of an insurance policy; in that event the company is subrogated to the cause of action of its insured against the one responsible for the damage for which the insurance company has paid.

EXAMPLE: While making a delivery, a home fuel oil company negligently performs its task and a home burns down as a result. If the home is protected by fire insurance, the insurance company will pay for the damages. The homeowner's claim against the oil company is then *subrogated* to the insurance company.

SUBROGEE one who, by **subrogation,** succeeds to the legal rights or claims of another.

SUBROGOR one whose legal rights or claims are acquired by another through **subrogation.**

SUBSCRIPTION RIGHTS the **contractual** right of an existing **shareholder** to purchase additional **shares** of **stock** of the same kind as that already held when and if new shares are issued by a corporation. Also called STOCK RIGHTS. Compare **stock option; warrant** [STOCK WARRANT].

SUBSIDIARY an inferior portion or capacity; usually describes a relationship between **corporations.**

SUBSIDIARY CORPORATION one in which another corporation owns a majority of shares and thus has control. It has all normal elements of a corporation **(charter, bylaws, directors),** but its **stock** is controlled by another corporation known as the PARENT CORPORATION.

SUB SILENTIO *(sŭb sĭ-lĕn'-shē-ō)* Lat.: under silence; silently. When a later opinion reaches a result contrary to what would appear to be controlling authority, the later case, by necessary **implication,** overrules sub silentio the prior holdings.

EXAMPLE: An early case holds that a homeowner has no obligation to remove the snow in front of his house. A later case ruled upon by a higher court then decides that the homeowner does have that obligation. The later case does not make specific reference to the earlier case. By necessary implication, the later case overrules *sub silentio* the prior case.

SUBSTANTIAL PERFORMANCE [or COMPLIANCE] **performance** of a contract that, while not full performance, is so nearly equivalent to what was bargained for that it would be unreasonable to deny the one who has promised to perform the full contract price, subject to the right of the one who agreed to pay for that performance to recover whatever **damages** may have been occasioned him by the promisor's failure to render full performance.

EXAMPLE: A student contracts to paint a neighbor's house during the summer. He has almost completed the task when he is overwhelmed by the desire to spend the rest of the summer at the shore. The only part of the house unpainted is the window moldings, which are the same color as the house but lack a fresh coat. The student is entitled to payment since there is **substantial performance** of the contract, but there will be a slight reduction in the price because of the unfinished moldings.

Compare **breach** [**BREACH OF CONTRACT**].

SUBSTANTIVE DUE PROCESS see **due process of law.**

SUBSTANTIVE LAW the **positive law** that creates, defines and regulates the rights and duties of the **parties** and that may give rise to a **cause of action,** as distinguished from **adjective law** that pertains to and prescribes the practice and **procedure** or the legal machinery by which the substantive law is determined or made effective.

SUBSTITUTED SERVICE see **service.**

SUBTENANT one who **leases** all or part of rented **premises** from the original **lessee** for a term less than that held by the original lessee; the original lessee becomes the sublessor.

EXAMPLE: A supplier rents space in a warehouse but finds that he does not need the full amount that he rented. He then leases part of the space to a large retail discount store that needs some extra storage space. The discount store, which is the *subtenant,* may pay rent to the supplier or to the warehouse owner. The supplier, though, is still liable for the full rent unless some other agreement with the warehouse owner is reached.

Compare **assignment** [**ASSIGNMENT OF A LEASE**].

SUCCESSION refers to the process by which the property of a decedent is inherited through **descent** or by **will.** See **intestate succession.**

SUCCESSOR one who succeeds to the role, rights, duties or place of another.

SUE OUT to apply for and obtain a **writ** or court **order,** as to sue out a writ in **chancery.**

SUICIDE the voluntary and intentional killing of oneself.

EXAMPLE: Suzanne is very upset over the loss of a boyfriend, so she goes out and drinks heavily. When she comes home, she decides to take some aspirin in the hope that there will be no hangover in the morning. Unfortunately, she never wakes up. Suzanne is not a victim of *suicide* because she had no intention of killing herself.

SUI GENERIS *(sū' ē jĕn'-ĕr-ĭs)* Lat.: of its own kind; unique; in a class by itself. See also **ejusdem generis.**

SUI JURIS *(sū'-ĕ jūr'-ĭs)* Lat.: of his own right. Describes one who is no longer dependent, e.g., one who has reached **majority,** or has been removed from the care of a **guardian.** Compare **emancipation; incompetency.**

SUIT any **proceeding** in a court of justice by which an individual pursues a **remedy** that the law affords.

CLASS SUIT see **class action.**

[STOCKHOLDERS'] DERIVATIVE SUIT see **stockholders' derivative action.**

SUM CERTAIN any amount that is fixed, settled, stated or exact. It may refer to the value of a **negotiable instrument,** to a price stated in a **contract,** or to a measure of **damages.** The sum must be ascertainable at the time the instrument is made and computable solely from examination of it.

EXAMPLE: A long-term contract includes a very technical formula for determining the cost of wheat. The formula allows for fluctuations in the market place, weather, demand and other factors. Although the price can therefore vary each time a price is paid, the fact that there is a formula means that the contract includes a *sum certain.*

SUMMARY JUDGMENT preverdict **judgment** of the court in response to a **motion** by plaintiff or defendant, rendered when the court perceives that only questions of law are in dispute, or that the court's decision must be the same regardless of which party's version of the facts is accepted. It is a device designed to effect a prompt disposition of controversies on their **merits** without resort to a lengthy trial.

EXAMPLE: Dale erects a structure on his property that almost completely blocks the sun from the pool area that his neighbor just built, and the neighbor sues Dale to remove the structure. Dale and the neighbor agree on that set of facts. The only question is whether Dale may do as he wants, which in this instance is a question of law. Both parties, therefore, seek a *summary judgment* supporting their respective positions.

Compare **directed verdict.**

SUMMARY PROCEEDING a method by which the **parties** to a legal controversy may achieve a more prompt disposition of their case by use of simplified **procedural** rules, usually involving more limited **discovery** or fact finding than is normally permitted in the particular type of proceeding. Summary proceedings have been commonly used in **arbitration, bankruptcy, landlord-tenant** and unlawful entry and **detainer** cases.

SUMMONS a mandate requiring the **appearance** of the defendant under penalty of having **judgment** entered against him for failure to appear. The object of the summons is to notify the defendant that he has been sued.

EXAMPLE: Nick sues a landscaper for installing a defective sprinkler system. His attorney prepares a *summons* notifying the landscaper of the court action. The clerk of the court stamps the summons, and it is then issued.

See **process; service.** Compare **subpoena.**

SUNDAY CLOSING LAWS any state or local laws that restrict activities on Sunday, as for instance forbidding the sale of goods on Sunday. Compare **blue laws.**

SUNSHINE LAWS laws requiring that government agencies and departments permit the public to attend their meetings. Often called **OPEN PUBLIC MEETINGS LAWS.**

SUO NOMINE *(sū'-ō nō'-mē-nā)* Lat.: in his own name.

SUPERSEDING CAUSE see **cause.**

SUPERVENING CAUSE see **cause** [INTERVENING CAUSE].

SUPPRESSION OF EVIDENCE a decision made by a judge not to allow certain evidence into a criminal trial because the evidence was obtained by illegal or improper means. See **unreasonable search and seizure.**

SUPRA *(sū'-prȧ)* Lat.: above. In a written work, refers to a part preceding that which is presently being read.

SUPREMACY CLAUSE popularized title for Article VI, Section 2 of the United States Constitution, which is the main foundation of the federal government's power over the states, providing that the acts of the federal government are operative as supreme law throughout the union.

EXAMPLE: The United States Supreme Court rules that no person can be arrested in his home without an arrest warrant issued by a judge. Regardless of the procedures the various states used before the Supreme Court decision, the *Supremacy Clause* mandates that the Supreme Court's decision govern future police practice.

SUPREME COURT the highest **appellate court** in most **jurisdictions** and in the **federal court** system. It is usually the appellate state court of last resort, and in the absence of a **federal question,** its decisions cannot be reviewed by other courts and must be respected. In some states this court is an inferior court and not the court of last resort.

In the federal court system, the United States Supreme Court is expressly provided for in the **Constitution,** which vests judicial power in "one Supreme Court" and such inferior courts as Congress shall establish. It consists of a Chief Justice and eight Associate Justices appointed by the President with the advice and consent of the U.S. Senate.

SURCHARGE 1. an additional charge that has been omitted from an account stated; 2. a penalty for failure to exercise common prudence and common skill in the performance of a **fiduciary's** duties.

3. SURTAX is a tax added to the normal tax, imposed on certain kinds of income.

SURETY one who undertakes to pay money or perform other acts in the event that his **principal** fails therein. See also **indorsement.**

EXAMPLE: A corporation wants to issue bonds so that it has sufficient money to develop a new product. If the reputation of the corporation is such that people are unwilling to buy the bonds without some guarantee, the corporation will seek a *surety* who in fact guarantees payment of the corporate bonds.

SURPLUS the remainder of a fund appropriated for a particular purpose. In corporations, surplus denotes **assets** left after liabilities and debts, including capital **stock,** have been deducted.

EARNED SURPLUS the portion of surplus derived from the net earnings, gains or profits retained by a corporation rather than paid to **shareholders** as **dividends.**

PAID-IN SURPLUS the portion of surplus derived from the sale, exchange or issuance of capital stock at a price above the PAR VALUE (see **par**) of the stock. Thus, the difference between par value and the actual price received is the paid-in surplus. In the case of **no-par stock,** it is the amount received that has been allocated to paid-in surplus. The term is sometimes used interchangeably with capital surplus, although the latter term is often used to denote the entire surplus of a corporation other than its earned surplus.

SURREBUTTER in **common law pleading,** a **plaintiff's** answer to the **defendant's rebuttal (rebutter).**

SURREJOINDER in **common law pleading,** a **plaintiff's** answer to the **defendant's rejoinder.**

SURRENDER the yielding or delivery of **possession** in response to a demand. In property law denotes the yielding of the **leasehold estate** by the lessee to the landlord, so that the TENANCY FOR YEARS (see **tenancy**) merges in the **reversion** and no longer exists.

SURROGATE a judicial officer of limited **jurisdiction,** who administers matters of **probate** and **intestate succession** and, in some cases, **adoptions.**

EXAMPLE: After the father's death, his will is submitted to a *surrogate,* who oversees the distribution of the estate. A question arises concerning a fraudulent transfer of money outside the estate, giving rise to possible criminal and civil liability. Since the surrogate is limited in what he can rule on, the question must be raised in a court that has broader jurisdiction.

SURTAX see **surcharge.**

SURVEILLANCE oversight or supervision. In criminal law, an investigative process by which police gather evidence about crimes or suspected crime through continued observation of persons or places. Wiretapping, electronic observation, tailing or shadowing are examples of this type of law enforcement procedure.

SURVIVAL STATUTE a statute that preserves for his **estate** a decedent's **cause of action** for infliction of **pain and suffering** and related **damages** suffered up to the moment of death. Compare **wrongful death statute.**

SURVIVORSHIP a right whereby a person becomes entitled to property by reason of his having survived another person who had an **interest** in it. It is one of the elements of a JOINT TENANCY (see **tenancy**).

EXAMPLE: A husband and wife own a house as tenants by the entirety. When the husband dies, the wife acquires full ownership of the house by her right of *survivorship.*

SUSPENDED SENTENCE see **sentence.**

SUSTAIN to support; to approve; to adequately maintain.

SYLLABUS a **headnote** preceding a reported case and summarizing the principles of law established in that case. Under the practice of the United States Supreme Court, the headnotes are prepared for the convenience of readers by the Reporter of Decisions; as such, the syllabus constitutes no part of the opinion of the Court.

SYMBOLIC DELIVERY see **delivery.**

SYNDICATE a group of individuals or companies who have formed a joint venture to undertake a project that the individuals would be unable or unwilling to pursue alone.

EXAMPLE: a large corporation frequently offers stock for sale. An underwriting *syndicate* made up of investment bankers and stockbrokers will first buy the stock, a step made possible by the fact that the syndicate can pool the resources of its individual members. The syndicate will then use the combined strength of its members to market the stock and sell it to the public.

T

TACKING to add together; 1. in property law, the uniting of the periods of possession of successive holders to complete the period necessary to establish title by **adverse possession,** which is possible provided that there is **privity** of estate between the successive adverse possessors. Thus, the original adverse possessor must transfer the property either by a voluntary **conveyance** or by **inheritance** for tacking to be permitted. 2. As a legislative phrase, tacking designates the practice of adding a measure that is of doubtful strength on its own merits onto a general appropriations bill in order to compel the legislature to vote for it. 3. As applied to mortgages, tacking is joining of a third purchaser's **encumbrance** with his original **mortgage** debt so as to close out the second mortgagee.

TAFT-HARTLEY ACT the popular name for the Labor-Management Relations Act of 1947, whose stated purpose is to protect employers' rights by broadening their rights to free speech on unionization; by permitting them to disregard unions formed by supervisory personnel; by outlawing the closed shop; by permitting employees to refrain from union activity; by limiting employee elections on whether to unionize to one per year; by prohibiting unions from forcing employees to join, from forcing an employer to discriminate against nonunion employees, from refusing to bargain collectively with the employer, from engaging in wildcat strikes, from charging discriminatory membership fees, and from extracting favors or kickbacks from employers.

EXAMPLE: A construction company is not allowed to send any trucks onto a construction site unless the driver is a union member. The company therefore cannot hire any drivers unless they belong to a union. The company has the right to bring a suit for a violation of the *Taft-Hartley Act*.

TAIL, ESTATE IN see **fee tail.**

TAINTED EVIDENCE [TAINT] see **fruit of the poisonous tree doctrine.**

TAKING THE FIFTH the popular term given to a person's assertion of his Fifth Amendment right not to give evidence that will incriminate himself. See **self-incrimination, privilege against; Fifth Amendment.**

TANGIBLE PROPERTY **property,** either **real** or **personal,** capable of being **possessed.** Tangible property is capable of being perceived by the senses, as distinguished from intangible property or incorporated rights in property, such as **franchises, copyrights, easements.** For taxation purposes, tangible property generally refers to (**personal property**) personalty, and is that movable property that has a value of its own, rather than merely the evidence or representation of value.

TAX a rate or sum of money assessed on a citizen's person, property or activity for the support of government, levied upon assets or real property (property tax), upon income derived from wages, etc. (income tax), or upon sale or purchase of goods (sales tax).

AD VALOREM TAX see **VALUE ADDED TAX.**.

CAPITAL GAINS TAX see **capital** [**CAPITAL ASSETS**]; **capital gains or losses.**

ESTATE TAX state death taxes imposed upon the net value of a decedent's **estate.** The same tax result is accomplished in some jurisdictions through imposition of a **TRANSFER TAX,** which is a tax upon the transfer of the property from the estate to the **beneficiary.**

ESTIMATED TAX income taxes that are paid periodically by a taxpayer on income that is not subject to **withholding** taxes, in an amount that represents a projection of ultimate tax liability for the taxable period.

EXCISE TAX see **excise.**

FRANCHISE TAX a tax generally imposed by the states upon **corporations,** often divided into two components: (1) a tax upon the net income of the corporation attributable to activities within the state, and (2) the tax on the net worth of the corporation located in the state.

EXAMPLE: A state imposes a tax on "the privilege of doing business" in the state. As long as the tax is only imposed on the income that the corporation earns in the state or on the value of the corporation's assets in the state, the tax is a valid *franchise tax* on the corporation.

INCOME TAX a tax imposed upon value received by the taxpayer, reduced by the allowable **deductions** and **credits.** See **return, income tax.**

POLL TAX see **poll tax.**

PROGRESSIVE TAX a tax whose rate increases as the amount subject to tax increases.

PROPERTY TAX a tax imposed by municipalities upon owners of property within their **jurisdiction,** based upon the **assessed** value of such property.

REGRESSIVE TAX a tax whose rate of tax remains the same regardless of the amounts involved, or decreases as the amount to which the tax is applied increases.

SALES TAX a tax imposed on the retail sale of certain items.

UNIFIED ESTATE AND GIFT TAX a federal tax imposed upon the net value of an **estate** and on **gifts** of certain amounts. Usually, the transferror is liable for gift taxes, but if the transferror fails to pay, the transferee may be held liable for payment.

USE TAX a tax imposed upon property when it is brought into the taxing jurisdiction, usually because the taxing jurisdiction has no jurisdiction over the sale and therefore cannot impose a sales tax.

EXAMPLE: A state requires a bus company to obtain certificates of title to operate their buses in that state. The certificates will not be issued until a tax is paid, based on the fair market value of the buses. The tax is permitted as a *use tax* to offset the cost of maintaining the state highways.

VALUE ADDED TAX [AD VALOREM TAX] a tax imposed upon the difference between the cost of an asset to the taxpayer and the present fair **market value** of such asset.

WITHHOLDING TAX the amount of income taxes that an employer is required to withhold from an employee's salary when the salary is paid. The amount withheld is a credit against the amount of income taxes the employee must pay on his income earned for the taxable year.

TAXABLE YEAR the period during which the tax liability of an individual or entity is calculated, or, in the case of certain nontaxable entities, the period for which tax information is provided. Compare **fiscal year.**

TAX BENEFIT DOCTRINE a theory that provides for the inclusion in GROSS INCOME (see **income**) of amounts deducted in earlier **taxable years** and recovered in later years, but only to the extent that the earlier **deductions** resulted in a reduction in income tax liability for the earlier years.

TAX COURT an independent sixteen-judge federal administrative agency that functions as a court to hear appeals by **taxpayers** from adverse administrative decisions by the **Internal Revenue Service.** Although such suits may be considered in federal district courts or in the Court of Claims, the Tax Court does not require the taxpayer to pay the alleged deficiency prior to suit. Headquartered in Washington, D.C., the Tax Court holds hearings in several principal cities as well. Tax court trials are **de novo** and an adverse decision may be appealed as of right to the Court of Appeals and in rare cases to the United States Supreme Court.

TAX CREDIT a dollar-for-dollar reduction in the amount of tax that a taxpayer owes. Unlike **deductions** or **exemptions,** which reduce the amount of income subject to tax, a credit reduces the actual amount of tax owed.

INVESTMENT TAX CREDIT tax credit allowed for investments in **personal property** devoted to business or income-producing activity, when certain specific requirements are met.

TAX EXPENDITURE revenue losses that are suffered by the federal government as a result of provisions of the **Internal Revenue Code** that grant special tax benefits to certain kinds of **taxpayers** or certain activities engaged in by taxpayers.

TAX EXPENDITURE BUDGET a compilation of various tax expenditures inherent in the tax system for the year in question.

TAXPAYER the person who is determined to bear the tax liability for a given **transaction,** activity or status.

TAX PREFERENCE ITEMS those items of **income, deduction** or **tax credit** deemed to reflect a preference in the tax law for the **taxpayer** benefited by the preference item. Since it is thought that these items result in preferential treatment that may result in minimal tax liability for certain taxpayers, notwithstanding substantial GROSS INCOME (see **income**), a minimum tax is imposed on the aggregate of the tax preference items in an attempt to insure a minimum tax liability for each taxpayer.

TAX RATE the percentage rate of **tax** imposed. Tax liability is computed by applying the applicable tax rate to the tax base.

MARGINAL TAX RATE the highest percentage at which any part of the taxpayer's income is taxed.

EFFECTIVE TAX RATE the rate at which the taxpayer would be taxed if his tax liability were taxed at a constant rate rather than progressively. This rate is computed by determining what percentage the taxpayer's tax liability is of the taxpayer's total taxable income. See **tax** [PROGRESSIVE TAX].

TAX RETURN see **return, income tax.**

TAX SALE see **sale** [TAX SALE].

TAX SHELTER any device by which a taxpayer can reduce his tax liability by engaging in activities that provide him with **deductions** or **credits** that he can apply against his tax liability. In such cases, the activities engaged in are said to shelter the taxpayer's other **income** from tax liability.

EXAMPLE: An individual in a high tax bracket may choose to make an investment in real estate or oil and gas in order to take advantage of tax losses that these investments create. The investor, in effect, uses money he would have paid in taxes to offset part of his investment. And if the investment is a good one, he may also make a profit when he sells his interest. These types of investments are referred to as *tax shelters*.

TEMPORARY INJUNCTION see **injunction; restraining order.**

TENANCY a **tenant's** right to possess an **estate,** whether by **lease** or by **title;** 1. refers generally to any right to hold property; 2. refers to holding in subordination to another's title, as in the landlord-tenant relationship.

HOLDOVER TENANCY see **TENANCY AT SUFFERANCE.**

JOINT TENANCY a single **estate** in **property,** real or personal, owned by two or more persons, under one **instrument** or act of the parties, with an equal right in all to share in the enjoyment during their lives; and on the death of a joint tenant, the property descends to the survivor or survivors and at length to the last survivor. Joint tenancy originally was a technical feudal estate in land, but now also applies, through **statutes,** to **personal property** (**stocks, bonds,** bank accounts, with right of **survivorship**).

PERIODIC TENANCY in landlord-tenant law, a tenancy for a particular period (a week, month, year or number of years), plus the expectancy or possibility that the period will be repeated. In contrast to a **TENANCY FOR YEARS,** a periodic tenancy must be terminated by due notice by either the landlord or the tenant, unless one party has failed to perform some part of his obligation. A periodic tenancy is considered a form of **TENANCY AT WILL** and is created either by express agreement or by implication from the manner in which rent is paid. A periodic tenancy is alienable.

TENANCY AT SUFFERANCE [HOLDOVER TENANCY] a tenancy that comes into existence when one at first lawfully possesses land, as under a lease, and subsequently holds over beyond the end of one term of the lease or occupies it without such lawful authority. A tenancy at sufferance therefore cannot arise from an agreement, distinguishing it from a TENANCY AT WILL. A tenant at sufferance differs from a **trespasser** only in that he originally entered with the landlord's permission. The landlord has a right to establish a landlord-tenant relationship (i.e., extend the lease) of a tenant at sufferance.

EXAMPLE: Lance has completed the one-year lease on his apartment. He continues to reside there although the landlord does nothing to acknowledge that he is there, including not accepting rent checks. Lance is a *tenant at sufferance*. He may have certain rights, though, depending on the state he is in, possibly including a right to one week's or thirty days' notice before eviction.

TENANCY AT WILL a leased estate that confers upon the tenant the right to possession that both parties agree is for an unpredetermined period and that either party may terminate upon proper notice. A tenancy at will may arise out of an express contract or by implication. Because a tenancy at will is determinable at any time, the tenant cannot **assign** or **grant** his estate to another.

TENANCY BY THE ENTIRETY ownership of property, real or personal, **tangible** and **intangible,** by a husband and wife together. Neither husband nor wife is allowed to **alienate** any part of the property so held without consent of the other. The survivor of the marriage is entitled to the whole property. A divorce severs the tenancies by the entirety and usually creates a **tenancy in common.** Under the MARRIED WOMAN'S ACTS each tenant by the entirety is a tenant in common of the **use,** and is therefore entitled to one half of the rents and profits while both are alive.

TENANCY FOR YEARS an estate in land created by a lease that is limited to a specified and definite term, whether in weeks, months or years. If the tenant stays beyond expiration of the term, the tenancy may be converted into a **TENANCY AT SUFFERANCE, TENANCY AT WILL** or a **PERIODIC TENANCY.** A tenancy for years is alienable, subject to lease restrictions against assignment or **sublease.**

TENANCY FROM MONTH TO MONTH see **PERIODIC TENANCY.**

TENANCY FROM YEAR TO YEAR see **PERIODIC TENANCY.**

TENANCY IN COMMON an interest held by two or more persons, each having a possessory right, usually deriving from a title (though perhaps also from a lease) in the same piece of land. Tenancy in common also applies to personalty. Though co-tenants may have unequal shares in the property, they are each entitled to equal use and possession. Thus, each is said to have an undivided interest in the property. An estate held as a tenancy in common may be **partitioned,** sold or **encumbered**.

TENANT 1. one who holds land by any kind of **title** or right, whether permanently or temporarily; 2. one who purchases an **estate** and is entitled to **possession,** whether exclusive or to be shared with others; 3. one who **leases** premises from the owner (**landlord**) or from a tenant as his **subtenant.** See also **tenancy.**

TENDER an unconditional offer to pay or **perform** in full an obligation owed to another, together with either actual presentation of the thing or sum owed, or some clear manifestation of present ability to pay or perform.

LEGAL TENDER any kind of currency or other such medium of commerce designated by law as one that must be accepted in satisfaction of monetary debt.

TENDER OFFER a publicly announced effort to purchase the stock of a company, not through open market transactions but through direct dealings with present shareholders, for the purpose of acquiring controlling ownership of that company.

TENDER OF DELIVERY the seller's placement at the buyer's disposal of goods sold to him. A seller's failure to tender delivery at the proper place, according to **contract,** may constitute a **breach** unless he has a lawful excuse; a buyer's refusal to take delivery at the proper place may constitute a breach on his part.

EXAMPLE: Scholarly Book Publishers contracts with a book wholesaler to distribute its books nationwide. Scholarly arranges to have the books shipped to the wholesaler's main warehouse on a specific date, and the wholesaler agrees to pick them up there. Scholarly fulfills its obligation, but the wholesaler does not take the books on the date agreed upon. Two days later, the books are destroyed by fire. Since Scholarly completed its *tender of delivery,* the wholesaler must pay for the damage.

TENDER OFFER a public offer made to **shareholders** of a particular **corporation** to purchase from them a specific number of shares of **stock** at a specific price. The price quoted in such an offer is payable only if the offeror is able to obtain the total amount of stock specified in the offer. The number is usually sufficient to give the offeror control of the corporation.

TENEMENT permanent and fixed property including both **corporeal** and **incorporeal real property.** In modern usage, tenement applies to any structure attached to land, and also to any kind of dwelling inhabited by a **tenant.** Tenement is frequently used to indicate dilapidated apartment dwellings.

TENURE right to hold; 1. in real property, an ancient hierarchical system of holding lands. 2. a statutory right of certain civil servants, teachers in the public schools and other employees to retain their positions permanently, subject only to removal for adequate cause or economic necessity.

TENURIAL OWNERSHIP see **ownership.**

TERM OF ART see **words of art.**

TERM OF COURT a definite time period prescribed by law for a court to administer its duties. Term and session are often used interchangeably, but, technically, term is the statutory time prescribed for judicial business and session is the time a court actually sits to hear cases. In general, terms of court no longer have any special significance, fixed periods of days having replaced the stated terms of court.

TESTACY the condition of leaving a valid **will** at one's death. Compare **intestacy.**

TESTAMENT strictly, a testimonial or just statement of a person's wishes concerning the disposition of his personal property after death, in contrast to a **will,** which is strictly a **devise** of **real estate.** Commonly, however, will and testament are considered synonymous.

TESTAMENTARY DISPOSITION a gift of property that **vests** (takes effect) at the time of the death of the person making the disposition. It can be effected by **deed,** by an **inter vivos** transaction or by **will.** All instruments used to make testamentary dispositions must comply with the requirements of the **statute of wills.**

EXAMPLE: A father owns one hundred shares of stock. He makes a gift to his son as follows: "To myself for life, then to my son." The gift to the son is a *testamentary disposition* since it does not take effect until the father's death.

TESTAMENTARY TRUST see **trust.**

TESTATOR [TESTATRIX] one who makes and executes a **testament** or **will,** testator applying to a man, testatrix to a woman.

TESTIMONY statement made by a **witness,** under oath, usually related to a legal **proceeding** or legislative hearing; **evidence** given by a competent witness under oath or **affirmation,** as distinguished from evidence derived from writing and other sources.

THEFT see **larceny.**

THIRD PARTY see **party.**

THIRD-PARTY BENEFICIARY a person having enforceable rights created by a **contract** to which he is not a **party** and for which he gives no **consideration.** The third person is a DONEE BENEFICIARY if the promisee expressed an intention to confer a benefit upon the third person as a **gift** in the form of the promised performance. He is a CREDITOR BENEFICIARY if the promisee, or some other person, is under an obligation under the contract, or the making of the **executory** contract itself, will satisfy and discharge that obligation. To be enforceable by the third-party beneficiary, the contract must be primarily for his benefit.

THRIFT INSTITUTIONS generic name for savings banks and savings and loan associations. See **bank.**

TIDE LAND land covered and uncovered by ordinary tides. See also **avulsion; reliction.**

TIME OF THE ESSENCE a term used in contracts that fixes time of **performance** as a vital term of the **contract,** the **breach** of which may operate as a discharge of the entire contract. The phrase emphasizes that prformance by one party at the time specified in the contract is essential in order to enable him to require performance from the other party.

TIME SHARING an arrangement by which either (1) multiple owners (or long-term **lessees**) of a **condominium** unit agree contractually to reserve to one another exclusively the use of the unit (and of the common elements associated with unit ownership) for a portion of the year, at the same time each year, or (2) individual owners purchase an interest in the unit (and associated common elements) that is limited in duration to a specified portion of each year and thereby divide the ownership of the unit into intervals, also referred to as INTERVAL OWNERSHIP.

EXAMPLE: A group of friends purchase a condominium at a ski resort. They develop a *time-sharing* arrangement to fit each person's desire, with Bill reserving two weeks in the spring. Unless the agreement states otherwise, as an owner Bill can do whatever he wants with those weeks, including renting to others.

TITHE in old English law, a right of the clergy to exact for the use of the Church one tenth of the produce of the lands and personal industry of the people.

TITLE ownership; a term used in property law to denote the composite of facts that will permit one to recover or to retain possession of a thing.

EXAMPLE: Marty's car is stolen, and the thief sells it to another person who pays a fair value for the car and has no knowledge or suspicion that it is stolen. Marty still has superior *title* to the car over the other person even though the person paid money for the vehicle. As a basic principle of law, ordinarily one cannot take title from a thief.

ADVERSE TITLE a title asserted in opposition to another; one claimed to have been acquired by **adverse possession.**

CLEAR TITLE see **clear title.**

CLEAR TITLE OF RECORD a title that the **record** shows to be an **indefeasible** unencumbered **estate.**

COLOR OF TITLE see **color of title.**

EQUITABLE TITLE ownership that is recognized by a **court of equity** or founded upon **equitable** principles, as opposed to formal legal title. The purchaser of real property can require **specific performance** of his contract for purchase and as a result, prior to the actual **conveyance,** he has an enforceable equitable title that can be terminated only by a **bona fide purchaser.**

MARKETABLE TITLE see **marketable title.**

QUIET TITLE see **quiet title.**

TITLE [OF A STATUTE] the heading of a **statute** or legislative bill, which introduces it by giving a brief description or summary of the matters it embraces.

TITLE JURISDICTION a jurisdiction in which **title** to **mortgaged premises** passes to the **mortgagee,** and only passes back to **mortgagor** when full payment is made. See **lien jurisdiction.**

TITLE SEARCH an investigation of documents in the public record office to determine the state of a **title,** including all **liens, encumbrances, mortgages, future interests,** etc., affecting the property; the means by which a **chain of title** is ascertained.

TITLE THEORY see **mortgage; title jurisdiction.**

TOLL 1. to bar, defeat. To toll the **statute of limitations** means to suspend the limitation.

EXAMPLE: State law provides that a person has 45 days to file an appeal from a conviction and that a judge must inform the person of that limit. At the end of Randolph's trial, the judge fails to inform him of the limit. When he is informed five months later, it is technically too late to file. A court may *toll* the 45-day limit until Randolph is informed of its existence, which in this case would be five months after the conviction. If an appeal is then not filed within 45 days, the opportunity will not be granted again.

2. charge for the use of another's property. 3. **consideration** for the use of roads, bridges, ferries or other public facilities.

TORT a wrong; a private or **civil** wrong or injury resulting from a **breach** of a **legal duty** that exists by virtue of society's expectations regarding interpersonal conduct, rather than by **contract** or other private relationship. The essential elements of a tort are existence of a legal duty owed by **defendant** to **plaintiff,** breach of that duty and a causal relation between defendant's conduct and the resulting damage to plaintiff.

EXAMPLE: Henry places an object on a railroad track to see what happens when it is hit by an oncoming train. The train derails in a set of circumstances that would not have occurred if there had been no object on the track. Henry has committed an intentional *tort* against the railroad and its passengers. He committed a crime as well.

TORTFEASOR one who commits a **tort.**

JOINT TORTFEASORS those who act together or independently to commit a **tortious** act, causing a single injury. See **contribution; joint tortfeasors.**

TORTIOUS describes conduct that subjects the actor(s) to **tort** liability; unlawful.

TO WIT namely; that is to say.

TRACT INDEX see **chain of title.**

TRADE FIXTURE property placed on or annexed to rented **real estate** by a **tenant** for the purpose of aiding himself in the conduct of a trade or business. The law makes provision for, and leases often expressly permit (or require), the tenant to remove such **fixtures** at the end of his tenancy, though the tenant is responsible to the landlord for any damage to the premises resulting from such removal. Other fixtures, which are considered **improvements,** the tenant must leave intact. Compare **waste.**

TRADEMARK any mark, word, letter, number, design, picture or combination thereof in any form, which is adopted and used by a person to denominate goods that he makes, is affixed to the goods, and is neither a common or generic name for the goods nor a picture of them, nor is merely descriptive of the goods.

Protection from infringement upon a trademark is afforded by the common law action for **unfair competition.**

TRADE SECRETS any formula, pattern, machine or process of manufacturing used in one's business that may give the user opportunity to obtain advantage over competitors; a plan or process, tool, mechanism or compound, known only to its owner and those of his employees to whom it is necessary to disclose it. A trade secret is distinguished from a **patent** in that the owner holds no exclusive rights to it as against the public, though the owner may seek an **injunction** or **damages** for trade secrets unlawfully obtained from him.

EXAMPLE: Ed works for a whiskey distilling company. There is no patent on the formula for making the liquor, although the formula has been used for over one hundred years. Ed leaves the company to work for someone else. The company can legally prevent Ed from using the formula since it is a *trade secret* that no one has ever been able to duplicate.

TRANSACTION an event or series of events that have **tax** consequences.

CLOSED TRANSACTION a deal in which all events have occurred to allow the transaction to be subject to tax.

OPEN TRANSACTION a deal in which events have not occurred to allow the transaction to be subject to tax.

SHAM TRANSACTION one that will be ignored because it is deemed to have no substance.

STEP TRANSACTION one that consists of a number of interdependent steps and will, generally, be subject to tax based upon all the various steps rather than upon each intermediate step.

TRANSACTIONAL IMMUNITY see **self-incrimination, privilege against.**

TRANSFER to **convey** or remove from one person or place to another; to sell or give; specifically, to take over **possession** or control as in the transfer of **title** to land.

TRANSFER AGENT individual or firm that keeps a record of the **shareholders** of a **corporation** by name, address, and number of shares owned. When stock is sold, the new owner through his agent presents the shares purchased to the transfer agent, who cancels the old certificates and issues new certificates registered in the name of the owner. Not every stock transaction results in a transfer, since a significant portion of most **issues** is held in **street name** to support **margin** or for the convenience of the owner.

TRANSFEREE LIABILITY a tax liability of a **taxpayer** that is imposed upon another person who is the transferee of property from the taxpayer under specified circumstances, in which the taxpayer is unable, because of the transfer, to pay his tax liability. In general, the transferee can be liable only to the extent of the value of the property transferred, although the liability is personal and can be recovered from any assets of the transferee. Transferee, for purposes of imposition of this liability, includes heirs, donees of **gifts** and **shareholders** of dissolved **corporations,** but does not include people who act as mere **agents** for others.

TRANSFER IN CONTEMPLATION OF DEATH see **cause [CAUSA MORTIS].**

TRANSFERRED INTENT a recognized concept in **tort** law, which states that if **defendant** intends harm to A but harms B instead, the intent is said to be transferred to the harm befalling the actual victim as far as defendant's liability to B in tort is concerned. In criminal law, the doctrine is chiefly applied to a situation where A, with MALICE AFORETHOUGHT (see **malice**), strikes at B, misses him and strikes C, resulting in death to C. Although A never bore any **malice** to C, he is nonetheless guilty of **murder.** In short, the law transfers the malice to the party slain.

TRAVERSE a common law **pleading** that denies the opposing party's **allegations** of fact.

GENERAL TRAVERSE a blanket denial, stated in general terms, intended to cover all the allegations.

SPECIAL TRAVERSE a denial that is not absolute, but that seeks to establish a denial through the presentation of supplementary facts (or **new matter**) that, if accurate, would render the allegations untenable.

TREASON a crime defined by the Constitution: "treason against the United States shall consist only in levying war against them, or in adhering to their enemies, giving them aid and comfort."

EXAMPLE: The United States is engaged in war with another country. A U.S. arms manufacturer sells munitions to a private party but with the express knowledge that the munitions will be transferred to the other country at war. The manufacturer may be guilty of *treason*.

Compare **sedition.**

TREASURY BILL a U.S. government **promissory note** issued by the U.S. Treasury, having maturity periods up to one year. Notes having longer maturities are called **Treasury notes** and very long maturities are called **Treasury bonds.** Treasury bills are sold at a discount to face value, which is paid at maturity. Denominations are $10,000 or multiples thereof, although smaller denominations are offered when money is in short supply. Money market trading is very active with large dollar amounts of Treasury bills, which are **bearer** instruments, changing hands daily.

TREASURY BOND 1. a long-term debt **instrument** issued by the U.S. Government. Issues of the U.S. Government have the highest rating among so-called fixed income or debt **securities** and, therefore, offer the lowest taxable yield of any **bonds.**

2. a bond that has been bought back by the issuing corporation. See **treasury stock.** Such Treasury bonds are usually retired as part of **sinking fund** requirements or held in the corporate treasury, which reduces interest expense.

TREASURY NOTE an intermediate term (one to five years) obligation of the U.S. Government that bears interest paid by **coupon.** Like all direct U.S. Government obligations, Treasury notes carry the highest domestic credit standing and thus have the lowest taxable yield available at equivalent maturity.

TREASURY STOCK common or preferred **stock** that had been issued by a company and later reacquired. The stock may be used for a variety of corporate purposes, such as a stock bonus plan for management and employees or to acquire another company, or it may be held indefinitely, resold or retired. While held in the company treasury, the stock earns no dividends and has no vote in company affairs.

TREATY a compact made between two or more independent nations with a view to the public welfare. Under the Constitution, the President has the sole power to initiate and make treaties, which must be approved by the Senate before they become binding on citizens of the United States as law. An EXECUTIVE AGREEMENT is often substituted for a treaty and does not require the advice and consent of the Senate, though it may be entered into pursuant to formal authority delegated by the Congress in particular legislation. Executive agreements, however, are restricted to narrower topics. Trade agreements, for example, are often executive agreements rather than treaties.

TREBLE DAMAGES the amount of **damages** awarded to an injured party, whereby the judge triples the amount that the jury awards; it acts to punish the wrongdoer in addition to compensating the injured party. This is a statutory remedy most often awarded in antitrust violations. See **damages [DOUBLE (TREBLE) DAMAGES].**

TRESPASS 1. in common law, a **form of action** instituted to recover **damages** for any unlawful injury to the plaintiff's person, property or rights, involving immediate force or violence; 2. the violent act that causes such injury; 3. most often connotes a wrongful interference with the **possession** of property and is applied to **personal property (personalty)** as well as to **realty.**

EXAMPLE: Len erects a fence that inadvertently crosses adjoining property. He *trespasses* on that property and is responsible for all damage that results from his action.

CONTINUING TRESPASS one that is not intermittent or transient, as where one dumps garbage upon the land of another. In such a case, there is a continuing wrong so long as the offending object remains.

TRESPASS DE BONIS ASPORTATIS *(dā bō'-nĭs äs-pôr-tä'-tĭs)* Lat.: trespass for goods carried off. A common law action brought to recover damages from a person who has taken **goods** or property from the rightful owner.

TRESPASS ON THE CASE one of the two early English actions at common law dealing with what are now known as **torts** (the other being simply trespass). Trespass on the case afforded remedy against injury to person or property indirectly resulting from the conduct of the defendant. The action of trespass covered only directly resulting injury.

TRESPASS QUARE CLAUSUM FREGIT see **quare clausum fregit.**

TRESPASS VI ET ARMIS *(vē ĕt är'mĭs)* Lat.: force and arms. 1. trespass with force and arms, or by unlawful means; 2. a remedy for injuries accompanied with force, or where the act done is itself an immediate injury to another's person or property.

TRIAL an examination, usually involving the offering of **testimony,** before a competent **tribunal** according to established procedures, of facts or law put in **issue** in a **cause** for the purpose of determining such issue.

TRIAL DE NOVO historically described an appeal from a decision of a court of **chancery.** It signifies a proceeding in which both issues of law and issues of fact are reconsidered as if the original trial had never taken place. Appeals from **probate** court or from minor courts, such as local municipal courts, are often by trial de novo. New testimony may be adduced or the matter may be determined **de novo** on the basis of the evidentiary **record** already produced. When the trial de novo is "on the record," no new evidence is taken by the reviewing court, but a fresh consideration of the law and facts is nevertheless undertaken without deference to the decision reached in the initial trial.

TRIAL COURT court of **original jurisdiction,** where matters are to be litigated first and where all evidence relative to a cause is received and considered. All states differentiate between trial courts and **appellate courts.** The distinction is that it is the function of the trial court first to determine the facts and the law in a case, with the appellate court acting predominantly as a court of review of law, but not fact.

TRIBUNAL an officer or body having authority to **adjudicate** matters. See also **court; forum.**

TRIER OF FACT see **fact finder.**

T.R.O. temporary **restraining order.**

TROVER an early common law **tort** action to recover **damages** for a wrongful **conversion** of **personal property** or to recover actual **possession** of such property. Originally, the action was limited to cases in which **lost property** had been found and converted by the finder to his own use. Later the action was expanded to include property not actually lost and found, but only wrongly converted. (Compare **detinue; replevin; tenancy** [TENANCY AT SUFFERANCE]; **trespass.**

TRUE BILL see **indictment.**

TRUST 1. an entity that holds assets (the **res** or corpus) for the benefit of certain other persons or entities. The person holding legal title or interest, who has responsibility for the assets and distribution of the assets or distribution of the income generated by such assets, is the **trustee.** The CESTUI QUE TRUST, or **beneficiary,** for whose benefit the trust is created, holds the EQUITABLE TITLE (see **title**) or interest. 2. any relationship in which one acts as **guardian** or **fiduciary** in relation to another's property. Thus, a deposit of money in a bank is a trust, or the receipt of money to be applied to a particular purpose or to be paid to another is a trust.

SIMPLE TRUST a trust that is required, by the terms of its creation or under state law, to distribute all of its income currently.

COMPLEX TRUST a trust that under the **instrument** of its creation or under state law may either distribute or retain income.

CHARITABLE TRUST a trust created to advance some public purpose, such as education, religion or science; also called a **PUBLIC TRUST.**

CONSTRUCTIVE TRUST [INVOLUNTARY TRUST] one that is found to exist by operation of law or by **construction** of the court, regardless of lack of express intent on the part of the parties. When one party has been wrongfully deprived, either by mistake, fraud or some other breach of faith, of some right, benefit or title to property, a court may impose upon the present holder of legal title to that property a constructive trust for the benefit of the wronged party. Thus, to prevent **unjust enrichment** of the legal holder, such person is deemed to hold the property as a trustee for the **beneficial use** of the party wrongfully deprived of rights.

EXPRESS TRUST [DIRECT TRUST] a trust created from the free and deliberate act of the parties, including affirmative intention of the **settlor** [the one granting the property] to set up the trust, usually evidenced by some writing, **deed** or **will.**

GRANTOR TRUST a trust that has beneficiaries other than the grantor but, because of retention of certain interests or certain powers over the trust, all income of the trust is taxed to the grantor.

IMPLIED TRUST one that is inferred from the parties' transactions by **operation of law,** in contrast to an **EXPRESS TRUST** that is created by the parties' deliberate acts or expression of intent. Implied trusts can be either **CONSTRUCTIVE** or **RESULTING.**

INVESTMENT TRUST see **investment company.**

LIVING TRUST an **inter vivos** trust; a trust established and in operation during the settlor's life. Compare TESTAMENTARY TRUST.

PRECATORY TRUST one frequently created by a **will,** arising from words of expectation, request or recommendation that are expressed therein. Though they do not amount to actual directives, such words are effective to create a trust so long as they are not so modified by the context as to amount to no more than mere suggestions, to be acted upon or not, according to the caprice of the supposed trustee.

RESULTING TRUST a trust arising by implication of law when it appears from the nature of the **transaction** that it was the intention of the parties to create a trust. Thus, a resulting trust involves the element of intent, which though implied, makes it more like an EXPRESS TRUST. A constructive trust, in contrast, is sometimes found contrary to the parties' intent, in order to work equity or frustrate **fraud.**

EXAMPLE: Mark purchases a piece of land, but the purchase agreement names a close friend as the purchaser. Since the friend is not considered a natural object of Mark's affection, which is usually a family member or relative, a presumption arises that Mark did not make a gift to his friend. Unless other evidence is shown to invalidate that presumption, a court finds that the friend holds title to the property as a *resulting trust* for Mark.

TESTAMENTARY TRUST a trust that is established during the settlor's life but is contained in the settlor's will and does not take effect until the settlor's death; created with the formalities necessary for a will.

SPENDTHRIFT TRUST see **spendthrift trust.**

UNIT INVESTMENT TRUST see **unit investment trust.**

VOTING TRUST see **voting trust.**

TRUST CERTIFICATE an **instrument** issued to finance the purchase of railroad equipment, under which the **trustees** hold **title** to the equipment as **security** for the load.

TRUST COMPANY a financial organization that provides **trust** services such as acting in the capacity of **trustee, fiduciary** or **agent** for both individuals and companies; **transfer agents** are typically provided by trust companies. Duties include administering **trust funds,** acting as custodian for property held in trust, providing investment management for trust funds, executing wills. Trust companies often engage in banking activities as well, and are regulated by state law.

TRUST DEED see **deed of trust.**

TRUSTEE 1. one who holds legal **title** to property in **trust** for the benefit of another person, and who is required to carry out specific duties with regard to the property, or who has been given power affecting the disposition of property for another's benefit.

EXAMPLE: A father creates a trust for his children. He wants to control the disposition of the money generated by the trust, so he names himself as *trustee*. In that position, he can be sure that his desires in relation to the trust are carried out.

2. also used loosely as anyone who acts as a **guardian** or **fiduciary** in relationship to another, such as a public officer towards his constituents, a state toward its citizens, or a partner to his copartner.

TRUSTEE IN BANKRUPTCY an officer, elected and approved by the **referee** or judge of a **bankruptcy** proceeding, who takes legal title to the property or money of the bankrupt and holds it in trust for equitable distribution among the bankrupt's **creditors.**

TRUST FUND **real property** or **personal property** held in **trust** for the benefit of another person; the **corpus [res]** of a trust.

TRUSTOR one who creates a **trust;** more often called the **settlor.**

TRUTH IN LENDING ACT a federal law, the provisions of which assure individuals applying for commercial credit information relating to the cost of credit, enabling them to decide which credit source offers them the most favorable credit terms. Under this law, the commercial lender must inform the borrower of the dollar amount of the interest charges and the interest rate, computed on an annual basis according to the specified formula, and must afford borrowers who pledge **real property** as **security** for the loan a three-day period in which to **rescind** the transaction.

EXAMPLE: A merchant allows his customers to buy goods on credit. He does not force them to sign any papers evidencing the debt, but, in return, he charges a fluctuating interest rate. This practice may violate the *Truth in Lending Act,* and the merchant may be liable for penalties.

TRY TITLE to submit to judicial scrutiny the legitimacy of **title** to property.

U

ULTIMATE FACTS the essential and determining facts on which the final conclusion of law is predicated. They are facts deduced by **inference** from evidentiary facts, which can be directly established by **testimony** or **evidence.** Compare **mediate data.**

ULTRAHAZARDOUS ACTIVITY an uncommon activity, giving rise to **strict liability,** that necessarily involves risk of serious harm to the person, land or **chattels** of others.

EXAMPLE: As part of the demolition of a building, a construction company uses various methods of blasting. These methods are permitted even though they may cause damages elsewhere because of the need to use explosive devices. But since blasting is an *ultrahazardous activity,* the company must pay any damage that results, whether or not the damage was forseeable.

ULTRA VIRES *(ŭl′-trä vī′-rēz)* Lat.: beyond, in excess of powers. That which is beyond the power authorized by law. 1. an action of a **corporation** that is beyond the powers conferred upon it by its **charter,** or by the **statute** under which it was created. 2. acts of public officials beyond their authority. See **quo warranto.**

UNCLEAN HANDS one of the **equitable** maxims embodying the principle that a party seeking redress in a court of equity (equitable relief) must not have done any unethical act in the transaction upon which he maintains the action in **equity,** since a court of conscience will not grant relief to one guilty of **unconscionable** conduct, i.e., to one with unclean hands.

UNCONDITIONAL DISCHARGE see **sentence [SUSPENDED SENTENCE].**

UNCONSCIONABLE so unreasonably detrimental to the interest of one party to a contract as to render the **contract** unenforceable. The term refers to a bargain so one-sided as to amount to an absence of meaningful choice on the part of one of the parties (typically as a result of greatly unequal bargaining power), together with contract terms unreasonably favorable to the other party.

EXAMPLE: Fern needs money quickly to meet her monthly car payments. She contracts with a company to work at extremely low wages in return for their making her car payments. The contract may be declared *unconscionable* because Fern entered into it in a distressed state and the company took great advantage of her position.

UNCONSTITUTIONAL conflicting with some provision of the **constitution.** A **statute** found to be unconstitutional is considered void or as if it had never been, and consequently all **rights, contracts** or duties that depend on it are void. Similarly, no one can be punished for having refused obedience to the **law** once it is found to be unconstitutional.

UNDERLEASE see **sublease.**

UNDERWRITE to insure the satisfaction of an obligation, such as by an **insurance** contract or sale of **bonds.** To underwrite an insurance contract is to act as the insurer, or assume the risk for the life or property of another.

EXAMPLE: Nocturn Company transports highly flammable liquids across the country. It locates an insurance company to *underwrite* an insurance policy, thereby shifting the risk and consequences of an accident onto another company. Nocturn will have to pay a high price for the underwriting, and the insurance company may require frequent supervision of Nocturn's safety practices.

To underwrite a **stock** or bond issue is to insure the sale of stocks or bonds by agreeing to buy the entire issue if they are not sold to the public before a certain date.

UNDISCLOSED PRINCIPAL see **principal.**

UNDIVIDED INTEREST that interest or right in **property** owned by TENANTS IN COMMON, JOINT TENANTS or TENANTS BY THE ENTIRETY (see **tenancy**), whereby each tenant has an equal right to make use of and enjoy the entire property. An undivided interest may be of only a fractional share, e.g., "an undivided one-quarter interest," in which case the holder is entitled to one quarter of all profits and sale proceeds from the property but has a right to possession of the whole. See also **partition; severalty.**

UNDUE INFLUENCE influence of another that destroys the requisite free will of a **testator** or **donor** and creates a ground for nullifying a **will** or invalidating an improvident **gift.** The exercise of undue influence is suggested by excessive insistence, superiority of will or mind, the relationship of the parties or pressure on the donor or testator by any other means to do what he is unable, practically, to refuse.

EXAMPLE: A mother has her son draft her will, which provides the son with most of her estate. The son is also her attorney. If the two other sons, both of whom had relationships with the mother equal to the attorney's, are virtually excluded from the mother's will, most courts will find *undue influence* on the part of the attorney and invalidate the gift to him.

Compare **duress.**

UNFAIR COMPETITION 1. unfair, untrue or misleading advertising likely to lead the public to believe that certain goods are associated with another manufacturer; 2. imitating a competitor's product, package or **trademark** in circumstances where the consumer might be misled; 3. representations or conduct that deceive the public into believing that the business name, reputation or good will of one person is that of another.

Unfair competition is a **tort** and a **fraud** for which the courts afford a **remedy.** Fraudulent or deceptive practices that are disparaging or injurious to the trade of a competitor may be **enjoined.**

UNIFORM COMMERCIAL CODE [UCC] a code of laws governing various commercial transactions, including the sale of **goods,** banking transactions, secured transactions in **personal property,** and other matters, that was designed to bring uniformity in these areas to the laws of the various states, and that has been adopted, with some modifications, in all states (except Louisiana) as well as in the District of Columbia and in the Virgin Islands.

UNIFORM LAWS laws that have been approved by the Commissioners on Uniform State Laws and are proposed to all state legislatures for their consideration and adoption. Some uniform laws are passed by only a few states; others are passed by all the states with minor differences in language.

EXAMPLE: The **Uniform Commercial Code,** a *uniform law,* has been adopted by almost all states, with some variations by several states. The UCC governs banking and secured transactions, and sale of goods.

UNILATERAL CONTRACT see **contract.**

UNILATERAL MISTAKE see **mistake.**

UNION SHOP a work place where all the employees are members of a union. Nonunion members may work in such shops provided they agree to join the union.

UNITIES the **common law** requirements necessary to create a JOINT TENANCY or a TENANCY BY THE ENTIRETY (see **tenancy**). A joint tenancy requires the four unities of interest, possession, time and title, and a tenancy by the entirety requires, in addition to the four unities, unity of person. Tenants in common, as a result of the kind of estate they hold, have a unity of possession, but no unity is required to create such an estate.

UNITY OF INTEREST the requirement that **interests** of the co-tenants in a joint tenancy or tenancy by the entirety be equal. An individual joint tenant cannot encumber his share by **mortgage** without destroying this unity; to preserve the joint tenancy the mortgage must be agreed to by all. Tenants in common are not subject to this unity of interest rule and may have unequal shares in the same property. See **tenancy** [**TENANCY IN COMMON**].

UNITY OF POSSESSION the equal right of each co-owner of property to the **use** and **possession** of the whole property.

UNITY OF TIME the requirement that the interests of the co-tenants in a joint tenancy or tenancy by the entirety must commence (or **vest**) at the same moment in time.

UNITY OF TITLE the requirement that all tenants of a joint tenancy or both tenants of a tenancy by the entirety acquire their interests under the same **title.** Thus, such co-tenants cannot hold by different **deeds;** their interests are created by the same instrument or event.

UNITY OF PERSON the common-law requirement for the creation of a tenancy by the entirety that the co-tenants be husband and wife, based on the conception that marriage created a unity of person.

UNIT INVESTMENT TRUST an unmanaged **portfolio** of **bonds** that is sold to investors in units of $1,000 each. A bank or **trust company** serves as custodian and **trustee** for the portfolio of bonds, and collects and periodically disburses interest payments and principal when bonds mature. Since the portfolio is fixed, the trust is self-liquidating because of both unit holder redemptions and bond maturities. Compare **nondiscretionary trust.**

UNIVERSAL AGENT an **agent** authorized to transact all the business of his **principal.**

UNJUST ENRICHMENT gain or benefit that is the result of another's efforts or acts but for which that other has received no recompense, and for which the one receiving the benefit has not paid. A person who is deemed by law to have been unjustly enriched at the expense of another is required to make **restitution** to the other. Restitution and unjust enrichment are modern designations for the older doctrine of quasi-contracts, which are not true contracts, but are obligations created by the law when money, property or services have been obtained by one person at the expense of another under such circumstances that in **equity** and good conscience he ought not retain it. The law then may impose a duty to pay compensation in order to prevent unjust enrichment.

EXAMPLE: Bart plants shrubbery under a contract with Joan. Joan dies before Bart is paid, and Gail then buys Joan's house. Gail must pay Bart for the shrubbery, for if she does not, she will be *unjustly enriched* and Bart will be out the value of the plantings.

Compare **quantum meruit.**

UNLAWFUL ASSEMBLY 1. a **misdemeanor** in common law consisting of a meeting of several persons with a common plan that, if carried out, would result in a riot; 2. a meeting of persons who intend to commit a crime by open force; 3. a meeting to execute a common design, lawful or lawful, in an unauthorized manner that is likely to cause fear of a BREACH OF THE PEACE (see **breach**). Compare **conspiracy.**

UNLAWFUL DETAINER the act of holding **possession** without right, as in the case of a **tenant** whose **lease** has expired. UNLAWFUL DETAINER STATUTES often create a right to oust, by summary **process,** a holdover tenant and to determine speedily the landlord's right to possession of real property. The **summary proceeding** determines only the question of possession; no ultimate determination of **title** or **estate** can be made in such a proceeding. See **tenancy** [TENANCY AT SUFFERANCE].

UNLISTED SECURITY a **stock** or **bond** that is not listed on a **stock exchange** and is therefore traded only in the **over-the-counter market.**

UNNATURAL ACT see **crime against nature.**

UNREASONABLE RESTRAINT OF TRADE see **restraint of trade.**

UNREASONABLE SEARCH AND SEIZURE a search and/or seizure of a person, a house, papers or effects that are protected against it by the Fourth and **Fourteenth Amendments** and state constitutions, where the basis for the search and/or seizure does not meet constitutional requirements.

EXAMPLE: An officer receives an anonymous tip that Sam is growing marijuana in his house. The officer waits until Sam leaves his house, and then the officer enters through an open window. Since the entry was conducted without a **warrant** and without **probable cause,** the *search and seizure* would be found *unreasonable* and evidence obtained thereby would be **suppressed** and would not be used to prove that Sam had marijuana in his house.

UP TICK [OR PLUS TICK] indicates that the latest trade in a **stock** is at a higher price than the previous trade. A ZERO-PLUS TICK is a trade at the last price with the preceding different price registered as an up tick.

USE the right to enjoy the benefits flowing from **real property** or **personal property; equitable** ownership as distinct from legal **title.** Historically in the law of property the term referred to every form of beneficial ownership enforceable in the courts of **chancery.** Historically, uses have been created by provision in a **deed,** by implication to the conveyer when property is transferred without **consideration** [called a RESULTING USE]; by **bargain and sale** deed or by a covenant to stand **seised.** Under the **Statute of Uses,** the party in whom a use was created was deemed to be the owner of legal title to a like **estate** as he had in the use; hence "A to B for the use of C for life" was operative under the statute to convey to C a life estate.

An important effect of the Statute of Uses was the validation **at law** of executory **interests** (a species of **future interests**) that had previously been recognized only in equity. A SHIFTING USE is a use that arises in derogation of another, i.e., shifts from one beneficiary to another, depending on some future contingency. A SPRINGING USE is a use that arises upon the occurrence of a future event and that does not take effect in derogation of any interest other than one that results to the grantor, or remains in him in the meantime. Thus, a shifting use is one that cuts short a prior use estate in a person other than the conveyor; a springing use is one that cuts short a use estate in the conveyor.

In patent law, use refers to the rights of the licensee of the patent.

PUBLIC USE see **public use.**

USE IMMUNITY see **self-incrimination, privilege against.**

USUFRUCT in **civil law,** the right to use and enjoy **property** vested in another, and to draw from it all the profit and utility it may produce, provided it be without altering the substance of the thing. See **beneficial use.**

USURY an unconscionable or exorbitant rate of **interest;** an excessive and illegal requirement of compensation for **forbearance** on a **debt;** a bargain under which a greater profit than is permitted by law is paid, or is agreed to be paid, to a **creditor** by or on behalf of the **debtor** for a loan of money, or for extending the maturity of a pecuniary debt. The state legislatures today determine the maximum allowable rates of interest that may be demanded in any financial transaction.

EXAMPLE: Don needs money but cannot obtain a loan from a bank. A close friend agrees to lend him what he needs but at an interest rate over the maximum allowed by law. Don agrees to the arrangement and in fact does not think it unfair. Still, the friend is guilty of *usury* and can be prosecuted for usury if the rate reaches a criminal level, which varies in each state. The friend may also be made to return any interest he has received. More importantly, the usurious rate of interest, and in some jurisdictions the debt as well, is not enforceable against Don in the event he has failed to make payments.

UTMOST RESISTANCE the degree of resistance that a woman traditionally has been required to offer her attacker in order to charge that she has been raped; the maximum resistance of which a woman is capable in resisting rape.

UTTER to put forth, to execute; especially, to offer, whether accepted or not, a forged **instrument** with representations by words or acts, directly or indirectly, that the instrument is valid.

The crime of UTTERING a forged instrument includes the element of fraudulent **intent** to injure another, and is distinguished from the crime of **forgery** by the requirement that the utterer pass or attempt to pass the forged instrument as genuine.

UXOR see **et ux.**

V

VACATE 1. to render **void;** to **set aside;** 2. to move out; to render vacant.

VAGRANCY general term for a class of minor offenses such as idleness without visible means of support, **loitering,** wandering around from place to place without any lawful purpose.

VARIANCE 1. in procedure, a discrepancy between what is **charged** or **alleged** and what is proved or offered as proof. A FATAL VARIANCE is, in both civil and criminal cases, a material and substantial variance: in criminal cases, it must also tend to mislead the defendant in making his defense, or tend to expose the defendant to the injury of **double jeopardy.**

EXAMPLE: Alice files a lawsuit against a package delivery service for damaging a package they delivered to her. At the trial, she offers proof to show that she never received the package. The difference between her original claim and the claim that she offers to prove constitutes a *fatal variance,* and Alice's case will probably be dismissed.

2. in zoning law, an exemption from the application of a zoning ordinance or regulation permitting a use that varies from that otherwise permitted. The exception is granted by the appropriate authority in special circumstances to protect against undue hardship wrought by strict enforcement. See **nonconforming use.**

VEL NON *(vĕl nŏn)* Lat.: or not.

VENDEE buyer, especially in a **contract** for the **sale** of **realty.**

VENDOR seller, especially person who sells **real property.**

VENIRE *(vĕ-nē'-rā)* Lat.: to come. Refers to the **common law** process by which **jurors** are summoned to try a case.

VENIRE DE NOVO *(dā nō'-vō)* Lat.: to come anew. Refers to summoning of a second **jury** for the purpose of proceeding to a second trial. Such a second trial is awarded where a **verdict** (by the jury) or finding (by the court) is so defective or ambiguous upon its face that no **judgment** can be rendered upon it. The term is sometimes used simply to denote a new trial.

VENUE a neighborhood, a neighboring place; synonym for place of trial; refers to the possible or proper place for trial of a **suit,** among several places where **jurisdiction** could be established. Venue essentially involves the right of the party sued to have the action heard in a particular judicial district, for reasons of convenience. In a criminal trial where publicity surrounding the crime would virtually preclude fair trial, the court will direct a CHANGE OF VENUE, or **removal** of the proceedings to a different district or county. See **forum non conveniens.**

VERDICT the opinion rendered by a **jury,** or a **judge** where there is no jury, on a question of fact. A verdict differs from a **judgment** in that a verdict is not a judicial determination, but rather a finding of fact that the trial court may accept or reject and utilize in formulating its judgment.

COMPROMISE VERDICT a verdict resulting from improper surrender of one juror's opinion to another on a material issue.

DIRECTED VERDICT see **directed verdict.**

GENERAL VERDICT ordinary verdict declaring simply which party prevails, without any special findings of fact.

PARTIAL VERDICT in criminal law, a finding that the defendant is guilty of certain charges but innocent of others.

QUOTIENT VERDICT improper and unacceptable kind of compromise verdict resulting from an agreement by the jurors that their verdict will be an award of **damages** in an amount to be determined by the addition of all jurors' computations of damages and its division by the number of jurors.

SPECIAL VERDICT one rendered on certain specific factual issues posed by the court. The special verdict requires the jury to make a specific finding on each ultimate fact put in issue by the **pleadings** rather than a general finding for one party or the other. The court will then apply the law to those found facts.

VERIFICATION confirmation of correctness or authenticity of **pleading** or other paper **affidavit,** oath or **deposition;** an affidavit attached to a statement insuring the truth of that statement.

VESTED fixed, accrued or absolute; not **contingent;** generally used to describe any right or **title** to something that is not dependent upon the occurrence or failure to occur of some specified future event (CONDITION PRECEDENT—see **condition**).

VESTED ESTATE a property **interest** which either is presently in possession or will necessarily come into **possession** in the future merely upon the determination, or end, of the preceding **estate.**

EXAMPLE: A mother conveys a house to her son, who will keep it until he has his first child, at which time the house is to pass to her daughter. Not until the son's child is born can it be determined whether the daughter will get the house. But immediately upon the birth, the daughter's interest in the house vests, giving rise to a *vested estate*.

VESTED INTEREST a present right or title to a thing that carries with it an existing right of **alienation,** even though the right to possession or enjoyment may be postponed to some uncertain time in the future.

VESTED REMAINDER a **remainder** that is limited to an ascertained person whose right to the estate is fixed, certain and not dependent upon the happening of any future event, but whose enjoyment of the estate is postponed to some future time.

VESTED RIGHTS in relation to constitutional guarantees, a broad shield of protection that consists of a vested interest that the government should in **equity** recognize and protect, and of which the individual could not be deprived arbitrarily without injustice. The term is frequently used to designate rights that have become so fixed that the owner cannot be deprived of them without his consent.

VEXATIOUS LITIGATION **civil action** shown to have been instituted maliciously and without **probable cause,** and that may be protected against by **injunction.** See **litigious; malicious prosecution.**

VICARIOUS LIABILITY **liability** imputed to one person for the actions of another, where the law contemplates that the other should be held responsible for a wrong in fact committed by someone else. Sometimes this doctrine is called IMPUTED LIABILITY.

EXAMPLE: Mel drives a truck for Speedy Delivery Service. While pulling out of a driveway, he hits a pedestrian. Speedy will be *vicariously liable* for the pedestrian's injuries under the doctrine of **respondeat superior.**

EXAMPLE: Sam agrees to drive the getaway car in a robbery. George, who enters the bank, kills a teller during the robbery. In most states, Sam is *vicariously liable* for the killing.

Compare **strict liability.**

VICINAGE neighborhood; vicinity. Contemporary meaning denotes a particular area where a crime was committed, where a **trial** is being held, or from which **jurors** are called.

VIDELICET see **viz.**

VI ET ARMIS see **trespass** [TRESPASS VI ET ARMIS].

VISA a recognition of the validity of a passport; issued by proper officials of the country that the bearer wishes to enter;

2. more broadly, a symbol made on a document certifying that it has been examined and approved.

VIS MAJOR *(vĭz mä-yôr′)* Lat.: a greater force. In civil law denotes an **act of God,** an irresistible natural cause that cannot be guarded against by ordinary exertions of skill and prudence. Once treated as equivalent to act of God, vis major now includes any insuperable interference.

VITIATE to **void;** to render a nullity; to impair.

VIZ *(vĭz)* Lat.: namely; that is to say; abbreviation of the Latin videlicet. Used in **pleadings** to specify or explain what goes before it.

VOID empty, having no legal force, incapable of being ratified.

VOIDABLE capable of being later **annulled;** refers to a valid act that, though it may be rendered void, may accomplish the thing sought unless or until the defect in the transaction has been effectively asserted or judicially ascertained and declared.

VOID FOR VAGUENESS a doctrine that renders a criminal statute unconstitutional and unenforceable when it is so vague that persons of common intelligence must guess at its meaning and differ about its application. A statute is **void** when it is vague about either what persons are within the scope of the statute, what conduct is forbidden or what punishment may be imposed. The principle derives from the requirement of the **due process** clause of the **Fifth Amendment** that criminal statutes give reasonably certain notice that an act has been made criminal before the act is committed and a person is charged with a crime for having so acted.

VOIR DIRE *(vwŏr dēr)* Fr.: to speak the truth. 1. A **VOIR DIRE EXAMINATION** by the court or by the attorneys of prospective jurors is to determine their qualification for **jury** service, to determine if there is cause to challenge (i.e., to excuse) particular jurors, and to provide information about the jurors so that the parties can exercise their statutory **peremptory** challenges (objections to particular jurors without need to state cause).

EXAMPLE: A doctor is on trial for performing an abortion. In a *voir dire* examination of potential jurors by counsel or the court, it is revealed that a prospective juror has strong religious beliefs concerning abortions that would bias any possibility of a fair and independent judgment. That juror will most likely not be used at the doctor's trial.

2. A voir dire examination during the trial refers to a **hearing** by the court out of the presence of the jury upon some **issue** of fact or law that requires an initial determination by the court or upon which the court must rule as a matter of law alone.

VOLENTI NON FIT INJURIA *(vō-lĕn'-tē nŏn fēt ĭn-jū'-rē-à)* Lat.: the volunteer suffers no wrong. No legal wrong is done to one who consents. In **tort** law, the principle that usually **damages** cannot be claimed by one who has consented to the activity that caused the damages.

VOLUNTARY APPEARANCE see **appearance.**

VOLUNTARY DISABLEMENT see **anticipatory breach.**

VOTING RIGHT the right of a common **shareholder** to vote in person or by **proxy** on the affairs of a company.

VOTING TRUST The accumulation in a single hand, or in a few hands, of shares of corporate **stock** belonging to many owners, for the purpose of exercising control over the business of the company. A device whereby two or more **shareholders** divorce the voting rights of their stock from its ownership, retaining their ownership but transferring their voting rights to **trustees** in whom the voting rights of all the depositors in the trust are pooled.

W

WAIVER an intentional and voluntary surrender of some known **right,** which generally may either result from an express agreement or be inferred from circumstances. See **informed consent.**

EXAMPLE: Spencer enters into a plea bargain with the prosecutor in the hope that he will receive a lighter sentence. Since the plea represents an admission of guilt and a *waiver* of the right to a jury trial, the judge must be sure that Spencer realizes the consequences of his actions. Therefore, the judge will inform Spencer that he has a right to have a trial and that there is no guarantee that a plea will necessarily result in any different sentence than from a trial. Without these precautions, the judge cannot be sure that Spencer's waiver is knowing and intelligent.

EXECUTORY WAIVER one that affects a still unperformed duty of the other party to a **contract.**

WANT OF CONSIDERATION see **consideration.**

WANTON grossly **negligent** or careless; with a reckless disregard of consequences.

WARD 1. a person whom the law regards as incapable of managing his own affairs, and over whom or over whose property a **guardian** is appointed. 2. one of the sections into which a town is divided for educational or election purposes.

WARRANT a written **order** from a competent authority directing the doing of a certain act, especially one directing the **arrest** of a person or persons, issued by a court, body or official. See also **bench warrant; search warrant.**

The word warrant is also used in commercial and property law to refer to a particular kind of guarantee or assurance about the quality and validity of what is being **conveyed** or sold.

WARRANT TO SATISFY JUDGMENT an authorization issued by the judgment **creditor's** attorney to the clerk of the court directing him to enter a **satisfaction** of the **judgment** in the official court records.

STOCK WARRANT a certificate that gives the holder the right to purchase shares of **stock** for a specified price and within a specified time. Unlike **subscription rights,** stock warrants offer the holder the right to purchase shares of a different kind from those already held. Thus a holder of common stock may purchase **preferred stock.** Stock warrants usually originate as a bonus with new **issues** of **bonds, notes** or preferred stock where they serve as an inducement to the buyer. Warrants so offered come attached to the new security and usually cannot be separated for a short period; once separated, the warrants can be traded like any other security.

WARRANTY an assurance by one **party** to a **contract** of the existence of a fact upon which the other party may rely, intended precisely to relieve the promisee of any duty to ascertain the fact for himself; amounts to a promise to **indemnify** the promisee for any loss if the fact warranted proves untrue. Such warranties are made either overtly (EXPRESS WARRANTIES) or by implication (IMPLIED WARRANTIES).

A COVENANT OF WARRANTY in **real property** is a covenant **running with the land,** insuring the continuing validity of **title.**

WARRANTY OF FITNESS a warranty that the goods are suitable for the special purpose of the buyer, which will not be satisfied by mere fitness for general purposes.

EXAMPLE: Constant Trucking Company orders a specially enforced truck for a new type of service it is starting. Constant places the order with a dealership with whom it has often worked in the past, and explains the need and purpose for the vehicle. The vehicle is delivered to Constant, which finds after one shipment that the truck is not built as specified. A *warranty of fitness,* which either is written in the contract between Constant and the dealer or is implied, has been breached. Constant can return the truck and demand its money back.

WARRANTY OF HABITABILITY a promise by the landlord that at the inception of a residential **lease** there are no **latent defects** in facilities vital to the use of the premises for residential purposes, and that these facilities will remain in usable condition for the duration of the lease.

WARRANTY OF MERCHANTABILITY a warranty that the goods are reasonably fit for the general purposes for which they are sold.

WARRANTY DEED a **deed** that warrants that the grantor has the **title** he claims he has. It purports to **convey** property free and clear of all **encumbrances.** As a guarantee of title, the warranty deed creates liability in the grantor if the title transferred is defective. Compare **quitclaim deed.**

WASH SALE a sale or other disposition of **stock** or **securities** as to which no loss is recognized for tax purposes, because within thirty days before or after the date of sale or disposition the taxpayer purchased substantially identical stock or securities.

WASTE generally, an act, by one in rightful **possession** of land who has less than a **fee simple** interest in the land, which decreases the value of the land or the owner's **interest** or the interest of another who has a future interest in the land (such as a **remainderman, lessor, mortgagee, reversioner**).

AMELIORATING WASTE a change in the physical structure of the occupied premises by an unauthorized act of the tenant that, though technically waste, in fact increases the value of the land.

EQUITABLE WASTE such acts as at law would not be deemed to be waste under the circumstances of the case but that in the view of a court of **equity** are so viewed because of their manifest injury to the property, although they are not inconsistent with the legal rights of the party committing them.

PERMISSIVE WASTE injury to the inheritance caused by the tenant's failure to make the expected reasonable repairs to the premises.

VOLUNTARY WASTE injury to the inheritance caused by an affirmative act of the tenant.

PHYSICAL WASTE in the law of oil and gas, a production practice that, in light of alternatives, reduces the quantity of hydrocarbons that may be produced from a reservoir.

ECONOMIC WASTE in the law of oil and gas, a production practice that, in light of alternatives, reduces net value of hydrocarbons that may be produced from a reservoir.

WATERED STOCK a stock **issue** that is offered to public investors by founders and promoters of a company at a greatly inflated price compared to **book value** or cost; stock that a company issues for property that is worth less than the stock. Stock may be identified as watered stock by comparison of market or offering value to net asset value of a share.

WEIGHT OF THE EVIDENCE a phrase that indicates the relative value of the totality of **evidence** presented on one side of a judicial dispute, compared to the evidence presented on the other side; refers to the persuasiveness of the testimony of the **witnesses.**

WHEN ISSUED short for "when, as and if issued," which is a conditional trading basis for a new **stock** or **bond** issue that has been authorized for issuance but does not actually exist. WHEN ISSUED SECURITIES can be bought or sold like ordinary securities, except that transactions do not settle until the actual security is formally issued and the **stock exchange** involved or the National Association of Securities Dealers decides on a specific settlement date. The most common occasion for when issued trading is in connection with stock splits. After the split is announced but before the new shares issue, the split stock may be traded on a when issued basis. Such trading has speculative appeal since a down payment of only 25 percent is required and since no **margin** or loan debt is required for the balance until settlement date, which might be weeks in the future.

WHIPLASH INJURY neck injury commonly associated with rear-end automobile collisions. Caused by a sudden, unexpected forced forward movement of the body while the unsupported head of an automobile occupant attempts to remain stationary consistent with the laws of physics, subjecting the neck to a severe strain while in a relaxed position.

WHITE-COLLAR CRIME a catch-all phrase connoting a variety of **frauds,** schemes and commercial offenses by business persons, confidence men and public officials; includes a broad range of nonviolent offenses that have cheating as the central element.

EXAMPLE: Directors of a bank arrange for friends of theirs to obtain large loans from the bank. The friends use fake names and businesses so that they cannot be traced when the loans are not repaid. The directors always approve the loans, and the money is split between the directors and friends. The scheme represents *white-collar crime* and each participant is liable for criminal prosecution.

Consumer fraud, **bribery** and stock manipulation are other examples of white-collar crime.

WHOLESALER middleman; person who buys large quantities of goods and resells to other distributors rather than to ultimate consumers. Compare **jobber.**

WIDOW'S ELECTION the right of a widow to elect to accept the stipulations of her husband's **will** or to object to the will and demand what is provided for a widow by **statute.**

WILDCAT STRIKE unauthorized strike; strike for which the representing labor union disclaims responsibility.

EXAMPLE: Working conditions have always been poor at a certain train yard, but the workers' representatives have never been able to get improvements. Tired of waiting for the representatives to negotiate something, the workers engage in a *wildcat strike* and take matters into their own hands. The success of the strike depends on how long it lasts and how many people participate, although such strikes are generally illegal. Even if the strike does not change conditions immediately, it indicates the workers' discontent and may prod both their representatives and their employer to change the conditions.

WILD'S CASE, RULE IN see **Rule in Wild's Case.**

WILL a person's declaration of how he desires his property to be disposed of after his death. A will may also contain other declarations of the **testator's** desires as to what is to be done after he dies so long as it disposes of some property. See **codicil; causa** [CAUSA MORTIS]. Compare **gift; testamentary dispositon.**

WILLFUL intentional, as distinguished from accidental. In a criminal statute, the term signifies an act done with a bad purpose and without justifiable excuse.

WINDING UP the process of **liquidating** a corporation. It consists of collecting the **assets,** paying the expenses, satisfying creditors' claims and distributing the net assets, usually in cash but possibly in kind, to **shareholders,** according to their liquidation preferences and rights. Compare **dissolution.**

WIRETAP the acquisition of the contents of communication through the use of any electronic, mechanical or other device. Use of wiretaps by government authorities is subject to the constitutional prohibition against unreasonable **search and seizure,** and they can be used only after a finding of **probable cause.** Use of wiretaps by private citizens against other private citizens may constitute a **tort** based on **invasion of privacy** and thereby give rise to a claim for **damages.**

WITHDRAWAL 1. removal of money or the like from the place where it is kept, such as a bank; 2. separation of oneself from a criminal activity to avoid liability for **conspiracy,** by conduct evincing disapproval of or opposition to the criminal activities. Compare **renunciation.**

WITHHOLDING that portion of wages earned that an employer retains, usually for income **tax** purposes, from each salary payment made to an employee. The amount so deducted is forwarded to the government to be credited against the total tax owed by the employee at the end of the **taxable year.** See **tax [WITHHOLDING TAX].**

WITH PREJUDICE see **dismissal [DISMISSAL WITH PREJUDICE].**

WITHOUT PREJUDICE see **dismissal [DISMISSAL WITHOUT PREJUDICE].**

WITNESS 1. one who gives **evidence** in a cause before a court and who **attests** or swears to facts or gives **testimony** under oath; 2. to observe the **execution** of, as that of an **instrument,** or to sign one's name to it to authenticate it (attest it).

ADVERSE [or HOSTILE] WITNESS one whose relationship to the opposing party is such that his testimony may be prejudiced against that party.

CHARACTER WITNESS a witness who testifies at another person's trial, vouching for that person's high moral character and standing in the community, but who does not have knowledge of the validity of the charges against that person.

EXAMPLE: the preacher testified as a *character witness* at Brian's trial, giving many examples of Brian's service to the elderly and poor. Looking only at the charitable work Brian had done, the preacher could not believe Brian would burglarize a house.

MATERIAL WITNESS one who can give testimony that might have a bearing upon the outcome of a cause and that no one else is able to give. In criminal law, the term refers particularly to a witness about whom there is reasonable expectation that he can give testimony bearing upon the defendant's guilt or innocence.

WITNESS AGAINST HIMSELF see **self-incrimination, privilege against.**

WORDS OF ART words that have a particular meaning in a particular area of study and that have either no meaning or different meanings outside that field.

WORDS OF LIMITATION words used in an **instrument** conveying an interest in **property** that seem to indicate the party to whom a **conveyance** is made, but that actually indicate the type of **estate** taken by the **grantee.** Compare **words of purchase.**

WORDS OF PURCHASE words in a property transfer that indicate who takes the **estate.** The term designates the **grantee** of the estate, while **words of limitation** define the property rights given to the grantee.

WORKERS' COMPENSATION ACTS **statutes** that in general establish **liability** of an employer for injuries or sicknesses that arise out of and in the course of employment. The liability is created without regard to the fault or **negligence** of the employer. Benefits generally include hospital and other medical payments and compensation for loss of income; if the injury is covered by the statute, compensation thereunder will be the employee's only **remedy** against his employer.

WORK PRODUCT work done by an attorney in the process of representing his client that is ordinarily not subject to **discovery.** It encompasses writings, statements or testimony that would substantially reflect or invade an attorney's legal impressions or legal theories about a pending anticipated **litigation,** including the attorney's strategy and opinions.

EXAMPLE: Rob is charged with tax evasion. He hires an attorney to prepare the case, and the attorney hires an accountant to compute Rob's income. Because the attorney hires the accountant, the accountant is working for the attorney, not for Rob. The accountant's report is the *work product* of the attorney and therefore cannot be obtianed by the Internal Revenue Service. If Rob hires the accountant and then presents the accountant's report to the attorney, the report would not be considered a privileged work product and would be discoverable by the IRS.

WORTHIER TITLE, DOCTRINE OF early **common law** rule whereby a **gift** by **devise (will)** to one's **heir** that amounted to exactly what the heir would have taken under the statutes of **descent and distribution** had his ancestor died **intestate,** was disregarded and the heir took instead by descent, which was considered as conferring a worthier (better) **title.**

The rule also has an application to transfer of property **inter vivos;** thus, a grantor may not grant a limited estate to another, with a remainder to the grantor's own heirs. This has been recognized in many American jurisdictions as a rule of **construction** in fulfilling the intent of the grantor. Thus, a **reversion** in the grantor is preferred to a **remainder** in his heirs.

WRIT a legal order issued by the authority and in the name of the state to compel a person to do something therein mentioned. It is issued by a court or other competent **tribunal,** and is directed to the sheriff or other officer authorized to execute it. In every case the writ itself contains directions for doing what is required.

WRIT OF CORAM NOBIS [WRIT OF ERROR CORAM NOBIS; CORAM NOBIS] *(kôr'-äm nō'-bĭs)* Lat.: before us; in our presence, i.e., in our court. The writ aims to bring the attention of the court to, and obtain relief from, errors of fact not appearing on the **record.** Knowing these facts in time would have prevented the **judgment** questioned. Thus, the writ does not correct errors of law. It is addressed to the court that rendered the judgment in which injustice was allegedly done, in contrast to **appeals** or review, which are directed to another court.

WRIT OF ERROR an early common law **writ** issued by the **appellate court,** directing the trial judge to send up the **record** in the case. The appellate court reviews only alleged errors of law. It is similar to a writ of **certiorari,** except that a writ of error is a writ of right and lies only where **jurisdiction** is exercised according to the course of the **common law.**

WRIT OF EXECUTION a routine court order by which the court attempts to enforce the **judgment** granted a **plaintiff,** by authorizing a sheriff to **levy** on the property belonging to the **judgment debtor,** which is located within the county, to satisfy the judgment obtained by the judgment creditor.

WRIT OF PROHIBITION a prerogative **writ** issued by a superior court that prevents an inferior court or **tribunal** from exceeding its **jurisdiction** or usurping jurisdiction it has not been given by law. It is an extraordinary writ because it issues only when the party seeking it is without other means of redress for the wrong about to be inflicted by the act of the inferior tribunal. Sometimes it is referred to simply as PROHIBITION.

WRIT OF RIGHT 1. a **writ** generally issued as a matter of course or granted as a matter of right, in contrast to **prerogative writs** that are issued only at the discretion of the issuing authority; 2. the name of an ancient writ for the recovery of real property.

WRONGFUL ACT any act that in the ordinary course will infringe upon the rights of another to his **damage,** unless the act is done in the exercise of an equal or superior right. Thus, the scope of the term is not limited to acts that are illegal, but includes acts that are deemed immoral, antisocial or tortious.

WRONGFUL DEATH STATUTE a statute that provides relief from the **common law** rule that the death of an individual cannot be the basis of a **cause of action** in a **civil** suit. Every U.S. state has a wrongful death statute, providing that action for damages can be maintained by the **executor, adminis-**

trator or **beneficiaries** of the decedent for the wrongful act, neglect or default that caused his death.

EXAMPLE: A hospital worker fails to follow a doctor's explicit instructions concerning which drugs to administer to Lucy. As a result, Lucy dies. Her husband can sue the hospital under that state's wrongful death statute.

Y

YELLOW DOG CONTRACT an employment **contract** expressly prohibiting the named employee from joining **labor unions** under pain of dismissal. Most state constitutions guarantee the right to union affiliation and to **collective bargaining.** Federal and state **statutes** now generally declare that such contracts will not form the basis for legal or **equitable** remedies.

YIELD the current return as a percentage of the price of a **stock** or **bond.**

YIELD-TO-MATURITY a calculation of **yield** on a **bond** that takes into account the **capital gain** on a discount bond or capital loss on a premium bond. In the case of a discount bond, the yield-to-maturity, YTM, is higher than the current yield or the coupon yield. The reverse is true for a premium bond with YTM lower than both current yield and coupon yield.

YOUTHFUL OFFENDERS youths accused of crime who are processed in the **juvenile court** system, and so are treated as delinquents rather than as adult criminals. The age beyond which an offender is considered an adult for prosecution and punishment purposes has not been uniformly established and so varies from state to state. See **juvenile delinquency.**

Z

ZONE OF EMPLOYMENT that physical area within which injuries to an employee are compensable by **workers' compensation** laws; it denotes the place of employment and surrounding areas (including the means of entrance and exit) that are under control of the employer.

ZONING legislative action, usually on the municipal level, that divides municipalities into districts for the purpose of regulating the use of private property and the construction of buildings within the zones established. Zoning is said to be part of the state **police power,** and therefore must be for the furthering of the health, morals, safety or general welfare of the community.

NOTES